PUBLICATIONS ON THE NEAR EAST

PUBLICATIONS ON THE NEAR EAST

Poetry's Voice, Society's Song:
Ottoman Lyric Poetry
WALTER G. ANDREWS

The Remaking of Istanbul: Portrait of an
Ottoman City in the Nineteenth Century
ZEYNEP ÇELIK

The Tragedy of Sohráb and Rostám
from the Persian National Epic, the
Shahname of Abol-Qasem Ferdowsi
TRANSLATED BY
JEROME W. CLINTON

The Jews in Modern Egypt, 1914–1952
GUDRUN KRÄMER

Izmir and the Levantine World, 1550–1650
DANIEL GOFFMAN

Medieval Agriculture and Islamic Science:
The Almanac of a Yemeni Sultan
DANIEL MARTIN VARISCO

Rethinking Modernity and
National Identity in Turkey
EDITED BY SIBEL BOZDOĞAN
AND REŞAT KASABA

EVERYDAY LIFE &

CONSUMER CULTURE

IN 18TH-CENTURY

DAMASCUS

James Grehan

UNIVERSITY OF WASHINGTON PRESS
Seattle & London

Publication of *Everyday Life and Consumer Culture in Eighteenth-Century Damascus* was made possible in part by a grant from the Institute of Turkish Studies, Washington, D.C.

Additional support was received from Portland State University.

University of Washington Press
P.O. Box 50096, Seattle, WA 98145
www.washington.edu/uwpress

The paper used in this publication is acid-free and 90 percent recycled from at least 50 percent post-consumer waste. It meets the minimum requirements of American National Standard for Information Sciences—Permanence of Paper for Printed Library materials, ANSI Z39.48–1984.

Library of Congress Cataloging-in-Publication Data

Grehan, James.
Everyday life and consumer culture in eighteenth-century Damascus/ James Grehan. — 1st ed.
    p. cm.
  Includes bibliographical references and index.
  ISBN—13: 978-0-295-98676-0 (hardback : alk. paper)
  ISBN—10: 0-295-98676-X (hardback : alk. paper)
  1. Damascus (Syria)—Social life and customs—18th century.
  2. Damascus (Syria)—Economic conditions—18th century.
  3. Consumers—Syria—Damascus—History—18th century. I. Title.
  DS99.D3G74 2007
  956.91'440—dc22   2006028857

For my parents, James and Arline Grehan

CONTENTS

TABLES

NOTE

ON

TRANSLITERATIONS

ALL ARABIC TERMS WERE TRANSLITERATED ACCORDING TO the system used by the *International Journal of Middle East Studies* (excepting the diacritical marks for velarized consonants and long vowels). Most words in the text appear in their singular form, sometimes explicitly marked (sing.). Plural forms (pl.) are specified.

Only in a few instances was it necessary to point out a Turkish word (Tk.) in circulation or identify individuals with Turkish names and spellings. Most of the latter were Ottoman officials such as governors and judges who were outsiders to local society. In general, their names were more easily and sensibly rendered into Turkish than the local Arabic equivalents.

In modern Turkish script, the letters below have the following pronunciation:

c j as in jam

ç ch as in church

ğ lengthens the preceding vowel

ı i as in cousin

i i as in elite

j s as in pleasure

ö the German ö

ş sh as in shape

ü the German ü

ACKNOWLEDGMENTS

No ONE CAN REALLY WRITE A BOOK ALONE. AS THIS project meandered through different archives, libraries, and history departments, I received crucial support from a number of individuals and staff members at various institutions who facilitated my research or offered valuable advice and direction.

The research for this book began with a Fulbright-Hays grant, which made possible my extended stay in Damascus, where I conducted archival research and learned the city's history at first hand. Timely assistance from the H. S. and Virginia Wallace Fellowship, awarded by the University of Texas at Austin, later enabled me to complete the writing of my dissertation during the final year of my graduate program. A subsequent fellowship, awarded jointly by the National Endowment for the Humanities and the American Research Institute in Turkey, allowed me to spend a year in the archives and libraries of Istanbul. At Portland State University, my book received publication subventions from the Department of History, the Friends of the Department of History, and the College of Liberal Arts and Sciences. A grant from the Institute of Turkish Studies further helped to defray publication costs.

In Damascus, I owe many thanks to the late Da'd al-Hakim, director of the Center for Historical Documents in Suq Saruja. She and her staff showed me many kindnesses and made my work in the archives a pleasant and memorable experience. The Institut Français d'Études Arabes de Damas, an important haven for all researchers in Syria, opened their doors to me as an associate researcher during the period 1995–96, and I am grateful for their welcome.

Along the way, I have accumulated many debts to fellow researchers who, however briefly, were willing to talk about my project and share their own reflections and experiences. Foremost among them was my mentor, Abraham Marcus, who introduced me to the field of Middle Eastern history, and with his usual dry humor, offered much calm counsel and sure guidance. From my days in the graduate program at Austin, I can never forget the kindness of Howard Miller, who showed faith in me at a time of great uncertainty and hardship; once more, I would like to express my appreciation. Among others who have offered help and asked probing questions, I would like to thank Kamran Aghaie, Engin Akarlı, Robert Blecher, John Curry, Jane Hathaway, Leila Hudson, Hidemitsu Kuroki, Brigitte Marino, 'Abd al-Razzaq Moaz, Jean-Paul Pascual, Richard von Lieuwen, Robert Morrison, Nasser Rabbat, 'Abd al-Karim Rafeq, Keith and Heghnar Watenpaugh, and Charles Wilkins. Their comments and suggestions have improved this book, even if I could not in the end expunge all its faults. Finally, the editorial staff at the University of Washington Press considerably eased the task of preparing the manuscript. Editors Michael Duckworth and Marilyn Trueblood were patient and reassuring and never seemed to mind my last-minute queries. Copyeditor Rachel Scollon read the text carefully and provided a much-needed set of fresh eyes.

For my wife, Pelin, words cannot suffice. Her love, patience, and understanding have made all the difference throughout a process which, by its very nature, is full of doubts, false trails, and unexpected detours. For our son Sinan, who no doubt wondered at his father's distraction and many hours hunched over keyboard and books, the completion of this project has probably come as the biggest relief. His bright smile and laughter were a constant source of solace, reminding me that the writing of books is not an end unto itself.

EVERYDAY LIFE &
CONSUMER CULTURE
IN 18TH-CENTURY
DAMASCUS

INTRODUCTION

THE OLD CITY OF DAMASCUS, WHICH NOW STANDS ON the eastern end of the modern metropolis, is an ideal place for contemplating the past. Here one finds, in remarkably preserved form, the physical vestiges of the medieval and Ottoman eras, which now house a mostly working-class population in ramshackle splendor. Even for those who have lived in Damascus all their lives, the sight of these old neighborhoods is still capable of arousing moments of wonder. One local author, reminiscing on his youth at the beginning of the twentieth century, exclaimed that "wherever you walk in its quarters and alleys and streets, a beautiful voice from the distant past calls to you, pulling you to it with a thousand and one beautiful and magnificent images."[1] Behind walls and roofs bristling with telephone wires and satellite dishes, all these haunting reminders have not lost their power to arrest the eye and vividly evoke an older way of life whose traces are rapidly vanishing.

The unprecedented affluence of the modern world has created a lifestyle of ease and luxury which, as numerous commentators have noted, would have been unimaginable to earlier generations. In the glare of these modern triumphs, which have occurred across the world, the material life of past centuries has seemed increasingly remote and acquired an almost timeless quality—an impression which is perpetuated in numerous guides to "traditional" cuisine, museum displays of household interiors, and collections of folk clothing. Yet such images are deceptively static. Every type of object has its own complicated career, its own story of how it was discovered, domesticated, and eventually popularized. The study of material life is the sum of thousands of these little histories which have to be painstakingly rescued from obscurity. To conjure up this lost world, whose challenges and constraints are fast receding from contemporary experience, we will have to steal into shops and homes and examine their contents in the minutest possible detail. A prayer rug, a pair of leather shoes, a set of coffee cups—all these objects and others like them, though seemingly inconsequential, have much to tell us about the people who bought and used them.

Such ordinary things have not always seemed worthy of close scrutiny, and until the last decades of the twentieth century were largely overlooked in historical scholarship. Sustained interest arose as a rather belated reaction to the advent of mass consumerism, which, in the affluent societies of the West, seemed to conquer all resistance and offer itself as the new future of humanity. In the years after the Second World War, demand boomed on an unprecedented scale, far outstripping the growth of population and inaugurating a very different kind of economic order, which invited, and indeed positively exhorted, people to seek comfort, satisfaction, and personal fulfillment in the acquisition of new possessions. Perhaps inevitably, much of the discussion about consumption turned into a debate about consumerism—the sources of these explosive appetites and the values which released and legitimized them.

In the initial search for answers, historians turned first to the factors of trade and production, which were seen as the real motors of economic life in the past. Consumption was de-emphasized. Variations in demand might occur, but functioned as an essentially passive response to variations in supply, brought about by innovations in manufacturing or extensions of commercial networks. In other words, consumption was treated quite directly as a "supply-side" problem.[2] Any breakthrough in the provision of goods would immediately call forth demand, which at all times was patiently awaiting new products and choices, if only consumers could obtain them at readily affordable prices. Resolved to a single main issue, the original debate centered around the origins of the industrial revolution, whose mechanized means of production, in turning out a flood tide of cheap goods, soon created their own markets and launched the modern era.

As interest in the history of consumption continued to grow, so too did dissatisfaction with supply-side explanations. Questions arose about the composition of demand and its interaction with ideas of taste, fashion, self-image, and manners. Consumers were recognized to have a far broader range of motives than a crude calculus of income and desire. In short, culture and politics entered the debate. Some of these critiques received their inspiration from the neighboring disciplines of the social sciences. As early as the opening decades of the twentieth century, theorists such as Thorstein Veblen and Werner Sombart began to investigate the link between consumption and cultural transformation.[3] This venerable, if somewhat eccentric, legacy was to find fertile ground in the historical literature of the late twentieth century. At first, the main emphasis lay on a reassessment of the wellsprings of the industrial revolution. Leading the way were historians of early modern Britain, who had begun to ask whether demand had simply followed dramatic expansions in output, or whether, in a long and stealthy movement, the "home market" had been gradually generating its own vigorous growth. As their arguments would have it, industrial innovation would have advanced not ahead of, but alongside, a budding consumer revolution. Even before the first mechanized factories, they insisted, much of England had already acquired a modern consumer culture.

In one form or another, the debate over consumerism has now passed to other parts of Western Europe and North America. Most heretical is the thesis of Jan deVries, who has subsumed the vaunted industrial revolution within an earlier "industrious revolution," which, in his telling, had reached full swing in the most precocious parts of Western Europe, urban and rural, by the seventeenth and eighteenth centuries. Households began working longer hours, increasing their output and income. Their enhanced purchasing power provided a new stimulus to consumption, which in turn called forth new and more efficient methods of production, ultimately giving rise to the industrial age. In deVries' hands, the old supply-side orthodoxy, now placed on its head, has given way entirely to the forces of demand.[4] His ideas have generated much controversy, but demonstrate the extent to which the tables have turned. Once relegated to the margins of historical discussions, consumption now stands firmly entrenched at the center of debates on the origins of the modern world.

Outside these favored regions of the West, where fewer hands are available to sift through the archives, consumption studies have made slower progress. One unresolved question is the scope and growth of non-European consumerism, which still needs to be described and assessed, as does its strength relative to demand in early modern Europe. Turning from debates about early modern Europe to the Ottoman Empire, one finds huge gaps in our knowledge of economic history. Some areas have been much better explored than others: fiscal policy, international trade, artisans and their guilds. From the vantage point of the archives, these were the most visible and glamorous sectors of the economy, connected with urban markets or the payment of taxes to the coffers of the state or its surrogates. A dense documentary trail leads through tax registers, cadastral surveys, legal disputes, and records of contracts and sales—wherever the sultan's subjects came within the purview of the state and its legal and bureaucratic apparatus. Far murkier are the currents of production, trade, and spending which flowed mostly outside the urban marketplace or had only irregular contact with it, or which took place on such a small and seemingly insignificant scale that they attracted little notice and generated comparatively few records. In the countryside, where the bureaucratic presence of the state was always attenuated, much of the economy passed well beyond the ledgers of scribes; but even in the towns, this zone of the unremarked and unmeasured was potentially vast. It is precisely because of such pervasive silences that the study of consumption is so valuable. The purchases that people made as part of their daily routines constituted the deep waters in which the more salient islands of economic activity were ultimately set. An awareness of this submerged consumer culture can correct serious distortions of scope and perspective.

One might conceivably object that a term like "consumer culture" is misplaced in the eighteenth century. Most often, it appears in discussions of contemporary economic life, which offers, by the measure of past generations, a seemingly bottomless cornucopia of choices. In the wealthiest societies, a very large proportion of the population stands ready to partake of this material abundance, which has become so inventive and ubiquitous that consumers now devote much of their energy to satisfying tastes, desires, and impulses which have nothing to do with the imperatives of survival. This freedom from the endless round of drudgery and necessity, from the obligation of toiling simply for the requirements of one's physical existence, has seemed to define the essence of consumer culture for many modern observers. But must we really restrict ourselves to such a narrow view of the matter, which takes account only of the overwhelming prosperity of modern times? Even in the eighteenth century, consumption took place within the framework of a consumer culture which, if not as fully mature and sophisticated as in contemporary societies, was no less essential in guiding demand. We should heed the warnings of Daniel Roche, who has called on historians not to reduce the consuming habits of even the poorest workers to the logic of bare subsistence.[5] In the most grinding poverty, one can still detect glints of fashion, self-expression, and other hints of social aspiration.

If sketched with enough detail, the study of consumption leads beyond strictly economic questions. It opens up new perspectives on social and political history that, in more orthodox accounts, might easily escape our notice.

In the first place, it allows us to look at basic issues of political economy with a very different pair of spectacles. In writing about the Ottoman Empire, few questions loom larger than the role of the state, which, because of its centrality in the documentary record, has attained towering proportions. An older school of historians saw it as an energetic and decisive presence. It had centralizing tendencies and intruded far into the lives of ordinary subjects, who took their place in a tightly defined social and political hierarchy. In its classical form, they argued, this system worked as a well-oiled machine in tax collection, price regulation, and oversight of commerce and industry. This model, of course, openly derives its inspiration from the economic activism of the twentieth-century state, whose own ambitions have been projected back onto the Ottoman political order. More recent scholarship has scaled back both the reach and grasp of the Ottoman state (as well as other early modern states). By the standards of its time, it possessed formidable capabilities in mobilizing men and material, and was admired by its European foes, who would not match its might and organization until the eighteenth century. Nevertheless, the central state faced definite limits on its practical authority, and was most active in the core provinces close to Istanbul. More distant regions such as Syria remained very much part of the Ottoman system, but were in practice granted more leeway. These trends became especially pronounced in the eighteenth century as the imperial leadership grappled unsuccessfully with external foes, most obviously in two disastrous wars with Russia (1768–74 and 1787–92) and the French occupation of Egypt (1798–1801).

The full implications of this eighteenth-century "decentralization," as most historians now prefer to call it, are still being assessed and debated. Distracted and weakened, Istanbul came to rely increasingly on local intermediaries, the provincial notables, who embraced the Ottoman order and yet had their own interests to safeguard. Most scholarship has concentrated on reconstructing their relationship with the central state and following the competition for control over provincial resources. By turning the spotlight on material culture, we can now look for the consequences of "decentralization" beyond these small cliques of elite families. What did this gradual swing in the balance of power between the center and the provinces mean for people in the lower social echelons—which is to say, the vast majority of the population? Material culture is a reliable and yet unassuming witness to this imperial retrenchment, which affected more than an administrative elite alone. Reverberating throughout the social order, structural shifts in political economy were bound to touch the lives of the sultan's humblest subjects. In the case of Damascus, this process of decentralization did not have the same significance for every segment of the urban population. Though local notables undoubtedly won new opportunities for power and profit, many other townspeople of lesser means would steadily enter an era of hard times. Most vulnerable, as we will see, were those who lacked some form of political entitlement, either through affiliation with local factions or through fiscal and legal privileges obtained from the Ottoman state.[6]

Aside from highlighting this link between politics and everyday urban life, the study of consumption is valuable simply for what it can reveal about the inner workings of culture. It paves the way for something like an economic ethnography—the patient accumulation of color, detail, and anecdote which alone can piece together premodern lifestyles. For no other culture is such a task more necessary or salutary than the Middle

East, mainly because no other culture has been bent and twisted to fit so many different ideological schemes, all searching for a single defining essence. Fashions have come and gone: "oriental despotism," modernization theory, "asiatic mode of production," and others whose luster has long worn away. One constant theme has been the application of outsized ideas, making outsized claims and thriving in the gaps of an underdeveloped historiography. Of all these theoretical panaceas, none has demonstrated a more enduring appeal than Islam. Due partly to modern nostalgia within the region, and partly to persistent tendencies within Western scholarship, commentators have repeatedly come back to it. They have rendered the Middle East as a reflection of a religion whose tenets and rules, they argue, impinge on nearly every aspect of everyday life, molding outlook and behavior in affairs both cosmic and mundane. Within this all-encompassing vision, the ambiguities of lived experience recede before the norms and conventions of religious and legal scholarship, which offer a ready-made framework of interpretation.

The idea of a profound connection between religion and everyday behavior is not new, and exercised an early fascination in the writing of European history, particularly on the early modern period. Contentious debates about the origins of capitalism once revolved around the rise of Protestantism. One of the most famous theses, formulated by Max Weber, held that a so-called Protestant "work ethic" was unusually effective in suppressing consumption and thereby promoting the accumulation of capital throughout much of northern Europe. Though seductive, this idea has come under attack. We now know that puritan ethics did indeed provoke a deep anxiety, even shame, over newly won wealth and security, but hardly dissuaded consumers from eating well and living comfortably in the privacy of their own homes.[7] An added problem, which further research is slowly clarifying, is the implication that non-Protestant cultures were somehow less inhibited, or perhaps less provident, in their consumption. As one study of early modern China makes perfectly plain, sixteenth-century commentators were already bemoaning the spread of high living and extravagant expenditure.[8] The assumption that these attitudes are somehow "Protestant"—or for that matter, distinctly European— no longer seems fully tenable.

The humble realities of everyday life will always mock such facile generalizations. Over the full range of their affairs, people's lives were simply too complex, improvised, and, most of all, self-interested to fall in line obediently with ideological schemes of any stripe. They were the sum of calculations and decisions that had their own pedestrian logic, remote from any absolute rules and doctrines. The key factor was the fundamental poverty of the premodern economy, which, in the Middle East and elsewhere, weighed heavily on thought and behavior and imposed a whole series of compromises to which consumers were both willing and compelled to submit. Stark and unsentimental, this victory of the real over the pure and ideal needs to be recounted. It has to be placed in an economic regime which had a very different spectrum of necessities, priorities, and luxuries. Most telling is the structure of this book, more than half of which, in one way or another, deals with food. Most of the eighteenth-century economy was a vast gastronomic enterprise on which everything else hinged. Though far from negligible, the other essentials of everyday life—most notably shelter and clothing—could never match the overwhelming concentration of people and resources in this single sector. In contemplating such lopsided distributions, and all the other basic terms of material existence, one begins to leave behind the pronouncements of the grand theories and see the world as people in the premodern Middle East once experienced it themselves.

Let us admit at the outset that the city of Damascus, as it stood on the brink of the modern era, was not quite a "typical" Middle Eastern community. To begin with, most of the people in Syria, as well as the Middle East as a whole, lived in villages in the countryside. Only about 20 percent of the nearby population took up residence in settlements large enough to be called towns (making Syria an unusually urbanized region of the empire), and most of these held little more than ten to fifteen thousand inhabitants. Measured by these regional standards, Damascus assumed immense proportions, which impressed Ottoman and European visitors alike. Home to some eighty to ninety thousand inhabitants, it easily ranked as one of the biggest towns in the Ottoman Empire (and, for that matter, in the wider Mediterranean basin). Among the urban centers of the Arab provinces, only Cairo (approximately 260,000), Aleppo (120,000), and Baghdad (100,000) could claim larger populations. To maintain its size, Damascus depended on a constant stream of immigrants, mostly from its immediate hinterland, which ensured that it would remain overwhelm-

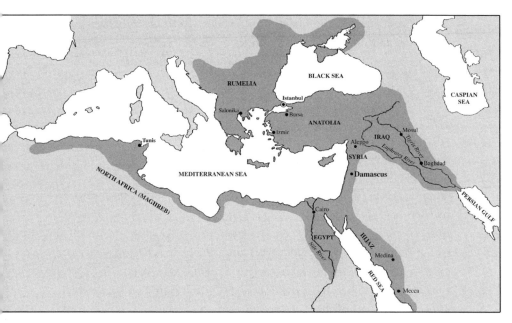

MAP I. The Ottoman Empire, c. 1750

ingly Arab in composition. But as a city of international renown, it was also an unusually cosmopolitan social world, which drew large numbers of Turks, Kurds, Persians, recently settled Arab and Turkoman bedouin, and Arab immigrants from as far afield as North Africa. Sustained by these diverse sources, Damascus was simultaneously Syrian, Arab, Ottoman, and Islamic.

In spite of its impressive size, the city did not, like Cairo or Aleppo, rank as a commercial or industrial city of the first magnitude. It made its fortune primarily as a thriving hub for local and regional markets, which, in any case, were almost certainly the largest sectors of the Ottoman economy. The nearest long-distance commercial artery ran north through Aleppo, which served as the main entrepot for the storied Levant trade. As a direct result, few Europeans ventured to Damascus before the nineteenth century. A small number of travel accounts survive, but almost entirely from the pens of brief sojourners who had, at best, only fleeting contact with residents. There is nothing to rival the meticulous description of eighteenth-century Aleppo put together by Alexander and Patrick

Russell, resident for a combined three decades as physicians for the Levant Company and fully conversant with the ways of local society. European sources from this period consequently have to be treated with great care.

More than for its role as a trading emporium, Damascus earned its fame for its long association, reaching back to the earliest centuries of Islam, with religious learning and worship. As late as Ottoman times, the city was still drawing students from around the Middle East to its scholars and Sufi adepts, who taught in mosques, religious schools (*madrasa*), and Sufi lodges (*zawiyya*; Tk. *tekke*) known far beyond the borders of the empire. Most visitors, however, arrived simply as Muslim pilgrims who had set out for the annual caravan to the holy cities of Mecca and Medina. It was one of two such escorts (the other originating from Cairo) gathering pilgrims from lands as distant as Central Asia and India and protecting them from predatory bedouin. By no coincidence, the fate of the caravan soon became a major concern of the Ottoman state, which, after the conquest of the Arab provinces in the sixteenth century, would present itself as the custodian of the holy cities and preeminent dynasty of the Islamic world.

The political importance of Damascus extended well beyond the pilgrimage. The city served as a provincial capital for most of southern Syria, including large parts of Palestine, and was therefore an arena of intense factional competition. Ottoman officials and members of the local elite vied for precious offices, privileges, and patronage dispensed by the central government in Istanbul. The chief representatives of the sultan were the governor (*wali*) and chief judge (*qadi al-qudat*). Overwhelmingly, these officials were outsiders who were largely unfamiliar with local conditions. Most were Turkish-speaking, cosmopolitan by training and outlook, and always on the move between provincial centers and Istanbul, where their careers were really based. The most notable exceptions, who only confirm the general rule, were the scions of the ʿAzm family. Originally holders of tax farms in the area of Hama, they later supplied a series of strong and ambitious governors: Ismaʿil (r. 1725–30), Sulayman (r. 1733–37, 1741–43), Asʿad (r. 1743–57), and Muhammad (r. 1771–72, 1773–83), who entrenched their family in local society even as they remained loyal instruments of the sultan.

Outside the highest posts of governor and chief judge, power was concentrated in the hands of the local notables (*aʿyan*). Unlike the Ottoman appointees, most of whom came and went with their brief terms and itinerant careers, the local notables provided continuous, if rather fractious, leadership in every field of urban life and functioned as indispensable links between the central and provincial administrations. They assiduously cultivated ties with the Ottoman state, and by the eighteenth century, were taking an increasingly assertive role in local politics. Subtle and discreet, they were masters of political ambiguity, acting as intermediaries between townspeople and Ottoman authorities, and, when their interests called for a little more independence, presenting themselves as the champions of local society. Most often, they confronted each other as rivals, skilled in the arts of bureaucratic intrigue and locked in constant maneuvering for offices and favors. Though disparate in background, they shared that combination of high status and outstanding wealth which placed them head and shoulders above their fellow townsmen.[9] Among the most prominent figures were the Janissary commanders, drawn from two competing corps: the locally recruited regiments (*yerliyya*) and the imperial troops (Tk. *kapıkulları*) sent from Istanbul to the citadel. Taking their orders directly from superiors in the capital, the Janissaries jealously guarded their prerogatives from encroachment by the governor, with whom they were frequently at odds. No less important were the grand merchants (pl. *tujjar*) who claimed preeminence in regional and long-distance trade. Their immense fortunes, which often reached far beyond commercial interests alone, automatically opened the door to power and, for the most influential among them, a seat in the governor's *diwan*, or informal council. Most prestigious of all were the leaders of the religious establishment (pl. *'ulama'*), consisting of the most esteemed scholars, teachers, religious functionaries (such as preachers and prayer leaders), and heads of Sufi orders. The highest positions passed within a small circle of long-established families whose names were synonymous with the city itself.

The immense political, administrative, and religious importance of Damascus has made it unusually visible to historians. Unlike the surrounding countryside, which remains sunk in historiographical shadows, surviving archives and libraries bring the city into sharp relief. Not only is Damascus, as a more literate and better documented society, more willing to give up its secrets; it simply has more of them to tell.

The most abundant records come from the archives of the Islamic courts, which were found in urban centers throughout the Ottoman Empire and dependent on Islamic law as the main basis for their proceedings. Damascus had six such venues: one main courthouse,[10] where the chief judge presided, and five branch tribunals supervised by deputy judges.[11] The deliberations were simple: most testimony was oral, and plaintiffs directly argued their own cases. Except on those rare occasions when the judge had to leave for direct inspections of evidence, justice seems to have been rendered on the spot, either with an immediate decision, or, less often, through a joint settlement mediated by the court. Unfortunately for historians, the judicial scribes composed their documents in a dry, formulaic language which rarely divulges anything more than the bare facts of the case. Thus our best witnesses are accidental guides, hasty and distracted, who require a great deal of careful handling and cautious inference.

The Damascene registers preserve a wide range of business and litigation. Browsing through the extant volumes, one finds cases of marriage, divorce, child custody, indebtedness, bankruptcy, inheritance, sales and rental agreements, and various other contracts and disputes. For the study of material life, the most useful records are unquestionably probate inventories (pl. *tarikat* or *mukhallafat*), which were kept in their own separate files. The backbone of this study consists of one thousand such documents drawn from the middle of the eighteenth century (1750–67). The estates can be broken down into two basic categories: "military" (250 entries) and "civilian" (750).[12] The "military" records were reserved for Damascenes who held the privilege of *askari* status, and constituted what we can call the "Ottoman class." The "civilian" inventories (kept in "indigenous" files, labeled *baladi* or *arabi*) were drawn from the general population, whom Ottoman political theory superciliously termed the "flocks" (*raʿaya*). The meaning of this distinction varied widely over the course of Ottoman history. In the early centuries of the empire, *askari* status applied to all members of the state apparatus: bureaucrats, ulama, and soldiers. But from the sixteenth century onwards, this social boundary dividing "military" and "civilian" spheres became increasingly blurred as the Janissaries, formerly slave-soldiers, were allowed to acquire all the prerogatives of local subjects, with whom they now freely intermixed.[13] Nothing was more revealing of these trends than the interior of the citadel, which had evolved into a commercial center in its own right. Besides having its own mosque, religious shrine, and several streets of houses, it contained a mint, a mill, a large number of shops and warehouses, and even its own bathhouse.[14] At the same time, many artisans and merchants were moving in the opposite direction, discreetly infiltrating the ranks of the military and acquiring Janissary pay tickets. These newcomers proved less than ideal soldiers—though, in truth, the Janissaries had already lost much of their discipline and élan—and often had little to do with either the administration or their nominal military units. What they really sought were the fiscal benefits of 'askari affiliation, namely full exemption from all imperial taxes (excluding those imposed by Islamic law). Membership in the Ottoman class was no guarantee of office and power, and generated nothing like "class consciousness" or a feeling of solidarity with which holders of 'askari status might agitate, make demands, or exert themselves as a single bloc. But as the inventories themselves amply demonstrate, it would continue to make a long-lasting difference in the Ottoman economic order.

Like the other court records, the probate inventories are rather taciturn sources, hinting more than explaining, and full of exasperating inconsistencies. Most of these difficulties stem from the rules governing probate procedures. According to Islamic law, the courts were responsible for drawing up inventories only when a person died intestate (in which case the treasury—i.e., *bayt al-mal*—claimed all assets) or when there were minor children among the heirs. Thus the records have really preserved a somewhat skewed sample of the adult population, who happened at the time of death to satisfy the criteria of Islamic inheritance law. Further clouding the sample is the consistent undercounting of women, who appear as a distinct minority of all estates.[15] The numbers inevitably raise suspicions. As legal commentators were well aware, some families wished to divide their property away from the prying eyes of the court, circumventing the laws of inheritance at the expense of female relatives.[16] Wealthy and prestigious families stood the best chance of getting their way. A leading Sufi shaykh, Mustafa ibn Sa'd al-Din al-Jabawi, openly deprived his daughter of her rightful share of her mother's estate, boasting that "the Banu Sa'd al-Din do not bequeath to women." One of the foremost spokesmen for the legal establishment, Muhammad Khalil al-Muradi, found his pronouncement "astonishing." He was personally familiar with these problems. Barely concealing his outrage, he recounted how his mother—who at the age of three had been her father's only heir—was quickly stripped of most of her inheritance, as was "the custom of [her] relatives" in the wealthy Safarjalani family.[17] Could such acts of dispossession have been widespread? We cannot be certain, but it seems unwise to assume that the law was regularly flouted. For many families, cheating would have been rather difficult, requiring extreme discipline and cooperation among a wide circle of relatives and, in all probability, a measure of political clout to keep representatives of the court at bay. If women turned up less frequently in probate records, moreover, we should not assume that legal evasions were entirely to blame. Reflecting trends across large parts of Eurasia (except Western Europe), the urban population itself may have been disproportionately male.[18]

More severely underrepresented were Christians (mostly Greek Orthodox) and Jews, who together made up roughly 15 percent of the urban population[19] and yet surfaced in much smaller numbers (3.4 percent) in probate documents. The discrepancy is puzzling because non-Muslims showed no hesitation in using the Islamic courts, faced no barriers in bringing cases to Muslim judges, and plainly recognized the advantages of doing business under the official law of the land.[20] One possibility is that religious minorities, who had their own sectarian courts governed by their own religious law, may have wanted (like some Muslim families) to dispense with Islamic laws of inheritance, which were more generous to women. This suspicion receives partial confirmation in the mention of only three women (out of a total of thirty-four non-Muslims) in our sample of mid-century inventories. The apparent determination of Christian and Jewish families to concentrate property in male hands has rendered the women of their communities among the least visible Damascenes of the eighteenth century.

Aside from issues of representation, the most frustrating limitations in probate inventories arise from the methods of the scribes, who as usual were not thinking of posterity in the course of their work. One must first remember that inventories were records of auctions, which were usually held in Suq al-Sibahiyya, in the central commercial district. Officials of the court gathered the belongings of the deceased and put them up for public bidding. Their notation can be maddeningly careless and imprecise. Items were often jumbled together haphazardly—probably as they were bought—without regard for systematic pricing or description. Indeed, as far as the scribes were concerned, their main duty was to appraise the estate, not to examine its contents in detail. In a small number of estates, the accounting is so sloppy and indifferent that the entries are obviously incomplete; the court apparently did what it judged necessary and overlooked the rest. One consequence is that we should not expect a false precision. Measurements, whenever they are possible, can only be taken as orders of magnitude—rough approximations of much broader trends and habits. And many other details of size, shape, color, texture, weight, and quality were never noted at all.

Nevertheless, these inconsistencies in record keeping should not be allowed to overshadow the enormous opportunities opened up by probate inventories, whose virtues (as well as pitfalls) are now increasingly recognized. Students of European history have been exploring them intensively for several decades as a rich source for premodern social history. Specialists on the Middle East, particularly on Ottoman history, have followed more recently in their wake, and the information to be gleaned from inventories will doubtless play a critical role in the writing of Ottoman and modern social history. No other documents have proven as useful in reconstructing material culture, mostly because inventories are essentially lists of personal possessions. Scribes mentioned everything from clothing and furniture to stocks of food and raw materials. They counted coins, jewelry, parcels of real estate, and outstanding loans and debts; and if the deceased was an artisan, the contents of his shop were also likely to appear. As a final obligation, the estate invariably contained a list of heirs, identified by name and blood relation. To a social historian, all these tiny details are invaluable assets which, taken in sufficient numbers, begin to tell an otherwise totally inaccessible story.

These terse and hastily scribbled records, speaking in their bureaucratic monotone, are not the only witnesses to the past. By the standards of the eighteenth century, Ottoman Damascus was an unusually articulate society, whose steady output of books, treatises, and poems circulated throughout the Middle East. Nearly all this literature was generated by the cultural elite—mostly ulama, together with a few educated officials, scribes, and soldiers. The range of their writings is quite broad, speaks in varied voices, and offers precious commentary on urban affairs.

Most knowledge produced by local scholarship revolved around the religious sciences, which made up the core of the educational curriculum.²¹ Among the most useful sources are the collections of legal opinions (*fatwa*) issued by the town's chief jurisconsult (*mufti*), who sat at the top of the local religious hierarchy. Often delivered as responses to moral and legal questions brought by ordinary townspeople, fatwas touched on nearly every aspect of religious and social life.²² Like most legal literature, however, they were couched in highly abstract language that never identified the questioners or exact circumstances under analysis. Legal treatises, another helpful source, suffer from the same limitations in language and content, but at least have the virtue of addressing topics in depth. The overriding concerns are always to demonstrate a mastery of Islamic scripture and tradition, and to build arguments on these unassailable foundations. For the social historian, the best commentaries are undoubtedly polemical broadsides fired in the midst of some controversy, barely concealing the passions of the day and bringing the discussion down from the ethereal realm of legal theory and into the jostle and hum of everyday life.

The picture of local society is somewhat fuller in literary sources. Though most authors were religious scholars—which means that some genres were as stylistically dry as legal literature—there is still much to be learned. Books on manners and etiquette belonged to a venerable tradition of polite letters (*adab*) which summarized the highest values of religion and learning—or, perhaps one should say, reflected the self-image of the literary segment of society. The travel account occupied the same position between religious and social commentary: partly a description of a journey, and partly a recitation of visits to mosques, shrines, Sufi lodges, and eminent teachers. Urban topographies likewise contained a dual focus. While explaining the layout of the city, they often lavished considerable attention on mosques, religious schools, and other sites connected with Islam. Summing up all these tendencies were the most monumental of religious-literary collections, the biographical dictionaries. The main purpose of these multi-volume works was to commemorate the great religious scholars and teachers of their day, supplemented by a smattering of state officials, poets, and folk saints. Varied in length, the entries devoted themselves mainly to recording accomplishments in the field of religion, together with a few details about their subjects' lives and times that contemporaries might have recalled.

Chronicles are perhaps the most difficult genre to characterize. Most were composed in the same literary milieu as other books—that is, by

Muslim men of religion—but there were some noteworthy exceptions. Ottoman officials and scribes occasionally penned their own accounts, and in one remarkable instance, we even have the notebook of Ahmad al-Budayri (d. 1763?), an ordinary barber. Non-Muslims, too, wrote down their own impressions, and within Syria, the tradition of Christian chronicles underwent a veritable renaissance during the eighteenth and nineteenth centuries.[23] What unites all these authors of disparate backgrounds is their focus on affairs of state, or at any rate, the activities of the social elite. When they sat down to record history, they regarded politics as the subject most worthy of their attention. But their eyes could easily wander. Other events around town, and sometimes from abroad, inevitably bubbled up in the narrative, turning chroniclers into invaluable witnesses on topics ranging from food prices to popular customs and beliefs. No social history can proceed without them.

One of the most surprising features of these Middle Eastern narratives, especially for those accustomed to the confessional style of European literature, is the absence of a personal voice. Even when writers referred to themselves, they almost always did so without disclosing their inner thoughts and feelings or dwelling on their intimate circle of family and friends. These self-effacing attitudes were deeply ingrained within literate culture. Indeed, chronicles were hardly the only genre which turned so resolutely outward. Most poetry exhibited the same emotional distance, appealing to a sensibility which prized verbal virtuosity over heartfelt expression. This decorous silence may be the most frustrating barrier facing social historians. In a society where few people knew how to read and write, the reluctance of even the literate minority to talk extensively about themselves seals off the last direct route into private life. All our materials have to be read with these shortcomings in mind. As we set off to explore the everyday world of eighteenth-century Damascenes, we need to remember this diffidence, which sprang from the heart of the culture, and recognize that we are invading areas of life where they would not have willingly allowed us to intrude.

Perhaps the biggest consolation is that, even under comparatively favorable circumstances, consumer culture can be hard to analyze. Contemporary researchers face their own recurring frustrations over sources and methodologies. One common (and rather optimistic) strategy is to put together questionnaires or simply ask people to monitor their own consumption in personal journals. But respondents can be sloppy and forgetful. Whether intentionally or not, they can misreport what they buy and consume, especially in the categories of food and drink, so closely bound to the unthinking routines of the day.[24] Thus the study of consumption has never been an exact science and cannot pretend to anything like statistical exactitude. It is worth remembering, as we peer back into the social life of an eighteenth-century town, that the material culture of our own times is full of anxieties and contradictions, mysterious fads and enthusiasms, furtive habits and addictions. As our own experience shows, ordinary things can simultaneously hold the most telling revelations and conceal the most elusive secrets.

I

CITY

&

ENVIRONMENT

THE STUDY OF CONSUMPTION NECESSARILY BEGINS WITH
the physical environment, interpreted in the broadest sense of the word.
This first step is to conjure up the city's former appearance, which demands more than a static portrait of streets and buildings. It also means
examining the natural forces and resources which shaped urban life, creating its preconditions while rendering it acutely vulnerable to sudden
setbacks and perennial insecurities. In exploring this relationship between city and nature, one inevitably moves from a strictly local orientation towards the broader regional environment. This is the domain of
geography, which held enormous implications for everyday life. Topography and climate were fundamental constraints on the eighteenth-century
economy, and their interaction set limits on the range and potential for
production, exchange, and consumption.

But can anyone really say that geography consists of physical elements
alone? On the contrary, Damascus was also part of a complex human

environment. The city has to be set against its regional and imperial backdrop, namely Syria and the Ottoman Empire, the larger units to which its destiny was inextricably joined. In the end, what emerges from these different legacies, ranging from the physical to the human and from the natural to the political, is a sort of logistical framework, explaining what the Damascene economy was capable of achieving and what lay beyond its grasp and imagination. Only after we first comprehend these basic realities can we begin to formulate broader questions about eighteenth-century material life.

THE LOCAL SETTING

The city of Damascus could never have existed without the blessings of nature. Some eighty kilometers (nearly fifty miles) inland from the Mediterranean Sea, it lies in a large oasis fed by the Barada River, which rises from the eastern slopes of Mount Lebanon some thirty miles to the west. From a height of more than 1,000 meters, the melting snows of the winter months drain into a valley which narrows suddenly as it descends to the east towards the Syrian Desert.[1] With the onset of warmer weather, these icy freshets would soon run dry were it not for 'Ayn Fijeh, a natural spring twenty kilometers (about twelve miles) west of the city, whose waters flow year-round from a large underground aquifer. Freshly recharged, the Barada runs eastward until it passes out of its valley and into the broad plain surrounding Damascus. As it approaches the city, it sends out six branches. Three bend sharply to the northwest suburbs and two toward the south, while another accompanies the main channel on its gradual progress through the city toward the swamps lying at the edge of the desert, where the river abruptly peters out and surrenders to the sands. The city owed everything to these waters. If Egypt was the "gift of the Nile," declared the early twentieth-century journalist Muhammad Kurd 'Ali, then Damascus was surely the "gift of the Barada."[2] On the surface, the comparison may seem derisory; the Barada, after all, is not at all a great river, and by Egyptian standards watered only a speck of arable land. And yet in sustaining settled life on the fringes of a vast desert, it performed a no less vital or remarkable role.

The Barada was the source of life not only for Damascus, but for its large oasis, which local inhabitants called the Ghuta. Within its verdant confines, which stretch about twenty kilometers from north to south and about ten to fifteen in width (a total of some 30,000 hectares), it is one of the most fertile patches of earth in all of western Asia.[3] In the eighteenth century, the landscape was covered with large orchards of olive and fruit trees as far as the eye could see. "The entire Ghuta," glowed Ibn Kannan (d. 1740), "is rivers and uninterrupted trees; seldom are fields found in it."[4] The fertile soil was made even more productive by a complex system of irrigation canals, developed and maintained through centuries of patient labor, and closely monitored by the local authorities.[5] Farther out from the city, the quality of the land steadily deteriorated. Along the east and south lay al-Marj, a thin belt of fields between the oasis and the desert. This outer zone was usually planted with grain, the only crop that it was capable of yielding consistently.[6] Less cultivated was the area to the north, which soon gave way to barren hills, and the western edge of the oasis, blocked by the steep barrier of the Anti-Lebanon range.

In the immediate vicinity of the city were sprawling orchards and gardens which extended for several miles in nearly every direction. Set within these lush surroundings, Damascus possessed an extraordinary beauty. Visitors never ceased to marvel at the immense expanse of green enveloping it, and the waters of its rivers and streams that sparkled everywhere. Passing through the area in the spring of 1697, the English traveler Henry Maundrell remarked with admiration:

Certainly no place in the world can promise the beholder, at a distance, greater voluptuousness. . . . [It] is encompassed with gardens extending no less, according to common estimation, than thirty miles around, which makes it look like a noble city in a vast wood. The gardens are thick-set with fruit trees of all kinds, kept fresh and verdant by the waters of the [Barada]. You discover in them many turrets, and steeples, and summer-houses frequently peeping out from among the green boughs, which may be conceived to add no small advantage and beauty to the prospect.[7]

Both men and women enjoyed the habit of visiting gardens for picnics and strolls with family and friends. Many of these places were so popular that they had their own names, which were sometimes preserved by geographers, who counted them among local landmarks to be extolled.[8]

The oasis was everywhere around Damascus. Yet where the two met,

one could not have distinguished a clear boundary. Urban expansion often meant the invasion and occupation of nearby orchards and fields which, far from retreating, continued to press against the settled areas and gave many outlying neighborhoods a semi-rural character. Along the southern limits of the city, in al-Shaghur, gardens had actually infiltrated

"General view of Damascus." The artist almost certainly made the sketch from Mount Qasyun, the high ridge overlooking Damascus from the northwest. L. Lortet, *La Syrie d'aujourd'hui: voyages dans la Phénicie, le Liban, et la Judée, 1875 1880.* Paris, 1884.

the city walls and reclaimed ground where houses and shops had once stood.[9] The conversion of agricultural land to urban space was never a permanent or irreversible process.

Rising from the midst of the oasis, somewhat towards its northwest corner, was Damascus itself. Viewed from the heights at the western edge

of the oasis, the city assumed an odd, asymmetrical shape, bulging at its northern extremities and tapering off in a long line towards the southwest, where it flared slightly at the end. As befitted one of the major urban centers of the Islamic world, the skyline was broken by the minarets of its many mosques and religious schools (*madrasa*). All other structures hung low to the ground, occupying no more than one or two stories.

At the core of this dense mass of stone and mud brick was an irregular, slightly rounded rectangle which marked the outline of the old city walls. This was the area of the medieval city, which had inherited the site from its ancient and Greco-Roman predecessors. Damascus did not begin to

The Barada River. The scene shows a portion of
the northwestern suburbs (probably by the Takiyya
Sulaymaniyya), where buildings and homes were
intermixed with gardens and orchards. W. H.
Bartlett, William Purser, et al., *Syria, the Holy Land,
Asia Minor &c., Illustrated*. London, 1836.

burst this centuries-old girdle of stonework until much later, from the
twelfth and thirteenth centuries onward, as a network of suburbs slowly
took root to the north, west, and southwest. To the far northwest, on
the slopes of Mount Qasyun, a high ridge which overlooks the city, the
neighborhood of al-Salihiyya sprang up at about the same time. It originally came into existence as a village of refugees from Crusader Palestine, but was soon drawn into the city's orbit, linked by an imperial road
through the intervening gardens.

After the Ottoman conquest of Syria (1516), Damascus entered a period of great prosperity and expansion.[10] The city's very layout bore wit-

ness to its security and success. Most of the medieval walls had crumbled from neglect under the long Ottoman peace, and in many places no longer acted as a meaningful barrier.[11] The extramural quarters had rapidly developed, and by the eighteenth century, at least one observer estimated that they accounted for most of the built-up surface area.[12] Two suburbs in particular had benefited. The neighborhoods to the northwest and west, notably Suq Saruja and al-Qanawat, had attained considerable size and affluence, due in large part to the many notables, Ottoman officials, and soldiers who made their home there.[13] Even more dynamic was al-Midan, the southwestern neighborhood, which had gained new prominence in the economic life of the city, above all as the center for the grain trade. Originally running as a long, thin band of settlement along the main route to the south, it was soon transformed into one of the most populous—not to mention turbulent—quarters in all of Damascus.[14]

Despite the steady expansion of the extramural quarters, the older structure of the city remained intact. The massive citadel, originally a Roman fortress and now the most visible symbol of Ottoman authority, continued to stand sentinel at the northwest intersection of the ancient walls and Barada River. The main business district began immediately to the south and extended throughout most of the southwest corner of the medieval core. Here lay most of the major markets (*suq*) and caravansaries (*khan*), which served the wholesale and long-distance trades. The most famous monument was the nearby Umayyad Mosque, which had undergone several incarnations throughout recorded history: first as a pagan temple, later as a church (ca. fourth century), and finally as the city's principal mosque from the eighth century onwards. Other important mosques and religious schools stood in the same central area, as well as the suburb of al-Salihiyya, which had been deeply associated with Islamic learning since its foundation. The Islamic character of Damascus was visible everywhere. Nearly every neighborhood had its own mosque or religious school, and many held Sufi lodges, which celebrated the mystical traditions of Islam. Popular religious practices, such as visits to the tombs and shrines of local folk saints, thrived in the vast cemeteries on the outskirts of town. Of the two largest, one was located to the north (al-Dahdah) and another to the south (outside Bab al-Saghir); smaller plots outside the eastern neighborhoods were reserved for the minority Christian and Jewish communities that tended to concentrate at this

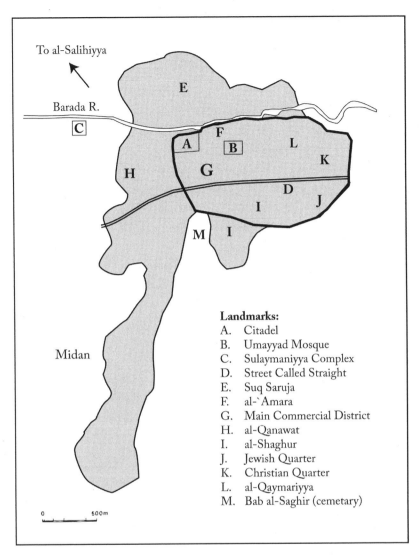

To al-Salihiyya

Barada R.

Midan

Landmarks:
A. Citadel
B. Umayyad Mosque
C. Sulaymaniyya Complex
D. Street Called Straight
E. Suq Saruja
F. al-'Amara
G. Main Commercial District
H. al-Qanawat
I. al-Shaghur
J. Jewish Quarter
K. Christian Quarter
L. al-Qaymariyya
M. Bab al-Saghir (cemetary)

0   500m

MAP 2. Damascus in the Eighteenth Century

far end of the city. Along with the surrounding fields and gardens, these burial grounds were among the few open spaces available to townspeople, and often doubled as recreational areas.

Like other Arab towns, Damascus was extremely compact. Most areas consisted of dense residential quarters which huddled together off the main routes. To outsiders, they seemed like impenetrable labyrinths. Back streets proceeded in a narrow, twisting tangle of alleys and cul-de-sacs that had arisen through centuries of constant modification supervised and initiated by residents themselves. No public agency engaged in urban planning or sought to impose a rational or geometric layout. Only in the twentieth century, with the active encouragement of French authorities during the mandate period (1920–46), were new urban forms, more regular and spacious, slowly implanted around the architectural fabric of the old city.[15] In earlier generations, no one could possibly have imagined this future revolution in building and design, or even thought it necessary. Obeying deep-seated cultural preferences, houses and other buildings stood packed together, side by side, with no room between them. As late as the lifetime of Nuʿman Qasatli (1854–1917), a native son who lived through the last decades of Ottoman rule, it seemed "as if the city were one building."[16] This spare use of space, which stood out as one of the most striking characteristics of urban life, would decisively shape everyday behavior and material culture in premodern times.

THE WHIMS OF NATURE

As much a part of Damascus as its buildings, streets, and gardens were the natural forces on which so much of urban life depended. Eighteenth-century townspeople were keenly attentive to the slightest shifts and disturbances in the rhythms of their environment. As they understood from long experience, earth, sky, and sun exerted a far-reaching power over their existence.

By far the greatest preoccupation was the weather. Nearly everything was connected with it: the supply of food, the prices of commodities, the prosperity of local markets. Geography had not been kind. It had endowed the city with its glorious oasis, but effectively placed it in the same climatic zone as the neighboring desert. Though winters were relatively mild and rarely brought freezing temperatures, summers were a long, hot succession of arid blue skies, made bearable only by the city's elevation and proximity to the sea. Between these two extremes, spring and autumn were no more than brief transitions, lasting perhaps three or four weeks.

Rainfall was scarce.[17] Most of the moisture carried by the Mediterranean winds never reached Damascus, falling instead to the west in the mountains of Lebanon. Only in the cool winter months did the city enjoy a short rainy season, which replenished local rivers and springs.[18] Storms at other times of the year were extremely rare—so rare, in fact, that chroniclers often took the trouble to note them. Agriculture had long adapted itself to these rhythms. Most sowing took place in the fall, in anticipation of the rains, and the harvest commenced in late spring. For this reason, winter weather became vital to the life of the city. In most years, it could be read as a short-term economic barometer. Adequate rains ensured that the harvest would not fail, which in turn held prices low and stimulated demand in local markets. Empty winter skies, in contrast, were an omen of difficult times ahead, leading in the worst years to widespread penury and hunger.

Dry weather was very much a communal affair, intimately bound up with popular religion and local politics. In the winter of 1696–97, the city experienced a prolonged drought which prompted elaborate appeals for divine intercession. Three days of general fasting were declared, and desperate peasants brought herds of cows, goats, and sheep from the countryside to be sacrificed. On the fourth day, amid the clamoring and wailing of a large throng of worshippers, a local holy man officiated at prayers which were instantly answered, we are told, by dark clouds on the horizon, which drenched the city for three entire days.[19] Rain thus acquired a psychological importance. The first showers of winter were a cause for rejoicing throughout the city. They even had the seemingly magical power to lower market prices, especially in the aftermath of a long drought.[20] So powerful was the symbolism of rain that it became associated with goodness itself. Muhammad al-Dikdikji was remembered for the great shower which soaked the city from the hour of his death until he had been washed and wrapped for burial. To a contemporary poet, it seemed that "the sky had wept upon him . . . as if it exulted in the ascent of his soul [to heaven]."[21]

These rains were not always so gentle. Even in a region of relatively low rainfall, the climate was capable of unleashing fierce and unpredictable storms. During one such torrent in October 1767, a great panic gripped the city; amid lightning, thunder, and an unusual cold, residents became terrified about the possibility of flooding.[22] Their fears were not groundless. Swollen with recent rainfall or melting mountain snows, the city's network of rivers periodically burst their banks and invaded the surrounding neighborhoods. In January 1747, the Barada overflowed in little more than half a night "until al-Marja [the area west of Suq Saruja] became like a lake" which climbed up the citadel wall "to the height of a man." The roaring waters filled the markets and carried away shops, merchandise, animals, even a few people.[23] Hardest to control were the Tura and Yazid Rivers, which were prone to flash flooding and required constant dredging and maintenance. Some residents, especially the owners of orchards near al-Salihiyya, tried to take regular precautions by hiring workers every February, during the height of the rainy season, to dam and scour their channels.[24] In October 1791, nearly all the northwestern suburbs of the city were inundated after heavy rains filled local rivers beyond capacity and pushed their waters as far as the foot of the citadel. Several bridges and grain storehouses collapsed and washed away. In the markets of Suq Saruja, as well as those outside the citadel, the currents swept away shops and homes and dragged a number of unfortunate residents and visiting pilgrims to their death.[25] In the aftermath of the disaster, the governor took decisive measures, ordering the residents of al-Salihiyya, together with those of the nearby villages of Harasta and al-Qabun, to reinforce the banks of the Yazid and repair the local devastation. They worked nearly two months at the task and covered most of the river's course.[26] Though flooding of this severity did not occur regularly,[27] memories lingered, particularly in the most vulnerable sections of the city, close to the rivers, where people lived with the greatest risks and consequences.

Perhaps the harshest problem posed by nature was the winter cold, which should not be underestimated. Contrary to the image of a balmy Mediterranean and desert climate, winter temperatures, which were typically cool, could drop quite suddenly.[28] In late autumn 1756, a deep freeze descended on Damascus for over three weeks. Many dogs, birds, and other animals died from exposure, and the water in local fountains turned to ice. Conditions were severe not just in Damascus, but throughout Syria. Reports reached the city that among the bedouin, many women and children had perished, and that, farther north, the Orontes River had frozen solid. In Hama, the famous waterwheels had stopped turning altogether, and camels and horses were able to walk across the ice.[29] Frigid weather visited Damascus during several other winters. Snow was unusual, but not unknown. At the worst times, such as January 1675, enough of it accumulated to clog the roads and cut communications with the outside world.[30] Snowfalls seem to have been especially frequent in the early years of the century (ten of the total of fourteen on record occurring before 1740).[31]

Was it a pale reflection of the "Little Ice Age" which held Europe and the Mediterranean world in its grip at about this time?[32] In any case, snow did not matter as much as freezing temperatures, which took a heavy toll on local orchards. During the period 1740–1813, large numbers of trees died in at least seven separate cold spells, an average of about once every ten years. Citrus trees always fared the worst.[33]

Even outside the winter months, Damascus was still vulnerable to sudden turns in the weather. The most unstable periods were the few short weeks comprising spring and autumn, which could produce startling effects.[34] A violent storm in April 1750 deposited hailstones "the size of chicken eggs." The end of April 1764 witnessed torrential rains followed by a "poisonous wind" that lasted three days; the unseasonable temperatures ruined much of the harvest and immediately touched off price increases.[35] The aftershocks of such a storm or cold snap could be much worse than the event itself, leaving behind weeks, if not months, of turbulence in local markets.

The extremes of summer weather presented their own challenges and disruptions. Located inland and close to the desert, Damascus often experienced periods of intense heat, which generally persisted from May into October, relieved only by the relatively cool nights of the desert climate. At its worst, this blistering weather could be dangerous, even life threatening. In August 1750, a ferocious heat wave dried wells and springs around the city, including one of the major canals of the Ghuta. As the supply of water fell, its price rose "until it became [as expensive] as flour."[36] This dire scene essentially repeated itself in the summer of 1764. Despite a wet winter, wells and springs again went dry. Rivers fell so low that nearby mills had to operate with mules harnessed to the grindstones; prices automatically shot up, and the markets entered a long recession from which they would not emerge for two whole years.[37] Only the ample reserves of water held by the Ghuta spared the city from more frequent crises, which were more likely to strike the pilgrimage caravan as it made its way over long tracts of desert wasteland.

Another scourge brought by warm weather was the periodic invasion of animal pests. Against these swarming enemies, the people of the eighteenth century were largely helpless, even in the face of relatively small-scale attacks. In 1727, for example, mice had little trouble devouring the harvest in several nearby villages.[38] Such incidents were little more than a passing nuisance compared to the cyclical infestations of locusts which, fortunately for the city, were few and far between. From the late seventeenth to the end of the eighteenth century, locusts appeared in four major waves, in 1680–82, 1708, 1747–48, and 1778.[39] Each time, the city went through the same motions. In the first stage, the governor would dispatch a team of Sufis to fetch water from a sacred spring in Persia.[40] Once they returned to Damascus, to the official welcome of local notables and parades of banners and music, the water was distributed throughout the city and suspended in pails from the highest points, such as Mount Qasyun and the minarets of the biggest mosques. The popular belief was that it would attract magical black birds (known as *samarmar*) that had a special appetite for locusts. In 1748 one energetic governor, perhaps skeptical of these time-honored defenses, assigned quotas of locusts to landowners and villagers, who had to collect and then bury them, at first in local cemeteries and later in nearby wells and caves.[41] These exertions proved absolutely futile. In the end, the only effective defense was the city's ability to draw on emergency supplies of food from a vast hinterland, covering most of southern Syria.[42]

Aside from locusts and other natural forces such as floods and droughts, Damascus faced disasters which had their origins not on the surface, but deep underground, in the imperceptible movements of the earth's crust. Syria straddles a major geological fault, which has made it highly susceptible to earthquakes throughout recorded history. Seismic activity was unusually intense in the eighteenth century. Low-level earthquakes shook the city several times, in 1705, 1712, 1723, 1735, and 1753. On the first and last occasions, the jolts were powerful enough to damage buildings and claim lives.[43] Nothing, however, matched the devastation of the final earthquake of the century, in 1759. The biggest in at least six hundred years, it laid waste to large areas of Syria and totally shattered Damascus itself.[44] Terrified of recurring aftershocks, many survivors lived under the open autumn skies or in makeshift huts and tents. Adding to the general misery was the weather, which brought rain, cold, and snow with the approach of winter.

Carrying away far more casualties than the earthquake itself was the plague which followed. The outbreak began around January 1760, while most Damascenes were still living outside their homes, and lasted until the summer months.[45] It was not the first visitation. Pestilence had a long history in the Middle East, dating far back into the ancient world. With the onset of the catastrophic Black Death (1347–49), it had returned for a new cycle of infections, violently flaring up at odd intervals. Though it had grown much less virulent in the intervening centuries, it remained a formidable and persistent menace. From the early seventeenth century until the great earthquake of 1759, epidemics swept through the city on no fewer than ten occasions.[46] Outbreaks were usually part of pandemics affecting all of Syria, so that plagues raging in cities such as Aleppo (1718) and Acre (1759) often spread sooner or later to Damascus.[47] In the worst epidemics, the loss of life could be quite heavy. Observing the plague of 1760 at its height, Ahmad al-Budayri swore that "nearly a thousand funerals" left the gates of the city each day—a figure that we should treat not as a precise count, but as a vivid expression of awe and despair.[48]

Plague was dramatic and highly lethal, but it was only one of the many diseases which beset the local population. Among the deadliest was smallpox, which overran Damascus in at least three separate epidemics, in 1748, 1754–55, and 1797–98.[49] It preyed mostly on children, who suffered high mortality rates, but was fully capable of cutting down adults as well. Survivors were often left disfigured or blind for life. In comparison, other diseases seemed less horrific, but exacted their own tribute in lives and debilitating illnesses. The local irrigation networks were a breeding ground for various fevers and infections. At least once during the century (1778) a full-blown epidemic of malaria (or something very much like it) seems to have erupted.[50] Most insidious were intestinal ailments such as dysentery, which could not be treated and often proved fatal. These low-grade diseases were ubiquitous and struck indiscriminately, afflicting both the rich and the poor, young and old. One of Ibn Kannan's sons lingered four months with such symptoms even though, as the grieving father later insisted, "his condition was not that of one who dies." As it turned out, he was the first of three sons whom the chronicler was to lose during his lifetime.[51] His experience was not unusual. High mortality from disease reigned not only in Damascus, but in cities throughout the premodern world.

PHYSICAL LIMITS: TIME AND DISTANCE

Famine, disease, drought, floods, earthquakes, pests—these are the most dramatic forces that shaped the fate of Damascus. Yet nature was also a

View of a market street. The throng of people and animals was typical of the main commercial districts. Rows of small shops, open to the air, lined the way. William Thomson, *The Land and the Book*. New York, 1886.

subtle presence, imposing limits that people of the city took for granted simply because they were such an obvious part of their existence. Nothing seemed less obtrusive or more permanent than the land itself: the surrounding oasis, the rivers watering it, the mountains to the west, the desert to the east. All these sights were a familiar part of the terrain and blended into the very personality of the city. More than background scenery, they also had profound cultural and economic consequences that the people of the eighteenth century were almost helpless to coun-

"The Street Called Straight." Paved and unusually wide, it functioned as one of the main thoroughfares within the walled portion of the city. Toward its western end, it became a major bazaar, known as Suq al-Tawil. William Thomson, *The Land and the Book*. New York, 1886.

ter. The folds and contours of regional topography alternately facilitated and obstructed movement, complicating attempts to overcome distance and link people and places. The resulting restrictions on transport and communications—in effect, a natural and technological "speed limit" on the circulation of people, goods, and ideas—repeatedly forced the local economy into fundamental compromises and impasses.

The difficulties of travel began in Damascus itself. Most back streets hardly allowed more than two people to walk abreast, and in the main commercial districts, the thoroughfares were regularly jammed with traffic and merchandise. Space was always at a premium. Shops were little more than cramped booths, rarely permitting more than one, or at most two, customers at a time. There were no storefronts, and apart from shutters, which were locked at night, no partitions marked off the interior. A few shopkeepers such as ʿAli Usta al-Hallaq, a barber of modest means, might keep a screen or "winter door" to block out inclement weather,[52] but as a general rule, shops were open to the air. Merchandise was frequently piled, as one traveler observed, in an "artful manner" around the shop, spilling out into the street.[53] This encroachment on public space was more than a convenient way for merchants to advertise; it was a virtual necessity owing to limited storage capacity that rarely amounted to more than a few shelves. Both law and custom tolerated this overflow as long as it did not impede traffic—a provision which was rarely enforced until nineteenth-century reformers sought to widen and straighten market thoroughfares.[54] Sidewalks were uncommon except in a few markets, where they consisted of wooden platforms raised two or three meters from the ground.[55] In most places, streets were unpaved and always at the mercy of the weather. Dust was a year-round nuisance. To keep the air clear, shopkeepers had to pay a special guild of workers to sprinkle water in the markets.[56] During winter, the main nemesis was mud. Few streets had adequate drains and gutters to carry away rainwater, and the ground soon melted into a thick bog.

The few paved roads were little better, having fallen into various stages of dilapidation. The main road through al-Bahsa (on the edge of the westernmost quarters) was typical; before it was restored in 1714 "it had disintegrated, riders and pedestrians having found hardship from it, especially in wintertime; seldom were riders spared from falling [into it]."[57] Repairs on such roads were costly, and despite the great prestige earned by sponsors, few officials took the initiative. It was always a noteworthy event whenever a notable stepped forward. Fathi al-Daftari, the city's treasurer, won praise for laying new stones on the imperial road to al-Salihiyya (1742).[58] Contemporaries were even more impressed by the governor Asʿad Pasha al-ʿAzm, who refurbished the pilgrimage route through the Midan in 1752 and "did not thereby wrong anyone, and did not take anything from anyone" to defray his expenses.[59] In both cases, the roads had been ignored for long periods (last paved, respectively, in

1675 and 1635).[60] And these were privileged routes. In comparison, ordinary streets received hardly any maintenance at all. In the absence of a municipal authority, the responsibility for upkeep devolved upon local neighborhoods, who carried out these tasks with uneven zeal. A few scattered areas were so neglected that travelers encountered mounds of rubble deposited by earthquakes and decaying buildings. "A few hours' labor would clear the wrecks away, but the passengers prefer to clamber up and down the piles of stones and fragments rather than to displace them."[61] Even inside the city itself, the streets could be full of obstacles and frustrations.

Outside Damascus, most routes were little more than tracks worn into the ground by successive generations of men and animals. The once extensive network of Roman roads had long ago crumbled. Referring to the former Antonine Way east of Tripoli, one traveler mourned that it was "so broken and uneven that to repair it would require no less labor than the wherewith it was at first made."[62] A British observer of the 1830s went further and declared, "Generally speaking the roads of Syria are in a deplorable condition."[63] Only the pilgrimage route received minimal maintenance. During the eighteenth century, 'Abdullah Pasha al-Aydinli was the first governor to oversee repairs (1732–34), paving it as far south as Qunaytra. 'Uthman Pasha al-Kurji later restored much of this work during his own term in office (1760–71) and added a number of forts along the way to bolster security.[64] Such measures made little difference. Communications remained precarious throughout the region, and it took little more than bad weather to paralyze all transport; "in the rainy season, indeed, traveling is nearly impossible."[65] Returning from Mecca in March 1743, the pilgrimage caravan was halted by flooding in Transjordan, near al-Qatrana. The racing currents swallowed up a number of men, women, and animals, as well as a considerable amount of baggage.[66] Elsewhere in the region, winter travel was equally uncertain. The difficulties were especially evident in the west, where the mountains of Lebanon formed an impenetrable barrier, due to the snows which inevitably blocked the roads at higher elevations. Summer too posed its own problems. Caravans taking desert routes preferred to depart either in winter or spring—definitely no later than May—to avoid the withering temperatures of summer.[67]

So the weather was always a factor. Like agriculture, travel responded to the rhythms of the seasons. Even the price of transport depended in part on the time of year. In contrast to summer, when rented animals were cheapest, rates were much higher during the trying winter months and remained so into spring, when animals were put out to grass.[68] Yet the effects of these natural cycles should not be exaggerated. Progress on eighteenth-century roads was always unpredictable, halting, and subject to setbacks and delays. By modern standards, time and distance moved forward at a crawl. Journeys which today require a mere afternoon once lasted many a weary day on the road. Ultimately, it was a question not of conditions, but of transport itself.

The first characteristic of eighteenth-century transport, and perhaps the one which best highlights the obstacles faced by the economy, was its high cost. Mobility was a luxury, and it was by no means accessible to everyone. Very few Damascenes possessed their own private means of transport, which required sizable outlays of capital, not to mention constant expenditures on maintenance, such as fodder and care for animals. Most residents therefore moved on foot, particularly the poor, who had little choice. Though walking was not a significant hardship within the city, it was usually impractical for longer journeys, which demanded animals, equipment, and supplies. All these preparations were synonymous with expense—often great expense—which rose incrementally the farther one traveled.[69] Long-distance travel required considerable resources and planning. It was not undertaken lightly or as a means of recreation; only the arrival of railways and motorcars encouraged these more frivolous attitudes.

Travel was so expensive and arduous that the state, in spite of its immense resources, had difficulty in meeting its own needs, which were almost invariably connected with warfare. Pressed for immediate solutions, officials resorted to the expedient of seizing pack animals from villagers, and indeed from anyone whom they encountered on the road, in exchange for nominal payments which were intentionally set at low rates.[70] Alerted by rumors along the highway, muleteers and caravan leaders often refused to approach cities where animals were being rounded up, preferring circuitous detours to losing their animals altogether with inadequate compensation. These disruptions point not only to the high costs of transport which prevailed, but to the chronic shortage of animals. The marketplace confirmed the intense pressures of supply and demand (see table 1.1). A single mount could cost tens, sometimes hundreds, of piasters (no doubt according to type, age, and condition). These steep expenses put them beyond the reach of most townspeople. In mid-century estates, only one out of every ten Damascenes owned an animal for transport.[71] The age of convenient mobility—the eighteenth-century equivalent of a car in every garage—was still very far off.

Most animals were essentially creatures of commerce, which depended heavily on their exertions. A large part of the economy moved on the backs of donkeys, mules, and camels, all of which functioned as the trucks and locomotives of their day. Their strength, speed, and stamina effectively determined the volume of trade and information that towns like Damascus exchanged with the outside world. Though all these animals were dependable and rugged, their capabilities were very different and gave rise to a certain division of labor.

Donkeys primarily carried local traffic. They were perfectly adapted to the narrow streets of the city and had the range to reach nearby villages. In several markets, particularly Suq al-Khayl (west of the citadel), donkey drivers rented their animals much like modern taxis, charging rates according to distance. Barefoot youths led riders to their destinations and then returned with the animals to market.[72] A few private individuals chose to keep donkeys, presumably for their own convenience in getting around town, but they represented only a tiny portion of the urban population.

Mules offered more range and endurance and seem to have performed a more strictly commercial role. They were perfectly useful as mounts, but were more valuable in transporting goods and supplies from local khans and grain warehouses, along desert caravan routes, or through twisting mountain footpaths, where they really excelled. Ownership tended to be highly specialized, probably because of their great expense; on average, the price of mules often ran well above 100 (or even 200) piasters.[73] Muleteers handled most of their breeding and sale, renting them to merchants and occasionally dabbling in an interregional trade in draft animals. Most carriers operated on a small scale, keeping one or two mules and offering their services as needed.[74] Individuals who possessed larger numbers (upwards of ten to twenty) tended to be merchants who had invested in private transport. One such entrepreneur left an estate which included nineteen mules at the time of his death in 1761, but his actual dealings were far more extensive, as indicated by the large quantities of olive oil on hand.[75] Was he originally a muleteer or an oil merchant? It is impossible to say with any certainty. The possession of mules inevitably led to commerce, which, for its own part, always demanded animals for transport.

For truly heavy lifting, merchants turned, above all, to camels, which were undoubtedly the most distinctive feature of Middle Eastern transport and the mainstay of the long-distance and regional routes. Their supply was handled by knowledgeable dealers (*jammal*), most of whom owned several animals (usually less than ten) and worked as carriers for hire.[76] Demand was always high owing to camels' unmatched combination of endurance and versatility. No animal was better able to withstand the rigors of the arid climate. Their unique physiology allowed them to store enormous quantities of water and march unfazed over large stretches of wasteland. Endowed with impressive stature and strength, they could hold between five and seven hundred pounds of baggage when properly harnessed, about the same capacity as three to five horses. As an added benefit, they were cheap to maintain, in some cases—notably with light commodities such as textiles—costing less than 1 percent of the value of their cargo for one trip.[77] It is no wonder that merchants esteemed them so highly; caravans simply could not function without them.

Ottoman officials were equally dependent on camels, which hauled most of the Porte's supplies during military campaigns. Sometime around 1757, innovative troops even managed to convert them into potent weapons, mounting small swiveling cannons onto their backs.[78] This idea was successful because of the great mobility of camels, deceptively masked by their bulky frames. As the bedouin had known for centuries, camels were swift enough to make excellent steeds if equipped with a suitable saddle. At a more leisurely pace, they could also function as the Middle Eastern version of a carriage, fitted with large wooden compartments hanging from one or both flanks.[79] The English traveler W. G. Browne, visiting Damascus at the end of the eighteenth century, noted that this was a popular way of undertaking the pilgrimage to Mecca. "Some of the more opulent hajjis, or pilgrims, were carried in litters, but the greater number in a kind of panniers, two and two, placed on the back of camels."[80] There were many porters who made a living by providing these comforts, as well as food and drink, for the duration of the journey. Only the ultra-pious tried to make the pilgrimage entirely on foot.[81]

Despite the great variety of roles that camels performed, they were never harnessed to wheeled vehicles. Unlike Europeans or villagers in parts of Anatolia, Syrians rarely used beasts of burden as draft animals. This preference had its roots in the late Roman and early Islamic periods, during the gradual shift from wheeled transport to animal haulage throughout most of the Middle East.[82] By the Ottoman period, wheeled vehicles had suffered a near extinction on the roads around Damascus. And yet they were never entirely forgotten. During construction of his famous palace (1750), As'ad Pasha al-'Azm removed columns from the madrasa of al-Malik al-Nasir in al-Salihiyya and ordered them loaded into carts, which were then hauled to their new site by teams of cattle.[83] Heavy and cumbersome, wheeled transport did not really mount a comeback until the late nineteenth century, when Turkomans and Circassians—respectively immigrants from Anatolia and refugees from the Caucasus—settled in large numbers in villages around Damascus and brought their ox-drawn carts, which they refused to give up.[84] Carriages pulled by horses, on the other hand, were a European innovation and had to await the opening of the Beirut-Damascus road (1863), run and monopolized by a French company.[85] Why was the wheel so long in returning? The main factor was the comparative cheapness of pack animals, which could carry more merchandise than carts and other vehicles, and could do so at lower rates. One further advantage was that animals did not require paved roads, which were expensive to construct and maintain. If transport nonetheless remained expensive, it was due to problems and limitations—such as slow speeds, chronic insecurity, and the high costs of raising and tending animals—which were common to all premodern economies.

Another legacy which had fateful consequences for Damascus was the overland orientation of its economy. This reluctance to travel by water was heavily influenced by geography. Apart from the Euphrates River flowing from the north towards Iraq, Syria had no major waterways. The Orontes, Litani, and Jordan Rivers were not navigable for the purpose of large-scale trade and provided relatively modest power for waterwheels and mills. From the coast, the Mediterranean beckoned as a natural outlet, but Damascus could not easily reach it. The main roads fanned out along a north-south axis, threading between the desert to the east and the Lebanese highlands to the west. Though the sea was in reality less than fifty miles away, it seemed far more distant—about three to four

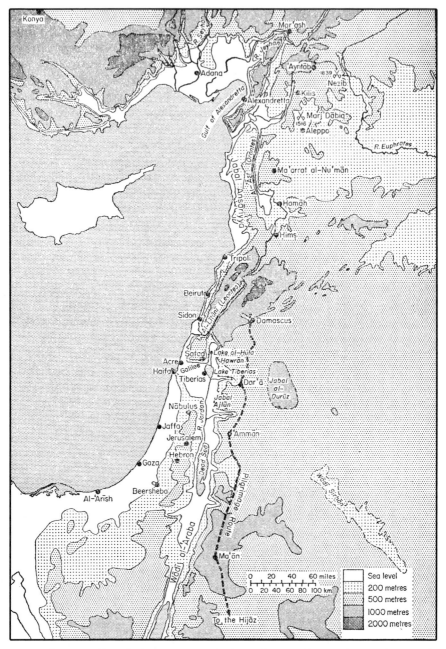

Reprinted from *Egypt and the Fertile Crescent, 1516–1922: A Political History*, by P.M. Holt. Copyright © 1966 by P.M. Holt. Used by permission of the publisher, Cornell University Press.

MAP 3. The Geography of Ottoman Syria. From Egypt and the Fertile Crescent, 1516–1922, by P. M. Holt. © 1966 by P. M. Holt; courtesy Cornell University Press.

days on the road through difficult and hostile terrain where the authority of Ottoman governors was no more than nominal. Caravans from Damascus to its closest ports, Sidon and Beirut, left at irregular intervals.[86] Between these departures, few dared to make the journey alone or in smaller groups on account of bandits and—what amounted to the same thing—the tolls levied by local Druze chieftains.[87] Communications with the coast did not begin to improve until the mid-nineteenth century, as Syria was progressively pulled into the European world economy. In the meantime, Damascus seldom looked towards the sea.[88]

Operating within its network of overland routes, Damascus made contact with the wider world primarily through its numerous caravans, which carried people, products, supplies, and that most precious commodity—news—into and out of the region. The overwhelming reliance upon overland transport imposed general limits on mobility—and, in a broader sense, the regional economy itself, which moved to a beat set by the caravans. In good conditions, caravans—or more precisely, their pack animals—could advance no more than twenty-five miles per day. In other words, the pace was tedious, and distance was only overcome through constant exertions. Even nearby destinations were not within easy reach. Tripoli, the largest Lebanese port, was six days away. Palestinian towns such as Jaffa and Acre were a journey of one to two weeks.[89] Travel to Aleppo, a distance that a bus can cover today in a mere five hours, required roughly two weeks.[90] To embark for more distant points, especially those outside the empire, one needed fortitude and, above all, patience. Pilgrims from Uzbekistan, befriended by Ibn Kannan in 1706, informed him that they had been on the road for nearly one whole year and had still not reached Mecca, their ultimate goal, another thirty-five days away.[91] As pilgrims, they were not traveling with any extraordinary urgency and, in fact, had arrived several months prior to the caravan's departure. But their speed was not essentially different from that of a foot soldier on campaign or a merchant accompanying his goods to the next market. Nearly everyone moved by the same means over the same familiar routes.

The only exception to these slow rhythms of movement and transport was the postal service managed by the Ottoman state. For its time, it worked with remarkable speed, cutting the distance between Damascus and Istanbul from upwards of forty days to only one week.[92] Its secret was twofold: swift horses (and sometimes dromedaries) combined with an elaborate network of relay stations scattered throughout the empire. In one highly instructive incident, an assembly of Damascene notables sent a formal complaint to the Porte (1675) about misconduct by the governor's soldiers. Learning of their protests, the governor sought to head off a potential scandal by warning his patrons in Istanbul and presenting his own side of the case. He immediately dispatched a courier, who, in spite of a late start, arrived in the sultan's summer palace at Edirne "many days" ahead of the original petition, which plodded through Anatolia with the pack animals (*dawab*) carrying it. As it finally entered Edirne, a report from the governor's emissary was already making its way back, only five days outside Damascus.[93] The difference was not lost upon the Damascene chronicler who recorded the dispute. Ease of communication was mainly an official privilege.

Private ownership of a horse was the next best alternative. It was one of the gaudiest status symbols, associated with wealth and military prowess. So great was the expense, and so alluring the image of appearing on horseback, that some owners, even among the affluent, contented themselves with a share of a single animal. In any case, speed was not the main attraction; horses rarely extended mobility beyond the average range of the caravans. This rule applied not merely to porters, who kept weary nags (*akdash*) for transport, but to the notables, soldiers, and merchants who filled local stables with the finest steeds in the city. During his many voyages around Syria, the eminent scholar 'Abd al-Ghani al-Nabulsi (1641–1731), together with his companions, proceeded not on foot, but on horseback, which said more about their fortunate social position than any desire to race across the countryside. Like other travelers, they proceeded at a deliberate pace. Their journey to Jerusalem, for example, lasted all of sixteen days—a little longer than most caravans taking the same route.[94] Their leisurely progress was less a choice than a necessity. Horses were a costly and yet fragile investment; in spite of their great strength and speed, they required constant care and attention. Travel at a gallop was impossible without a frequent change of mounts to avoid injuring or killing animals. Since only the state was in a position to establish such a chain of replacements, it alone was able to tap the full speed of its steeds and thereby exceed, albeit marginally, the normal barriers which weighed so heavily on economy and society.

Contact with the outside world involved more than transport. As one of the major cities of the Ottoman Empire, Damascus participated in economic, religious, and administrative networks reaching far beyond its immediate hinterland. In all these capacities, it acted as a point of attraction and accumulation, absorbing food, taxes, raw materials, manufactures, and immigrants from around the region. Yet this position was achieved only with constant effort and vigilance. The city continually had to project itself over its hinterland, as well as a large province, while simultaneously checking rival centers of authority that sprang up with increasing frequency over the course of the eighteenth century. The domination of such a wide area was, in practice, uneven, and often remained a question determined essentially by geography, distance, and the local balance of power.

Damascus exerted its firmest control over its economic hinterland, close to home, where its rulers and leading families were able to maintain the most vigorous presence. The core of this hinterland was, of course, the Ghuta. But Damascus had long outstripped its oasis. As the principal city of southern Syria, it extended its economic and political grip to neighboring territories to feed its people and enrich its markets. To the south, it exploited the wealth of the Hawran plain; to the northwest, between Mount Lebanon and the Anti-Lebanon range, it summoned the resources of the Biqaʿ Valley. In each of these areas, the city's paramountcy was unquestioned, or at any rate, very difficult to subvert. Damascene merchants and Janissaries invested heavily here in local trade and lucrative tax farms (the right to collect taxes on behalf of the Ottoman government), and the provincial administration collected a major portion of its revenues.

Beyond these immediate districts, the city's hold was more tenuous and fluctuated sharply throughout the Ottoman period. The outer reaches of the province, particularly the settlements of Palestine and Transjordan, largely ran their own affairs.[95] During the eighteenth century, the governor and his troops rarely intruded here except to gather taxes during the *dawra*, the annual military expedition through southern Syria and Palestine whose proceeds funded the pilgrimage caravan.[96] In the small towns of Palestine, a handful of notable families maintained themselves in office and won regular reappointments from the imperial bureaucracy,

which resorted to indirect strategies of manipulating rivalries and enticing recalcitrant leaders with offices and honors. Although Damascus occupied a privileged position, its authority was hampered at every turn by
unavoidable compromises.

More troubling to the provincial administration was a gradual swing
in power towards the Mediterranean coast, where a succession of warlords established themselves.[97] The first was Zahir al-ʿUmar (d. 1775), a
bedouin chieftain who served originally as a tax farmer in the area of Lake
Tiberius (the Sea of Galilee). By the 1740s, he had assembled a private
army, fortified his base at the port of Acre, and built up his own fiefdom
covering northern Palestine. His shoes were later filled by Ahmad Pasha
al-Jazzar ("The Butcher"), a Bosnian soldier renowned for his ruthless

Interior view of the Khan of As'ad Pasha. Upon its completion in 1753, it immediately ranked as the biggest caravansary in the city. W. H. Bartlett, William Purser, et al., *Syria, the Holy Land, Asia Minor &c., Illustrated*. London, 1836.

and brutal methods. Appointed governor of Sidon, he settled instead in Acre, where he ruled over the peasantry with a heavy hand and became the region's main powerbroker (1775–1804), interfering often in Lebanese politics and successfully cowing the governors of Damascus. As a crowning triumph, his forces turned back Napoleon Bonaparte's invasion of Syria (1799), staged from Egypt, which the French would briefly occupy (1798–1801). Under his two successors, Acre remained a regional stronghold until the Egyptian occupation of Syria (1832–40) under Muhammad Ali.

The fundamental limitations of provincial administration were both the cause and effect of chronic insecurity in many parts of the countryside. Local strongmen, soldiers of fortune, and marauding bedouin made their presence felt through banditry, which the governor's troops worked relentlessly to stamp out. Yet military campaigns, no matter how frequently conducted, produced few long-term improvements. Highwaymen were an essentially ineradicable element of premodern society, often lurking in inaccessible highlands or close to the fringes of the desert. They were so elusive that a former mercenary commander who had fallen afoul of authorities and run away was able to win reinstatement after returning to the city with the heads of four brigands, which he presented as a peace offering.[98] It was a gesture that the governor, rarely successful in apprehending bandits himself, was likely to appreciate.

All except the most foolhardy travelers knew of the dangers which haunted every journey, and eagerly sought the latest news whenever they entered a new region. On the road, the exchange of greetings among fellow wayfarers was a necessary precaution for gathering intelligence and planning emergency detours.[99] Those who ventured out alone or unarmed gambled with their lives. Mikha'il Burayk (fl. 1782), a Greek Orthodox priest, relates the tale of two priests, riding by themselves, who were murdered by Lebanese villagers; he offers their fate as a stern example to those who would underestimate the risks by "taking confidence in themselves and traveling alone."[100] Safety, more than speed, was the highest consideration on the road.

The solution to this perennial problem was the caravan, which offered the advantage of numbers and mutual protection. Specific arrangements varied with the size and destination of each group of travelers, but the chief concern was always security, which they had to provide for themselves. Ensuring a further measure of safety was the vast network of khans, which were constructed not only inside towns, but along the main routes at intervals representing about one day of travel. Most were sturdy buildings, typically consisting of two stories of rooms set around an open courtyard. In urban markets, they might serve simultaneously as a workshop, commercial depot, and stable. On the road, they functioned first and foremost as small fortresses, designed almost exclusively for shelter and defense. Many Europeans considered them altogether too spartan. Drawing an unfavorable comparison with English inns, Henry Maundrell warned that one "must expect nothing here but bare walls. As for other accommodations of meat, drink, bread, fire, provender, with these it must be every one's care to furnish himself."[101] Arab travelers complained of similar discomforts. During his grand tour to Jerusalem in 1690, 'Abd al-Ghani al-Nabulsi recorded a difficult night of fleas and intense cold in a khan south of Damascus.[102] There were no alternatives. Hotels and inns in the Western style did not appear until the late nineteenth century, and took root very slowly in cities like Damascus, where they catered mainly to a European clientele.[103] In the meantime, caravans did without such conveniences. What they required, more than comfortable accommodations, was a secure haven from the perils of the road.

Nearly all caravans faced some degree of risk, but none were more vulnerable than the big convoys, loaded with merchandise and coin and planned according to well-known routes. The dangers not only shadowed the pilgrimage caravan, whose fate was one of the great anxieties of the imperial administration, but nearly all major expeditions, such as the commercial caravans to Aleppo and Baghdad, whose long columns of animals advertised their size and wealth. The chief concern was the bedouin. Though they constituted little more than 5 percent of the population of the Fertile Crescent, their political and military weight far exceeded their numbers and could not be ignored. Most bedouin tribes were willing to allow safe passage in exchange for a payment (*surra*), which became a regular part of the desert economy and a necessary supplement to their own meager livelihood. The Ottoman state sought further cooperation by granting official titles to their leaders and nominally integrating them into the provincial administration. But such incentives did not always work. When payments were inadequate or entirely withheld, the bedouin quickly turned into formidable foes. Few caravans could withstand the concerted attack of tribal armies, such as the 'Anaza federation of the Syrian Desert, which totally overwhelmed one of the lucrative caravans to Baghdad in 1774.[104] Other areas were more or less permanently unsettled, making it nearly impossible to advance without military escorts, as al-Nabulsi discovered on his way through the Sinai (1693).[105] Few travelers could count on the cavalry to save the day, and in fact troops appeared for al-Nabulsi's party only because Egyptian forces maintained a regular presence along the route from al-'Arish. Most caravans had to practice self-reliance, which meant that, in addition to arming themselves, they had to negotiate as they moved from one territory to the next. Through tolls, payments, casual trade, and other blandishments, bedouin tribes were inevitably drawn into regional commerce, helping to ensure the safety of the traffic from which they profited. This uneasy and parasitic relationship was a type of banditry that the regional economy had tamed and absorbed, but at a definite cost, which complicated the circuits of exchange and added what was tantamount to an unofficial tax onto transported goods.

During the eighteenth century, the problem of banditry grew ever more serious throughout the Fertile Crescent. Some regions, like the Lebanese highlands, were especially notorious for brigandage and other forms of political insubordination, but no corner of the province was entirely safe.[106] Many of the worst troubles originated in the Syrian Desert, where the political and demographic regime of the bedouin was undergoing a profound upheaval. New arrivals, mostly from the 'Anaza confederation, had pushed northward from their original Arabian grazing areas and displaced many of the previously established tribes. As competition for water and pasture intensified from the late seventeenth century onwards, the bedouin became ever more bellicose.

The most alarming development was the increasing number of attacks on the pilgrimage caravan, which was harassed no fewer than nineteen times in the period 1674–1752, and was actually pillaged in 1671, 1691, 1711, 1740, and 1757.[107] The last of these disasters was by far the worst, and certainly inspired the most vivid accounts. In the aftermath of the ambush, thousands of pilgrims perished in the desert from thirst, exposure, and exhaustion.[108] Officials in Istanbul greeted the news with outrage, regarding it as an affront to the Ottoman dynasty, whose image as the divinely ordained guardian of the Holy Cities was badly tarnished. On the local scene, the damage was immense and transcended narrow political and ideological considerations. Returning with precious stones, textiles, spices, and above all Yemeni coffee, the pilgrimage caravan was also a lucrative source of trade.[109] Merchants and Ottoman officials, the latter of whom were not at all hesitant to dabble in commerce, invested large sums in the expedition. Though it was a special caravan, it fulfilled a commercial purpose just like any other, and indeed many pilgrims paid their way by bartering merchandise carried from their homeland. Their sheer numbers—between twenty and forty thousand in a typical year[110]—provided Damascus with an enormous injection of people, goods, and capital. In 1765, state expenditures alone exceeded 300,000 piasters on troops, their provisions, and sundry subsidies to the bedouin.[111] Any disruption in this annual cycle immediately convulsed local markets, which could sink into prolonged slumps or experience sharp price fluctuations. For good reason, people eagerly awaited the latest news of the pilgrimage. Unexpected delays were the occasion for wild rumors, and spread a sense of panic throughout the city.

Towards the end of the century, the pilgrimage faced unprecedented dangers due to the emergence of a new political order deep within central Arabia. An obscure bedouin dynasty, the house of Saʿud (forerunners of the modern Saudis), had made common cause with the adherents of a puritanical religious sect known as the Wahhabis. Their guiding light, the jurist Ibn ʿAbd al-Wahhab (1703–92), called for the purification of Islam and a return to what he regarded as the norms of early Islamic society. By the beginning of the nineteenth century, Wahhabi power extended over a large part of Arabia, and raiding parties struck as far away as the settlements of southern Syria and Iraq. Rejecting the legitimacy of Ottoman rule, the movement culminated in the sack of the Shiite holy city of Karbala (1802) and the capture of Mecca (1803) and Medina (1805). The victors smashed local religious shrines and effectively barred the pilgrimage caravan. By 1810, they had grown bold enough to operate in the vicinity of Damascus.[112] The Ottomans organized several campaigns, all of which ended in futility. Imperial authority returned only with the arrival in 1811 of the Egyptian army, newly reorganized under the formidable Egyptian viceroy Muhammad Ali, who defeated the Wahhabis and later broke up their state in the interior.

PRIMACY OF THE LOCAL

These local reverses—warlords, restless bedouin, French invaders, Wahhabi raiders—coincided with a series of severe challenges for the Ottoman Empire as a whole: a string of military defeats in the Balkans and Egypt during the second half of the eighteenth century; loss of territory in the Crimea (1783); the rise of powerful notables and warlords throughout much of the sultan's domains; and grave fiscal and monetary instability (from the 1770s). Were Damascenes fully aware of these ominous connections? Local accounts rarely mention the gathering crisis, which so alarmed the imperial leadership that it launched the first (and ultimately unsuccessful) administrative and military reforms—the so-called New

Order, which ended with the murder of Selim III (r. 1789–1807). Their inattention was not a matter of indifference. From the standpoint of eighteenth-century Damascenes, the doings of city and province generally obscured these more distant imperial horizons. Popular consciousness was primarily local, and external affairs intruded only fitfully into this relatively closed universe. News from more distant lands arrived with the caravans and imperial messengers, and was sometimes announced with official celebrations that might honor the birth of children to the sultan or some military victory on the frontiers. These events might briefly cause a commotion, but rarely occupied center stage for long. Reports reaching ordinary Damascenes were often garbled or imperfectly understood. When Ahmad al-Budayri recorded in his journal in 1743 that the Persian king Tahmasp had besieged Baghdad, he was unaware that Tahmasp had died many years earlier, having fought against the Ottomans in the 1720s. In fact, it was Nadir Shah, not this earlier ruler, who was then leading the assault on Iraq.[113] Such faulty knowledge was the product of eighteenth-century communications, always difficult and intermittent. Rapid and reliable links with the outside were a modern achievement, which followed the spread of steam shipping, mechanized transport, and telegraphy. Even then, mentalities were slow to change. Reflecting on his childhood at the beginning of the twentieth century, one Damascene author recalled that "the people were in ignorance and knew not a thing about political matters which took place abroad."[114] His eighteenth-century forebears were no better informed. Though not oblivious to the wider world, Damascenes were thoroughly preoccupied with their own corner of the empire.

All these barriers to the flow of news and information were fully reproduced in the circulation of goods. Most production and consumption relied on materials which were obtained from local or regional sources. The result was a kind of parochial diversity. Each town and region boasted its own distinctive styles and tastes. Strong local identities manifested themselves in building, costume, even the smallest consumer goods. Returning from a visit to Jerusalem, al-Nabulsi stopped at Bethlehem and took the time to purchase one of its renowned specialties: prayer beads carved from local olive trees and sold by peddlers at the side of the road.[115] Damascene consumers, as he well knew, could not count on finding such things at home. And he had not yet left southern Syria.

This tendency towards localism did not arise from the Ottoman decentralization of the eighteenth century, which exacerbated rural insecurity in many areas, but certainly did not create the unsettled conditions. Rather, it was the outcome of long-term technological deficiencies in transport and communication, which predated Ottoman rule and to eighteenth-century Damascenes seemed more or less permanent and normal. These structural bottlenecks encouraged a large degree of self-reliance. Though goods and materials were continually flowing into Damascus from regional and international trading routes, urban markets faced insuperable ceilings on the quantities that they could realistically import. The transport sector was condemned to low speeds and capacities, which ensured that Damascus and other towns would have to draw their sustenance primarily from their hinterland. One other corollary, to which we will turn next, was that the city was exposed to potential shortfalls in its most essential supplies. The prospect of such catastrophic failures, which were almost impossible to rectify, would constantly haunt the premodern economy.

I I

BREAD

&

SURVIVAL

THE COMMOTION CREATED BY THE HARVEST OF 1749 was like nothing Damascus had seen in more than a generation. When the grain finally arrived from the fields in June, at the traditional time, the entire city exploded in demonstrations of thanksgiving and joy. Most of the markets were strung with decorations, and a festive air filled the streets. As one eyewitness recounted, "due to their great happiness, the people of Damascus, especially the poor, began to weep and shout with joy inasmuch as God had delivered them" from their suffering.[1] The popular reaction was particularly exultant that year because it followed a long period of hard times and scarcity, which had lasted through the winter and spring. The infusion of new grain changed the life of the city at one stroke, lowering prices and ensuring that everyone would have enough to eat.

Even when times were not so desperate, townspeople eagerly awaited news from the countryside. A successful cereal harvest was always a cause for relief, if not raucous celebration, whereas the failure of crops cast a pall over the city, raising the specter of want, misery, and perhaps even starvation for the poorest. Everything was linked to this annual chain of events in which grain was planted, gathered, stored, and eaten. But can we really talk about these various stages, in which grain was slowly transformed into daily bread, as if they were merely the outcome of a "natural" process? On the contrary, grain occupied a huge share of local and regional markets, making it the focus of continuous struggle, profit, and manipulation. As an object of investment, trade, taxation, and consumption, it served as the indispensable fuel to the local economy, which had to direct most of its energies into the complex and uncertain task of simply feeding itself. More broadly, the story of bread raises basic questions about Ottoman political economy in the eighteenth century. Food and politics were deeply intertwined. As city and empire entered an unusually stormy period in their history, the reverberations from setbacks experienced by the Ottoman state would be felt throughout the social order, far from the battlefields and official chanceries. For many townspeople, these imperial travails would usher in a new era of hardships.

THE PREDOMINANCE OF CEREALS

To speak of the harvest in the singular, as if it consisted of a single crop, would be entirely misleading. In reality, there was not merely grain, but a whole hierarchy of different grains, each of which had a distinct identity in local culture.

At the apex stood wheat, the perennial favorite among the entire population. "Wheat is the best type of grain," as one local authority explained without bothering to add the slightest qualification.[2] In tribute to its popularity, it was grown nearly everywhere in the Syrian countryside. Damascus received a good portion of its supplies from the Biqaʿ Valley, east of Mount Lebanon. But the real granary of the city was the Hawran plain to the south, which was renowned for the high quality and quantity of its yields.[3] Much less esteemed was the output of the Damascene oasis itself, which as a mark of its inferiority might be fed to animals in times of plenty.[4] As an imperial army in Syria prepared for the campaign against Napoleon (1799), it naturally requisitioned stocks of flour not from the nearby villages of Damascus (which were asked instead to contribute barley), but from the more distant districts of the Hawran.[5]

Among other cereals, only rice had a reputation comparable to wheat, appearing as a favorite complement to feasts and celebrations. But as a relatively pricey import from Egypt, it never established itself as a regular feature of the daily diet, and for many Damascenes very much remained a luxury dish.[6] Far more common, both in quantity of stocks and frequency of consumption, was barley, the consolation of the peasantry and urban poor (table 2.1).[7] In confirmation of its lowly status, it was often used as fodder for animals. ʿAbd al-Ghani al-Nabulsi expressed little surprise when his horse was given barley at a local village.[8] The same aversion was shown to sorghum (*dhurra*) and millet (*dukhn*), ancient rivals that were cultivated far less widely than barley, and satisfied identical patterns of consumption. Occupying the bottom rank were crops reserved exclusively for animals, mostly leguminous plants such as vetch.[9]

This hierarchy of grains showed remarkable stability throughout the Ottoman period and almost certainly dated from earlier centuries, stretching far into the remote past. Like all Syrians, Damascenes demonstrated a stubborn preference for wheat and switched to other grains (apart from rice) only when it lay beyond their means or fell into short supply. Alternatives to these traditional choices were slow to appear. The potato, an import from the New World, had reached Syria by the eighteenth century,[10] but struggled to gain popularity; even at the end of the nineteenth century, unscrupulous millers used it mainly as a means of adulterating their grain, adding yet another ruse to their already extensive bag of tricks.[11] Maize (*dhurra safraʾ*), another arrival from overseas, was embraced with equal reluctance.[12] This resistance can be explained partly as a matter of established tastes, and partly as an outgrowth of demographic trends. In other areas of the Old World where maize flourished on a large scale, notably Europe and China,[13] a population explosion of unprecedented proportions was taking place; as the number of mouths grew beyond the capacity of the old agricultural regime, peasants had to adopt new crops—above all, maize, potatoes, and sweet potatoes—to ward off starvation. In contrast, eighteenth-century Syria—and, for that matter, nearly all of the Ottoman lands—faced no such emergency. Syrians thus had little reason to alter their habits of the hearth. Thanks to this continuity in taste, supply, and demand, wheat remained "the noblest of foods" (*ashraf al-aṭʿima*). Other grains continued to take their traditional places behind it.[14]

TABLE 2.1 Grain and Diet

Amounts of Grain and Fodder Found in Damascene Estates, ca. 1750–67

GRAIN/FODDER	QUANTITY (IN *GHIRARA*)
Wheat (*hinta/qamh*)	180.2
Rice* (*aruzz/ruzz*)	56.51
Barley (*sha'ir*)	238.4
Sorghum (*dhurra*)	4.8
Vetch (*julbanna/kirsinna*)	5.99

SOURCE: Islamic Court Records.

*Converted from the standard *qintar* normally used for rice

What was true among cereals can equally be said for their products, for grain was merely the first link in a long chain of processing and refining that led to flour and, finally, to bread. Many families, especially among the peasantry and urban poor, commonly ate wheat (or barley) bulgur. It was a familiar ingredient in many local dishes: mixed with yogurt, it became *kishk*, one of the fixtures of rural life and a popular meal during the chill of winter; with lentils, it yielded *mujaddara*, another food of the working population.[15] More than anything else, though, it was bread which was the true staple of the diet. Looking out upon the countryside, Damascene chroniclers sometimes referred to the broad expanses of agricultural land as "bread."[16] This simple and direct equation was more than a convenience of vocabulary; it said everything about the priorities of everyday life, in which bread was not merely a food among foods, but an endless obsession. No other food excited the same devotion among the townspeople, who exulted when it was cheap and abundant. It was identified with life itself and acquired a connection with the divine. To sell bread on the streets, a vendor merely had to shout, "God is generous!" (*Allah karim!*), and passersby instantly knew his trade.[17] In the popular imagination, nothing mattered as much as bread. It was "the pillar of religion, the support of the spirit, and the life-blood of the soul."[18]

Damascenes were quite fortunate, then, to enjoy a supply which was not only ample, but of excellent quality as well. "Nowhere have I seen bread in such perfection as at Damascus," exclaimed the French poet

Lamartine during a visit in the early nineteenth century.[19] It was not a false impression. The people of Damascus, like other townspeople of the Middle East, typically ate bread made from wheat flour, and had been blessed with this privilege since antiquity.[20] When local writers referred to "bread," they meant exactly this wheat bread, which always came in the shape of flat, round loaves. It was the implicit standard, and the best indicator of overall price and supply.

But not all loaves were alike. The simple word for bread (*khubz*) concealed the many varieties which were actually available. Like the grain from which it was made, bread too conformed to a larger scale of taste and prestige.

The overwhelming preference was for white bread. This rule was absolute and applied even to non-wheat bread, such as white barley bread, which also had a high reputation.[21] Whatever the exact ingredients and proportions, white bread marked off the upper end of the market. It was "special bread" (*khubz khass*), and therefore fetched an invariably high price, putting it well beyond the reach of the poor.[22] And there were even more refined (and expensive) variations, all of which paid homage to the same time-honored principle of white bread and wheat flour. For those who liked crispy bread, and were willing to pay the extra price for it, there was the ring-shaped treat known as *ka'k*.[23] Much harder and drier was *buqsumat*, a long biscuit. Baked in large quantities for expeditions like pilgrimage caravans and military campaigns, it was able to survive long voyages without rotting. When ready to eat, travelers "steep it in water, and find it as good as if new made. Both rich and poor prefer it to all other sort of bread," explained an enthusiastic Englishman.[24] Another favorite was *ma'ruk*, consisting of white bread coated with clarified butter, and costing roughly 50 percent more than ordinary white bread.[25] Providing a similar effect on both palate and purse were sesames and sesame oil, the key ingredients to *khubz al-abariz*.[26]

Compared with these specialties, other refinements differed primarily in their manner of preparation. Among the finest Damascene breads were those baked in a *tannur*, a kind of small oven sunk into the ground. Al-Nabulsi touted this bread as superior to all others.[27] In a closely related method of baking, stones were placed along the inside of the oven; a convex iron plate was then laid on top and covered with animal manure, which was prized as a slow-burning fuel. Baked without this lid, the same bread was called *khubz al-milla*, for which, however, Damascenes showed considerably less relish, for "no one bakes it unless destitute."[28] The most lavish praise was reserved for "doctors' bread," whose secret was a heavy dose of garlic. Ibn Kannan rhapsodized that it prevented sickness, aided digestion, restored the skin to its natural ruddy tones, and, if eaten regularly, extended longevity "until [one] reaches the natural age of one hundred twenty."[29] If bread was a necessity, good bread was a passion and delight.

Cheap bread, on the other hand, offered little more than affordability. The difference was immediately noticeable in the color and texture of the loaves, which grew progressively darker and coarser as one moved down the scale of price and taste. Brown bread (*khubz asmar*), which took its hue from a higher content of bran and other impurities, was almost synonymous with inferior quality. The same verdict, moreover, applied to any bread not made from wheat. Typical of this prejudice was barley bread, whose popularity among the peasantry and the poor was a sure sign of its humble status and limited appeal. Echoing a widely held opinion, Ibn Kannan declared that it was a beneficial food, but less nourishing than wheat bread, whereas al-Nabulsi claimed that it "dries and constipates the constitution and gives rise to winds."[30] Among the wheat-eaters of urban society, it was associated with sacrifice and self-denial. Recounting the austere lifestyle of a twelfth-century scholar, al-Nabulsi noted that the pious *shaykh* had slept on a simple mat and eaten nothing but barley bread.[31] No better was bread made from sorghum, which evoked the same unappetizing image. It was regarded as a poor man's food and eaten mostly as a cheap substitute for wheat. So fastidious were Damascenes that they even looked askance at mixed grains—usually some combination of wheat and either barley or sorghum—which stood at roughly half the price of ordinary wheat bread.[32] Beneath these second-rate alternatives were the true indicators of desperation. Indeed, the poorest of the poor sometimes had to settle for repulsive "black bread" (*khubz aswad*), a last resort which was universally despised. More than unpalatable, it often contained so much foreign matter and filth that it resembled not so much bread as disemboweled "livers."[33] Only starvation was worse.

In any event, the kind of bread that people ate often had less to do with its reputation and taste than the state of local supplies. Quality and quantity were very much interrelated. Whenever stocks of grain dwindled, due to drought or other disruptions, prices inevitably leapt upwards, spreading misery and tempting millers and bakers to adulterate their flour and thereby stretch both ingredients and profits. Contemporaries recognized, and dreaded, both of these signals, which were tantamount to a declaration of economic crisis. As wheat became ever more precious and difficult to find, Damascenes soon resigned themselves to cereals that they normally scorned. "During this year," wrote Ahmad al-Budayri in his journal in 1747, "rain has been scarce, and prices high. Most of the food of the Damascene people has been bread of sorghum and barley, and the poor have had nothing but God."[34] In the worst years, such as 1758, even black bread gradually disappeared, leaving swarms of beggars to starve in the streets. Many of these miserable refugees were peasants who had given up all hope and fled from their homes in the countryside. "We saw them entering the city in hordes, barefoot and naked, like those who have emerged from the grave," remembered Mikha'il Burayk.[35] In such dire extremities, survival sometimes meant sacrificing all the usual standards and adopting the most unorthodox solutions. A prolonged drought in 1792 was so severe that the city had to improvise bread made from vetch, which resembled clover more than wheat.[36] But at least there was bread, no matter how distasteful or repugnant. Without it, the situation was truly hopeless.

ESTIMATING CONSUMPTION

Having observed the centrality of bread in the local diet, our next step is to examine how much of it Damascenes were actually eating. Was it enough to provide ample sustenance? Or were many people merely existing in a state of chronic malnutrition? Almost no firsthand evidence survives from the eighteenth century. There are no scraps of paper which preserve shopping lists or household budgets. Nor were Damascenes in the habit of keeping diaries or recording other personal testimonials which might allow us to reconstruct the popular diet in all its minute details. All these uncertainties are highlighted by the offhand comment of al-Budayri, who mentioned during Ramadan in 1750 that he had kept the fast (enjoined for able-bodied adults from dawn to dusk during the entire month) for the first time in many years.[37] Did most Muslims faithfully observe this religious duty? Did consumption of food drop during Rama-

TABLE 2.2. The Distribution of Wealth

(in 1000 selected estates, ca. 1750–67)

GROSS VALUE OF ESTATE (IN PIASTERS)	NO. OF DAMASCENES	AGGREGATE VALUE (IN PIASTERS)
<100	285 (28.5%)	14,943 (1.2%)
100–499	418 (41.8%)	100,231 (8.5%)
500–999	116 (11.6%)	83,447 (7.1%)
1000–4999	136 (13.6%)	270,357 (23.0%)
>=5000	45 (4.5%)	705,590 (60.0%)
Total	1000	1,174,568

SOURCE: Islamic Court Records

dan, or did they simply make up the difference with late-night feasting? Existing sources have almost nothing to say on the matter.

Our best chance at calculating consumption is to work with those who had the fewest choices, namely the poor of Damascus, whose meals consisted mostly of bread. Their simple eating habits, dictated by economic constraints, permit relatively straightforward, albeit rough, calculations about their daily intake of food, as well as its equivalent in calories. Living at the level of bare subsistence, they can help us to determine the minimum amounts of food required for survival. So even if the diet of the wealthy is beyond our ability to reconstruct in detail, we can still offer judgments about the lower reaches of society, which, after all, held the majority of townspeople.

The gulf between rich and poor was enormous. One way of appreciating the true magnitude of this difference is to examine the personal fortunes of a random group of eighteenth-century Damascenes, drawn from the surviving probate inventories for the period 1750–67. Their collective testimony reveals one glaring and irrefutable fact: an extreme, even staggering, concentration of wealth (table 2.2). The richest individual, a long-forgotten dignitary named Hasan Çelebi (d. 1763), died in possession of assets worth more than 118,000 piasters. At the bottom of the economic scale was Shaʿban al-Misri, a pauper who departed his life in

1757 with little more than seven piasters to his credit.[38] Equally sugges-
tive is the aggregate evidence. Though the average fortune amounted to
roughly 1,249 piasters, only some 15 percent of the group (181 out of 1,194)
surpassed this figure. The top 3 percent controlled a little over half the
wealth; meanwhile, at the other end of the spectrum, Damascenes who
held less than five hundred piasters (70.4 percent of the group) could
claim less than a tenth (9.1 percent). Overall, more than one out of every
four inhabitants (28.3 percent) may have lived in dire poverty, possessing
resources worth less than one hundred piasters.

These imbalances were partly reinforced by political distinctions,
which had everything to do with the distribution of wealth across Damascene society. Particularly decisive was membership in the "Ottoman
class." It is difficult to estimate the size of this social group, which the
central state itself may not have accurately known, but ʿaskari Damascenes
must have formed a significant minority, several thousand strong, within
the urban population. In addition to local officials, dignitaries, and soldiers, they included an outer circle of pensionaries, hangers-on, and others
who had probably inherited various privileges and honors from earlier
generations. Their economic weight was disproportionate to their numbers. On average, they held fortunes which were nearly three times as
valuable as those of their "civilian" counterparts (table 2.3).[39] Having
more money to spend, ʿaskari Damascenes were, on the whole, better
fed than other townspeople; no less critically, they were better insulated
against the price shocks periodically delivered by food shortage and
speculation. Hence the most imperceptible political privileges, such as
tax exemptions, could yield very real economic dividends.

All these figures clearly show the vast inequalities which prevailed
throughout Damascene society. Yet they tell us very little about the resources which were at the disposal of townspeople on a daily basis. The
ideal solution would be to estimate disposable income, which could be
extracted from data on wages and other earnings. Such evidence would
allow us to make calculations about expenditures, including the amount
of food that an ordinary person could possibly have purchased over a
given interval. Regrettably, the practical obstacles are insurmountable.
Perhaps local guilds kept information on wages and work schedules, but
like so many other papers from the premodern Middle East, their records (if they ever existed) have entirely vanished. More disappointing

TABLE 2.3. "Military" (*'Askari*) vs. "Native" (*Baladi*) Wealth

GROSS VALUE OF ESTATES (IN PIASTERS)	NO. OF *'ASKARI* ESTATES	NO. OF *BALADI* ESTATES
<100	34	251
100–499	81	337
500–999	46	70
1000–4999	60	76
>=5000	29	16
Total	250	750
Total Wealth	576,269	598,299
Average Value	2,305	797.7

SOURCE: Islamic Court Records

still, there are few other sources which are likely to prove helpful. Among the remaining documents, the most useful are the registers of the Islamic courts, which contain occasional references to contracts and, somewhat more frequently, official appointments. The chief difficulty is that both of these sources suffer from flaws which make generalizations hazardous. Contracts are scattered throughout the thousands of pages of other cases, offering few hints about the terms of labor. Records of appointments seem to hold more promise, but ultimately reveal too little. Most were simply declarations that a job had changed hands, either by inheritance or through a formal act of transfer, together with a few additional pieces of information, such as the salary and schedule of payments. Since the vast majority of appointments were connected in some way with pious foundations attached to mosques, religious schools, bathhouses, and the local hospital (the *bimaristan* of Nur al-Din, founded in the twelfth century), the recipients were most often ulama, who were not entirely representative of the working population. Another problem is that one can never be sure whether the occupant of a particular position had a claim on others as well. Many members of the religious establishment held multiple appointments and were not the least bit hesitant in their search for further honors and promotions. One outcome of this intense competition was the practice of awarding fractions of positions. Ulama might easily share jobs with other individuals, thereby gaining a portion of the overall salary. A man who held enough partial grants could provide a significant boost to his income, earning far more than the salary listed on any single document.

Given the general lack of data on wages, the only alternative is to infer disposable income through other kinds of payments. Such evidence can be found elsewhere in the Islamic courts, primarily in the official accounts (pl. *muhasabat*) drawn up for orphans—that is, all children whose fathers had died. Islamic law stipulated that all orphans were to be placed under the protection of a court-appointed guardian (*wasi*), who was almost invariably a close relative. The guardian assumed responsibility for managing the children's wealth and was fully empowered to make investments, extend loans, and even borrow money for personal use. To discourage abuses, the court was supposed to conduct annual reviews until the children were declared adults, which usually happened at some time during their mid-teens. In the meantime, they received a regular allowance, which was established by the judge and deducted from their estates.

Judges never explained their rulings with elaborate opinions, but it seems likely that they considered the economic status of the family before fixing the rate of payment. Orphans who inherited large sums tended to receive the most generous grants (table 2.4), often in excess of fifty piasters annually for accounts audited at mid-century. In contrast, poor children had to manage with much less support. Apart from three exceptionally low cases, the bottom range hovered between twelve and thirty piasters per year, with the great majority of these children (forty-two out of forty-seven) receiving at least eighteen piasters. The court scribes rarely specified how this money was spent, listing it as no more than "maintenance and clothing" (*nafaqa wa kiswa*). In all probability, the overwhelming share of the stipend was devoted to food rather than clothing; in fact, sizable payments for the latter sometimes appeared in a separate category, apart from the everyday expenses of nafaqa, which had more to do with nourishment.[40] If food enjoyed the same priority in the accounts of other children, as seems likely, it would reflect patterns observed for other areas of the premodern world, such as European cities, where artisans and common laborers spent nearly all of their income on food.[41]

Whatever the spending habits of guardians, one can safely assume that

TABLE 2.4. Estimating the Minimum Standard of Living: Orphans' Estates
(*muhasabat*), ca. 1750–67

	ANNUAL PAYMENTS (IN PIASTERS)								
Value of Estate	42	12–17	18–23	24–30	31–36	37–42	43–48	>48	Total
<100	1	0	6	6	0	1	0	0	14
100–499	2	3	9	17	5	4	2	8	50
500–999	0	2	1	2	4	1	2	12	24
>1000	0	0	0	1	2	3	1	28	35
Total	3	5	16	26	11	9	5	48	123

SOURCE: Islamic Court Records

the proportion of funds set aside for non-dietary expenses must have shrunk as budgets grew smaller. Among the least fortunate orphans, the level of support must have verged on bare subsistence, making their stipends an ideal reference for the minimum cost of living. These figures cannot, of course, be taken as a precise index of poverty. Due to the unpredictable fluctuations of prices, only the most lavish incomes could guarantee a fixed standard of living. Nevertheless, the records are extremely useful for identifying the financial *limits* at which everyday life became increasingly difficult and precarious. Converted to daily installments, the lowest allowances averaged between two and three misriyyas per child (one piaster being equal to forty misriyyas). Let us assume, first, that the stipends were spent entirely on food, and that whatever was purchased with these funds went entirely into the mouths of the children. Measured against the price of bread, always the mainstay of the poor, we can then produce a rough estimate of consumption (disregarding, for the sake of our calculations, variations in prices according to season, as well as other conditions affecting the market).

For the price of bread, we are fortunate to have a fairly regular series extending throughout the two middle decades of the century, thanks mainly to the journal of Ahmad al-Budayri. During most of this time, the annual average for bread hovered around four to six misriyyas per *ratl* (1.85 kilograms, or a little over four pounds). For the poorest children, who received only two misriyyas per day, daily consumption of bread would have therefore been no more than one-half to one-third of a ratl: expressed in energy, the equivalent of 1,550–2,350 calories.[42] Naturally, there were other sources of calories in the daily diet, but the poor had to content themselves with relatively simple fare, which meant a monotonous routine dominated by bread and more bread. As a result, they were unlikely to receive significantly higher levels of energy except when they were able to obtain meat, fats, and oils in substantial quantities. It was a pattern which endured until quite recent times. One twentieth-century survey discovered that grain always constituted at least half of what people ate, and for the majority, the figure could climb as high as 90 percent.[43] Another study, confined to urban households of "functionaries and wage-earners" during the 1930s, concluded that some three-quarters of the diet (excluding seasonal produce) was devoted to grains and starches.[44] Apart from the addition of potatoes, it was a balance of foods that eighteenth-century Damascenes would certainly have recognized.

Despite the deficiencies of such a diet, the poor of the mid-eighteenth century may not have been so terribly fed. This is a problem which really concerns nutrition as well as energy, and therefore requires a much fuller discussion of eating habits, beyond bread alone. But if we confine ourselves to basic requirements for energy, it is possible to say that, even with consumption as low as 2,000 calories or so, Damascenes were not suffering from unusual deprivation.[45] They were certainly doing no worse than Parisian workers who, shortly before the French Revolution (1789), were living at roughly the same level of sustenance.[46] At about the same time, in Tokugawa Japan most peasants enjoyed a diet which, though centered on rice instead of wheat, provided about 1,800–2,300 calories, putting them in an identical range.[47] More research needs to be conducted on other parts of the world, and for as many different periods as possible, but each of these cases points towards a common daily minimum on the order of 2000 calories. Damascenes who filled themselves at this rate may have enjoyed a meager lifestyle, at least in comparison with societies in the modern West, where diets under 2500 calories are considered trying or altogether insufficient for adults on an active work schedule.[48] But insofar as we take bread as our single measure, Damascenes seem to have enjoyed a standard of living which was fully comparable with the rest of eighteenth-century Eurasia.

The local economy devoted most of its resources to meeting this hunger for bread. The supply, storage, and refinement of grain involved immense amounts of capital and employed most of the Syrian population, four-fifths of whom were peasants growing food on the land. From this broad hinterland flowed the vital stream of grain which animated the regional economy and functioned as its most essential commodity, even acting on occasion as a substitute for money.[49] But it was never a stream which flowed freely; rather, it was subject at every turn to the dictates and demands of urban wealth and power. This control was part of a much wider pattern of domination in which a subordinate rural world provided taxes, raw materials, and immigrants for the maintenance and enrichment of the urban economy. Measured against the villages within its orbit, the city was an island of affluence and security.

Nothing confirmed these advantages like a bad harvest. Whenever grain ran short, the Ottoman administration carefully diverted supplies to Damascene warehouses.[50] Governors spared no pains in finding emergency relief. In an attempt to alleviate the scarcity and high prices which prevailed in 1751, Asʿad Pasha al-ʿAzm obtained deliveries of grain from as far away as Hama, where he and his family had established themselves as tax farmers and continued to wield considerable influence.[51] Other consignments arrived by sea, usually through Lebanese ports such as Sidon, which in 1708 relayed some 675 tons (3,000 *ghirara*) of grain to Damascus after locusts had devastated the harvests of the interior.[52] When the swarms again returned in 1747–48, Asʿad Pasha converted their ravages into a pretext for launching raids against Druze communities in the Biqaʿ. Showing utter indifference to the fate of villagers, he timed his campaign for the harvest and plundered local crops, which he brought back to Damascus and placed on the market.[53] But the city could not always count on such timely infusions from the outside and was often thrown back on its own resources, however desperate the situation threatened to become. As the French traveler Volney observed (1784), the main effect of this policy was to transfer the brunt of the crisis to the countryside, which was compelled to release its stocks of grain to the Damascene market.[54] It was perhaps the greatest urban privilege: peasants might starve, but Damascus had to be fed.

In other words, grain was not simply another branch of commerce. Its centrality to both diet and economy made it a thoroughly political affair in which Ottoman and local authorities intruded at every level. The state reserved the right to set prices for grain and other foodstuffs, and was charged with monitoring local storage facilities and ensuring that weights and measures were accurate. Public opinion expected diligent inspections, which, barring natural catastrophes and social upheavals, were held directly responsible for fluctuations in prices. Townspeople had little faith in the laws of supply and demand. The urban imagination populated the marketplace with sinister forces bent on manipulating stocks of grain at public expense and suffering. So unshakable was this conviction that, in the spring of 1706, Ibn Kannan could only express amazement when wheat suddenly became cheaper "by itself" without the intervention of the authorities; it was all the more remarkable, he asserted, because "the rulers" had been hoarding supplies.[55]

Townspeople really believed that small groups of officials and merchants could hatch elaborate schemes to fix prices and fill their pockets. But was there any truth to these perceptions of mischief and collusion, or to the widely shared assumption that a few individuals could control the fate of a single commodity? Unfortunately, the structural sources of hunger and privation—the actual chain of causes and events which contributed to a sense of misery and crisis—are not always easy to sort out and identify. Amid the swirling rumors that frightened contemporaries all too willingly reported, many claims can hardly be regarded as more than hearsay or stock invectives against "speculators" and "hoarders." Historians of early modern Europe, who have grappled with the same problems, have generally echoed this skepticism and dismissed allegations of manipulation as the phantoms of terrified imaginations. Not everyone agrees. The main dissenter, Steven Kaplan, has studied the grain trade of eighteenth-century Paris in exhaustive detail and warned that profiteering constituted a very real threat to urban consumers. Merchants, he argues, could exercise a pernicious influence over the supply of grain.[56]

Does Damascus vindicate his defense of public paranoia? By way of illustration, we can take the events of the spring of 1749. Grain had become very expensive in the months preceding the harvest, which, much to the relief of the populace, turned out to be quite plentiful. But when prices hardly seemed to fall after the first shipments of new wheat, outraged crowds began to plunder some of the bakeries. As part of the effort to quell the rioting, price controls were immediately instituted, leading to reductions of 20 to 40 percent. For a short time, these measures proved so effective that a grateful population began to celebrate. Their joy was short-lived, for the governor, As'ad Pasha al-'Azm, had learned what was happening and become publicly enraged. In the presence of many notables, he and his agents began to tour the markets and threaten anyone who did not revert to the higher rates, which, in view of his own immense stockpiles of grain, would have ensured handsome profits. In subsequent days, the bakeries bent to the pasha's will, but not exactly as he intended. As a result of his interference, "bread became blacker and changed" in quality, if not price, allowing for the continued skimming of profits. But his victory was only temporary. Due to the glut of wheat, prices soon began to fall again, touching off further festivities.[57] This episode in failed profiteering would seem to demonstrate that simple administrative edicts, or the crudest schemes for maintaining shortages, could not overcome the forces of supply and demand. More specifically, everything depended on sufficient supplies. Large surpluses allowed the market to brush off attempts at extralegal manipulation; the more grain became available, the less influence predatory dealers could hope to exert over prices.

When supplies faltered, the rules were very different. Contemporaries eagerly attributed rising prices to official negligence, which, as they saw it, was most critical in opening the door to hoarding and manipulation. As food became ever dearer throughout the autumn of 1742, Ahmad al-Budayri was certain that the real problem was a "lack of inspections by the rulers," who allowed merchants to charge whatever they pleased. As prices crept ever higher during the following year, he again leveled the same complaint (to be repeated many times in the future) that "there was neither dearth nor locusts nor drought, but [only] want of inspections and tours [of the markets]."[58] Governors and judges were often rated simply for their success in keeping down prices. Rajab Pasha, who served as governor in 1720–21, carried out frequent tours of the markets and was fondly remembered for many years, as was 'Uthman Pasha al-Kurji (r. 1760–71), who earned similar praise for his own efforts to regulate commerce.[59] So powerful was the psychological effect of inspections that officials sometimes resorted to them as a means of restoring public confidence and easing social unrest. During the prolonged turbulence which followed the sack of the pilgrimage caravan in 1757, the qadi roved the markets in person, checking equipment and dispensing justice on the spot. All violators promptly received the bastinado, whereas honest merchants earned a silver misriyya for obeying regulations.[60] The state, whether represented by the qadi or its other officials, rarely made such dramatic appearances. But for all its discretion—and occasional complicity in unlawful practices—it was never far from the scene.

One of the most frequent targets of official supervision—and deservedly so, in the bitter estimation of contemporaries—were the bakers. As the last link in the refining and marketing of grain, they were viewed with a mixture of envy and mistrust, especially during times of scarcity, which offered opportunities to profit from hunger. Local wisdom characterized them as "persons of dispute and contention," as troublemakers who were always sowing discord with their underhanded practices.[61] The authorities held them in the same low regard and kept close watch over the bakeries, making public examples out of a few unlucky miscreants. In the most notorious cases, bakers might be hanged or humiliated in the marketplace.[62]

Millers fell under the same suspicion and were treated with equal severity. Fueling popular cynicism were various rumors, always widespread during shortages, which whispered of millers who adulterated their flour with inferior grains.[63] By far the most damning allegations had to do with hoarding, which stoked public anger like no other issue. Ibn Kannan once noted (with evident satisfaction) the strangling (1736) of a miller who was caught hoarding grain and conspiring to raise prices. Shortly afterwards, two Janissary millers from the yerliyya corps were hanged for the same offense.[64] These small fry paid the price for the far more serious manipulations committed at higher levels, where violators enjoyed the immunity conferred by wealth and power.

At the root of this antagonism towards millers and bakers was their very centrality to everyday life. In the course of obtaining their provisions, Damascenes almost unavoidably met with one or the other. The degree of interaction varied from household to household, each of which had its own routines and needs.[65]

Some families, especially among the poor, bought their loaves straight from local ovens and were therefore entirely at the mercy of their bakers. As a result, they were particularly vulnerable to disruptions in the marketplace. During the brief Egyptian occupation of Damascus in 1771, staged as part of a short-lived and eccentric rebellion (1770–72) by ʿAli Bey al-Kabir, shops throughout the city closed their shutters in expectation of heavy fighting and looting. But the outcome was not what the populace had imagined. Local notables persuaded the Egyptian commander to restrain his troops and declare a safe conduct for all townspeople except a contingent of imperial Janissaries, who were holding out in the citadel and vowing not to surrender without the express order of the sultan. When markets reopened soon afterwards, it was primarily the poor who rushed out to buy food.[66] Living from hand to mouth, these were the families whose meager incomes and cramped quarters made it nearly impossible to stockpile flour and other foodstuffs. At the bottom rungs of the economic ladder, closure of the local markets was more than an inconvenience; it was the prelude to hunger and privation.

As always, wealthier households were in a better position. They routinely kept reserves of food in cellars or pantries (*kilar* or *bayt muʾna*) designed expressly for the purpose of storing dry goods. In the grandest homes, there might even be a private granary.[67] The impulse to hoard was so thoroughly imprinted in local minds that it might reach bizarre proportions. The chronicler al-Budayri was stunned to hear of a man who had committed suicide, apparently on account of heavy indebtedness, even though he had accumulated enormous quantities of wheat in his home and could easily have sold them.[68] Such behavior, albeit an extreme aberration, is a reminder of the underlying anxieties with which people lived. The specter of hunger was never totally absent, encouraging stockpiling as a sensible precaution against unforeseen crises.[69] It was a solution which also lent flexibility to daily routines. By keeping extra supplies, families were able to regulate the quality of their bread by kneading their own dough and sending it out for baking. Neighborhood bakeries took a small fee and perhaps one or two loaves as commission for their services.[70] This option was most popular—and feasible—among middling and affluent households.[71] The ideal was always the same: to minimize dependence on the market.

Only a handful of residents attained anything like self-sufficiency or absolute security in regard to supplies. Even those who did not buy bread directly from bakeries still had to contend with millers, who were the main source of flour for the general population. Within this category of tradesmen, Damascenes broadly distinguished between two types. The first were "commercial millers" (*tahhan suqi*), who operated the biggest mills and dealt directly with the granaries. In popular imagery, they were sinister figures who hoarded grain and battened on the misery of others. Less vilified were the "residential millers" (*tahhan bayti*), whom Damascenes were more likely to patronize. They enjoyed a reputation as "persons of trust," perhaps because their dealings were easier to monitor and more likely to create intimate ties between artisan and consumer. The arrangements were simple and flexible. For their own part, households were responsible only for washing and cleaning their grain. Whenever they needed flour, they summoned a local miller, who would come with his familiar sack and take away a small amount of grain for grinding. The fees were modest, and the small scale of the trade probably offered fewer opportunities for mischief.[72]

Only a few Damascenes tried to take matters into their own hands. Poor households, like many of their counterparts in Aleppo, may have kept crude hand mills for their own use.[73] But the search for convenience really favored the wealthy. One solution was to install a private mill (presumably a small grindstone) right inside the home.[74] Others simply purchased shares of commercial mills. Though some of these properties were held by small groups of investors, most belonged to members of the urban elite, who showed an insatiable appetite for real estate.[75] The best mills adjoined local rivers, which provided the optimum source of power, whereas those driven by animals had a reputation for grinding mediocre flour.[76] Milling techniques were quite versatile and produced several grades of flour, from fine to coarse. Varieties were made available according to demand, which was mostly determined by the bakers, who formed the biggest clientele.[77]

Far more than the millers and bakers, the real beneficiaries of the grain trade were the people who owned the grain and stored it. Their fortunes were visible in the many granaries (*bayika* or *hasil*) located throughout the city, especially in extramural quarters such as al-Midan and al-Salihiyya.[78] These structures came in many different sizes, from unassuming storerooms consisting of little more than four walls and a roof, to imposing warehouses built around as many as four or five stone vaults and multiple rooms.[79] The variety of facilities was a direct reflection of the grain trade itself, which involved individuals from across the social spectrum.

Even Damascenes from modest backgrounds helped to provision the city. They were the small-time dealers (*'allaf*) who held relatively incon-sequential stocks of grain.[80] At this level, the grain trade was merely an extension of the instinct to hoard; without sufficient capital, it was im-possible to entertain grander ambitions. Other townspeople accumulated grain outside the market, primarily through pious foundations (*waqf*)—that is, properties that various benefactors had set aside in perpetuity for the funding of private (*ahli*) or pious (*khayri*) causes. Most consisted of urban real estate such as shops and houses. But it was also possible to incorporate rural land, such as the waqf of Nur al-Din, a twelfth-century ruler whose name was attached to large tracts of land in the nearby village of Darayya. Shares in this "wheat of the poor" (*hintat al-fuqara'*) circulated widely in the eighteenth century. Their obvious economic benefits, as in-surance against hunger and inflation, explain the concern of many families to preserve their entitlements from one generation to the next.[81] Other shares changed hands between strangers, presumably for a price, and were carefully registered in the local courts. The quantities of grain were often substantial, and in several cases exceeded one ton per year.[82] Many ben-eficiaries, however, seem not to have been very poor at all, and at least a few were prominent ulama.[83] Despite the pious intentions of the waqf, the attraction of grain proved too powerful to be left to the poor alone.

Indeed, wherever grain accumulated, the affluent soon followed in pursuit. At no time was it a field of commerce which lay open to all, or even most, Damascenes. On the contrary, most of the grain trade was concentrated in the hands of a small group of wholesalers (*bawayiki* or *khazzan*), who tended to belong to the "Ottoman class."[84] Wealth flowed, above all, to those Damascenes who had access to the power and resourc-es of the state—that is to say, Ottoman officials and local notables. It was primarily members of this privileged social circle, not 'askari Damascenes as a whole, who reigned supreme in the grain market. In one sense, their investments in grain made them almost indistinguishable from mer-chants. But they really owed their fortunes to political connections, for control over grain required control over the countryside.

Closest to the levers of power, as well as the potential profits that they yielded, were the city's governors, who rarely hesitated to dip their hands into commerce. They routinely—and almost unavoidably—mixed duty with business, managing vast amounts of wealth which had to be collect-ed, forwarded to Istanbul, or disbursed on the spot. Taken to extremes, the pursuit of profit sometimes shaded into open malfeasance. In 1713, the ruthless Nasuh Pasha confiscated all local grain without warning and transferred it to his private warehouses, leading to an immediate shortage of bread and the closure of most of the city's shops.[85] Fueling the temptation for administrative abuse was the eighteenth-century Ottoman policy (adopted by many other large states of the era) of auctioning offices to the highest bidders, for whom bureaucratic posts then became a kind of private investment which had to be recouped and, if possible, turned to profit. There is a danger, however, in placing too much emphasis on tales of venality, which obscure the more legitimate paths to wealth that were readily available to governors. As the commanders of the pilgrimage caravan, for instance, they were ideally placed to join local merchants in long-distance trade and share in its immense rewards. And since taxation was practically inseparable from the fate of the harvest, governors found themselves constantly handling grain and dealing with questions concerning the latest state of supplies.

These administrative functions opened the door to profit for lesser officials, such as Mustafa Agha, a deputy commander (Tk. *kethüda*) in the entourage of 'Uthman Pasha al-Kurji (r. 1760–71). The former used his position to trade extensively in wheat, barley, and vetch, not to mention livestock, and accumulate property and possessions valued at more than 52,000 piasters upon his death in 1765.[86] The potential for hefty earnings helps to explain the enduring appeal of service in the Ottoman state in spite of its latent perils: sudden dismissal, confiscation of assets, and in the most precipitous falls from grace, a speedy and ignominious execution.

The rewards of power also lured local notables, who eagerly sought the wealth of the countryside. Some families pursued a calculated strategy of buying up parcels of urban and rural real estate connected with the grain trade. They snapped up mills, warehouses, and village fields, which allowed them to siphon off considerable stocks of wheat and barley. A second option was to purchase rural tax farms (*iltizam*), which were usually leased for short terms ranging from one to three years. The successful bidder paid for the right to collect taxes on behalf of the imperial treasury, which was chronically short of cash. As an added inducement, the Ottoman state had begun to offer lifetime tax farms (Tk. *malikane*) by the end of the seventeenth century.[87]

Among the biggest participants in the grain market were prominent ulama, many of whom built impressive portfolios of investments. Ibrahim Efendi al-'Ajlani, who belonged to one of the most distinguished religious families in the city, earned at least part of his fortune from the countryside, investing heavily in wheat and barley.[88] Operating on an entirely different scale was the illustrious mufti Hamid al-'Imadi, undoubtedly one of the richest men in Damascus at the time of his death. His estate comprised ninety-three properties, including a mill, an olive press, and a large number of fields, orchards, shops, and houses scattered throughout eleven villages, mostly in the Ghuta, but also as far away as the Hawran.[89] Inevitably, he dealt in grain, an interest which did not escape the notice of his fellow townspeople. In the difficult days before the harvest of 1749, while prices were steadily climbing, persistent rumors accused him of hoarding supplies "like the grandees and notables who do not fear [God]."[90] It was not the worldliness of the mufti which disturbed Damascenes, so much as the blatant injustice that he was seen committing. They saw no contradiction between religious authority and commercial ambition. Material gain was an entirely legitimate pursuit, as long as it was not sought with excessive ardor or in violation of Islamic precepts.

These ethical niceties were irrelevant to the commanders of the Janissary corps, who had long established their hold over large areas of the Damascene hinterland, particularly in the Hawran. Testifying to their extensive rural interests were the many granaries which dotted the suburb of al-Midan, stronghold of the yerliyya troops.[91] The wealthiest officers, such as Mustafa Agha al-Hawasili, were so successful that they were practically indistinguishable from the grand merchants (pl. *tujjar*) of the bazaars. Al-Hawasili's estate, assessed at more than 22,000 piasters, held over one ton of barley, but also gave proof of his wide-ranging interests in coffee, livestock, cloth, silk, and household supplies.[92] Yet, only the biggest dealers ventured far beyond the grain market. More representative of the military was Husayn Agha ibn Hijazi Agha, who owned rural land and focused his attention on wheat, barley, and sorghum.[93] Indeed, Janissaries became so closely identified with the grain trade that they became stock figures in local culture as the instigators of high prices and dearth. Among his entries for 1745, al-Budayri carefully devoted space to curse one of the foremost yerliyya officers, Mustafa Agha ibn al-Qabani, who had died during the year:

He was one of those who hoard food and desire high prices for the people. May God hasten [his] torment and punishment. Truly, I heard about him that when they wanted to bury him and dug a grave for him, they found a great serpent in it, and so they dug another, and likewise found [another serpent], until they had dug several graves and found serpents [in all of them]. . . . Moreover, they found in his estate one hundred ghirara of sesames even though in the entire country there was not a single *mudd*[94] available. They found, too, a great deal of wheat. It had been requested of him that he sell the wheat for forty-five piasters per ghirara, but he refused and swore that he would only sell for fifty. Then he expired without having sold anything. Thus [the wheat] was sold with his estate, and God showed mercy upon His people through his death, because He is the most forgiving.[95]

Al-Budayri spoke for many of his contemporaries, who nourished a deep hatred for the big grain merchants. It was a popular axiom that speculation, along with abuse of power, was one of the primary causes of food shortages. As bread grew harder to find, people were quick to blame the wealthy and powerful, and Janissary officers were a favorite target.

AN EIGHTEENTH-CENTURY CRISIS?

Complaints about hoarding and speculation were standard fare in local chronicles. Normally preoccupied with local politics, their pages also reveal the concerns of everyday life, which were never far removed from the affairs of the high and mighty. Nearly all writers were united in the conviction that the times were getting worse. Food was becoming more expensive, they insisted, and tyranny, corruption, and violence were on the rise, causing shortages to occur more frequently. Were things really as bad as they seemed? Or was it a misleading impression—a widespread conceit, repeated throughout Middle Eastern letters, that the current generation was living through an age of decline?[96]

Nothing tells the story better than the price of grain. Viewed over the eighteenth century, its behavior reenacts the fortunes of the market, which determined how much food Damascenes could ultimately put on their plates. Any crisis in the urban economy should be immediately apparent in the persistence of high prices, which in turn would indicate general want and scarcity, or at the very least, constant pressure on the market.

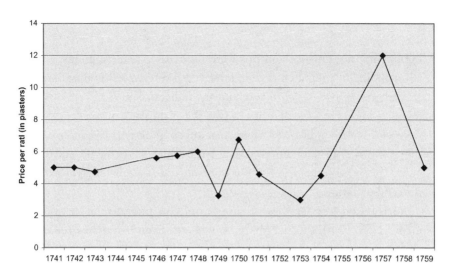

CHART I. The Uncertain Price of Bread, c. 1741–1759
Source: Ahmad al-Budayri, Hawadith Dimashq al-yawmiyya

As with any other commodity, the price of grain fluctuated over time, obeying hidden rhythms of which people were largely unaware. These variations were most characteristic of short-term conditions, which could demonstrate extreme volatility (chart I). Good prices in one year were no guarantee of what the next would bring. So unpredictable was the market that its shifting moods were noticeable even from season to season. The cost of grain normally fell after the June harvest and slowly climbed over the remainder of the year, especially during the winter and spring months, as stocks ran low again; but it might also move up and down according to the state of supplies, the prospects for the harvest, unexpected or ominous weather, and news from the outside world. It was one of the great uncertainties of eighteenth-century life.

Since Damascenes were forever adjusting their diets according to local prices, feasting when bread was cheap and tightening their belts as the market contracted, they developed an obsession for tracking the cost of living. It was a subject of constant speculation, a pretext for poetic verses,[97] a spur to fortune-telling and magical weather forecasts,[98] and a favorite theme of commentators who longed for the good old days. What townspeople understood, above all else, was that the grain trade was unusually sensitive to the slightest shocks and setbacks. Yet this sensitivity was not tantamount to confusion. Amid all the mercurial swings of the market, prices generally adhered to a basic set of relationships. Reflect-

ing popular taste, wheat and rice were the most expensive grains, usually standing at roughly the same level.[99] As less favored grains, barley
and other substitutes such as sorghum and millet occupied a lower range,
fetching anywhere from one-half to two-thirds the price of wheat. Violations of this ratio indicated a wider crisis affecting the entire economy. In
the spring of 1749, sorghum peaked at levels which were roughly equal to
wheat.[100] By no coincidence, it was remembered as a time of great hardship and privation.

Such episodes of dearth were never so infrequent or distant that their
memory was altogether forgotten or ignored. Even periods of relative
abundance were interspersed with occasional crises that operated as a
more or less permanent feature of the premodern economy. After a series of bad harvests in the late sixteenth century (particularly 1577–91),
Syria entered upon a long succession of good years that lasted into the
early eighteenth century. But at no time was the economy entirely free
from the threat of shortages and high prices, which struck hardest in
1642, 1661, 1676, and 1689.[101] Even so, the seventeenth century was exceptional for having, on average, no more than one famine every two to
three decades. It was a remarkable stretch of good fortune that was not
to be soon repeated.

Indeed, the eighteenth-century economy was more conspicuous for
its tribulations than triumphs. Despite periodic recoveries that temporarily lowered the cost of grain, prices were moving inexorably upwards.
Throughout the period 1680–1800, the grain market advanced through
several cycles (chart 2). After several years of plenty in the 1680s, the final
decade of the century (or at least the first half of that decade) registered
significant price increases. But before this trend could fully take hold,
the average value of wheat began to decline somewhat at the opening
of the new century. Except for shortfalls in 1708 and 1713, the city had
little difficulty feeding itself.[102] Only with the 1720s did the first intima-
tions of trouble begin to shake local markets. Instead of subsiding like the
high prices of the 1690s, the pressure on the food supply deepened into
a more or less permanent drain on the economy. By the 1740s, when our
information becomes much fuller, the cost of grain had already climbed
to unprecedented levels. Prices began to accelerate once again during the
1770s and 1780s. Most dramatic were the convulsions of the last decade

of the century, which witnessed at least one spectacular failure of the harvest, and a doubling of the cost of grain.

One of the most striking features of these trends is that they closely parallel the grain market in Egypt. There too, from the late seventeenth century till the arrival of the French Expedition in 1798, the price of wheat steadily rose, even when allowances are made for the depreciation of local coinage. Equally interesting is the coincidence of cycles. Egyptian grain experienced two peaks. The first occurred at the end of the seventeenth century, just as Syrian grain was showing increases, and was followed by a partial fall in prices over the next two decades. By mid-century, grain was again becoming noticeably more expensive. Prices continued to gather momentum upwards, cresting at record highs in the 1790s.[103] The timing and magnitude of these fluctuations were roughly identical and may have been a long-term structure of the regional economy. As far back as the fourteenth century, the geographer al-'Umari remarked that prices for grain were usually similar in both Egypt and Syria.[104] To some degree, then, geography was destiny.

Yet secular trends, however distinct and regular, do not constitute an explanation for the movement of markets; they merely demonstrate patterns whose underlying causes have to be uncovered and analyzed. Prices alone cannot reveal what propelled them up or down, alternately disrupting and invigorating the eighteenth-century economy.

Any discussion of grain prices has to begin with the regional climate, which worked its unalterable will on the market long before humans set about the task of reaping, dividing, and storing the harvest. There were no administrative remedies for drought, flooding, and freezes, whose periodic visitations were all too familiar to premodern populations. Some of the most memorable weather of the eighteenth century occurred in the 1740s and 1750s, the very decades which marked the onset of permanently high food prices.[105] Despite a wet autumn in 1742, a succession of winter freezes ruined crops and initiated a severe food shortage, as well as social unrest.[106] Irregular rainfall led to the same predicament in the winter and spring of 1745, once again throwing the markets into turmoil.[107] At their worst, subsistence crises were enormous catastrophes which affected the entire region. The hard times of 1758 were reported throughout the Levant and as far north as Diyarbakir, on the banks of the Tigris, whence

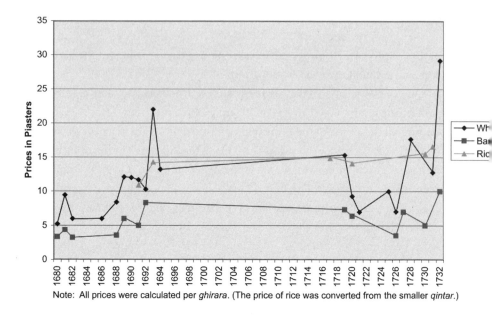

Note: All prices were calculated per *ghirara*. (The price of rice was converted from the smaller *qintar*.)

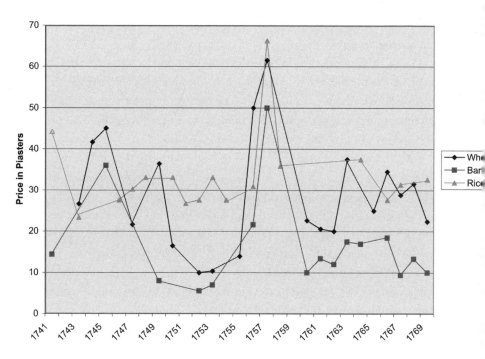

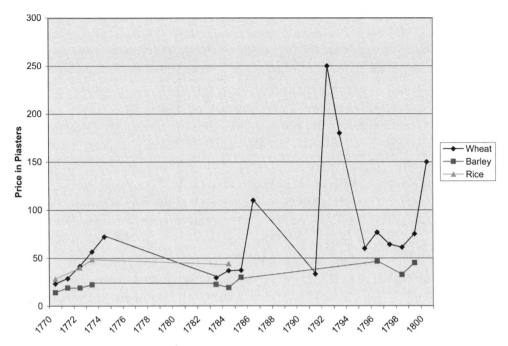

CHART 2. The Price of Grain in Damascus
(top) 1680–1732; (bottom) 1741–1769; (right) 1770–1800
Note: All prices were calculated per ghirara.

horrific tales of cannibalism reached the ears of Damascenes. Identical rumors of starving mothers eating their children had circulated during a previous shortage in 1688–89, suggesting that they were not so much factual accounts as the projections of terrified imaginations.[108] Their very repetition, however, suggests that bad harvests occasionally struck on a wide and devastating scale. During the worst afflictions, such as those of the late 1580s, drought and famine might cover the entire Mediterranean basin.[109] Receiving so little moisture, Syria was especially vulnerable to these untoward shifts in the weather.

Plentiful rainfall, on the other hand, easily translated into a bumper crop. The excellent harvests of 1677 and 1730, for example, benefited from superb weather, which almost invariably meant ample moisture during the winter and spring months.[110] The arrival of storm clouds was hailed as the promise of cheap bread and good living. Heavy snows at the end of 1711 prompted open rejoicing among the people of Damascus, especially since little rain had fallen in the preceding months.[111] The winter of 1751–52 was so wet, noted al-Budayri in his journal, that people had told him of wheat growing on the roof of a neighbor's house. He excitedly wrote that it was "a year of much rain and many benefits and blessings."[112] The popular reaction was nearly always the same; as precious moisture accumulated in the ground, spirits rose in anticipation of good times ahead.

Unfortunately for the people of the eighteenth century, good weather had little effect in reversing cumulative increases in the price of grain. Especially after mid-century, no amount of moisture was capable of returning markets to the levels of earlier decades. By the 1790s, prices had leapt so high that even the kindliest weather, such as the rains which graced Damascus in the spring of 1796–97,[113] led only to a partial recovery, leaving the cost of grain at well above the average for the 1780s. Thus the weather exerted its most decisive influence in the short term, where its caprices can be seen on price graphs as sudden spikes and tremors along a relatively smooth slope. As a factor in the vicissitudes of the urban grain market, it would seem to offer only a partial explanation.

Seeking a fuller answer, Antoine Abdel-Nour maintained that the food shortages of the eighteenth century were exacerbated, if not entirely caused, by a breakdown in the Ottoman administration. During the worst years of dearth, governors might have to draw on reserves of grain from neighboring provinces. In the case of Damascus, the usual sources were Egypt and Anatolia. Since grain was a bulky commodity, extremely expensive to move overland (doubling in price about every hundred kilometers), it nearly always arrived via sea routes. Local chronicles, Abdel-Nour notes, mention shipments of grain arriving in Lebanese ports in 1708 and 1725.[114] But after this last date, we hear nothing more about such transfers. As'ad Pasha brought grain from Hama to ease a shortage in 1751,[115] but haulage by pack animal over such a long distance was an extraordinary measure, made possible by his dual preeminence as governor of Damascus and a leading tax-farmer and grain merchant in central Syria. With the waning authority of Istanbul and mounting political turmoil within the Fertile Crescent, Abdel-Nour argues, provinces like Syria were gradually forced to fend for themselves by the middle of the eighteenth century.

But is such a bleak picture of administrative collapse really credible? During the very period when the Ottoman political system was placed under the greatest stress—the mid-century war with Russia (1768–74)—the governor of Damascus was ordered in 1771 to cooperate in provisioning two shiploads of grain for the island of Rhodes, which was suffering through its own shortage.[116] At the same time, the governor of Tunisia still found it possible to send several consignments of grain to the Lebanese coast in the period from 1769 to 1773. Moving again in the other direction, Syrian grain was rushed to Egypt in 1784 to cover shortfalls caused by low flooding along the Nile.[117] The demand for grain, which was constant and essential, found its own solutions, whether or not Istanbul was in full control of the situation. More important, it seems highly unlikely that administrative links between provinces ever deteriorated to such an exaggerated extent.

Nevertheless, the political struggles of the eighteenth century cannot be lightly dismissed. Despite the empire's impressive resiliency and cohesion, it faced serious problems which touched nearly every province. To take one example, frequent warfare, even on distant fronts, was capable of producing entirely local repercussions. In Damascus, the arrival of Egyptian troops on their way to the Persian frontier in 1727 was sufficient to spark an increase in the price of food, aggravating the hardships of a bad harvest.[118] The city also felt the effects of regional conflicts, which became particularly virulent in the second half of the century. Zahir al-ʿUmar, the powerful bedouin chieftain operating out of Acre, made one of his boldest moves in 1772, seizing a large portion of the Hawran and preventing the provincial governor from undertaking the dawra to finance the pilgrimage. For the next two years, prices remained high in Damascus, which temporarily lost one of its main sources of grain. To make matters worse, troops sent to punish Zahir in 1773 were defeated and soon began ravaging villages along their path of retreat.[119] A nearly identical chain of events was set off by Napoleon's invasion of Syria (1799). As reinforcements poured into Damascus, prices once again began to inch upwards. In scenes now familiar to residents, the soldiers proved resistant to discipline, and showed more enthusiasm for plundering nearby villages and orchards than organizing the defense of Syria.[120]

Accompanying the political turbulence experienced by the city was a marked increase in social unrest, which was most visible during the middle decades of the century. Clashing openly in the streets were the two feuding Janissary corps, who were constantly at odds with one another. The presence of several different bands of mercenaries—Kurds, North Africans, and others who also joined local struggles—only added fuel to the fire. Other forms of unrest, which were not necessarily violent, involved ordinary townspeople under the leadership of local notables. The tactics were as varied as the circumstances. If soldiers and their clients were quick to draw weapons, ulama and merchants tended to resort to more peaceful means to register their disaffection. Nothing suited this indirect, cautious style of protest better than the premodern equivalent of the general strike: merchants and artisans, often with the formal blessing of religious leaders, would close their shops and refuse to do business until the authorities addressed their grievances. In 1724, residents in the neighborhood of al-Salihiyya shut down their markets and called on the qadi, whom they accused of "much oppression," to revoke a series of provocative rulings; faced with a wave of open discontent, the qadi soon yielded.[121] So the local population was by no means passive, cowed, and resigned to its lot. Once rallied behind a cause, it was fully capable of pressing its own demands and bringing unpopular officials and other targets of its displeasure to account.

Whereas some protests were mobilized in this fashion from above, others were essentially popular uprisings, which received no instigation or direction from local leaders and could not be identified with any single faction. It is not easy to categorize these movements, which had many causes and lived only the most ephemeral existence. Most often, they took the form of tax revolts, protests against corruption and extortion, and, above all, the fury and despair of bread riots.

No issue was more incendiary than bread, which prompted popular protests on at least five separate occasions: in 1734, 1743, 1745, 1749, and again during the extended disorders of 1757–58. As mass movements, these bread riots appear with a startling suddenness and are difficult to explain with much precision in the absence of readily identifiable leaders and parties. What we can safely say is that protesters offered nothing like a revolutionary program. Their main concern seems to have been the price of bread, as well as the usual insistence that the authorities regulate the marketplace.

The first recorded bread riot occurred in the winter of 1734, shortly after Sulayman Pasha al-'Azm had taken up his new post as governor. It was a time of high prices, and perhaps as a rebuke to his perceived inaction, an unnamed group of Damascenes attacked grain storehouses that belonged personally to the pasha. He responded quickly and ruthlessly, hanging four of the demonstrators and infuriating popular opinion.

When he soon afterwards left as commander of the pilgrimage caravan, "no one greeted him" in public. He later restored his good name only by embarking on a campaign of energetic reforms, abolishing unspecified "abuses" that harmed local artisans. Perhaps most critical to his rehabilitation in the eyes of the populace was the arrival of a plentiful harvest that spring.[122]

The next major bread riot, in July 1743, erupted in the aftermath of another bad harvest. Bread had become scarce and expensive, and as the situation within the city worsened, a hungry mob attacked the courthouse, driving out the *qadi*. After venting their rage at the authorities, they then turned to the more urgent task of finding food, and pillaged local bakeries, which in preceding days had become the scene of long lines and importunate crowds. Aside from the high prices and shortage of bread at the ovens, the chronicler al-Budayri attributed the uprising to the "infrequency of inspections over the owners of grain, the millers, and the wholesalers." The governor, Sulayman Pasha al-ʿAzm, had apparently reached the same conclusion (and perhaps learned a lesson from his earlier experiences about placating popular discontent). After he issued threats against suppliers, bread suddenly appeared on the market again; in gratitude for this prompt and stern action, "the people prayed for His Excellency [the Governor]."[123] To contemporaries, the reason for the breakdown in civil order was simple and obvious. Powerful and wealthy individuals had been tampering with the food supply; once these culprits were restrained, bread immediately became available again.

The same events more or less repeated themselves in July 1745. A bad harvest in the spring had resulted in a severe shortage of bread, culminating in street protests on July 21. A large crowd, "raising their voices with wails and entreaties," gathered outside the governor's residence, where they accused Asʿad Pasha al-ʿAzm, who had earlier succeeded his uncle, of failing to regulate the markets. It was the same logic displayed two years earlier, equating high prices with official misconduct. Eager to place the blame elsewhere, the governor made a brief speech and suggested that protesters take their grievances to the courthouse, insisting that it was the qadi who was truly responsible for their suffering. Amazingly, the crowd agreed and immediately set out for the city's main tribunal. Reinforced by Janissaries, they would go on to expel the qadi and kill several members of his entourage.[124]

Each of these disturbances illustrates important characteristics of popular protest, which, in most cases, followed fairly consistent patterns and adhered to the same underlying set of beliefs and assumptions. Some demonstrations, it is true, were more unruly than others, and soon got out of hand. Rioters might give way to high emotions, and, like those who plundered the governor's storehouses in 1734, content themselves with sheer vengeance or the seizure of precious supplies of food. But they more often showed a rough discipline of purpose, which was concerned not with overturning established authority, but with activating it on their own behalf. Their main grievance, visible in the protests of 1743 and 1745, was not that the political order itself had failed, but that particular officials had been negligent in carrying out their duties. Coming under the most intense scrutiny was the chief judge, who, by the eighteenth century, had become the most frequent target of popular protest and retribution in Ottoman Damascus.[125] We have already seen how judges periodically patrolled the marketplace themselves, providing ample precedent for popular notions of justice and official accountability. In the bread riot of 1745, the governor himself essentially reaffirmed these expectations when he urged rioters to take their case to the courthouse. In effect, he conceded the legitimacy of the protest; if injustices had been committed, townspeople had an implicit right to confront officials and demand an end to corruption or negligence. The authorities could not appear indifferent—or even worse, downright complicit—in the suffering of the populace.

Bread was not merely a commodity; it functioned as an entitlement, which was, to one degree or another, extended to the entire community. Popular opinion expected that the price of grain would be regulated and held in check, even during shortages, so that no one could profit from the desperation of others. All these attitudes bear a striking resemblance to what E. P. Thompson has called the "moral economy" of eighteenth-century England, where consumers remained wary of the ascendant "free-market" doctrine, which favored lifting all such customary and legal restrictions on trade.[126] In Damascus, too, a kind of economic paternalism prevailed. Officials were responsible for ensuring adequate supplies of grain, and for monitoring shops and storehouses. If townspeople resorted to violence, they understood it as a reaction to intolerable provocations, such as rumors of artificial shortages and profiteering by grain dealers, which would have nullified these precious protections. This mentality helps to explain the timing of bread riots, which were never a straight-forward response to privation and scarcity. Shortages have to be seen as a necessary, but not entirely sufficient, precondition for demonstrations in the marketplace. To understand why popular resentments and suspicions suddenly flared into open protest, we have to look beyond the movement of prices and examine the political situation which reigned in the city at mid-century.

As a major administrative center, Damascus was already an arena of intense rivalries, which revolved mostly around the triangular intrigue of the governor and two Janissary factions. The local political order had become increasingly unstable by the early eighteenth century, most notice-ably in the rising violence of the 1720s and 1730s, and was totally upset in 1740 by an imperial decree which ordered the removal of the impe-rial Janissaries. This decision, which enjoyed a great deal of local support at the time, created radical imbalances in local political alignments that were to last for most of the next two decades.

Within this heightened concentration of power lay the future woes of the grain market—and, consequently, of ordinary townspeople. In the immediate aftermath of the imperial Janissaries' expulsion, the dominant faction in Damascene politics was headed by the city's treasurer, Fathi al-Daftari, who in turn derived most of his support from the yerliyya.[127] Having no counterweight at their disposal, the governors could do little more than bide their time for much of the 1740s. Despite a show of bra-vado that Sulayman Pasha al-ʿAzm made against speculators in 1743, he had really fallen into a policy of appeasing Fathi and the yerliyya. His nephew, Asʿad Pasha, proved even more helpless during the early years of his own rule (1743–57). Facing no effective checks on their power, the yerliyya officers seized control over a large part of local foodstocks.[128] Only toward the end of the 1740s did they lose their newfound preemi-nence. Announcing this next swing of the pendulum was the return of the imperial Janissaries, recalled to Damascus in 1748, two years after the execution of Fathi al-Daftari, the patron of the yerliyya, who was ulti-mately outmaneuvered by Asʿad Pasha in his struggle for control over the city. Having neutralized the local Janissaries, Asʿad Pasha then entered nearly a decade of political supremacy throughout southern Syria. He as-sembled a huge fortune which allowed him to build a magnificent palace (1751) and caravansary (1753) in the heart of the city. Accompanying much of this wealth were popular suspicions of rampant profiteering in the grain market, which, as we have already seen, helped to ignite at least one full-blown bread riot in 1749. The unbridled power of the governor, unchecked by local rivals, produced the same mistrust and resentment as the earlier ascendancy of the yerliyya.

The connection between popular violence and broader political currents was again apparent in the chaotic events of 1757–58. The immediate cause was the dismissal and reassignment of As'ad Pasha, who had ultimately lost the trust and support of Istanbul. After his replacement, Husayn Pasha al-Makki, settled down in the city in February 1757, old rivalries soon reasserted themselves and ushered in what was, for Damascus, the most tumultuous period of the eighteenth century. Feeding discontent were local prices, which had risen to alarming levels during a harsh winter. Popular anger did not take long to express itself. On the day after the governor's entry into the city, a delegation of notables approached his palace to offer their formal greetings. They were intercepted by a crowd that denounced them for hoarding grain and scheming "to exploit the poor and miserable." Other bystanders expressed their outrage by flinging rocks. Impressed with this display of hostility, the governor demanded inspections of the markets. Prices soon fell, but only temporarily, prompting townspeople to complain that the new pasha had begun to "engage in oppression, like his predecessors." After several months of calm, the city exploded into a chain reaction of violence over the summer of 1757: street battles between Janissary factions; a popular uprising that resulted in the expulsion of a large number of mercenaries; and further clashes in which Janissaries mobilized their clients in surrounding neighborhoods.[129] On the heels of all these setbacks, the crowning misfortune was the annihilation, in October, of the pilgrimage caravan in the desert to the south. The subsequent flight of the governor, who chose not to return with the surviving pilgrims, deepened the political void in the city. Amid a revolt by yerliyya Janissaries at the end of the year, shops closed and the price of bread soared 140 percent in less than a month.

The continuing turmoil nearly set the stage for more popular rioting. When the new governor, 'Abdullah Pasha Çeteci, assumed his post in January 1758, he began hunting down the defiant Janissaries in the Midan. The battle turned quickly in his favor, but his troops were undisciplined.

Looting was extensive, and many men, women, and children were either killed or taken prisoner, paying the price for their neighborhood's allegiances. The effect on the local economy was devastating. Most of the Midan's bakeries stood empty, and bread soon disappeared from markets elsewhere in the city. With a disappointing harvest in the spring, the plight of the population reached emergency proportions. Fearing bread riots, the governor posted soldiers at all the bakeries, which were besieged by "great crowds of men, women, and children, from whom heart-breaking cries and wails were heard."[130] Nature had conspired with political conflict to bring the city to its knees.

In taking these last precautions, the governor instinctively understood the conditions which produced bread riots. Hunger alone was never enough to drive people into the streets. Both before and after the events of the 1740s and 1750s, there were several bad harvests, such as the shortfalls of 1732 and 1764, and yet none of them resulted in popular demonstrations. The spark required to light all this potential tinder was generated by two separate forces. The first was a sudden and sustained rise in the price of grain, such as the wave of increases which overtook the city in the middle decades of the century. Striking at the basic staple of the diet, this persistent erosion of purchasing power, which raised the cost of bread—and thus the cost of living—to unaccustomed levels, undermined public confidence in the marketplace and bred rumors of secret plots to hoard grain. The other trigger for popular violence was a crisis in the local political order, which made fears about hoarding and speculation seem all the more plausible and urgent. What distinguished the shortages of 1734, 1743, 1745, 1749, and 1757 was precisely their timing with deeper waves of strife within the city.[131] Throughout most of the 1740s, and again in the wake of Asʿad Pasha's departure in 1757, the balance, not only among Damascene factions but between the province and the imperial center as well, underwent radical and unforeseen shifts, enabling one faction to suppress the others, or initiating an open free-for-all. It is interesting to note that, despite blatant attempts at market manipulation in the latter portion of the century (most notably under al-Jazzar) the next bread riot did not occur until February 1806. Though food prices remained high throughout most of the first two decades of the nineteenth century, the population again chose a time of extreme political agitation to fill the streets and overrun the courthouse. From the south, the Wahhabis were raiding the Ghuta and barring the way of the pilgrimage caravan. Inside the city itself, the governor was unable to restrain the two Janissary corps, still feuding with one another decades later.[132] Bread riots were thus linked to wider conflicts in urban society, and often coincided with other manifestations of street violence. One has to look far beyond the fate of the harvest to understand how hungry crowds were incited.

THE SOCIAL COSTS OF DECENTRALIZATION

All this turbulence has to be seen as an outgrowth of the forces of decentralization within the Ottoman Empire. During the eighteenth century, the balance of power between Istanbul and the provinces was steadily shifting in favor of the latter. To maintain its authority and prestige, Istanbul had to rely increasingly on negotiation, enticement, and, perhaps most skillfully, the manipulation of local rivalries. Local elites, on the other hand, continued to work within the Ottoman system, which bestowed legitimacy on their position and allowed them to advance their political and economic interests through its administrative apparatus. By the time the empire began to face its most serious external challenges, in the final decades of the century, they had deepened their extensive financial, administrative, and ideological attachments to the Ottoman order. Even as the central state grew weaker, the imperial system as a whole retained hidden sources of vitality.

In its own corner of the empire, eighteenth-century Damascus reproduced all these trends. Even at the height of decentralization, society and economy continued to bear the stamp of Ottoman power. The urban elite prospered, mainly by seizing new opportunities in the fiscal system, which, in turn, would further unlock the resources of the countryside. Participation in the imperial administration offered its own rewards most obviously in the grain trade. Except for a thin stratum of petty dealers, this crucial sector had fallen solidly into the hands of Ottoman officials and local notables, whose 'askari status made them part of what was, in effect, an "Ottoman class" within the urban population. Not all members of the urban elite held these credentials, but the correspondence between wealth and access to state offices and privileges was unmistakable. Even beyond the highest social circles, the golden touch of the state, however slight or indirect, continued to matter. The smallest offices and emoluments could be converted into long-term financial and fiscal gains, which, in one way or another, created a skewed distribution of wealth in favor of 'askari Damascenes. The presence of such entitlements and their associated benefits, even at lower economic levels, shows how effectively the Ottoman order was able to penetrate urban society. The turbulence of the eighteenth century would have left these more fortunate Damascenes relatively unscathed, and in the case of the urban elite, positively promoted their interests.

For the rest of the population, Ottoman decentralization came at a rather high cost. It heightened political competition at the local level, which often generated unforeseen social and economic aftershocks. One can easily observe the rising wave of violence and open factionalism, especially in the second half of the eighteenth century, in other big Arab towns such as Cairo and Aleppo.[133] As the markets of Damascus demonstrated, these conflicts were a blight on the local economy, hitting hardest at the poorest and most vulnerable sectors of the urban population. Again, the fate of the grain trade is most revealing, as consumers, most notably in the second half of the century, were forced to pay ever-higher prices for their daily supply of bread. If the eighteenth century was indeed the heyday of the provincial notables, the benefits did not necessarily "trickle down" the social ladder. In considering the standard of living enjoyed by ordinary townspeople, we need to remember these disparities in consumption, which probably worsened as a result of political transformations that contemporaries seem to have only partially understood.

III

LUXURY

&

VARIETY

EVERYDAY

FOOD

T HE PEOPLE OF DAMASCUS DID NOT, OF COURSE, EAT bread alone. For reasons of nutrition, taste, and prestige, they were constantly trying to enrich their diet with other foods. Compared with townspeople in many other parts of Eurasia, they were quite fortunate. The city could count on obtaining a wide range of foodstuffs: meats, dairy products, cooking oils, an abundance of fresh produce, spices, and sweets. Its well-stocked markets were a tribute to the riches of its hinterland and the highly productive orchards and gardens of its suburbs. Other supplies entered from the nearby desert economy or arrived with the long-distance caravans which cut across the Fertile Crescent. Provisions reached the city from nearly every direction.

We have to think of all these supplemental foods as the flexible part of the diet, expanded as the means and opportunities for consumption arose, but never entirely in the power of families to fix for themselves. What people ate was partly a matter of their resources, which is to say that the rich, as always, enjoyed a much fuller diet than the poor. But wealth was not the only factor which determined the precious ability to choose. Eighteenth-century lives were much more closely tied to the rhythms of nature, which dictated when many foods would be available. As a result, the Damascene diet could be very uneven from season to season, compounding variations which inevitably occurred in the quality and quantity of foods from one year to the next. Other distortions flowed from the grain trade, which cast a shadow over the entire economy. The price of bread usually told the whole story: high levels were a symptom of hardship and misfortune throughout the city, frequently causing a chain reaction in the marketplace and dragging other prices up or down in their wake. And as the cost of bread rose, the amount of money set aside for other things was bound to shrink. Other lessons from the grain trade are worth recalling as well, for supply responded to more than strictly economic pressures. Once again, political forces extended their control over key elements of the diet, which helped to highlight and reproduce the larger social hierarchy.

MEAT: FIRST AMONG LUXURY FOODS

No food was more coveted, or better epitomized the balance between desires and constraints, than meat. Damascenes recognized it as a rich source of nutrition and sought to include it in their diet whenever possible. By eighteenth-century standards, it was a costly item, typically fetching five to six times the price of white bread (let alone humbler varieties). Daily consumption was thus restricted mainly to well-to-do households, for whom meat advertised social status as effectively as riding a horse, sporting fine clothes, or buying a big house. As a prized delicacy, it was also a powerful expression of hospitality, often being served on special occasions such as weddings, circumcisions, and religious feasts. In short, it was part of the very image of the good life. As one local author explained, to dream of eating cooked meat was a sure promise of material gain.[1] His fellow townspeople needed no persuasion. The poor rarely saw it on their plates, or at most enjoyed small portions.[2] Rural diets were even more impoverished, or, to be more precise, condemned to the tedium of barley bread.

This identification of meat with power and privilege was sanctioned by the Ottoman state, which devoted considerable resources to furnishing Istanbul, its capital, with sufficient quantities from provincial herds. Meat was openly regarded as an official perquisite, to be reserved above all for dignitaries and their households.[3] The imperial Janissaries stationed in the citadel received it, along with wheat, as part of their regular rations.[4] Bypassing the butchers, local mercenaries were accustomed to taking payments in sheep, as well as their usual wages, and jealously guarded their claims.[5] In the worst moments of disorder, they might simply help themselves to local supplies. After troops under the command of Husayn Pasha al-Makki had crushed the yerliyya Janissaries and restored his authority as governor (1758), they proceeded to terrorize the Midan, where their adversaries had organized local resistance. After an extended looting spree, the victors "ate nothing but meat, and rice, and good bread, until meat became scarce and there was no bread to be eaten."[6] As a token of raw might and arrogance, their choice of food was hardly coincidental. These connotations help to explain the reaction of the Christian community in 1766 to their new patriarch, who had been seen shamelessly eating meat in church during a feast. "The Orthodox Christians were very distressed and uneasy because of this situation," reported the priest Mikha'il Burayk, "because it had previously not been the custom of Orthodox priests to eat meat openly."[7] Such pleasures were denied to the men of the cloth, who were expected to show an outward modesty in conformity with their spiritual calling.

All these attitudes correlating meat with social status found support from religious authorities. 'Abd al-Ghani al-Nabulsi argued in a fatwa that butchers and others who sold meat could, in effect, charge higher prices to non-Damascenes. His logic rested on two fundamental distinctions. One concerned the difference between essential and nonessential foods, and the other dealt with the rights of local residents (ahl al-balad) as opposed to "foreigners." In any given place, observed al-Nabulsi, residents would be familiar with all the prices on the market and were therefore entitled to receive food at the going rate. Foreigners, too, enjoyed this same protection, but only with respect to bread, which was so central to survival that everyone would know its value. "One who enters a country first asks, in most cases, about the price of bread there." Meat was a different matter because it was unnecessary as long as sufficient bread was available on the market.[8] In other words, bread was for everyone, but the same expectation did not apply to meat, which was clearly defined as a luxury food. Damascene culture had long resigned itself to this inequity: though everyone wished to eat meat, only a few could taste it whenever they pleased.

These carnivorous longings were satisfied with a comparatively narrow selection of meats. Beef was available, but did not inspire great demand. The Frenchman Volney was disappointed with what he tasted, both in Egypt and Syria, complaining that local cuts were "lean and bad, like all the meat of hot countries."[9] Local consumers apparently agreed, for it was sheep, not cattle, that held pride of place in Damascus. When people spoke of eating meat (lahm), they usually meant mutton, which clearly ranked as their favorite choice. If butchers turned to other animals, it was usually a signal of disruption in supply and, in many instances, the accompaniment to a much wider subsistence crisis. During the general food shortage of 1743, mutton grew so scarce that butchers began to slaughter water buffalo, goats, and camels.[10] For contemporaries, such choices were unimaginable as long as there were alternatives.

Aside from red meat, only poultry had anything like wide appeal. The biographer of Zahir al-ʿUmar praised the bedouin chief for his austere lifestyle, which consisted of a frugal diet of chicken and gravy in the morning.[11] Most chickens, however, were raised for their eggs, which offered a cheaper and more regular supply of protein. Some Damascenes kept chickens in their homes, tending them as a supplementary source of income; one unfortunate neighbor of al-Budayri lost twenty-two during a severe cold spell in November 1756.[12] As for fish, small amounts were available from local rivers, but the sea was much too distant to enable consumption on a larger scale.[13] Proscribed by both Islam and Judaism, pork was never a practical alternative, and was considered utterly loathsome and inedible.[14]

So local markets were mostly dependent on the supply of sheep, stimulating one of the main links to the broader regional economy. It was a far-flung trade, which put the city in touch with bedouin tribes who roamed the lands of the Fertile Crescent and wandered as far as the pastures of Anatolia. Since the commodities in question essentially walked themselves to market, distances were easily overcome. Most of the sheep sold in Damascene markets, in fact, originated in the region of Erzurum near the Black Sea. This northern territory was the homeland of Turkoman and Kurdish tribes who spent their summers in the eastern highlands and then marched their herds south to the Syrian Desert with the onset of winter. Playing a somewhat lesser role in sheep breeding were Arab tribes, who followed a similar schedule in moving between the cities of the Fertile Crescent and the interior of the Syrian Desert. Nothing was more important to the bedouin economy than this annual cycle, gateway to the indispensable urban markets where they purchased cloth, textiles, utensils, and all the other manufactures that they could not provide for themselves.[15] At the same time, their migrations were one of the central features of the urban economy. In most years, the price of mutton followed an annual cycle similar to that of grain, falling in spring with the arrival of the bedouin and slowly climbing as the seasons progressed. The end of spring was also the time when the bedouin sheared their sheep, providing most of the raw material for the manufacture of woolens.[16] All these activities were tied together, touching many different people throughout local society, which watched the movement of its flocks almost as eagerly as the outcome of the harvest.

The key intermediaries in the sheep trade were Damascene merchants, who followed several basic strategies in obtaining animals. The most direct route was to make contact with the tribes in their summer pastures, either in person or through private agents who could place orders. More convenient was the establishment of year-round partnerships, which allowed merchants to request a specific number of sheep each spring. For those who preferred small-scale operations or instant exchanges, it was equally possible to make purchases without advance arrangement, greeting the bedouin as they arrived outside the city and conducting business on the spot. Other merchants left private flocks with local tribes who circulated on the fringes of the desert, or else kept their animals in nearby villages, whence shepherds led them to market as often as needed.[17] One such dealer was Yusuf al-Sawwaf, who owned fifty sheep, not to mention his thirteen cows and shares in eighteen horses, all of which he kept scattered throughout several villages in the Ghuta.[18] But Yusuf was a merchant of relatively modest means. He lacked the full range of investments available to his wealthier counterparts, who really dominated the trade. Among these captains of commerce were officials and well-connected members of their families, like the son of Muhammad Pasha al-'Azm, who by 1790 had converted his "renown" into partnerships with various bedouin who supplied the city with sheep and cows.[19] His profile was typical of the biggest livestock merchants, who, much like the leaders of the grain trade, tended to combine wealth and 'askari status.[20] Big herds did not come cheap, and access to bedouin tribes and pasturage was often facilitated by administrative contacts and military prestige.

The alignment with power was no less visible at the lower levels of the meat trade, especially among the local butchers. One of the most powerful figures in the marketplace was the head of their guild, who bore responsibility for provisioning the kitchens of local officials. He directed one of the largest craft organizations in the city, and exercised considerable influence over other professions connected with the meat trade.[21] Perhaps inevitably, many members of the trade were yerliyya Janissaries, who ranked among the city's most devoted gourmands. These social connections were obvious in the geography of the southwestern suburbs such as al-Qanawat, which was not only a favorite residence for officials and merchants, but for a large number of butchers as well.[22] Partly because of such affiliations, local opinion viewed the lot of butchers as enviable and secure.[23] But not all members of the trade were prosperous. Mirroring the grain market, small-time dealers and craftsmen coexisted with much wealthier figures.

Business seems to have been steady. For most butchers, one or two sheep per day were sufficient, but the biggest operations needed as many as three or four. At this rate, they would have required large numbers of animals. From his vantage point at the end of the nineteenth century, Muhammad Sa'id al-Qasimi estimated Damascene consumption at approximately one hundred fifty head of sheep each day.[24] Since the population of the city then stood at about 150,000, this would have meant that about one sheep was slaughtered for every thousand inhabitants. If we assume the same rate of consumption for the eighteenth century, the corresponding total would come to eighty or ninety sheep per day, or something on the order of 30,000 sheep annually. And this figure may actually represent a gross underestimate, for one contemporary report (1777) claimed that the annual appetite of Aleppo, with as many as 120,000 inhabitants, stood between 80,000 and 100,000 sheep.[25] If Damascus, which had roughly three-quarters of this population, devoured mutton with the same relish, our estimate would then reach 60,000–75,000 animals. Even if we simply split the totals and take 45,000–60,000 sheep as an approximate range, the numbers still show a considerable demand—at least from those who could afford to indulge their tastes. And as long as prices were low enough, Damascenes could prove very stubborn about eating as much meat as possible. In 1747, the ʿAnaza bedouin defeated a rival tribe and rewarded themselves by seizing sheep whose "number could only be counted by God." The booty was brought to Damascus and quickly sold even though "the people knew that it was unlawful plunder." A few morally fastidious consumers—"who were quite insignificant [in number]"—refused to touch the meat, but "the others, who were most of the people, did not care."[26] Nothing could suppress these appetites, which guaranteed a virtually bottomless demand that asserted itself at the first opportunity and kept prices high.

The lucrative nature of the trade, together with the involvement of officials and soldiers, made it a tempting target for chicanery and abuse. One of the most flagrant manipulators of the meat supply was Ismaʿil Pasha al-ʿAzm. Soon after his installation as governor (1725), he closed all but ten butchers' shops and two slaughterhouses and established a virtual monopoly on the supply of mutton, setting artificially high prices (as much as 50 to 100 percent above previous costs) and collecting handsome profits.[27] His nephew, Asʿad Pasha, proved even more adept at squeezing the market. While campaigning against Druze forces in the Biqaʿ in 1747, he turned a complaint against a local Druze into a pretext for confiscating his five hundred sheep, which he then sold to Damascene butchers at inflated prices.[28] Two years later, the governor again organized a military expedition, which was aimed this time against Zahir al-ʿUmar and his allies among the bedouin. Victorious in battle, his troops seized large flocks of sheep, which, upon his order, were distributed among the butchers of Damascus and nearby villages whom the bedouin had been harassing. Yet it was no gesture of generosity; the governor exploited his triumph entirely for personal gain, charging five times the price that prevailed on the open market.[29] It was impossible to disentangle the workings of the meat market from the demands and pressures of the local political system. The two of them converged at too many points and shared too many interests.

This interdependence meant that meat prices, which were much less affected by climatic conditions than grain, were unusually sensitive to the city's political fortunes. Like every other commodity, meat was caught up

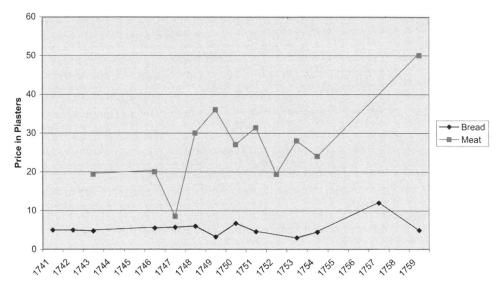

CHART 3. The Price of Bread vs. Meat, c. 1741–1759
Note: All prices for bread represent yearly averages.
Prices for meat are based on the average for mutton.

in the broader currents overtaking the Damascene economy. During the eighteenth century, the cost of living—as reflected, above all, in the price of wheat—was gradually rising. The correspondence between wheat and mutton was not exact, but they followed the same upward trend. If we look, for example, at prices for the 1740s and 1750s (chart 3), wheat served as an unreliable predictor for the price of meat, whose supply, after all, was ultimately tied to the vicissitudes of the bedouin economy, far from Damascus. But over the long term, each was really responding to similar pressures, which, if anything, exerted themselves more intensely in the market for livestock, where the political turbulence of the eighteenth century seems to have proved especially disruptive. Mutton stood at seven to eight misriyyas per ratl in 1699, but had skyrocketed to eighty by 1774.[30] In contrast, the price of wheat had merely doubled over the same period.

The pressures on the meat market manifested themselves as early as the 1720s, at the very moment when the price of wheat was first beginning its prolonged ascent. Contemporaries viewed the two sets of increases as a consequence of the same problem, namely, a lack of inspections in the marketplace. Popular opinion incessantly called on the authorities to act, and the latter periodically carried out campaigns to curtail abuses and maintain a fair price for meat, just as they did for bread and grain. After As'ad Pasha al-'Azm left the city with the pilgrimage caravan in August 1752, his lieutenant governor began to enact strict controls in the market-place, beginning with the price of meat, which was rapidly escalating. To demonstrate his sincerity, he publicly humiliated a group of butchers who were guilty of violations.[31] These measures were more notable for their infrequency than effectiveness, but townspeople never lost their attach-ment to forceful demonstrations of justice, even when the primary issue was the cost of meat. Though not as central to the diet as grain, it was still regarded as one of the commodities which set the trend for the rest of the market, and therefore warranted official attention and intervention.

ALTERNATIVES AND SUPPLEMENTS TO MEAT:
FATS AND PROTEINS

No matter how thoroughly shops and artisans were supervised, meat remained an expensive source of protein. Prices were rising constant-ly throughout the century, and the bottom line was inescapable. Most people had no choice except to search for alternatives and supplements, which might provide a similar level of nutrition, but at much lower costs. The attempt to meet this chronic deficiency explains, in large part, the pop-ularity of dairy products, such as milk, cream, cheese, yogurt, and butter.

All sectors of the dairy trade ultimately originated in the bedouin and rural economies, the sources of nearly all the city's milk. As with meat and grain, the overwhelming bulk of supplies moved under the direction of urban merchants, most of whom held 'askari credentials.[32] In plan-ning their investments, they had two main options. The first was to deal directly with the bedouin and share ownership of cows and goats. In contrast to the city's mutton, which came from as far away as Anatolia, these imports originated mostly in the vicinity of the city, which usually required merchants to enter into partnerships with local Arab tribes. Hi-jazi al-Misri held half of twenty-nine cows and thirty-one water buffalo that he left with the Banu Sha'bi, who acted as partners and caretakers. But he was also careful to exercise the other option of keeping animals closer to the city, for he owned another seventy cows that he had put out to pasture in the village of Khadr in the Ghuta.[33] In fact, most merchants preferred to adopt this latter solution, which offered more flexibility and control. A further incentive was that, in comparison with sheep, cows and goats were easier to maintain and needed less land for grazing, for which gardens and orchards around the city or in surrounding villages were usually sufficient.[34] Anyone who had a patch of land in the suburbs or some distant village might invest in a small number of animals. Muhammad Beshe al-Qaziri placed his six goats in the village of al-Barza, just north of Damascus, presumably among the extensive olive groves that he owned there.[35] Some people even bought a fraction of a single animal, or a portion of the animal's produce instead of the animal itself.[36] The market for cows, which were more numerous than goats, was especially active. Every Friday (as reported in the nineteenth century), merchants auctioned cows imported from provinces as distant as Erzurum. Peasants from the Ghuta also participated, driving small herds into town and arranging terms with buyers through special brokers.[37]

In fact, it was these humble peasants who accounted for most dairy production. Shepherds arrived in the city early every morning and wandered the back streets, calling to customers and dispensing milk straight from their animals. Others simply set up stalls and sold their milk in the marketplace.[38] Local opinion regarding the latter seems to have gradually deteriorated. Writing in the late seventeenth century, al-Nabulsi associated the trade with "excellence of conduct and gentleness of speech";[39] two hundred years later, al-Qasimi accused these same merchants of shamelessly diluting their milk with water, claiming that "they seldom sell it pure."[40] Was it perhaps due to the growth of the city and the subsequent strain on supplies? A more certain observation is that Damascenes could obtain milk throughout the year. Like everything else connected with the city's herds, production of milk varied with the seasons, reaching its peak in spring and ebbing during the trying winter months.[41] Nearly all dairy products conformed to these annual rhythms, which seemed so natural and inevitable that, in the spring of 1754, al-Budayri expressed disbelief at the high prices for butter "in the days of [its] season."[42] Only sheep, much less popular as a source of milk than cows and goats, followed a different schedule, giving their highest yields in October rather than the spring.[43] Besides milk, the city received regular deliveries of cream, which was the specialty of the nearby villages. A large part wound up in the shops of sweet sellers, who used it in making pastries, but it was also sold in the marketplace.[44]

Another product of the oasis was cheese. The merchants who handled it generated so much business that they had their own khan (Khan al-Jubn), from which they maintained direct links with the villagers who manufactured it. Some of these dealers had their own shops in the market, where they sold their supplies directly to the public, but many were content to act as middlemen for neighborhood grocers. The city and its hinterland were practically self-sufficient, consuming and producing several different varieties of cheese, which differed mostly in the manner of preparation and storage. Among the most popular products was "white" or feta cheese (*jubn abyad*), but Ahmad al-Budayri, who jotted down the prices of his favorite foods, was also partial to *qarisha* (a kind of sour cheese) and "green cheese" (perhaps on account of its mold).[45]

Like cheese, yogurt came primarily from local villages. It was made from the milk of both cows and goats, and stored in skin pouches, which were transported to the city on the backs of pack animals. The yogurt vendors (*labban*) fanned out through the countryside each morning, collecting supplies and bringing them to market, often to the shops of grocers. Many others, however, dispensed with these intermediaries and circulated in the streets as common peddlers.[46] In performing one of his celebrated "miracles," the local saint Husayn al-Hamawi accosted one such tradesman and ordered him to empty the contents of a container into the street; as dogs devoured the spilt yogurt, a serpent crawled out from inside, to the amazement of nearby spectators.[47] The popular diet reflected the heavy demand that these itinerant vendors helped to meet. Yogurt was one of the most versatile elements in local cuisine and could be mixed with herbs, grains, sauces, and meats. It was especially important in the meals of the poor, for whom it served as a leading source of nutrition.[48]

Damascene cooking also relied heavily on clarified butter (*samna*). More than any other food except mutton, it was closely associated with the bedouin, who enjoyed a virtual monopoly over its production. The best butter was reputed to come from the region of Hama, where certain tribes made it from sheep's milk; but most supplies in Syria were processed from a mixture of milk and yogurt, which was churned in sheepskin bags.[49] The trade formed one of the regular links between the urban and bedouin economies, in which each partner frequently called upon the services of the other. A bedouin and his bags of butter were a familiar sight, hardly worthy of notice, unless he was Saʿid al-Jaʿfari, a scholar and poet who had abandoned his career following the death of his Sufi mentor. Lost in grief, he joined a bedouin tribe, with whom he spent the rest of his life; his former colleagues saw him only when he came to the city to sell samna with his fellow tribesmen.[50] Like that other famous export of the desert, mutton, the cost of butter rose progressively over the course of the eighteenth century—not as dramatically as meat, but in line with the overall increase in the cost of living (chart 4). Many of the poor could not always afford the real thing. They instead learned to acquire a taste for imitations, such as the fat which was extracted from boiled sheep's heads, which were famous for filling the markets with their malodorous vapors.[51] In the search for nourishing protein, fat, and "richness" (dasim), people were willing to try almost anything.

Olive oil was a more palatable alternative. When people could not afford clarified butter, which always commanded higher prices (chart 4), they usually turned to olive oil as the second best choice. Among the poor, it must have seemed like a godsend—almost literally, since olive trees were considered blessed, and in many places functioned as shrines where people recited prayers and made votive offerings.[52] As an added practical advantage, it stored well and could be easily transported. When soldiers retook the desert fort of Qalʿat Jibril from bedouin marauders (1706), they found not hidden booty, as they had hoped, but stockpiles of wheat and olive oil.[53] In this remote location, where resupply was difficult, it proved itself as an essential commodity.

Like all countries of the Mediterranean basin, Syria had a long association with the olive, which was cultivated nearly everywhere, from the villages of Aleppo down through the coast of Palestine, where it was especially important to the local economy. The Ghuta, too, was a center of production, and provided Damascus with most of its oil. But the oasis by itself was unequal to the requirements of the city, which had to turn to other sources, mainly in Lebanon.[54] The local trade followed a familiar pattern: the biggest dealers tended to hold ʿaskari credentials, duplicating "military" preeminence in the handling of other foodstuffs such as grain and meat. These ʿaskari magnates owned many of the nearby olive orchards, and nearly all of the presses that crushed the fruit and extracted

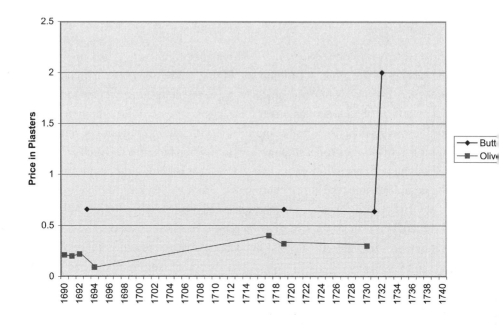

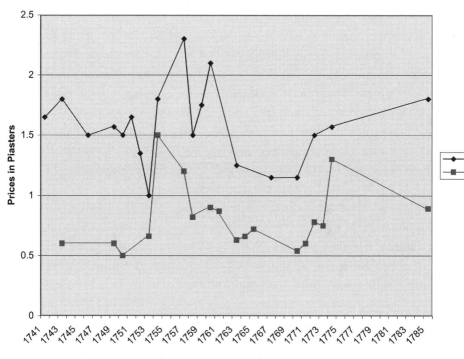

CHART 4. The Price of Butter vs. Olive Oil
(top) 1690–1740; (bottom) 1741–1785
Source: Islamic Court Records

the oil. From the presses, the oil then passed to middlemen, who held their supplies in deep wells shielded from the sunlight and outside air.[55] For the wealthiest among them, it was only a short step to the soap industry,[56] which in most regions of Syria was a spontaneous outgrowth of olive cultivation, the source of the main ingredient. But soap never really became a major industry in Damascus. Due to its regular shortfalls in olive oil, the city had to rely on imports from Lebanon and Palestine—most notably Tripoli and Nablus—to cover its own deficiencies in production.[57] As for the oil which was destined for human consumption (drawn from the clearest layers of fluid) most of it reached the market through wandering peddlers, who purchased small amounts from wholesalers. These humble middlemen toured the markets with their pack animals, pouring out oil to grocers and other clients from the large skin bags which distinguished their trade.[58]

Unlike olive oil, which was valued mainly as a fat in cooking, pulses served as a cheap (albeit incomplete) source of protein, and thus made a significant contribution to the diet of ordinary Damascenes. Among the varieties known to Damascene palates were fava beans (*ful*), chickpeas, cowpeas (*lubiya*),[59] and lentils, the latter of which were usually imported from Egypt.[60] Sacks of beans were one of the common sights at grocer's shops, but one could just as easily buy from street peddlers.[61]

Damascenes were especially fond of chickpeas, which were widely regarded as a specialty of the city. Writing in the late nineteenth century, al-Qasimi noted several ready-made dishes available from street vendors, who were most active during the winter months, when hot food was in greatest demand. The simplest recipe (*hummus bi-zayt*) consisted of mashed chickpeas mixed with olive oil, thyme (*sa'tir*), and cumin. Others were a variation of *musabbaha*: mashed chickpeas and sesame paste (*tahina*) sprinkled with lemon or pomegranate juice, melted butter, and pistachios or pine nuts.[62] But were all these dishes, however cherished and celebrated in various incarnations today, actually eaten by eighteenth-century Damascenes? Contemporary sources make no mention of them. Equally interesting is a comment by al-Qasimi, who claimed that, in his lifetime (1843–1900), they were virtually unknown outside of Damascus, whether among the towns of the Syrian coast or those of the Hijaz.[63] It seems likely, therefore, that these recipes not only originated in Damascus, but were relative latecomers to local kitchens. The people of the eighteenth century had to settle for much plainer fare, boiling their chickpeas and flavoring them with olive oil or salt; the latter was recommended by al-Nabulsi, who thought that it eased the digestion of an otherwise difficult food.[64] As an alternative, Damascenes feasted on *qadama*, roasted and salted chickpeas whose fame reached across all of Syria. An entire profession (*qadamani*) arose to handle production, which, like the businesses of other food vendors, required almost no capital; "no street was without one or more," al-Qasimi later observed.[65] So prevalent were chickpeas in the local diet that (presumably during food shortages) they might even be ground and baked as an ingredient in cheap bread.[66] Served in nearly any way, they enjoyed universal favor as a healthful and invigorating food which "strengthened the heart" and "eliminated melancholic ideas."[67] The comparative simplicity of cooking in no way diminished their appeal.

Other pulses were held in lower esteem. Medical authorities credited lentils with promoting sound intestines and a sense of well-being, but overindulgence, they claimed, would lead to "melancholic diseases such as depression, leprosy, and cancer." Fava beans, on the other hand, were viewed with outright suspicion and blamed for producing "dullness of the senses" and "dim-wittedness";[68] one saving grace, acknowledged al-Nabulsi, was their ability to cleanse the breath of garlic.[69] In any case, we should not make too much of these learned pronouncements, at least in relation to actual eating habits. Butrus al-Kibrisli, the Greek Orthodox patriarch (d. 1764), was careful to keep quantities of both chickpeas and fava beans (in fact, twice as much of the latter) on hand in his cellar.[70] Local appetites, it seems, obeyed their own rules, whatever the doctors might say.

SEASONAL FOODS: VEGETABLES AND FRUITS

Nearly every food was seasonal in nature, responsive to its own annual cycle of supply and demand, but none to the degree of fresh produce, which was available only part of the year before it soon vanished again. The consequences for the daily diet were both obvious and profound. A large proportion of the nutrients found in vegetables and fruits could be eaten only during the few weeks that they were gathered from gardens and orchards and brought to local markets. So in considering whether the local diet was sufficiently healthful and varied, one needs to remember these seasonal breaks and fluctuations, to which no kitchen was immune.

Let us begin with vegetables, which followed an annual progression that, even in the twentieth century, Damascene markets continued to observe with few alterations. The warm months were naturally the period of the greatest variety. Starting from the last weeks of spring and extending throughout the summer, the stalls of greengrocers (*khadari*) filled with onions, squash, eggplant, asparagus, lettuce, and cucumbers, followed in the first weeks of autumn by a wave of radishes, cabbages, and turnips. Winter, never an entirely barren season, brought spinach, cauliflower, carrots, beets, leeks, and parsley. Of all these items, the most common were onion, squash, and eggplant, which appeared regularly even in the meals of the poor. The journal of Ahmad al-Budayri offers confirmation of their importance; aside from one reference each to cabbages and cucumbers, these three were the only vegetables for which he bothered, at one time or another, to note a price. Several other vegetables which have since become integral to Syrian cooking made only the most belated advances into the Middle East. The tomato, whose lineage stretches back to the New World, spread in the wake of the Egyptian occupation of the 1830s.[71] Other nineteenth-century newcomers were string beans and green peppers, which also made slow progress.[72]

Damascus received nearly all its vegetables from nearby gardens, which came in every imaginable size. Some of this produce was obtained from the villages of the oasis, such as al-Nabak, which won renown for its garlic.[73] Many other gardens were located on the outskirts of the city, or even in its very heart, wherever space and opportunity permitted. In an age of slow transport, this commitment to self-sufficiency was virtually the only option, especially with regard to perishable goods. Additional provisions, such as cucumbers from Egypt or eggplant from the Lebanese coast, might come from the outside, but the city was for the most part dependent on its hinterland.[74]

It was no different with fruit, grown in immense quantities in orchards covering much of the Ghuta. Local writers had been celebrating this prodigious output for centuries, proclaiming it as one of the city's great virtues. Indeed, fruit was a familiar, if transient, part of the local diet, and not a luxury which had to be imported at considerable effort and expense.[75] Summer brought a profusion of peaches, mulberries, grapes, apricots, plums, apples, pears, quinces, watermelons, and figs. The winter fruits, of course, were less numerous, but no less important, consisting chiefly of pomegranates, lemons, and bitter oranges (narnaj). These were supplemented by dried fruits such as raisins and dates, and small caches of apples, quinces, and pears that fruit vendors had hoarded in preparation for the cold weather and bare shelves.[76] What little the city lacked, it easily summoned from markets around the Fertile Crescent. Dates arrived from Iraq and, in lesser quantities, the Hijaz as well; many of these shipments were then reexported to the Lebanese coast as part of a centuries-old commercial circuit. Among the goods which came in return were oranges, lemons, and bananas, which flourished at the lower elevations.[77] In short, Damascus was a veritable cornucopia. By the eighteenth century, nearly all the fruits that residents take for granted today were familiar to the local diet. Only cherries and strawberries, two items which appear today in even the smallest markets, struggled to make their way into Syria, remaining quite rare even into the early twentieth century.[78] In view of the Ghuta's bounty, the city hardly missed them.

Orchards were a prominent feature of the local landscape and, like nearby fields of grain, functioned as a major outlet for urban wealth, which was always seeking secure investments. Many properties were located on land adjacent to the city, most notably toward the western and southern districts; attracting nearly equal interest were neighboring villages such as al-Mezze, Barza, and Kafr Susa, whose fields nearly overlapped those of the suburbs. Though wealthy landowners held many of these orchards, a large number of petty cultivators (bustani) made a living by tending fruit on smaller patches of land, usually around the neighborhood of al-Salihiyya, whose position as the most distant suburb made it an ideal outpost for agricultural activities.[79] To these full-time laborers, one can add the many homeowners from nearly every part of the city who raised grape vines and lemon, orange, palm, fig, and mulberry trees in and around their homes.[80] Some sales deeds specifically mention the presence of irrigation channels to water these domestic plots.[81] More distant areas of the oasis also served the Damascene market and might acquire their own renown. The village of Darayya, for example, was widely considered the finest source of grapes in the entire region, and traded them as far afield as northern

Syria and the Lebanese ports.[82] Such exports were part of a larger surplus which gained a market throughout southern Syria, which was enamored with both the quality and quantity of the city's fruits.

Living at the heart of such a fertile land, Damascenes made the most of their good fortune and consumed fruit with a passion whenever it was available. Prices were relatively low, making fruit affordable to all but the poor. Figs and apricots, for example, were two of the cheapest fruits, at most times no more expensive (by weight) than bread. Higher prices immediately gave rise to suspicions of market manipulation. During the summer of 1746, al-Budayri could not contain his doubts about the high cost of figs "in spite of the abundance of fruit."[83] In better times, Damascenes gave themselves over to their appetites. Ibn Kannan was so devoted to fruit that his journal included regular observations on the growing season, the state of supplies, and trends in prices, which were always a concern. The early weeks of summer were fondly recalled as the "days of mulberries" (ayyam al-tut), and among the advice confided in one entry of his journal were directions for removing peach and mulberry stains from clothes.[84] This appreciation for fruit extended to the rites of hospitality. When al-Nabulsi and his companions spent the night with the governor of Tripoli (1700), they received pomegranates, watermelon, and grapes as an offering of esteem and an expression of good manners.[85] Fruit was the perfect complement to such pleasantries. It was one of the joys of the palate and, while the season lasted, a welcome and nutritious addition to the daily diet.

Damascenes went to great lengths to preserve fruit and prolong its availability. Few activities stimulated more ingenuity or required more care. People converted various fruits into jams, made with either sugar or honey. Easy to manufacture and store, jams were a solution to which both households and grocers frequently resorted.[86] Also popular were dried fruits. Browsing through a contemporary agricultural manual, one finds a wide array of methods for drying and storing apples, grapes, quinces, peaches, pomegranates, oranges, plums, pears, and figs.[87] For grapes alone, the advice runs to several pages.[88] The range of experimentation offers proof of the constant effort devoted to the problem of storage.

Damascenes waged the same struggle against time and nature with vegetables, which were preserved primarily through pickling. It was an operation familiar to all households, as it remains even today in working-class neighborhoods. Nor was it confined to domestic chores, in which women assumed a leading role. In nearly every neighborhood, there were tradesmen who devoted themselves exclusively to the pickling of foods,[89] as well as grocers and street peddlers who sold their own stocks of vinegar and pickles.[90] Especially famous for their expertise were the people of al-Salihiyya, who took advantage, as always, of their semirural location to excel in the preparation of foods. Demand quite naturally peaked during the winter, when vegetables were scarcest, but nothing prevented customers from enjoying pickles throughout the year. Damascenes showed a special fondness for pickled cucumbers, radishes, beets, eggplant, turnips, and olives.[91] Most recipes for pickling were simple and revolved around the use of vinegar obtained from fermented grape juice.[92] Indeed, the need for vinegar accounted for much of the importance of the grape harvest.

PRESERVATIVES: SALT AND SPICES

One of the other major substances used as a preservative was salt. In both popular and learned lore, contemporaries saw numerous applications and recommended it for all kinds of foods. Among his tips for storing fruit, al-Nabulsi suggested sprinkling salt over figs and soaking pomegranates in salt water before hanging them to dry. Salt was even effective in maintaining vinegar; in the event that worms appeared, he advised, the addition of small quantities would be enough to kill them.[93] Most urgent was the need to salt meat, which easily spoiled. One of the horrors of the pilgrimage caravan in 1757 was that survivors of the bedouin attack had to slaughter many of their camels for food. What made the ordeal even worse, added the chronicler Burayk, was having to eat this meat unpreserved because all their salt, along with their other supplies, had been depleted.[94] It was more than a question of taste. In an age before dependable refrigeration techniques, Burayk's reaction reveals an abiding concern with the preservation of food.

Since salt was so critical to the extension of food supplies, and indispensable to both human and animal life, Syria was fortunate to have a number of sources at its disposal. One of the biggest fields was east of Aleppo, on the way to Mosul.[95] But this was too distant to serve Damascus, which had to secure its own supplies from southern Syria. In the sixteenth century, most shipments arrived from the Lebanese coast, drawn from the salt marshes of Sidon and Acre or hauled from the wharves at Tripoli, which acquired its cargoes from Cyprus. This coastal trade, which operated as a state monopoly, seems to have gradually lost its prominence, perhaps succumbing to the pressures of geography, which must have favored inland sources over the long term.[96] By the eighteenth century, the saltworks located in the Syrian Desert around Palmyra seem to have emerged as the central supplier. Annual accounts from the provincial treasury indicate that it formed one of the most lucrative tax farms, held for nearly a quarter of a century by a single Janissary officer.[97] Supplies found their way to local markets through a variety of middlemen. Some were active in other branches of the economy, such as the all-important grain trade;[98] others were small-time retailers, like the many grocers who sold lesser quantities for everyday use.[99]

More glamorous than salt was the trade in spices, which Damascus had been importing for centuries. Like other big commercial centers in the Middle East, the city had originally acted as an entrepot for European merchants, who by 1500 had accounted for most of the demand in western Eurasia. By the mid-seventeenth century, the volume of traffic had declined precipitously due to the European circumnavigation of Africa, which bypassed Middle Eastern suppliers. The loss of European markets put the Middle Eastern end of the spice trade on a new footing. No longer did it serve as the path to fabulous wealth, as it had during its medieval heyday. Yet spices did not simply disappear from Syrian markets. Towns like Damascus continued to receive annual cargoes with the return of the pilgrimage caravan from Mecca and Medina, which maintained regular links with Jedda, the main Arabian port along the Red Sea and the westernmost emporium for the riches of the Indian Ocean.[100]

So even after Europeans turned their attention elsewhere, the ancient commercial circuits remained in place, operating on a reduced scale, and yet stimulating exchange all the same. For some merchants investment in spices was an outgrowth of the lucrative coffee trade, to which they really owed their fortunes.[101] More representative were the petty retailers, most of whom could be found in their shops lining Suq al-Buzuriyya, southwest of the Umayyad Mosque, where they still cluster today. For centuries, they had doubled as purveyors of incense, perfumes, and pharmacological herbs and drugs (as many spices were originally classified). The biggest dealers stocked the equivalent of a general store. Peering into the shop of Isma'il al-'Attar, one finds many features resembling a neighborhood grocery.[102] Aside from the usual array of spices and fragrances, he kept dry goods such as rice, and a collection of sundry materials: candles and matches for households; paper and ink for scholars and scribes; and alum, ammonia, and borax for industrial purposes. Yet all these supplies were essentially sidelines to the central, defining concern, which always remained spices. In Isma'il's stall alone, customers would have seen an assortment of cinnamon, ginger, saffron, cloves, turmeric, rhubarb, and anise. Other shops contained nutmeg, cumin, cardamom, sumac, safflower, mint, mustard, pepper, and others which were far less common.

A longtime presence in local markets did not mean that spices were everyday items in the kitchen. Few were used solely to flavor food. The cheapest and most popular expedient was garlic, which was one of the truly constant elements of the diet. It was available nearly everywhere, from both local grocers and itinerant peddlers who still make their rounds in the streets of the old quarter today.[103] Doctors extolled it as an aid to digestion that killed lice and intestinal worms, but warned against mixing it with onions and fatty meats (*al-shahm*), which in combination were purported to "cause insanity."[104] Sumac and cumin were other additives,[105] along with marjoram and water-lily (*nufar*), that earned praise for improving meat dishes.[106] What is perhaps most striking is the relative lack of interest in pepper, whose reputation and appeal were worldwide. In Europe, the craze for pepper had seduced upper-class appetites from the early medieval period into the late seventeenth century, and the spice had found its way into everything from drinks to jams.[107] This enthusiasm never reached the same frenzy in the Middle East, probably because its people had enjoyed far easier access to East Asian spices over a much longer period. In the eighteenth century, local stocks must have been fairly ample. Once the linchpin of the east-west trade, pepper was still "widespread among the people. Both the high and low use it," yawned al-Nabulsi.[108] In his agricultural manual, he mentions it only as an ingredient in recipes for pickling turnips, eggplants, and olives.[109] In other respects, Damascene authors seem to have shown no special deference to pepper, which functioned merely as one spice among others.

On the whole, contemporary sources say very little about the culinary properties of spices. This silence was doubtlessly connected to their relatively high cost, but also had to do with broader attitudes which assigned them a lesser role in cooking and eating than today. Townspeople tended to prize spices mainly for their practical uses. In the search for effective preservatives, which was endless, they eagerly turned to the most ordinary condiments. One of garlic's virtues, according to al-Nabulsi, was its ability to prevent food from spoiling.[110] Even more effective was mustard. Not counting vinegar, it was the "mainstay of pickled vegetables ['umdat al-mukhallal], and the best of it is white, pounded with a little bit of salt so that it does not become bitter."[111] Also celebrated was the medicinal value of spices. The literature is extensive and occupies large sections of medical and even agricultural manuals. To come back to mustard: it had acquired a reputation as a powerful and versatile drug. According to contemporaries, it prevented the loss of hair, stopped nosebleeds, suppressed belching and nausea, and offered the added benefit of eliminating the odor of garlic and onion from the breath. Dangled over the head of a woman in labor, it was reputed to ease a complicated delivery.[112] And the list of spices and their applications could easily go on.

LOCAL DELIGHTS: NUTS AND SWEETS

Signs of variety can be detected elsewhere in eighteenth-century eating habits, which by modern standards were insipid and restricted, but not unceasingly bland. The full range of local resources appears in the other goods that spice merchants frequently kept in stock.

Most of their shops, and those of many grocers as well, contained several different kinds of nuts, which were one of the great diversions of the Damascene diet. Like fruit, nuts could often be purchased at a relatively modest cost, in large part because they were found all over Syria. Hazelnuts and walnuts grew in the vicinity of Damascus, whereas pistachios and almonds were brought from the orchards of northern Syria, which to this day remain famous for their produce. Only almonds really qualified as a luxury food, fetching prices which (by weight) exceeded those of mutton. Also expensive, but eaten mostly as garnishes, were pine nuts and sesame seeds; the latter were commonly pressed and converted into sesame oil, a costly substitute for olive oil, or ground into tahina, widely consumed today.[113] In addition, local shops carried quantities of cucumber and watermelon seeds, which were also roasted and sold on the street by vendors. Most exotic were coconuts,[114] which presumably came from the Persian Gulf or tropical areas further east. From the standpoint of nutrition, none of these nuts and seeds were a major component of the diet. Easily stored and transported, they must nonetheless have provided a useful supplement to proteins and fats found in more expensive foods.

Nuts such as pistachios were sometimes dusted with sugar, which was another major commodity in the shops of spice merchants. Sugar had been known throughout Syria since its introduction from India soon after the Islamic conquest, and was grown in small quantities, primarily around the coastal region and central plains.[115] Until the emergence of the Atlantic economy during the seventeenth century, Syria had actually been sending a modest surplus to Europe.[116] As the output of Brazilian and Caribbean plantations continued to rise, the former relationship was reversed, and Syria became a net importer, mostly via French and Austrian merchants. This "Frankish sugar" (*sukkar ifranji*), cultivated with slave labor, was usually cheaper than the homegrown variety, sometimes by as much as 30 to 40 percent, and had already captured much of the Ottoman market by the middle of the eighteenth century. Most imports consisted of brown sugar, which was less costly and therefore more popular than the highly refined white sugar.[117]

Despite its longtime presence in the Middle East, sugar was not an article of mass consumption in the eighteenth century. It seems more likely, in fact, that production and use had actually dropped from medieval levels. One historian has placed the turning point at the beginning of the fifteenth century, but the decline was probably more gradual and old habits harder to break. As late as 1481, Damascene consumers, demonstrating their heartfelt attachment, staged sugar riots when prices reached intolerable peaks.[118] In later periods, the production of sugar seems to have partly recovered, at least in Ottoman Egypt, but it collapsed again under competition from Caribbean sugar in the eighteenth century.[119] Unlike their late-medieval forbears, Damascenes hardly seemed to notice the second time, for the market had long ago shrunk to a rather exclusive domain. Counted as one "spice" among others, sugar was treated as much as a medicine as a dietary condiment.[120] And fashioned into candy, it was now enjoyed mostly by the affluent, like all luxury products. One governor was so fond of sugar that he carried it with him on the pilgrimage caravan (1705). When he foolishly provoked a bedouin tribe during the return to Damascus, they killed him and pillaged his camp; to their delight, they found a hoard of sugar and sweets among the horses, donkeys, mules, tents, and baggage.[121]

The limited nature of demand was reflected in the inventories of local merchants, who showed little interest in entering the sugar trade. For the most part, it remained a marginal venture, functioning as a sideline to other commodities such as textiles or coffee, which drew much greater amounts of capital.[122] In contrast to Western Europe, where sugar was beginning to transform diet and notions of taste for rich and poor alike, no similar revolution was underway in the Ottoman Middle East. For most households, sugar remained an infrequent visitor even into the early twentieth century, and it seems to have gained ground only after the First World War.[123]

In the meantime, most people sweetened their food with honey and grape syrup (dibs). Both were commonly sold by neighborhood grocers, but grape syrup was certainly more widespread, appearing more frequently among personal possessions and costing two to three times less than honey, which was in turn about half as expensive as sugar. Most of the grape syrup consumed in Damascus came from the villages of the Ghuta.[124] Damascenes were often active in the trade as rent-collecting landlords, such as Muhammad Bey al-Kurdi, who operated a grape press in the village of al-Damir. Honey was a simpler matter. Much of it was gathered by landowners like Mustafa al-Sharawi, an unusually affluent bustani who put five beehives on his properties.[125] It was scarcer than grape syrup, and to satisfy popular cravings the city had to comb a much wider region, extending far into its hinterland. These ties were well known and occasionally stimulated the avarice of local officials. Contemplating a punitive campaign against the settlements of the Biqaʿ (1709), the ruthless Nasuh Pasha ordered every village to pay specified amounts of grain, bread, sheep, and butter, while not neglecting to demand large quantities of honey as well; the terrified peasants were spared only at the last minute when the governor suddenly cancelled the expedition.[126] This eagerness to reach out, by one means or another, to more distant suppliers is one of the best indications of the popularity that honey enjoyed.

All these sweeteners—sugar, honey, and grape syrup—were the indispensable raw materials for the city's favorite confections, which brought it fame and envy throughout the eastern Mediterranean. Among the local specialties were rose-petal pastes and jams, prepared with sugar or honey.[127]

Others were based on apricots, which might be stuffed with pistachios or converted into *qamr al-din*, a paste which was produced around the Ghuta.[128] On the urban market, it was handled mostly by sweet sellers, but it seems that many other nonspecialists also participated in the trade.[129] Another group of confectioners prepared a mixture known as *hilawa*, which was made from sesame paste and nuts and sweetened with sugar or grape syrup.[130] Pastries were perhaps the most beloved of all Damascene sweets. Eighteenth-century sources mention names which are still familiar to modern ears: *kunafa, qata'if, bughaja,* and *baqlawa,* which offered various combinations of sugar, honey, butter, and nuts, as well as doughs of different textures and shapes.[131]

Sweet foods such as pastries were among the quintessential symbols of privilege and easy living. According to al-Nabulsi, kunafa in a dream signified "knowledge and guidance."[132] Soldiers and officials took a less refined view and regarded it simply as one of the pleasures reserved for the high and mighty. In 1788, rebellious Janissaries who had temporarily expelled the governor paraded through the streets, feasting on meat, rice, and, not least, kunafa.[133] Not everyone held such a favorable opinion of these foods. The most extreme conservatives reacted with suspicion and even outright hostility, deploring them as decadent and morally tainted. As early as the seventeenth century, Muhammad al-Ustuwani (d. 1661), a puritanical preacher aligned with the Kadızadeli movement, had (unsuccessfully) proposed a ban on the sale of pastries.[134] His campaign for gastronomic morality was later renewed under Genç Yusuf Pasha (1807), a governor who was determined to enforce his own strict interpretation of Islamic law and propriety. In a series of regulations that affected nearly every facet of everyday life, he went so far as to outlaw the consumption of pastries.[135] The decree proved highly unpopular. "Great vexation befell the people of Damascus, for nothing like this order had occurred since time immemorial."[136] In any case, the drive for a more righteous diet was in vain. With the blessings of the ulama and acquiescence of the governor himself, Damascenes were soon allowed to return to their cherished pastries. To escape the tedium of the daily diet, there was no governor whom they were not willing to defy.

All of these controversies bring up an inevitable question: exactly how sweet was the eighteenth-century diet? Our sources from this period make quantitative estimates virtually impossible and, at best, reveal little more than the foods that people were actually eating. Let us take the journal of Ahmad al-Budayri, our humble barber and most talkative witness to the tribulations of eighteenth-century life. As an artisan, he was somewhat representative of the working population. There are other clues about his economic status: as the owner of a house, he cannot be considered desperately poor, but his numerous complaints and weary supplications to God indicate a man who felt hard-pressed by the times, in which prices were rising and, as he saw it, morals were declining. What did such a man and his family eat? He offers no information about the amount of food purchased for his family's kitchen. Rather, his most useful service was simply to note prices from local markets. Counting these jottings, we can indirectly determine his priorities (table 3.1). Not surprisingly, bread and grains ranked at the top of his list—nothing else came close. Next in importance were meats and dairy products (especially butter), to be followed only then by sweeteners—mostly grape syrup, together with a few comments about honey and total silence on sugar. Seasonal foods receive only a few scattered references, no doubt owing to the reliable output of Damascene orchards and gardens, close at hand and supplying local kitchens with virtually everything that they needed at affordable prices.

In citing grape syrup almost as often as meat and butter, al-Budayri provides a tantalizing piece of evidence about eighteenth-century eating habits, which were by no means uniformly bland and monotonous. But it was really more than a question of craving for heightened taste and more interesting variation. The foods most frequently mentioned by al-Budayri share the all-important characteristic of a high caloric content. Bread and grain were the most economical sources of energy and, for that reason, had long formed the core of the Syrian diet. Meat and butter came next in his journal, glamorous foods standing at the high end of local fare, expensive to obtain and consumed in limited quantities. Within this dietary scheme, grape syrup (and to a lesser extent honey) may have performed an underappreciated role, offering hidden reserves of energy, easily and eagerly tapped by a population which could never get enough to eat.

The importance of such cheap supplements to the diet should not be underrated. As some historians have suggested, people in many parts of early modern Europe probably made up caloric deficiencies through the consumption of alcohol—which effectively meant drinking grain or

TABLE 3.1. References to Food Prices in the *Journal of Ahmad al-Budayri*, ca. 1741–62

GRAIN AND GRAIN PRODUCTS	NO.	SEASONAL FOODS	NO.
Bread	31	Onion	7
Wheat	11	Eggplant	4
Barley	5	Squash	3
Rice	16	Cucumbers	1
Sorghum	2	Cabbage	1
Flour	2	Apricots	2
Bulgur Wheat	1	Apples	2
Biscuit	1	Mulberries	1
Proteins and Fats		Pears	1
Meat	18	Pomegranates	1
Fish	1	Dates	1
Eggs	4	Figs	1
Cream	1	Watermelon	1
Yogurt	1	*Preservatives and Spices*	
Cheese	3	Salt	3
Butter (*samna*)	17	Garlic	6
Olive Oil	5	Sumac	1
Sesame Oil	2	*Sweeteners*	
Chick Peas	4	Grape Syrup	13
Lentils	4	Honey	4
Cowpeas (*lubiya*)	1		
Indian Peas (*mash*)	1		

SOURCE: Ahmad al-Budayri, *Hawadith Dimashq al-yawmiyya.*

grape products instead of eating them. In a predominantly Muslim so-ciety like Ottoman Damascus, where alcohol was officially banned, this was not a workable solution. Thus in meeting shortfalls in energy, sweet foods would have stood out as an ideal alternative. By weight, grape syrup and honey delivered almost as many calories as bread and yet remained an affordable component of the popular diet. Among other foods avail-able to Damascenes, only nuts such as pistachios, walnuts, hazelnuts, and almonds held a greater caloric value. Though al-Budayri's journal shows no great interest, Damascenes probably consumed many of the cheapest varieties of nuts in confections such as qamr al-din, whose apricot paste would also have been very nourishing. In this way, preference and necessity managed to meet furtively at many points in the eighteenth-century diet. Tastes which seem at first glance to have arisen from a natural "sweet tooth" beckoned no less seductively with the promise of precious extra calories.

HOW NUTRITIOUS WAS THE EIGHTEENTH-CENTURY DIET?

All these observations stand as a useful corrective to estimates ventured in the last chapter, where calculations depended merely on the consumption of bread and grain. We can now see that many Damascenes—not among the truly poor, but certainly those living above bare subsistence—enjoyed a diet which was probably a little more substantial than their obsession with bread would at first indicate.

Even by the standards of the early twentieth century, most townspeople may not have been eating so badly. We have already learned that the families of "functionaries and wage-earners" living in Syrian cities in the 1930s devoted about three-quarters of their diet to grains and starches (table 3.2). Looking at the remainder of this shopping list (which, as noted previously, does not include fruits and vegetables), we find that meat, eggs, and fish constituted less than 10 percent of annual intake; and dairy products such as milk, cheese, and butter comprised a share which was only slightly larger. These proportions may well have been greater than what eighteenth-century families were accustomed to eating, but in the absence of comparable data from the past, it is impossible to calculate with any accuracy. Curiously enough, the per capita yield of energy from basic starches—wheat, bread, (wheat) flour, rice, and potatoes—stands around 2,100 calories, putting it in the same range as estimates for the eighteenth-century diet. When the other listed foods are added, this "working-class" diet seems positively rich, exceeding 3,000 daily calories, mostly on account of meat and dairy products, which acted as a crucial supplement.

TABLE 3.2. Monthly Consumption of Food by Urban
"Working-Class Families" in Syria, ca. 1930s

FOOD	AMOUNT (IN KILOGRAMS)
Wheat	15
Bread	31
Flour	30
Rice (Egyptian)	13
Potatoes	8
Mutton on the bone	5
Mutton (deboned)	4
Fresh Fish	3
Eggs	50 (no.)
Fresh Milk	10
Cheese	2
Butter (samna)	2
Olive oil	4
Onions	4
Sugar	11

SOURCE: Youssef Khoury, *Prix et monnaie en Syrie*, p. 161

These projections raise interesting questions about the diet in earlier times, and reinforce the importance of proteins, which even in fairly
limited quantities and as a fairly small proportion of the total diet could
dramatically improve overall levels of nutrition. Indeed, the first priority of eighteenth-century consumers, once basic caloric needs had been
met (mostly through bread) was to secure as much protein as possible.
This was not an easy task, for access was highly uneven. Though the city
slaughtered tens of thousands of sheep every year, most of this bounty
was destined for official and elite households, as well as the plates of soldiers and others connected with the state. Among the general population,
dairy products and legumes would have made up some of the difference,
but low levels of protein consumption were, to one degree or another,
probably the norm. Here a broader perspective is needed. Within the
wider experience of the eighteenth century, were Damascenes suffering

from unusual deficiencies? In fact, meat seems to have been scarce and expensive across much of the early modern world. In continental Europe alone, per capita meat consumption had been falling since the sixteenth century and would not recover till after 1870.[137] So low levels of protein, in Damascus or elsewhere, were not particularly glaring. It is quite likely, moreover, that Damascenes were doing better than townspeople in most other parts of Eurasia. In standing so close to the bedouin economy, they were able to obtain comparatively regular and plentiful supplies of animals. The notations on the price of meat found throughout the journal of al-Budayri suggest that even a barber might—undoubtedly in small quantities—partake with some frequency in this urban mania.

Taking their place below meat, for which urban consumers so endlessly pined, other foods were both cheaper and less esteemed, and therefore attracted much less political control and manipulation. On balance, the major preoccupation seems to have been the search for ever more energy. Damascenes were happy to consume anything which could have contributed to this requirement: nuts, sweeteners, pastries, confections. The difference in caloric intake may have been small, but in extending labor and endurance, could have been significant enough to be felt. Harder to judge is the role of fruits and vegetables, which, as cyclical foods, may have been too ephemeral to represent a substantial portion of the diet over the course of a year. Only the pickling of vegetables ensured that, even in the depths of winter, there would be some minimal source of valuable vitamins and nutrients. Cheap and abundant, the produce of the nearby gardens and orchards may have actually been one of the biggest dietary advantages exploited by residents. It was certainly noticed by visitors from more northerly societies, which would be slow in matching this sufficiency. As late as the 1830s, John Bowring was expressing his approval of the Damascene diet, which he found more varied and nourishing than the fare available to workers in industrializing Britain.[138] Though his assessment probably reveals more about conditions in London than Damascus, it still evokes a standard that even the leading economy of western Europe, flush with the profits of early industrialization, could not immediately surpass.

IV

LUXURY

&

VARIETY

EVERYDAY

DRINK

W HAT PEOPLE DRANK WAS NO DIFFERENT FROM THEIR
choice of food, insofar as it was not merely a matter of physiological necessity but of social and religious significance as well. The universal drink
was water, which was simultaneously one of the most routine, complex,
and daunting issues of urban life, posing its own problems of supply,
regulation, and distribution. But water was not the only option. With
varying degrees of enthusiasm, Damascenes were also able to enjoy several
popular beverages. These alternatives acquired a deeply social character,
which ensured that the act of drinking was rarely a solitary pleasure and,
almost by definition, implied companionship and conviviality. More disturbing to religious opinion, drinking provided outlets for stimulation
and escape. Especially popular were two fairly recent commodities, coffee and tobacco (the latter of which is "drunk" in popular speech).[1] Their
introduction in the Ottoman period (in the sixteenth and seventeenth
centuries respectively) stirred passionate debates about their morality

and legality within Islamic culture. More than any other innovations that overtook Ottoman Damascus, their inexorable victory helped to transform patterns of everyday life, which, by the eighteenth century, had become unimaginable without them.

WATER: MEANS AND SOURCES

By eighteenth-century standards, Damascus stood in a particularly favorable position. It lay in the midst of an oasis, sustained not merely by its own river system, but also by a large underground aquifer that was continually replenished. It had no need of cisterns, and, unlike Aleppo, Tunis, and Algiers, no aqueducts were required to tap distant sources.[2] Thus water, so indispensable to humans and animals alike, was always available, either from local rivers or from the springs and wells which dotted the Ghuta.

The largest part of the city's water was drawn from the Barada River and its six branches. Much of it was diverted to irrigate orchards, gardens, and fields, but it was also a major source of drinking water, for which local residents such as Nu'man Qasatli had boundless praise: "in all my travels in Syria, I have never seen water like it in purity and goodness."[3] These qualities did not, however, protect Damascenes from the many species of bacteria and parasites which made the river their home. In addition to lethal fevers, other unpleasant realities of eighteenth-century life included debilitating sicknesses, especially intestinal problems such as dysentery and worms, which afflicted a large percentage of the population. Medical wisdom had little to offer. Against the miseries of diarrhea and dysentery, it could only recommend lavender, watercress, sumac, and myrtle,[4] and, for the truly faithful, water from the holy well of Zamzam in Mecca.[5] Putative cures for worms and other intestinal parasites were no better: cumin, garlic, mint, and peaches.[6] Practical solutions were late in coming. Only after a severe outbreak of cholera in 1907 did local authorities install the first pipe at 'Ayn Fijeh, the Ghuta's aquifer, from which water was pumped to storage facilities on the northern end of the city. Rates of sickness reportedly dropped 70 percent in the following years.[7] The system was later expanded throughout the city during the French Mandate, allowing underground water to be sent directly to nearly all neighborhoods by 1932.

Until that time, water had to be brought through an elaborate network of earthen pipes (pl. *qasatil*), most of which were buried out of sight. "Under the earth there is another city of water channels. The pipes, mains, and drains are all underground. If a person were to dig anywhere below, he would find water ducts joined in layers, left and right, one over another."[8] Much of this system served local mosques, bathhouses, and fountains, but it also extended to many homes. A special guild of overseers looked after the pipes, which, if neglected, had a tendency to fill, ultimately causing them to crack and explode. Constant care had to be taken to clean them of the mud and debris which accumulated throughout the year, especially in winter. Local methods were effective, but left much to be desired in the way of sanitation. Clogged pipes required little more than scouring from a long rod to remove blockages; with leaks, on the other hand, workers often restored water pressure by jamming bits of animal manure into the cracks.[9] Other pieces of equipment requiring maintenance were the distribution sites (*tali*) found in nearly every quarter.[10] At each of these conduits—small compartments attached to the sides of buildings, sometimes raised to add water pressure—water flowed from a main pipe into smaller ones that branched off to individual homes, which thereby gained access to their own private supply of water.

Because there was no municipality to carry out repairs, residents had to assume the burden of providing for upkeep and apportioning the costs amongst themselves. The courts always upheld the principle of communal responsibility, insisting that everyone who benefited from the pipes had to contribute to their maintenance. Inherent in these obligations was a corollary principle of communal welfare: no one could "own" the drinking water that flowed in local rivers or pursue activities that might hinder others' access. When a man proposed to build a house along one of the rivers passing near al-Salihiyya (probably the Yazid), his neighbors organized to block construction on the grounds that it would reduce the amount of water available to them.[11] Water was a serious question, affecting nearly every facet of everyday life, from drinking and cooking to washing and cleaning. Residents needed little incentive to agitate for their rights.

Disruptions in service, though rare, did occur periodically along the smaller branches of the Barada and outlying streams. Water levels might fall from a lack of maintenance, allowing channels to fill with silt and debris and choke off sections further downstream.[12] In 1753, the culprit was a boulder which fell into the Qanawat River and cut water supplies to the western suburbs for three days.[13] At least one major blockage was deliberate: during the construction of his famous palace in 1750, Asʿad Pasha al-ʿAzm temporarily halted the flow of the Qanawat, depriving mosques, fountains, bathhouses, and numerous homes downstream of their customary water.[14] Such high-handed interference was extremely unusual. The authorities took great pains in overseeing a highly sophisticated distribution system throughout the Ghuta. Inside the city, where supervision was no less strict, households were forbidden from taking more than their allotted share (as determined by informal communal agreements).

Most homes attached to the water system came equipped with a courtyard fountain (*birka* or *bahra*), which was the preferred means of delivering water. Ideally, the fountain was fed directly from public pipes, but in some houses the water arrived via a more circuitous route, from the runoff (*faʾid*) of a neighbor's fountain—an arrangement which sometimes created tension and conflict when neighbors wished to make changes or repairs.[15] The most fortunate residents might have several fountains at their disposal, but such extravagances were possible only in the biggest homes, which contained two or even three courtyards.[16] Equally rare was the presence of a decorative fountain (*fisqiyyat maʾ*), another sign of opulence.[17] The most lavish specimens were works of the highest craftsmanship, which might even be celebrated in verse. ʿAbd al-Ghani al-Nabulsi dedicated one of his poems to a fountain which enveloped four candles in a ball of water, as if to form "a lantern made of water."[18] Few homeowners, however, could afford such charming diversions. Most fountains answered to everyday household needs, in which aesthetic considerations were minimal. As court descriptions indicate, residents often found it sufficient to place tiling around the bottom edge of the basin and plaster the inside with lime.

The main alternatives to private fountains were wells (*biʾr maʾ*), which were fairly easy to dig because the water table in Damascus was close to the surface. Unlike fountains, which were at the mercy of connecting pipes, wells required little maintenance apart from periodic cleaning and dredging.[19] They were present in every quarter of the city. Even in homes with fountains, owners sometimes took the precaution of digging wells as insurance against drought, which occasionally struck with enough se-

TABLE 4.1. Fountains vs. Wells
(in a sample of Damascene homes, ca. 1738–63)

VALUE OF HOME (IN PIASTERS)	FOUNTAIN (BIRKAT MA')	WELL (BI'R MA')	BOTH	NEITHER
<100	6	10	0	13
100–499	35	64	2	35
500–999	19	7	2	4
1000–4999	22	0	0	0
>=5000	2	0	0	0
Total	84	81	4	52

SOURCE: Islamic Court Records

verity to threaten the supply of water.[20] Nevertheless, wells were never the ideal, due primarily to their impure and often brackish water. Local opinion assumed the worst. In explaining how to plant gillyflowers (*khayrí*), Ibn Kannan cautioned that well water, like saltwater, would be fatal to the seeds.[21] Only a few wells, which managed to tap into local rivers, brought up water of a higher quality.[22] Such experiences account for al-Nabulsi's surprised reaction in Latakia, where he noted (1693) that the people drank excellent water that was drawn entirely from wells.[23] To a native of Damascus, it hardly seemed possible.

Despite these reservations, wells remained a necessity in a large number of homes. For many of the poor, there was little choice. Though the city contained roughly as many fountains as wells, the ratio quickly shifted in favor of the latter as the value of real estate dropped. Overall, the least expensive homes were twice as likely to come with a well as a fountain (table 4.1). Conversely, wells were almost entirely shunned at the upper end of the residential scale, where the well-to-do had the freedom to install whatever they wished. Geography, too, played a part in determining how households obtained their water. In general, fountains were a more feasible option in sections of the city close to rivers and their subsidiary canals, whereas the number of wells increased as these sources became more distant. Thus, fountains were most common in the northwestern suburbs, including al-Salihiyya, which took advantage not only

TABLE 4.2. Fountains vs. Wells, According to Location

(From a sample of sales deeds, ca. 1738–63)

	FOUNTAIN (BIRKAT MA')	WELL (BI'R MA')	BOTH	NEITHER
Intramural (including all of al-Shaghur)	35	28	3	7
North/ Northwest (including al-Salihiyya)	37	5	1	4
Southwest (upper)	10	17	0	18
Southwest (lower)	2	31	0	23
Total	84	81	4	52

SOURCE: Islamic Court Records

of the main channel of the Barada, but of several other branches—the Yazid and Tura to the northwest, and the Qanawat, winding through the westernmost neighborhoods. In all these areas, the percentage of wells was extremely low (table 4.2). In the intramural quarters, also located near the Barada, the ratio between fountains and wells was slightly lower—about even—and reflected the local availability of flowing water. Only in the southern reaches of the city—particularly the Midan—did the preponderance of wells become unmistakable. And the farther south one lived, the more difficult it was to maintain fountains.

Complicating access to water were the cramped housing conditions that prevailed among a large portion of the population. Many houses were divided among two or more families, each of which received its own partitioned section of the property. Detailed arrangements determined how the use of the courtyard and its fountain or well would be shared.[24] In the search for water, some went so far as to purchase part of a neighbor's facilities.[25] All these rights were jealously guarded; if not explicitly mentioned in a deed or some other formal document, occupants in effect ceded residential water entirely to their housemates. This was the worst predicament: to have neither a fountain nor a well. Examples of such households, of which the overwhelming majority were poor, could be found throughout the city, but most were concentrated, as one might expect, in the southern suburbs, where water was always scarcest. In such extreme circumstances, the search for outside supplies was not merely a necessity of life, but a requirement of the law. No wife, for example, was obligated to live in a home which was not in some way provided with water.[26] One solution was to hire water-carriers, who patrolled the streets with their brass cups and skin pouches and did a steady business whenever the rivers ran low.[27] But most families simply could not afford this service on a daily basis, and had to fetch their own water from public sources. Among the most reliable were the Ghuta's numerous springs, many of which lay on the outskirts of the city. Along one stretch of the Barada, from Bab al-Salam to Bab Tuma, there were reportedly three hundred and sixty such sites, which owed their existence to the adjacent river. So popular were springs that they might even serve people who had their own fountains and wells. During the winter months, the rivers tended to carry large amounts of sediment, making their water less palatable and causing disruptions in many areas as pipes filled up and burst. Summertime made springs even more appealing to a population which thirsted for cold water; scorching temperatures soon heated most water flowing near the surface, especially as the volume of the rivers inevitably dropped.[28]

In addition to springs, cold water could be obtained from regular deliveries of snow. Thanks to the efforts of enterprising peasants and teams of carriers, snow was available in Damascus year round. Most of it was brought from the village of Manin, north of the city in the heights of al-Qalamun, where the local inhabitants collected snow in wintertime, packed it into storage vaults, and sent off "more than a hundred loads each day during the summer."[29] Some orders came from as far away as Cairo. Regardless of destination, the expense was considerable and frustrated the thirst of all but the wealthy. Most frequently, snow was reserved for medical uses. It was prescribed for toothaches, fevers, intestinal disorders, and mange, and was even given to animals to help fatten them.[30]

Far more important than either local springs or shipments of snow

"A fountain next to the market." Most neighborhood fountains were smaller and would not have featured such elaborate decoration. L. Lortet, *La Syrie d'aujourd'hui: voyages dans la Phénicie, le Liban, et la Judée, 1875–1880*. Paris, 1884.

were the public taps (*sabíl*), which, like many private homes, drew their water entirely from rivers and canals. But unlike residential fountains, whose flow was strictly regulated, these communal sources were open all the time to anyone who needed water. They were located around the city, even in the surrounding gardens and orchards, and acted as major landmarks that often had their own names, known throughout nearby quarters.[31] The state played no role in maintaining them. Repairs had to be sponsored by local neighborhoods, wealthy donors, or pious foundations. Such charity and cooperation provided indispensable relief for those Damascenes who enjoyed only the most rudimentary housing, lacking water and many other conveniences.

A home without water was, of course, a great hardship. But by regional standards, even the poorest Damascenes, who bore the brunt of these privations, fared quite well compared to other eighteenth-century townspeople. At the very least, water was nearly always available, whereas in many other Syrian cities it was a constant problem, either because there were few sources or because local rivers were insufficient for local needs. The people of Gaza, for instance, were entirely dependent on their wells, for which the southern Palestinian coast provided no alternative.[32] A less precarious case was Aleppo, which nevertheless staggered beneath the twin burdens of an enormous population (about a third larger than Damascus) and an inadequate river (the Quwayq, which was inferior in volume, if not length, to the Barada). The city suffered from chronic shortages, aggravated by brackish groundwater, an aqueduct which repeatedly fell into disrepair, and unscrupulous landowners who illegally diverted river water for irrigation.[33] In contrast, Damascus had virtually all the water that it needed. Even during the worst heat of the summer, shortages occurred infrequently, thereby sparing residents from one of the persistent anxieties of premodern life.

LOCAL BEVERAGES

Apart from water, Damascenes had few choices about what they could drink. One factor was expense. Water was nearly everywhere, easily drawn from fountains, wells, or springs, whereas alternatives offered a change of taste, but at a price which effectively put them in the class of luxury items. To serve something other than water, moreover, was an automatic break with routine, and on most occasions stood out as a gesture of hospitality, conforming to the demands of etiquette or promoting the desire for good fellowship.

Turning first to the more innocuous pastimes, we find the sweetened beverages known as sherbets (*sharab*). The simplest version was nothing more than honey or sugar added to water. For Zahir al-ʿUmar, the powerful bedouin chief, sugar water was one of the few luxuries that he allowed himself in an otherwise strict dietary regimen.[34] But there were also more elaborate mixtures. Among the favorites were citrus drinks such as lemonade, and sherbets made from apple juice, myrtle water (*shar-ab al-as*), tamarind juice (*tamar hindi*), and, perhaps most highly esteemed of all, several kinds of rose water.[35] Customers could buy from itinerant vendors in the streets or from the shops of spice merchants, who might keep their own reserves on hand.[36] Demand was fairly restricted. Only wealthy townspeople, like Sulayman Pasha al-ʿAzm, would have enjoyed these drinks on a regular basis. Before leaving the bathhouse one afternoon (1743), he was allegedly poisoned by a brother of Zahir al-ʿUmar, who knew that the governor would unwind with a cup of sherbet.[37] Other notables served sweet drinks as a token of hospitality. Summoning several Janissaries who had antagonized him, one governor (1699) was unable to act against them before showing the requisite courtesy; only after he had seated them and dispensed the usual sherbets did he read out the imperial warrant for their arrest and execution.[38] The poor, on the other hand, resorted to sweet drinks mainly as a treatment for illness,[39] and did not develop the habit of consuming them until fairly recently. As late as the 1920s, the Christian quarter of Bab al-Musalla, in the southwest, had no seller of lemonade and other fruit drinks.[40] It was not an oversight, but the remnant of a much older pattern of consumption.

Alcohol was the most infamous beverage, which Islamic law sternly condemned as an intoxicant. These very explicit strictures, however, did not amount to a full ban on its manufacture.[41] Local Christians and Jews, who remained free to make and drink it within the bounds of discretion, accounted for some of this output.[42] But most production was handled by nearby villages, especially Saydnaya, located to the north of Damascus.[43] Grapes were the basis of all alcoholic drinks, either fermented as wine or distilled as arrack, a licorice-flavored spirit known by various names throughout the eastern Mediterranean and taking its distinctive taste from anise.

Aside from religious minorities, whose drinking habits were exempt from Islamic prohibitions, the most devoted tipplers were Ottoman officials and members of the local military. The entourage of Fathi al-Daftari, who briefly challenged Asʿad Pasha for preeminence in the city, were rumored to give themselves up freely to alcohol, among numerous other vices that enemies attributed to them.[44] No more temperate was the Ottoman official (a "pasha") posted to Damascus in 1805 to defend the city from Wahhabi raiders in the south; instead of going out to meet the enemy, he remained in the Tekke (Sufi lodge) of al-Marja, "perpetually intoxicated, night and day" until the departure of the pilgrimage.[45] Janissaries were particularly notorious for drunkenness. Seen through the eyes of the Englishman Henry Maundrell, who encountered them in 1697, they were a true terror to behold. "A drunken Janissary, passing under the window where we were, chanced to have a drop of wine thrown out upon his vest, upon which innocent provocation he presented his pistol at us in the window; had it gone off, it must have been fatal to one or both of us, who sat next the place. But it pleased God to restrain his fury."[46] So uncontainable was the thirst of imperial Janissaries that, in 1776, they extorted wine and arrack, in addition to more conventional tribute, from local Christian communities.[47] Those who kept company with soldiers, such as prostitutes, showed the same partiality to alcohol. In 1744 one prostitute, drunk and unveiled, attacked the qadi on the street with a knife; in response, the mufti issued a fatwa authorizing the execution of all "daughters of sin and desire," most of whom temporarily fled the city or went into hiding.[48]

In defiance of Islamic norms, many prominent figures connected with popular religion were also known to consume alcohol. In one entry for 1750, the chronicler al-Budayri mentions the death of a revered folk saint, who, like many holy men, was noted for his bizarre antics and astonishing "marvels." Though the saint occasionally drank wine, it never diminished his standing among his followers.[49] The same tolerance was shown towards Sufis, some of whom engaged in their own outlandish behavior, including the use of wine in rituals. Indignant and appalled, leading religious scholars repeated tales of Sufi rituals that degenerated into drunken debauchery, complete with rumors of homosexual orgies.[50] But unlike official Islam, popular religion made allowances for intoxicants such as alcohol, and among its most heterodox practitioners, even sanctioned them as a means for promoting spiritual ecstasy.

Against these open and suspected violations of Islamic law, the authorities railed in vain. Governors now and then made attempts to enforce the letter of the law, but these campaigns had no lasting effect.

The middle decades of the eighteenth century appear quite tolerant of public drinking, at least for members of the minority communities. Mikha'il Burayk judged the rule of As'ad Pasha al-'Azm as most lenient: Christian families drank wine and arrack openly in the gardens and orchards around the city without the slightest harassment.[51] Only towards the end of the century did the push for stricter compliance became more noticeable, as the city felt both the military and ideological pressure of the Wahhabi movement welling from the heart of the Arabian Peninsula. In 1804, Ibrahim Pasha al-Muhassil forbade Christians and Jews from drinking wine and arrack; to ensure cooperation, the governor's troops searched the houses of suspected dealers and dumped whatever alcohol they found into the streets.[52] Genç Yusuf Pasha repeated the ban (but not the inspections) three years later during his own sweeping promulgations against immorality.[53] But such measures remained exceptional throughout most of the Ottoman period, finding support only among the most inflexible conservatives, who formed a small but vocal minority within the religious establishment. Always watchful of social mores and quick to claim falling standards, they viewed not merely alcohol, but all intoxicants as a major threat to society and religion, for the sake of which compromise was unthinkable.

THE PASSION FOR COFFEE

Conservatives were equally outspoken against coffee after it first arrived from Yemen towards the end of the fifteenth century. It was immediately identified as an intoxicant—or denounced simply as an impious "innovation" (*bid'a*)—and aroused further suspicions due to its popularity among Sufis, who appreciated its virtues as a stimulant during all-night vigils.[54] All these objections soon proved irrelevant, however, as popular opinion was quickly won over to the pleasures of caffeine. By the late sixteenth century, the religious authorities in Damascus and many other cities of the empire had fully legalized the new beverage.[55]

The stridency of the early disputes (which, if the muted reaction in Europe is any indication, seem not to have flared up beyond the Islamic world)[56] found only the most distant echoes in the work of eighteenth-century scholars. Al-Nabulsi hailed both the mental and physical benefits of coffee, stressing the many good works which could be performed under its invigorating influence, not least of which were Sufi rituals and the study of religious literature. Even if it was capable of producing euphoria or overly animated behavior, this condition was not the same as outright intoxication and resulted mostly from the "meeting of religious brothers, either for the *dhikr* or the *sama*ʿ [Sufi rituals], or merely the recital of poetry or pleasant late-night conversation. Most of the cheer, in reality, is not from coffee [itself], but rather from the conversation of friends."[57] In his own life, he had no qualms about the habit, as revealed by his travel accounts, in which episodes of hospitality and relaxation were sometimes accompanied by cups of coffee.[58] In his blasé acceptance, he was not alone. Noting the death of Ahmad al-Salami (d. 1714), who had suddenly collapsed one Friday after imbibing coffee, the biographer al-Muradi offered not a single moralizing comment.[59] Indeed, except for sporadic denunciations from ultraconservative quarters, the original controversy was long dead. Coffee had come to stay.

The newcomer soon established itself as a lucrative commodity. For local merchants, coffee was the basis of untold wealth—or, to observe the same process from the opposite point of attraction, possession of a large fortune often led, sooner or later, to investment in coffee. In either case, the scent of coffee lured many of the richest men in the city, including a disproportionate number of ʿaskari Damascenes, who, as always, dominated the most remunerative sectors of the economy.[60] Profits were impressive even though Cairo functioned as the true center of the trade.[61] Damascus distinguished itself mainly as a regional entrepot; what it did not consume for its own needs, it shipped northward to Aleppo and other cities in Syria and Anatolia.

Most of this coffee originated in Yemen, which remained the major source for Damascene markets throughout the eighteenth century. To obtain their supplies, local merchants followed the annual pilgrimage, making their purchases in the holy cities of the Hijaz and hauling back their cargoes with the main caravan. The only challenge to this route came from Atlantic coffee, which was imported from the Caribbean via France. This "Frankish coffee" (*bunn ifranji*) first reached Cairo in 1737[62] and arrived in other parts of the Ottoman world over the next decade;[63] in Damascus, it had definitely appeared in local markets by the early 1750s.[64] Cheaper to produce, owing to the ruthless exploitation of African slaves, it quickly made inroads against its Yemeni competition, whose prices were roughly 30 to 35 percent higher around mid-century.[65] It may seem surprising, then, that the demand for Yemeni coffee, or mocha (named after Mukha, the main coffee port), remained strong. One factor in its continuing popularity was the reduction in prices which occurred for all types of coffee around the middle of the eighteenth century (chart 5). Just as crucial was the quality of mocha, which in both the Ottoman Empire and Europe was regarded as superior to all other varieties.[66] In towns like Cairo, an unmistakable snobbery developed. The well-to-do refused to drink the cheaper imports and insisted on Yemeni coffee. For the lower end of the market, which could not afford to be so discerning, merchants adulterated their stocks of mocha with the less costly and esteemed Caribbean coffee. In Damascus, the same practices probably prevailed as well.

Trade and taste were further intertwined in the methods for preparing coffee. Especially important was the trade in spices and incense, which brought cardamom and ambergris. Cardamom was often ground into coffee to mask its bitterness.[67] Ambergris performed a double function, enhancing flavor and odor. As a parting courtesy, noted Henry Maundrell, many notables would have their guests' beards fumigated with censors of smoking ambergris.[68] Dissolved in small quantities, it was equally prized as an additive to coffee.[69] Other ingredients were not widely used. During Napoleon's occupation, Egyptians mocked the French for sweetening their coffee with sugar. Milk, too, was unthinkable for Ottoman tastes.[70] Damascenes, like other Middle Easterners, always drank their coffee hot and strong. Individual portions were poured into small china cups (*finjan*) "generally not holding quite an ounce and a half of liquid."[71] No one used saucers. These first achieved popularity in Europe, where people originally drank out of their saucers instead of their cups, which were treated as small reservoirs for the hot liquid.[72]

Like the coffee itself, the service conformed to its own scale of taste and prestige. The most admired cups were of "Chinese" (*sini*) porcelain, imported from East Asia via the Red Sea, whereas others were European imitations.[73] Cheaper and less esteemed was the output of Kutahya, the western Anatolian town that, by the eighteenth century, had become the center of production for Ottoman tiles and ceramics. As regional elites turned increasingly to imported wares (especially from Europe), the qual-

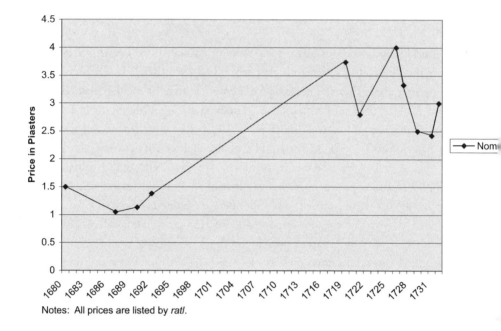

Notes: All prices are listed by *ratl*.

Nominal Price

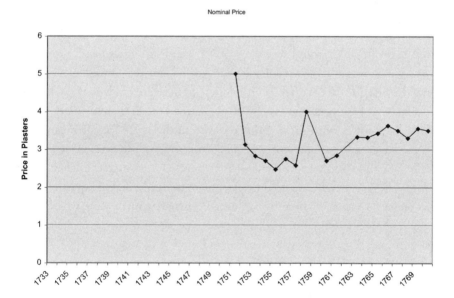

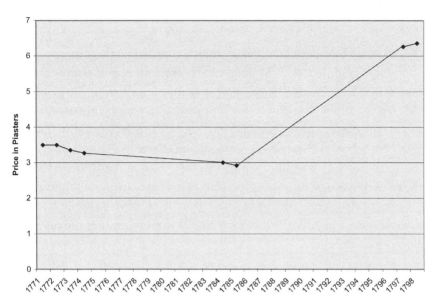

CHART 5. The Price of Coffee
Left: (top) 1680–1731; (bottom) 1733–1769; Above: 1771–1798
Note: All prices are listed by *ratl*.

ity of its manufactures steadily declined. As confirmation of this trend, affluent households in Damascus largely shunned the Kutahya wares, together with any copies that local artisans may have produced.[74] It is no coincidence that, at roughly the same time, the Damascene porcelain industry was beginning to die out; by the end of the nineteenth century, there were no workshops to attract al-Qasimi's attention in his dictionary of local crafts and trades.[75] This subtle shift in demand was probably a response to superior manufacturing techniques, as well as the expansion of international trading networks, rather than the emergence of new decorative tastes. And since the Middle East had been using porcelain for centuries (unlike Europe), it can hardly be regarded as a new form of consumption;[76] at most, the age of coffee may have stimulated an interest in finer grades of chinaware.

By the eighteenth century, all these accessories had become both commonplace and necessary in domestic life, thanks to the universal enthusiasm for coffee drinking. Damascenes of nearly every social rank enjoyed it as often as their means allowed. The situation was comparable to Aleppo, where Alexander Russell calculated "few of the lower people drink less than three or four cups of coffee in twenty-four hours; their superiors drink more; and persons who frequent the great drink perhaps twenty cups daily."[77] For many Damascenes, early mornings were incomplete, even trying, without a cup of coffee.[78] Surveying the belongings of ordinary townspeople, one is unavoidably struck by the prevalence of coffee pots (ibriq qahwa) at nearly every socioeconomic level.[79] The wealthy, of course, accounted for a disproportionate share, but it is equally clear that all except the poorest townspeople eagerly participated in one of the great pastimes of eighteenth-century life. The triumph of coffee was complete. Across the city's population, it had established itself as one of the fixtures of the social scene.

The craving for coffee was apparent not merely inside the home, but in public places as well. Some bathhouses kept their own supplies for customers, who might relax with a cup after a refreshing bath.[80] The Frenchman Volney discovered that merchants on the road viewed coffee as an indispensable part of travel; "the baggage of a man who wishes to be completely provided consists . . . above all [of] coffee-berries with a roaster and a wooden mortar to pound them," among many other items judged essential.[81] In the marketplace, coffee lubricated the wheels of commerce. Shopkeepers frequently offered it to customers as an accompaniment to bargaining, which always proceeded at a leisurely pace.[82] In nearly all social situations, the rites of hospitality simply could not do without it. When the Egyptian commander Muhammad Bey Abu'l-Dhahab received a delegation of ulama who had come to surrender the city (1771), he did not forget to present them with the obligatory welcome of coffee.[83] These habits were imitated everywhere, even in the countryside. During his celebrated trip to Jerusalem, al-Nabulsi encountered a "possessed" hermit, who lived in a cave and had a reputation for working miracles. Despite the rugged accommodations, the hermit kept his own mortar and roasting pan. Nearby villagers claimed that, with this simple equipment, he was able to make "delicious coffee" from wheat, barley, sorghum, or chickpeas.[84] Nothing other than the craze for coffee could inspire such behavior, even in the most improbable settings.

The most public expression of this devotion was the coffeehouse, which was one of the great social innovations of the Ottoman period. By his own day, estimated Nu'man Qasatli (1876), Damascus had about one hundred ten such establishments scattered throughout the city.[85] In the eighteenth century, many were still being built, and the opening of a new one always attracted public attention. The chronicler al-Budayri found the construction of four coffeehouses in 1756 to be one of the newsworthy events of the year.[86] Ibn Jum'a showed the same interest when he reported that the al-Munakhiliyya coffeehouse had caught fire and burned to the ground (1716) as the city was being decorated with lights.[87] In the local mind, it was the destruction of a familiar landmark known to everyone. In 1750, al-Budayri reported the attempted suicide of a man who had thrown himself from the walls of the citadel "in the direction of al-Munakhiliyya coffeehouse," which had of course been restored much earlier.[88] Contemporaries would have immediately recognized the location.

Coffeehouses could be found in nearly every part of the city, in both residential quarters and markets. There was even one at the gate of the citadel.[89] The majority were modest operations which might accommodate one or perhaps two dozen customers.[90] In contrast, the biggest coffeehouses could hold literally hundreds of people at a time.[91] As a general rule, the latter were restricted to the extramural quarters, where there was more space, as well as an abundance of water and greenery which added pleasant scenery. Some of these establishments, like the one recalled by Henry Maundrell, reached impressive dimensions and created a striking effect:

[It was] a coffee house capable of entertaining four or five hundred people, shaded over head with trees, and with mats when the boughs fail. It had two quarters for the reception of guests, one proper for the summer, the other for the winter. That designated for the summer was a small island, washed all around with a large, swift stream, and shaded over head with mats and trees. We found here a multitude of Turks upon the divans, regaling themselves in this pleasant place.[92]

The rustic ambience was one of the main attractions of these outlying coffeehouses, and their popularity seems to have fluctuated according to the weather. After many of the coffeehouses in al-Marja had been renovated in the 1870s, Qasatli was surprised to find that several of them, in the midst of winter, continued to bustle during the daylight hours.[93] For knowledgeable observers, this off-season appeal seemed odd and out of place. In the intramural quarters, on the other hand, the business of

coffeehouses followed the opposite cycle, tending to peak during cold weather as people withdrew indoors, showing little inclination to venture out to nearby gardens.[94]

To operate a coffeehouse, one needed little capital. Some individuals actually owned their premises, but like all urban real estate, it was an expensive investment. Having no other choice, many coffeehouse attendants (*qahwajî*) rented from private individuals or pious foundations.[95] Apart from a license (Tk. *gedîk*) for the shop, they required only the simplest implements: cups, plates, pots, and a few benches or divans in the smallest establishments. Some entered the coffee trade on their own behalf,[96] but many others obtained their supplies from middlemen (*bunnî*) who sold in small amounts and offered their services as roast-

"Cafés in Damascus, a branch of the Barada flowing between." This bucolic scene shows several large coffeehouses set in the gardens, probably in the western suburbs, where patrons might stay well after dark. Business was most brisk here during the spring and summer months. W. H. Bartlett, William Purser et al., *Syria, the Holy Land, Asia Minor &c., Illustrated.* London, 1836.

ers and grinders.[97] Proprietors came from all economic levels.[98] Partnerships were fairly common, and the few financial obstacles were easily surmounted. But it remained, for the most part, a field of petty commerce in which the accumulation of wealth was slow and irregular, rarely if ever building a fortune.

Most proprietors of coffeehouses were distinguished by their affiliation with the Ottoman class.[99] Several were actually soldiers, such as Muhammad Usta al-Baghdadi, who served as a member of the imperial Janissaries while running his own coffeehouse with a partner.[100] The military attachment to coffee was famous throughout the Ottoman Empire. Even on patrol, soldiers would never dream of leaving their coffee behind.[101] Inside town, there was no question of going without it. Especially in the western and southwestern neighborhoods, where most soldiers resided, regiments often had their own coffeehouses that they had either assimilated into their network of colleagues and clients or claimed through outright occupation. After arriving in the city, the first imperial troops dispatched against Napoleon in 1799 immediately seized a number of coffeehouses for themselves, hanging their insignia as an informal way of marking the territory.[102] Another practice, observed mostly among local units, was to inscribe their regimental number over the hearth, treating it like a banner to be protected against all challengers. These symbols announced to everyone that the coffeehouse was no longer open ground; henceforth, the interior was to be quite literally transformed into a sanctuary. Whoever committed a crime—even murder—might seek asylum if the soldiers granted their consent.[103] It was their own space, held on their own terms.

Yet many other coffeehouses had little to do with soldiers. They were public places where men (but rarely women) of nearly every social background came together to pass the time over a few leisurely cups. News, gossip, and conversation were the standard diversions, but by no means the only fare. Patrons might fritter away the time with chess, backgammon, and games of chance, whose devotees were often betrayed by the presence of dice in their estates.[104] Many coffeehouses also staged regular entertainment, sometimes lasting late into the night. One of the prime attractions was music, for which Damascenes displayed a keen appreciation. Among his other jottings for 1747, al-Budayri mentioned the arrival of three Jewish musicians from Aleppo who toured the local coffeehouses to popular acclaim.[105] Other performers were storytellers (*hakawati*)[106] and puppeteers; their stock of pungent tales and humor complemented the traditions of elite literature, whose poets found their own pleasant refuge amid coffee cups.[107] No other establishment could rival the coffeehouse as a hub of social life. Since its first appearance in the sixteenth century in towns throughout the Middle East, it had become the bastion of an unapologetic culture of leisure and idleness. Popular culture had welcomed the new social opportunities, and by the eighteenth century took them fully for granted.

So irresistible was the spell of coffeehouses that many men were known to spend a good deal of their spare time inside. One such regular was Muhammad al-Mughassil, a resident of al-Salihiyya who led an anti-corruption campaign in 1730 that resulted in the dismissal and execution of a neighborhood headman (*shaykh*); when the latter's supporters finally caught up with him and exacted their bloody revenge, he was naturally enjoying himself in a coffeehouse.[108] The authorities regarded these social addictions as something of an epidemic. One frustrated governor, informed that many patrons were refusing to leave the coffeehouses for Friday prayers (1699), repeatedly ordered their closure until they were "almost ruined by the lack of people coming to them, out of fear of the pasha."[109] It was perhaps a belated answer to the Kadızadeli movement, which had led to a ban on all coffeehouses in Istanbul (but not, curiously enough, the provinces) during the middle decades of the seventeenth century.[110] With the normalization of coffee, such extreme measures became increasingly difficult to carry out. In Damascus, the last attempt to curb the popularity of coffeehouses was left to Genç Yusuf Pasha, who ordered them to shut down at sunset (1807); like the rest of his campaign for public morality, it proved to be nothing more than a temporary inconvenience.[111]

Each of these unpopular decrees reflected lingering suspicions about the social role of coffeehouses. Their unabashed air of pleasure, worldliness, and escapism made them anathema to respectable social circles. In the fanciest homes, residents might install their own "coffee room" (*udat qahwa*), allowing them to entertain in privacy and comfort and avoid the unseemly necessity of mingling with social inferiors.[112] Much of this distaste, especially pronounced among leading religious authorities, was rooted in the conviction that coffeehouses promoted behavior and entertainment which were vulgar, immoral, and, at their worst, downright un-Islamic. Most disturbing of all was the availability of wine and other intoxicants, particularly in establishments near the Christian quarter.[113] The painful awareness that many Damascenes were partaking of these forbidden temptations in the heart of the city roused the pious to personal action. 'Abd al-Rahman al-Kurdi, a Sufi shaykh, won praise for converting a coffeehouse near his home in al-'Amara into a Sufi lodge. His biographer, the mufti al-Muradi, minced no words in describing the former patrons, whom he dismissed as "the rabble and riff-raff from among the people, the deviant and dissolute, and gamblers." He hailed the rededication of the building as a pious deed by which "God drove [the former coffeehouse] from the shadows and into the light."[114] Thus the battle lines remained drawn. Though coffee drinking had long ago become a legal and acceptable pastime, it continued to haunt the imagination of the moral authorities indirectly, in the image of the coffeehouse itself.

TOBACCO: THE GUILTIEST PLEASURE

It is difficult to mention coffee without also touching on the subject of tobacco, which provoked another of the great religious controversies of the Ottoman period. From the standpoint of conservatives, the two were twin evils, frequently consumed together and ultimately posing the same threat to the moral order. When al-Muradi observed that Khalil al-Misri was "infatuated with drinking coffee and [smoking] tobacco," he was not speaking of an isolated case, whose behavior was unique or startling.[115] It was, as far as such commentators were concerned, an all too popular combination. That tobacco was often smoked in coffeehouses only confirmed its dubious reputation, placing it among the other vices that patrons merrily flaunted.

Unlike coffee, which arrived from the region of the Red Sea, tobacco (*tutun*)[116] had to cross an entire ocean from the New World. It had first appeared in the Ottoman Empire at the beginning of the seventeenth century, not long after its introduction into Europe. As its popularity grew, it became an important crop in Anatolia, along the coast of the Black Sea and throughout several regions in the Mediterranean south. In Syria, it soon gained a foothold in the hills of the northwest, mostly around the port of Latakia. An active trade immediately developed with the cities of the interior, which relied primarily on this "coastal tobacco" (*tutun sahili*). So tightly bound were source and market that some of the biggest Damascene dealers, such as one ʿUmar al-Hamawi (d. 1732), were able to arrange purchases of tobacco even before the harvest.[117] Tobacco was also grown farther down the Syrian coast, around Tripoli and Tyre, and by the nineteenth century would reach several villages around Damascus.[118] Syrian tobacco, however, never held a monopoly over the regional market, which also drew on "Kurdish" and Persian varieties, the latter of which, known locally as *tunbak*, earned the highest reputation among consumers.[119] To enhance their experience, some connoisseurs liked to flavor their tobacco with grape syrup, an improvement which was said to have come westward from India and Iran.[120]

"Pipes, nargilehs, coffee-cups, and trays." A coffee pot appears on the tray, along with small cups of a standard size. Completing the ensemble are long pipes, set with small bowls at the end, and hookahs of various designs. William Thomson, *The Land and the Book*. New York, 1886.

On the whole, the tobacco trade was profitable, and supported its own class of wholesalers (*tutunji*), who were joined by other merchants to whom tobacco appealed mainly as a rewarding sideline.[121] Equally telling was the construction of a specialized caravansary (Khan al-Tutun) in Suq al-Silah, located near the heart of the main commercial district. Helping to stimulate demand was the overall affordability of tobacco.

Prices remained relatively low over the long term (lower by weight, for example, than coffee) and actually declined somewhat during the middle decades of the eighteenth century (chart 6). As an added inducement, the equipment for smoking was straightforward and cheap. A standard pipe (*qasaba*) rarely fetched more than one or two piasters, and often less. The simplest versions were usually fashioned out of a long stick of rosewood, which extended as much as four or five feet; some were assembled from several smaller segments, which made them ideal for traveling.[122] An alternative was the earthen *ghalyun*, a funnel-shaped water-pipe; a small bowl held the plug of tobacco, which was burned with hot coals, and the smoke was drawn up to the mouth in decorated tubes. Other models were made from brass, or, at the bottom end of the market, polished coconut shells. Best of all were the hookahs designed with glass or crystal bottles, which could be quite extravagant.[123] For most Damascenes, such refinements were an impossible luxury that they might have been able to see only at coffeehouses.[124] Other ways of taking tobacco were almost entirely unknown. Snuff, which was to grow into a craze throughout Catholic Europe in the eighteenth century, had not yet reached Syria.[125] The worldwide fad for cigarettes would not begin until the middle of the nineteenth century.

It is nearly impossible to estimate the proportion of townspeople who smoked. Probate inventories offer few clues, probably because smoking implements tended to be cheap, somewhat fragile, and difficult to auction for reuse. Contemporaries leave only the general impression that, by the eighteenth century, tobacco had already become very popular. Volney found that it was readily available in the countryside.[126] Al-Nabulsi treated it as an all-conquering force which had reached the far corners of the globe and seduced adherents from all walks of life:

[Tobacco] has now become extremely famous in all the countries of Islam: in the Holy Cities, Damascus, Cairo, Aleppo, Anatolia [*al-Rum*]. Indeed, it was diffused and spread until it reached from North Africa to the Middle East and to India and the Indus Valley. People of all kinds have used it and devoted themselves to it: those who are known for goodness and piety [i.e., the Sufis]; those from among the doctors of law, the chief shaykhs of the muftis and teachers, and [students]; those who possess the positions of commanders, judges, prayer leaders, preachers, and muezzins; the rulers

"Syrian ladies." They have most likely come together for a private party in a local garden. Sustained by coffee, tobacco, and musical instruments, the entertainments have reached full swing. William Thomson, *The Land and the Book*. New York, 1886.

of the state; and finally the general population in the markets and homes, as well as soldiers and slaves, from among the elderly, adults, youth, and children. I have even seen young children of about five years applying themselves to it.[127]

To these swelling ranks of smokers, one can also add many of the city's women, whom al-Nabulsi had overlooked (or perhaps been unwilling to mention). "Smoking has become one of the greatest scourges in Damascus. Men, women, and even girls have begun to smoke," lamented al-Budayri (1749), who generally spoke in the most conservative tones. He was particularly startled by the sight of women daring to indulge in the habit publicly. While relaxing with friends in al-Marja in the spring of 1750, he noticed a number of them "greater than the men, sitting along the bank of the [Barada]. They were eating and drinking, and drinking coffee and [smoking] tobacco just as the men were doing."[128] Mikha'il Burayk, a Greek Orthodox priest, shared this reaction and expressed amazement (1759) at women who "smoked tobacco in homes, bathhouses, and gardens, even along the river while people were passing by."[129] All this self-professed shock and horror issued from two main sources. The first was an offended male sensibility which had regarded tobacco as an essentially male prerogative. Women were "crossing boundaries," as Burayk put it; they were acting like men and needed to be stopped, especially outside the home, where these transgressions were all the more embarrassing to public mores. The other objection, which transcended the issue of gender, was an offended sense of propriety. Women were engaging in an activity which had not yet escaped moral taint and suspicion. Far more than coffee drinking, smoking continued to be seen as disreputable.

This air of controversy may have been unavoidable. Despite all the successes achieved by tobacco, it was a relatively new commodity. Protracted and emotional legal debates, which had raged ever since its arrival in the Islamic world, were still running their course. Many personal enmities sprang from this one question alone, which divided religious circles throughout the empire. The venerable al-Nabulsi, a defender of tobacco, was not at all surprised to find himself in at least one heated discussion about smoking during his stay in Jerusalem (1690).[130] More perilous to his career was a feud that he started with the future chief mufti (Tk. şey-hülislam) of Istanbul, who had strict views on the issue of tobacco. He later penned a sarcastic essay with his adversary's name in the title ("The Sharp Sword in the Neck of 'Ata' Allah the Qadi"). The latter never forgot, and after ascending to high office, briefly stripped al-Nabulsi of a teaching position at the Madrasa Selimiye (1713).[131] As such public squabbling demonstrates, the dispute over tobacco was more than an abstract point of law; it was a celebrated cause in which scholars identified themselves personally with one side or the other.

To clarify the positions in this debate, let us examine the arguments of al-Nabulsi, who was the foremost spokesman for the toleration of tobacco. His aim was not to encourage smoking, but to criticize conservatives for their excessive "zeal" (ta'assub) and prevent them from applying an overly strict version of the law. The banning of tobacco, he insisted (1682), was the same kind of mistake that earlier authors had made with coffee, which had elicited identical condemnations and yet won approval

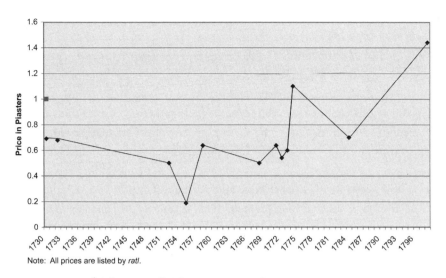

Note: All prices are listed by *ratl*.

CHART 6. The Price of Tobacco, c. 1730–1800
Note: All prices are listed by *ratl*.

in the long run as more flexible attitudes prevailed. Claims that coffee was an intoxicant had proven to be false, and were no more accurate with regard to tobacco.[132] Nor did he make the slightest concession to those who argued that smokers undermined their own health. If smoking was so harmful, he asked, why did people not suffer the same consequences from the smoke given off by fires in the marketplace or by burning garbage in the bathhouses?[133] On the contrary, tobacco was a benign substance. Even people who did not smoke, like al-Nabulsi himself (until he became an avid smoker eleven years later), often found its aroma more pleasant than incense. Clinching the argument were the medical benefits of tobacco, which was especially effective in treating "bilious disorders."[134] The only harm to be feared from smoking was the trauma of sudden withdrawal, which was capable of producing "sicknesses and maladies" and, in the case of a personal friend, had led to "a condition resembling insanity." It was therefore in the public interest to permit the habit rather than imposing restrictions which would incapacitate smokers.[135]

Many scholars adopted a less lenient view of smoking, and even if they hesitated to condemn it altogether could never quite suppress their visceral hostility or accord it respectable status. Murad al-Muradi (d. 1720), great-grandfather of the famous biographer, purchased a local khan in Suq Saruja whose tenants had offended the neighborhood with their "immorality and dissolution." He promptly converted it into the madrasa which afterwards bore the family name, and specifically stipulated in the deed of foundation that anyone who was a "bachelor, youth, or smoker of tobacco" was prohibited from residing there.[136] Even as late as the eighteenth century, after the stormiest years of debate had passed, a vociferous minority continued to take a more extreme position, inveighing against tobacco as a blatant intoxicant. The most unyielding critics were renowned for their shrill tone and puritanical antics. So strenuous were the objections of one Aleppan scholar, Hasan al-Tabbakh, that if someone tried to smoke during gatherings where he was present, he would pinch his nose shut and refuse to breathe until the offender had extinguished his pipe. The cruel irony of his life was to contract an illness for which his doctor found no effective treatment except tobacco; after ignoring this advice for a time, he found the pain unbearable and soon had to accept it as a last resort. Another scholar, Qasim al-Bakirji, was remembered for his even more adamant rejection of tobacco. When he later lost an eye to a disease, his doctor ordered him to begin smoking to preserve the other; the fearful patient obediently submitted, as his colleagues in Damascus could not refrain from noting.[137] The reluctance of such conversions reveals the depth of feeling which animated the debate. Opponents were absolutely sincere and demanded action to uphold what they regarded as the rightful interpretation of Islamic law.

Local authorities occasionally complied with these wishes and sponsored campaigns to abolish smoking. One pious governor, Hasan Pasha, was so determined to stamp out tobacco that in 1699 he conducted a tour of al-Salihiyya in disguise, destroying the pipes of offenders before returning to pray at the Umayyad Mosque.[138] The crackdown was apparently short-lived, for it had to be resumed under Nasuh Pasha, who in 1711 outlawed all smoking in local markets, where shopkeepers had taken up the practice with particular enthusiasm. Unhappy with the results of the first decree, the governor not only repeated it two years later, causing "extreme hardship" to habitual smokers, but even extended it to women, whose fondness for tobacco was now raising alarms.[139] It seems, though, that smokers soon found ways to circumvent the restrictions and reassert themselves in public. After these early lessons in popular resistance, there was only one more attempt at prohibition. As'ad Pasha al-'Azm issued a proclamation to all the markets and coffeehouses (1749), threatening smokers with strangulation and hanging; however, he quickly reversed the decree, perhaps aware of its futility.[140] No other governor would again concern himself with the matter, which proved beyond the power of the state to contain.

It is interesting that the same authorities made no move to root out narcotics such as opium, laudanum, and hashish. To some extent, this inaction was the reflection of a broader ambivalence within official culture. Although Islamic law ruled that such drugs were clearly intoxicants, it also recognized that they might sometimes have a legitimate purpose. In making this distinction, scholars showed a fair degree of flexibility. They gave explicit approval for medical treatments involving narcotics, which were never really as controversial as tobacco, partly because they had been known and used in this way for centuries in the Middle East. Opium, which was mostly imported from India and Yemen, was routinely listed as a painkiller.[141] In the case of henbane (*banj*), al-Nabulsi readily conceded that it was an intoxicant, but in the next breath had no qualms about recommending it for nosebleeds, earaches, and toothaches.[142] As an act of compassion, scholars also allowed addicts to continue taking narcotics in the event that sudden withdrawal might lead to death.[143]

Many Damascenes paid little heed to these medical and legal niceties. It was an open secret in towns all over the Middle East that many people, including otherwise respectable shopkeepers and artisans, enjoyed mixing their tobacco with opium and other narcotics (whose various combinations were known as *barsh*). To the chagrin of moralists, they often smoked it quite publicly in their shops or in local coffeehouses.[144] Husayn al-Rumi, a seller of household wares (*khurdaji*), was one shopkeeper who kept small amounts of tobacco and opium on hand (presumably for his own use and not for sale).[145] But it was not simply denizens of the marketplace who succumbed. Carousing soldiers showed the same appreciation for these intoxicants as for others, and took an active part in replenishing local supplies.[146] So prevalent was the habit that, as al-Nabulsi lamented, it even seduced members of the religious establishment. For Mustafa al-Safarjalani, scion of a notable religious family, barsh was apparently an addiction, for it "tempted him all the time."[147] Ibrahim ibn Saʿd al-Din, a profligate Sufi shaykh, was even more reckless. His fondness for barsh and other pleasures took him into local shops and coffeehouses, where he used to sit in his finest clothing, giving rise to many scandalous jokes and rumors. Appalled and disgusted, al-Muradi could only comment that "his fortune was greater than his intellect."[148] But such rebukes rarely found their mark. Intoxicants, however defined, were a permanent part of the local culture.

THE TRIUMPH OF PLEASURE

One can go even further and question whether the definitions themselves, on either side of the argument, were ever really fixed or permanent. Nearly everyone might agree in principle that intoxicants were abhorrent and ought to be banned, but the application of such high-minded ideals was another matter, producing much discord and revealing little common ground. What is indisputable is that the ulama, as the custodians of Islamic law and tradition, were not the final arbiters. Conservative opposition to the new substances was doomed not because of the inherent merits and flaws of their legal arguments, but because of public opinion, which effectively overrode all objections. In the end, the religious authorities had to bow to the social realities of the day. Islamic law, particularly through the field of Islamic jurisprudence (*fiqh*), had to adapt itself to maintain its relevance. Even as late as the Ottoman period, it was constantly accommodating the needs of ordinary believers, whose everyday attitudes actively shaped their religion.

Nevertheless, the flexibility of Islam hardly explains why so many people embraced coffee and tobacco with such eagerness. So complete was their devotion that it appears more like the manifestation of a much deeper impulse, which was endlessly searching for release. Much of this restless appetite can undoubtedly be traced to the relative monotony of the eighteenth-century diet, from which Damascenes sought relief wherever they could find it. But this answer is not entirely adequate, for it cannot tell us why there was not a similar urge to find new foods, or a reluctance to accept them when they did arrive, as with the potato and New World vegetables. What made beverages different? It was, in short, exactly their ability to "intoxicate," which in most cases meant merely to stimulate or alter mood and perception. This did not apply, of course, to sweet drinks such as sherbets; but in Damascus, as in nearly every other premodern culture, most beverages served as a means of mental escape or exhilaration. No religious edict could entirely suppress this yearning, which the guardians of morality constantly aimed to thwart. Their responses produced mixed results. The ban on alcohol was mostly effective, but other drugs such as opium and hashish enjoyed an underground popularity. And when Damascenes discovered coffee and tobacco (and later tea, which was popularized in the twentieth century),[149] they quickly gave themselves up to the new pleasures.

One of the main achievements of the eighteenth century was to entrench these more relaxed attitudes about fun and leisure. The consumption of coffee and tobacco now seemed normal and, for the most part, uncontroversial. All that remained of the older, more priggish objections was a conservative undercurrent which was incapable of defusing popular enthusiasm for the two novelties. One cannot assume that this outcome was a foregone conclusion. The fierce debates which greeted coffee drinking in the sixteenth century, and smoking in the seventeenth, ought to remind us how threatening and subversive these breakthroughs first appeared to contemporaries. As conservatives recognized, coffee and tobacco liberated a new strain of hedonism within Middle Eastern culture, which was now unwilling to repent. A revolution in lifestyle soon took place. As more people came to demand these goods as one of the decencies of everyday life, opportunities for pleasure and recreation became more frequent and accessible. In short, escapism was becoming downright routine, and even a bit respectable.

V

DOMESTIC

SPACE

E VEN FOR A WALI, OR LOCAL FOLK SAINT, HUSAYN AL-
Hamawi was remarkable for his exceptionally odd behavior. He used
to roam the streets of his neighborhood, eventually making his permanent home in one of the back lanes, where he lived atop piles of "garbage
and stones." Most astonishing to contemporaries were the dogs which
followed him everywhere. He treated them like companions and even
used to eat with them, emptying his container of food on the ground
and sharing his meals.[1] These scenes were particularly outrageous to a
Middle Eastern sensibility, which regarded dogs as unclean animals, but
in a culture which prized domesticity, it was no less shocking to live in
the streets, utterly homeless. Damascenes had a deep attachment to their
homes, which provided not only a shelter from the elements, but a safe
harbor for family life.

Unfortunately for historians, Damascenes were jealous of their privacy, and did not willingly surrender the secrets of this innermost social

world. They took the organization of their homes entirely for granted, as if people had always lived the same way and could not possibly choose any other lifestyle. Most visible in the surviving documents are the physical traces of domesticity. We can reconstruct the lodgings that people inhabited and, perhaps a little more intimately, the different objects that they owned. All this physical evidence inevitably leads back to prevailing notions of wealth and well-being. As this chapter will once again demonstrate, the balance of resources and expenditures was heavily tilted in favor of food and drink, blunting most other consumerist impulses and, in particular, leaving townspeople with relatively little to lavish on their living spaces. Standards of comfort and taste had to be correspondingly adjusted and diluted. More than any other field of material culture, the domestic arena would make the greatest concessions and claim the fewest consolations.

TYPES OF HOUSING

The great majority of eighteenth-century Damascenes lived in their own houses, which came in all sizes, from the most richly appointed mansions to the meanest hovels on the outskirts of town. Some rented their premises, but for the most part Damascus was a town of homeowners. Indeed, one of the highest aspirations of every family was to acquire residential property. It was one of the steps that signaled integration into the local community and symbolically announced to everyone that a family had definitively put down roots. That a significant number eventually attained this goal is confirmed by our sample of probate inventories: more than a third (37 percent) mention at least a portion of a house among recorded assets. Though most owners were wealthy, poorer households were by no means excluded from participating in the real estate market (table 5.1).[2] And since residential property tended to concentrate in male hands (often by intentional design of families, who sought to circumvent Islamic rules of inheritance),[3] one can more readily see how a large percentage of the urban population—including all the spouses, children, and relatives who might have lived under the same roof as the deed-holder—occupied owned, and not rented, quarters.

The layout of houses in Ottoman Damascus was characteristic of nearly all Arab cities: one or two stories of rooms surrounding a court-

TABLE 5.1. Distribution of Residential Property

VALUE OF ESTATE	ESTATES INCLUDING RESIDENTIAL PROPERTY*	TOTAL NUMBER OF ESTATES	ESTATES INCLUDING RESIDENTIAL PROPERTY (%)
<100	75	285	26.3
100–499	127	418	30.3
500–999	55	116	47.4
1000–4999	81	136	59.5
>5000	32	45	71.1
Total	370	1,000	37.0

SOURCE: Islamic Court Records
*At least a portion of a house

yard, which served as the focal point of the living space. There were occasional violations of this principle, as in houses which lacked a courtyard altogether, but it remained the overwhelming tendency, regardless of modifications in design. For the people of the eighteenth century, this was the only architecture they knew. As in other towns of the greater Mediterranean region, particularly its eastern half, houses had been adhering to the same traditions for centuries, extending into the remote past well beyond the Islamic period.[4]

Viewed from the streets, the typical residence revealed almost nothing of its interior plan. It sheltered behind high blank walls, symbolically turning its back on the life of the city and giving mute expression to the ideal of familial intimacy, which explains much of this design. Sounds might escape now and then from behind these "high towers," as Nu'man Qasatli called them,[5] but at street level, passersby had no hope of peering inward and glimpsing the lives of the occupants. On this matter, local culture was adamant: domestic life was not for display.

The facades, though prominent, were usually bare of decoration or any other outward sign of ostentation. At most, homeowners might resort to an occasional whitewashing. Techniques were simple, but effective. The affluent prepared a coating of lime thickened with gum, which was very expensive and reserved for the finest buildings, whereas the poor, who had to be less discriminating, used a mixture of chalk and water.[6] Regular maintenance was uncommon. Mikha'il Burayk thought it worthwhile to record the whitewashing of a Greek Orthodox church in 1756, and showed the same pride when another church received a fresh coating of lime twenty-five years later.[7] In 1759, the entire city underwent a whitewashing, but only at the behest of the governor, who was preparing official festivities and had already ordered the decoration of markets and streets.[8] Only a few walls, typically on wealthy homes and bathhouses, were graced with elaborate paintings and designs "like the drawing of a wonderful country, beautiful places, or a sea and a ship, or cypress trees, or flowers such as roses."[9]

As the outward face of the home, walls were not designed for aesthetic gratification; rather, their purpose was to serve as the first line of defense for private life. To build these sturdy sentinels, residents used everything at their disposal—and really had little choice in the matter. Unlike many other Syrian towns, Damascus suffered from a dearth of key construction materials such as stone and wood. Stone was present in most walls only to a height of about one or two meters—enough, that is, to provide a firm foundation, but little more. Additional amounts were an extravagance. To 'Abd al-Ghani al-Nabulsi, it came as a shock to see the houses of Nablus (1690), which were built entirely from blocks of stone and gypsum, even as high as their vaulted roofs.[10] The shortage of stone around Damascus was so severe that it drove As'ad Pasha, while constructing his famed palace in 1750, to cut the flow of the Banyas River for twelve days, thereby allowing workers to dismantle an abandoned mill. No less frustrating was his search for wood, which took his agents all over Syria, where it was in chronically short supply.[11] Inside the city, wood appeared most notably in the roofs of several covered markets, which of course posed their own hazards. When Suq al-Dhira' went up in flames in 1709, the destruction was so complete that nothing remained afterward except "a mound of earth"; a second fire at the end of 1711 convinced waqf administrators, who controlled the market, to rebuild it with a stone vault, the only one of its kind in the city.[12] In residential architecture, wood was used in the form of thin beams, which typically served as the frame for an upper story or roof. Though fires might break out in individual homes,[13] they never caused the widespread devastation that periodically struck towns like Istanbul, where wooden houses were the norm.[14]

In view of the expense of building with stone and wood, Damascenes used them sparingly and often had to fall back on other techniques. In the records of the Islamic courts, one can find contracts for the repair of dilapidated or abandoned properties which reveal the standard materials that went into homes: "red earth" (*turab ahmar*), mud, mud brick, straw, nails, pegs, and mortar.[15] For many of the poor, necessity demanded simplicity, which often meant building from top to bottom with sun-dried mud brick, which was solid, cheap, and easily repaired. Much less favored was packed earth (*dakk*), which was normally used for the walls around orchards or gardens. Though sturdy, it had a tendency to melt under the relentless onslaught of wind, rain, and snow. Mud brick was more durable, but to prevent erosion had to be covered with a plaster of lime.[16]

Many of the same precautions had to be taken with roofs, which were repaired according to a seasonal cycle. Every autumn, in preparation for the winter rains, teams of peasants from as far away as the Hawran descended on Damascus and hired themselves out to homeowners, who turned to them as the unsurpassed experts in patching and restoring worn and leaky roofs. The best weather-proofing was *zariqa*, which was composed of mortar (*qusrimill*),[17] lime, and straw. One application was said to last ten years, but "required money that the middle classes—let alone the poor—were likely to find unbearable."[18] For most homes, a simple coating of mud had to suffice, with the drawback that it had to be repeated every two years on account of its inferior quality. The repairmen generally continued making their rounds until the end of autumn, when they went back to their villages to sow grain before the arrival of the rains.[19] Their annual migration was one of the myriad ties binding the city to its hinterland, and offered further proof of the constant intermingling which took place between urban and rural worlds.

If we turn from the structure of houses to the interior space, the main feature was undeniably the central courtyard, which can still be found today in nearly all the buildings of the older neighborhoods. Rooms were ranged around this single open space, which, as we have previously noted, almost always contained a fountain or draw well. The most expensive properties might hold two courtyards, sometimes even three or four, each of which had its own ensemble of rooms. In the mansions of notables, each of these spaces performed a specialized function within the life of the household. The outer courtyard (*barrani*) was typically devoted to public functions, such as receiving guests and clients, whereas the middle (*wastani*) and especially the inner (*juwwani*) areas were the domain of the family, kept separate for the honor and convenience of the women. Most houses also had an upper story (*tabaqa*), placed over the rooms on one side of the courtyard, and less frequently extending over a second or even third side. Access was provided by a staircase, usually made of stone (less often of wood) and set off along one of the courtyard walls. In addition to one or two rooms at the top, many documents mention a small patio (*mashraqa*); but in other respects, the upper apartments were generally narrow and confined. Structures taller than two floors, like some of the tenements in big European cities, were simply not built. Damascenes judged it better to expand outward rather than upward—no doubt a wise decision in a region prone to earthquakes.

Viewed from overhead, houses were most conspicuous for their density of construction. Most walls were shared with neighbors, placing houses side by side. No space was left for alleys or yards. Living quarters were so close that some families were able to purchase neighboring rooms and knock down partitioning walls—in effect, merging part of the adjacent property with their own household. Streets were so narrow that it was even possible to extend rooms overhead to properties across the way. All these arrangements were perfectly legal; at most, the authorities might require that a certain window or door be blocked up for the sake of privacy, which, in the huddled dwellings of the back streets, was notoriously hard to protect.

The quest for privacy was built into the very design of residential architecture, which not only shut out the gaze of outsiders but marked off separate living spaces on the inside as well. There were no hallways. Rooms communicated directly with the courtyard, minimizing traffic and unwanted intrusions. But if we try to look beyond the spatial divisions of the house and uncover the unspoken rules of domesticity—when people were entitled to privacy and how they distributed their activities within the household—only frustrations lie ahead.

The most lasting impression left by records is that privacy was precious. Few homes were large, and throughout the urban population, the incidence of crowding was high. As always, poverty induced the biggest compromises. Among the urban poor, whole families might occupy one or two rooms, sharing their house with relatives or even total strangers.

TABLE 5.2. A Crowded City: Joint-Ownership and Patterns of Exchange (in a Sample of Damascene Residences, ca. 1738–63)

VALUE OF HOME IN PIASTERS	<100	100–499	500–999	>1,000	TOTAL
Portion of Home Exchanged Beween Relatives	13	39	8	5	65
Portion of Home Exchanged Between Nonrelatives	8	64	10	9	91
Exchange of Entire Property Between Relatives	0	5	0	3	8
Exchange of Entire Property Between Nonrelatives	14	51	13	17	95
Total	35	159	31	34	259

SOURCE: Islamic Court Records

Eighteenth-century sales deeds demonstrate that joint ownership—and by implication, joint residence—was a fairly common social reality (table 5.2).[20] More to the point, most of these transactions took place between nonrelatives, proving that the constraints of poverty could overcome the sternest moral and cultural inhibitions. These pressures were not unique to Damascus. Crowding was no less prevalent, for example, in eighteenth-century Aleppo, where these unpleasant sacrifices were normal and, for many families, quite unavoidable.[21]

To appreciate the scale of the problem, we need only consider the alternatives to residential property, such as the city's mosques and madrasas, which often had their own complexes of rooms and annexes. None of these spaces were allowed to lie idle or vacant. Despite the compromises entailed by private residence in a public place, many Damascenes eagerly sought these accommodations even though they could rarely hope to obtain more than a single room—or even part of a room. Many of these rooms passed by inheritance from father to son, especially among custodians and other low-ranking functionaries. But nothing prevented others from acquiring their own apartments, often through voluntary concessions from previous tenants—if we can take the documents at their word and assume that no other favors changed hands.[22] Among the most notable occupants of religious buildings were scholars and Sufis, who, like Mustafa al-Bakri, the famous mystic, sought refuges where they could devote themselves wholly to study and meditation.[23] Others were visitors, whether students or pilgrims, who had come to participate in local religious life, sometimes settling down permanently in the community.[24] Compensating for the lack of comfort and privacy was a measure of financial security, insofar as occupants were freed from the burden of paying rent. The privilege was therefore a useful asset, which had to be guarded and preserved. The records of the Islamic courts are full of cases in which individuals carefully registered or transferred their rights of residence.

Providing similar lodgings were many of the city's khans, which often won notoriety in popular lore as dens of iniquity. Most of these suspicions arose from the marginal status of the inhabitants, who tended to consist of outsiders and rootless figures such as bachelors, travelers, and migrants.[25] But we should not accept this image too uncritically. Even respectable ulama and merchants might have temporary recourse to these quarters.[26] One Christian merchant, Abdullah walad Sarkis, felt comfortable enough to leave his wife and young daughter in Khan Hasan Pasha while he went away on business to Beirut.[27] In many other khans, the population seems to have been much more transient. Khan al-Haramayn, located near Bab al-Barid, was one of the most popular accommodations for Muslim pilgrims, who began pouring into the city every year around the time of Ramadan.[28] As in the fortresses along the caravan routes, the trappings were quite bare: two stories of unfurnished rooms (the bottom ones usually reserved for commerce) enclosing an open courtyard.

At the bottom end of the market, one final option was to settle in large tenements (hawsh), which seem to have been present in nearly all big Arab towns.[29] For a pittance, occupants rented or bought rooms set in one or two stories around a common courtyard, preserving the essential form of Damascene homes, but throwing neighbors together with little thought for privacy, comfort, or security. These accommodations represented the absolute minimum, paying only token homage to the ideals of residential architecture, and yet testifying to their enduring appeal. Poverty could demand concessions and sacrifices, but could not overcome deep-seated preferences in building and design.

BASIC AMENITIES: HEAT, LIGHT, AND HYGIENE

The existence of courtyards in all types of housing meant that they were constantly admitting air from the outside in every season. The people of the eighteenth century thus faced much greater exposure to the heat and cold, which easily penetrated to every room and corner. As a matter of necessity, they were constantly adjusting their habits according to the weather and time of day. During the daylight hours of winter, families tended to migrate upstairs in search of sunlight, whereas summer saw a retreat to the lower level, out of the harsh desert glare.[30] Nighttime patterns were different. In winter, it was better to sleep downstairs, where the drafts were less intense. During warmer weather, people quickly fled the stuffy interiors and laid their beds outdoors, making a place in the courtyard or climbing to the rooftop.[31] It was one of the few solutions to the perennial discomforts of summer.

Of the two extremes of climate, winter undoubtedly posed greater difficulties. Heat might be an inconvenience, but even at its worst was almost never life-threatening, unlike the cold. Though freezing temperatures were unusual, people struggled to keep themselves warm. In spite of the thickness of their walls, Damascene homes provided only the feeblest insulation. Against the drafts which were continually invading their rooms, residents sometimes hung drapes (*burdaya*) in their doorways, but these crude barriers were not very popular (and in all likelihood not very comforting).[32] Heating, too, was ineffective. Few houses had chimneys or hearths, which operated almost exclusively in bakeries and were in any case viewed as dangerous nuisances in residential quarters.[33] For many people, especially among the affluent, the main source of heat was a copper or iron brazier (*manqal*);[34] in the poorest households, it might be a small earthen stove (*kanun*).[35] Apart from these simple techniques, families had no means of generating warmth. Unlike Europe and parts of East Asia, there was no discernible evolution in heating technology during the early modern period.

To provide themselves with precious heat, households required regular quantities of fuel, which in the eighteenth century consisted of a basic choice between wood and charcoal. Always scarce, wood was gathered from dead or dying trees, which were chopped and sold mostly by local peasants. People were willing to use almost any wood for this purpose, but olive trees were the most highly prized.[36] According to al-Qasimi, "most of the people, rich and poor," regularly consumed at least some amount of firewood for heating and, above all, cooking and cleaning.[37] But because of its expense, few households could depend solely on this one source of heat. For this reason, the universal fuel was really charcoal (*fahm*). Though it generated less energy and was not as useful for cooking, it burned more efficiently and was always cheaper and more plentiful than wood. Especially in the autumn, as the cold weather approached, households across the city began the annual task of stockpiling supplies, which were available from vendors who circulated in all the neighborhoods and markets.[38] Prices depended on the time of year and showed tremendous sensitivity to the weather. The chronicler al-Budayri, ever watchful of the market, recorded a more than fourfold increase during one particularly severe freeze in December 1741. A second shortage occurred during February 1749, when a "harsh, painful cold" descended upon the city, attracting peddlers who wandered the streets and markets with crates of charcoal atop their heads. Some shortages were entirely artificial. At the end of the summer of 1752, the price of charcoal suddenly began to rise due to mysterious hoarding that the lieutenant governor, in spite of vigorous inspections, was unable to check. "No one got charcoal except those who were powerful, like the imperial Janissaries and the Dalatiyya [the band of mostly Kurdish mercenaries allied with them]," who were no doubt aware of the approaching winter.[39] Manipulation of charcoal supplies was a serious matter for the entire city because, aside from wood, there was essentially no other fuel. Artisans sometimes burned hemp and even olive pits,[40] and in small ovens residents were known to use manure;[41] but for those who had a choice, these alternatives were of course out of the question for domestic heating.

Difficult to heat, eighteenth-century homes were also difficult to light. Interiors were permanently dim, mostly due to a lack of windows. On the ground floor there were few openings, and none of these was more than a narrow slit located high on the wall, filled with either a wooden grate or a fixed plate of glass. Rooms were further darkened by the poor quality

One of the earliest photographs of Damascus (c. 1857), here showing a group of homes. The exteriors were typical in their blank simplicity, broken only by a few tiny windows at ground level. Among the most notable features were the wooden shutters that sometimes looked onto the street from the upper floor. From the Otrakji collection, www.mideastimage.com.

of local glass, which was distinguished by its greenish tint; starting from the late eighteenth century, it rapidly lost ground to European imports, which owed their transparency to better materials and more advanced techniques.[42] Large windows (*shubbak*) were reserved for the upper story and were quite rare. In the few homes where they had been installed, they usually faced inward toward the courtyard to safeguard the privacy of the family and discourage thieves from entering. Some of these windows held iron grates, but they were never fitted with glass panes. Far more common were ornate wooden grills which allowed occupants, above all the women of the family, to look out without being seen themselves. The room was thus exposed constantly to the open air which could "play freely through the apartment."[43] Unquestionably, it was an arrangement which was best suited to warm weather. The search for comfort and ventilation seems to have been a bigger concern than any desire to illuminate the room.

At night, Damascenes had to submit to the darkness. The means of illumination at their disposal were few and, at least to modern eyes, utterly derisory. Street lighting was nonexistent except during important celebrations such as Ramadan and Laylat al-Nisf (staged during the middle of Sha'ban, the month preceding Ramadan), when the markets would be strung with lanterns and kept open late.[44] The ulama were highly suspicious of all such nighttime festivities. They objected to the illumination of public spaces mostly on the grounds that it subverted public morality and encouraged people to gather for questionable purposes, especially "youths and idle persons," who were accused of engaging in dubious entertainments, disturbing the peace, violating the sanctity of mosques, and committing other intolerable offenses.[45]

After nightfall, it was to difficult to move about the city because each residential quarter sealed itself off behind heavy gates. Anyone who ventured outside had to carry lanterns or torches—if they were prudent. The only lighted sanctuaries were the major mosques, whose pious foundations often set aside funds for lanterns and their maintenance. Special workers extinguished the lamps in the morning, polished and refilled them, and then lit them again for evening prayers. The best lanterns (*qindil* or *fanus*) were made of glass or crystal and burned olive oil, which served as the basic fuel until the modern transition to European gas lamps, which began around the mid-nineteenth century. Cheaper models used coarse cloth or paper, and instead of burning fuel held a simple candle.[46]

In private households, all these distinctions were irrelevant, for lanterns were a very uncommon possession. Most people had to make do with candles, which besides being more affordable were readily available from neighborhood grocers. But let us not imagine rooms lined with flickering candles, in which residents carried on with their routines well after dark. Though most estates held at least one candlestick, few were listed with more than two or three, testifying to the severe constraints placed upon nocturnal life. Damascenes might occasionally stay up late, particularly in warm weather, but they had to keep company in the dark, or at best under the thin rays of the moon. Few families could light enough candles to illuminate a room and permit activities requiring good visibility.

To further appreciate this link between natural and domestic rhythms, one need only consider the cleanliness of eighteenth-century homes. Floors typified the predicament of Damascene housekeepers. A fully tiled courtyard was an extravagance, automatically ranking a home among the most elegant in the city. For the mufti 'Ali al-Muradi, who had been building a new home with marble tiles and wooden engravings, the death of his son Ahmad al-Saʿid was a devastating loss; as a measure of his grief, the inconsolable father stopped all work on the property and sold it for a fraction of its worth.[47] Such a gesture made a deep impression on his fellow townspeople, whose homes rarely contained tiles of any sort except around the base of their courtyard fountains. Due to the prohibitive cost of laying tile, the most practical option was to coat the courtyard with a mixture of lime and ash, which was said to last upwards of twenty years.[48] For the poorest, there was nothing but packed earth.

Among the most unpleasant features of eighteenth-century homes was their odor. The combination of cramped quarters and tiny windows ensured that rooms were musty, even stifling places—as one can infer from the popularity of censers (*mibkhara*) at nearly every socioeconomic level. Adding to the pungency and discomfort of many ordinary homes was the presence of animals, which often had to be tethered inside the courtyard. Only the grandest houses had their own stables (*istabl*), which were usually set aside for horses—another indication of substantial wealth.

A bigger problem was the infestation of insects, which thrived in the warm environment. Townspeople lived under a nearly constant siege from which they could find little relief. Countermeasures were notable mostly for being both elaborate and utterly futile. Against the annual torment of fleas, al-Nabulsi recommended the juice of leeks mixed with the blood of a billy goat; if placed inside a hole, the potion would act as a fatal lure. But nothing seems to have been as effective as the scorching weather of midsummer, when fleas naturally took shelter and disappeared.[49] One popular remedy against ants was to dust the house with cumin, which was also supposed to be effective against bedbugs.[50] To drive out other pests, such as scorpions and flies, local wisdom touted an array of ointments, fumigants, incantations, and repellent leaves and flowers.[51] Perhaps the greatest scourge of every neighborhood was its numerous rats, against which there was no real defense. One belief was that onions would ward them off,[52] but others placed their faith only in poisons, which were sometimes blended with grape syrup and other enticing foods.[53]

The existence of a large population of rats, not to mention the innumerable dogs and cats which prowled everywhere, was an inevitable consequence of the prevailing methods of household sanitation. Throughout the city, people disposed of their garbage by simply depositing it in the street. The Ottoman authorities took no part in supervising local sanitation and left it to more informal solutions. The small corps of sweepers and garbagemen who met this need toured the markets and residential quarters daily in search of refuse. Much of this material was collected and stored in al-ʿAmara, particularly in Khan al-Thulj, whence it was sold as fuel to local bathhouses.[54] The garbagemen brought manure, loaded into baskets on the backs of donkeys, to gardens and orchards on the outskirts of town,[55] or supplied tradesmen such as tanners, who sometimes used animal feces in the curing of hides.[56]

Similar teams of sanitation workers served private homes. Nearly every household had a latrine (*murtafaq*), which required periodic maintenance. In villages and the most distant parts of the city, it was likely to be little more than a covered pit, but in most urban neighborhoods it was connected to a rudimentary sewage system, which was actually quite advanced by the standards of the day. As a general rule, the latrine was an enclosed space within the courtyard (more rarely on the upper floor) from which waste was carried through underground pipes, often flushed by runoff from fountains toward open drains running throughout the neighborhood. All these channels formed a network of fetid tributaries, ultimately emptying into either the Barada River or a large canal known as the Qalit River (Nahr Qalit) that flowed through the heart of the city and into the fields southeast of al-Shaghur. If any of the public sewers became blocked, the problem was treated like any other involving the supply of water, which is to say that maintenance was a collective responsibility: whoever benefited from the channel was obligated to help defray the costs of dredging and repairing it. When pipes became clogged inside homes, residents had to call teams of drain cleaners. In houses not equipped with proper latrines, these workers performed the thankless task of exhuming the excreta which gradually filled makeshift pits.[57] Among their other clients were the city's mosques, which operated their own public toilets. The funds for upkeep were typically drawn from pious foundations, such as the one created by Asʿad Pasha al-ʿAzm (1756) for the renovation of latrines in Yalbagha Mosque, northwest of the citadel.[58] Together with the pools for ritual ablutions, these facilities were essential to preparations for daily prayers, and provided a public convenience to local markets.

All these elaborate arrangements reaffirmed the high value that local culture placed on personal cleanliness and grooming, made all the more desirable by the noisome sights and smells which constantly surrounded townspeople. In treatises on Islamic ethics, which showed a scrupulous concern for the body, authors were unafraid to address the most sensitive and awkward subjects. They spoke quite frankly, and in considerable detail, about the correct way of performing the excretory functions, which ought, they stressed, to take place in complete privacy and silence.[59] One recurring theme was the division of labor between the hands: the left hand for unclean tasks, while the right one received priority in eating and other everyday situations where pollution was to be absolutely avoided. The same principle applied to the feet. When entering the sacred precincts of a mosque, the right foot came first; latrines and other noxious places called for the left foot.[60] The ulama urged that mothers teach their children these rules, which were undoubtedly ritualistic, but must have nonetheless reinforced a certain minimal hygiene.[61]

Of all the habits cultivated by townspeople, none was as popular or as effective in promoting cleanliness as regular bathing, which in practice meant visiting the neighborhood bathhouse (*hammam*). This was one of the great traditions of both the urban and rural Middle East,[62] dating back to antiquity and thriving throughout the Islamic period. Every part of the city had at least one such establishment. In Ibn Kannan's lifetime (1663–1740), there were five in his neighborhood of al-Salihiyya alone; for the entire city, Nuʿman Qasatli later gave an estimate of fifty-eight (1876).[63] Further heightening their appeal was the prominent role of bathing in social life, particularly for women, who enjoyed access to many bathhouses at predesignated hours or on specific days of the week when men were barred from entering. Bathing at home was a privilege only of the wealthy, who owned the biggest homes and had the space and resources to install their own facilities.[64] Many households kept basins and bowls and small amounts of soap for washing before meals and prayers, but not for more extensive grooming and cleaning of the body.

On the whole, eighteenth-century plumbing fulfilled fairly modest functions. It brought water to many homes and helped to evacuate waste, but did not yet rise to the standard of running water, available upon demand at any time. Though latrines of one kind or another were a basic feature of nearly every house and provided some measure of sanitation, the concept of a bathroom or private bathing was virtually unknown. These partial suc-

"Washing the hands." Preparing for a meal, polished diners required nothing more than a simple pitcher and bowl. As a pleasant accompaniment, no one has forgotten his tobacco. William Thomson, *The Land and the Book*. New York, 1886.

cesses were typical of living standards throughout the city. Though in many ways admirably adapted to their environment, domestic arrangements represented a series of compromises in which ideals of comfort and cleanliness had to be sacrificed to the overwhelming realities of poverty, crowding, and minimal infrastructure. In imagining the daily routines of Damascenes, we need to keep these everyday conditions—so common that contemporaries barely thought of mentioning them—fixed firmly in our minds.

COOKING AND EATING

Mirroring the priorities of the broader urban economy, none of these routines occupied as much time and energy as the basic task of acquiring and preparing food. Among the household objects registered in probate inventories, nearly two-thirds were in some way connected with cooking and eating. Documents mention a plethora of pots (*tanjara, maʿun, hilla*, often appearing with a *ghita*, or cover) and pans (*miqlaya, luhuq*, and *tawwaya*). Other common objects were ladles (*kabja*), strainers (*misfaya*), skimmers (*kafkir*), mortars (*hawun*) and pestles (*yadd*), kettles for boiling water (*kukum*), and sacks (*ʿidl*) and containers (*ʿulba*) for storage. Every household needed this equipment, which was simple and varied little across the population.

For both rich and poor, moreover, the methods for preparing food were laborious and time-consuming. Every meal required a succession of tedious but essential chores—shopping in the markets, drawing water, gathering fuel, lighting fires—before the process of cooking could ever begin. Nearly everything had to be made from scratch, cleaned by hand, and carefully tended over an open flame. Eighteenth-century households were simply not equipped to ease these burdens. One need look no farther than the kitchen (*matbakh*), which was found in the floor plans of most homes (table 5.3). Due to the sketchiness of deeds, their exact layout and dimensions are nearly impossible to determine, but in most cases they were probably rather cramped. A small number were furnished with a water tap (*masnaʿ maʾ*) connected to a household fountain, but this was an extravagance that most homeowners never bothered to install.[65] Whenever they needed water for anything, nearly all households had to fetch it in pails (*satl*), store it in great basins (*lakan*), and replenish it regularly. Most kitchens existed simply as separate rooms or annexes. Bare of conveniences, their main function was to provide extra space for cooking and storage. Given our limited information about domestic habits, we can only assume that families prepared their food there, but in the absence of fixed stoves and hearths, nothing prevented them from moving to the courtyard or even to another room if they wished. High demand for space may have turned some kitchens into little more than depots. Few homes could boast a small cellar (*kilar* or *bayt muʾna*) for supplemental storage.

In prosperous households, cooking might be performed by servants and slaves. As regards domestic service, the existing records make it difficult to judge the extent of hiring. Only elite households, where wives actually had a legal claim to servants,[66] would have kept large domestic staffs. In addition to cooks and washerwomen, leading families had their own attendants, flunkeys, and various hangers-on whose superfluous presence,

TABLE 5.3. Prevalence of Kitchens and Cellars

(in a Sample of Damascene Residences, ca. 1738–63)

VALUE OF HOME, IN PIASTERS	2 KITCHENS	1 KITCHEN	NO KITCHEN
<100	0	12	23
100–499	1	83	58
500–999	1	25	6
>1000	0	21	4
Total	2	141	91

	2 CELLARS	1 CELLAR	NO CELLAR
<100	0	2	32
100–499	0	6	136
500–999	0	3	24
>1000	1	11	0
Total	1	22	192

SOURCE: Islamic Court Records

made possible by cheap wages and a surplus of idle labor, announced the social importance of their employer.[67] Slaves, on the other hand, represented a much weightier expenditure, usually requiring (depending on age and physical condition) over a hundred piasters at the time of purchase alone. Almost by definition, then, slaveholders were well-to-do, and few could afford to own more than one slave.[68] As in other Ottoman towns, the market trafficked mainly in women.[69] Inventories rarely mention distinguishing characteristics, but most were probably brought from Africa (either the Sudan or Ethiopia, via Egypt). As a percentage of the urban population (in which they were almost exclusively found), slaves were not very numerous, and turned up in barely more than 2 percent of mid-century inventories. Most of the owners (eighteen out of twenty-three) were male, and may have used their female slaves as concubines, as they were entitled under Islamic law. But the most common fate seems to have been domestic service, which male slaves might also be expected to perform.[70]

Most Damascene families could not begin to contemplate such alternatives. They had to handle their own household chores, which, in the family economy of the eighteenth century, fell squarely on the shoulders of women. And among the most "feminine" tasks was the preparation of food for daily meals. What is surprising, however, is that personal estates did not necessarily reflect this broad division of labor. Apart from the baskets (*sabat*) used in shopping and other errands, many kitchen utensils were distributed fairly proportionately between men and women and seem not to have been identified as exclusively "feminine." Heavy pots and pans, together with other metal equipment such as ladles, strainers, and skimmers, actually turned up overwhelmingly in male hands.[71] Probably on account of the size or expense of these objects, men may have been expected to contribute them to the household, even if they had no intention of personally using them in the kitchen. More important, they had much greater wealth at their disposal than women, who simply had fewer choices in what they could buy. In our sample of one thousand inventories, women held a mere 13 percent of recorded assets, even though they represented 39 percent of the total group.[72] In view of this skewed distribution of wealth, which tended to leave women with cheaper goods like textiles, the heavily feminine connotations of domestic cooking seem not to have surfaced in patterns of ownership, which conformed to an economic rather than a social logic.

Turning from cooking to eating, only the roughest sketch of dining habits is possible. Particularly difficult to pinpoint is the timing of meals, which probably resembled that of Cairo and Aleppo, where most people liked to eat three times a day: a light breakfast around dawn, the main meal at midday, and then an early-evening dinner which might consist of leftovers.[73] The physical arrangements are simpler to reconstruct. Diners sat on the ground and ranged themselves around a large tray (*tabsiyya, sufra, siniyya,* or *sadr*) which was sometimes elevated on a small wooden stool (*kursi*[74] or *iskamla*); if the family was poor, a simple cloth might take the place of the tray.[75] Food was served in various bowls (*tasa* and *zabdiyya*) and plates (*sahn, tabaq* and *lankari*), which were ubiquitous in personal estates. Water might be brought in pitchers and jugs (*ibriq* and *batiyya*), but individual cups (*kasa* and *kubbaya*) were not especially numerous, most likely because family members drank from only a few shared receptacles. Most of this tableware was made from tinned copper, which offered the irresistible combination of cheapness and durability.[76] There were also more elegant variations: pitchers, bowls, cups, and trays fashioned from silver, lapis lazuli, glass, and crystal. At the low end of the market, trays might be designed with leather or cloth; and for the poorest clientele, there were plates of straw.[77]

Other utensils were harder to find. Damascenes had nothing like individual cutlery, which at this time was only beginning to spread throughout the affluent populations of Western Europe.[78] Most people were not even recorded as owning a knife (sikkin), the most widespread dining implement. Evidence from personal estates, which rarely held more than one knife, suggests that it was probably shared by diners for tasks like carving and cutting. Another refinement was the wooden spoon (ma'laqa). Found mostly in affluent estates, it appears as one of the minor luxuries of eighteenth-century life, not so much as a personal utensil as an instrument for serving food.[79] Forks (shawka), also wooden, were even rarer and were probably used for cooking (and perhaps serving) rather than eating. The majority of Damascenes ate with their hands or, as one sixteenth-century author disapprovingly noted, scooped up their food with folded pieces of bread.[80] Since people touched their food directly, many households provided small washbowls (tasht) and hand towels (bashkir) for the rinsing of hands. As an extra touch of elegance, perfume might be dispensed after meals (as evidenced by a qumqum, or perfume bottle, in a large number of estates).

Seated around the food, polite diners observed a scrupulous etiquette. Ranking high among offenses was carelessness in emitting sounds: gulping loudly from cups, chewing noisily, blowing on hot food, smacking or licking the lips "like a cow." Neatness was an imperative. Fingers were to stay out of the mouth and hair, and beards were to be kept clean of half-eaten morsels and other debris.[81] Good manners dictated that only the right hand be used in handling food, and that people content themselves with moderate portions.[82] One cannot generalize for the entire population, which must have conformed in varying degrees according to social status, piety and learning, and the constraints imposed by actual living conditions. Yet the manuals of etiquette reveal ideals of elegance and sophistication which were no less appreciated by diners of the premodern era.

What is certain about all these fine manners is that authors presupposed an essentially domestic dining culture. The city had a weak tradi-

"Sitting at meat—party at dinner." The diners help themselves from a common bowl in the center of the tray. Everyone has his own plate, and sits comfortably on a divan or cushion. A servant holding a pitcher is a reminder that this is no ordinary social scene. William Thomson, *The Land and the Book*. New York, 1886.

tion of public eating establishments, and restaurants as we know them today would not arrive until the last years of the nineteenth century. Although professional cooks worked in the markets, and sometimes catered to the households of notables, they sold mostly to a narrow circle of customers: travelers, residents of khans, and those who lived alone and had no domestic help. Other dealers in food were little more than itinerant peddlers. Families might, for instance, call on the services of bean sellers, who roved the streets and were especially popular in winter.[83] All this business, however, took place strictly on a take-out basis. The most direct consequence was that families and groups of friends had to organize their own meals if they wanted to dine outside the home. The most popular destinations were nearby gardens and orchards. Ibn Kannan's notebook is full of these extramural visits with his colleagues, with whom he read poetry, discussed scholarship, and passed the time with pleasant conversation and meals.[84] Traffic peaked in spring as the flowers came into bloom and both men and women ventured out "day and night." To meet this seasonal clientele, a number of informal services sprang up. Especially around al-Salihiyya, there were various places which rented plates, spoons, pans, blankets, carpets, cushions—all the necessities for a pleasant meal outside.[85] The lack of eating facilities or urban amenities such as parks or public squares never prevented townspeople from improvising other outlets for dining and socializing, which always went hand in hand.

Pervading all these meals and excursions was a strong ethos of hospitality, which expressed itself mainly in the form of food and drink. The significance of these exchanges was more than sentimental, and transcended the simple pleasures of sharing food and company. Meals helped to cement social networks of trust and reciprocity, and highlighted relations of obligation and dependence. No one understood these expectations better than the urban elite, who used visits and meals to shore up both horizontal and vertical solidarities. With social peers, they might throw lavish entertainments at home. Attaining the suave ideal was ʿAbd al-Muʿti al-Falaqansi (d. 1710), the chief scribe (katib), acknowledged as the city's finest connoisseur of the good life. He stocked his house with the best food and finery, and surrounded himself with musicians who played and sang continuously.[86] Other notables owned property in the Ghuta and invited colleagues for extended village retreats, often for several days at a time.[87] Social inferiors, on the other hand, required demonstrations of munificence which projected status and influence through feasts and festivities. Notables might convert private rites of passage into public spectacles promoting broader social and political aims. Among the grandest occasions were weddings, which, in addition to forging alliances between households, offered an obvious pretext for flaunting power and wealth. In the biggest celebrations, the feasting might last over several days.[88] Circumcisions were another milestone which might, in a moment of ambition, become a communal as well as a family affair.[89] Even households of lesser means tried to mimic these gestures. Ibn Kannan mentions several celebrations thrown by his neighbors and fellow ulama, all of whom wished to assert themselves within their own social networks.[90]

The code of hospitality suffused the entire culture. No less than the urban elite, ordinary Damascenes were eager to advertise their commitment to these values through offers of food and drink and other displays of generosity. Even the poor incorporated little flourishes into the most common social encounters as marks of goodwill and esteem. Henry Maundrell, an English traveler, was deeply struck by these habits, which he observed (1697) throughout Syria:

It is counted uncivil to visit in this country without an offering in hand. All great men expect it as a kind of tribute due to their character and authority, and look upon themselves as affronted, and indeed defrauded, when this compliment is omitted. Even in familiar visits amongst inferior people, you shall seldom have them come without bringing a flower or an orange, or some other token of their respect to the person visited.[91]

Sensitivities ran deep. Failure to cultivate the proper social graces, or show appreciation for any hospitality that guests received, was an affront to dignity and could lead to scandal.[92] The real burden, of course, fell on the host. Few insults stung as badly as an accusation of stinginess, which touched directly on sense of honor and social rank. Speaking for this popular mentality, which had definite expectations about social obligations to be discharged and largesse to be shared, Mikha'il Burayk deplored, in 1747, the spread of a new marriage custom among local Christians. In the past, the groom had traditionally dispensed charity to the poor "so that they could eat," but many families, even among "the middle classes" (awsat al-nas), had begun to post armed guards (Tk. tüfenkçi) at their doors to keep unwanted guests away. Burayk called down divine punishment on the originator of the practice, who was "very stingy" even though his family was quite affluent.[93] The clear implication was that such miserly behavior was a threat to the solidarity of the community, and that these social bonds required the rich to help the poor, needy, and vulnerable.

The danger was expressed in popular lore, which told stories of individuals or whole settlements who had courted misfortune by ignoring their social obligations. Passing by a deserted Syrian village with his entourage in 1693, al-Nabulsi learned that it had once prospered, but that hard times struck after the villagers denied hospitality to a North African traveler; in retaliation, the spurned Maghribi had tossed a talisman into the nearby well, which dried up within a few days and left the area desolate.[94] The learned scholar offers not a word of doubt.

Educated and self-conscious, ulama were particularly attuned to the niceties of etiquette. Treated with respect and courtesy, they were also the recipients of much hospitality themselves. Hosting an illustrious scholar or Sufi reflected immense prestige on the sponsor, who thereby linked his name with the patronage of Islam.[95] Hospitality was staged not merely for the benefit of particular ulama, but in the name of religion itself, which preached the virtues of generosity.[96] The biggest gestures, which invariably brought out large quantities of food, tended to accompany religious holidays. The Muradi family used to commemorate the birthday (mawlid) of the prophet Muhammad by opening their home in Suq Saruja to the public and inviting notables such as the governor and qadi.[97] Such acts of piety and charity were more or less expected from all the highest religious officials. In the words of the biographer Muhammad Khalil al-Muradi (d. 1791/2), one of several muftis produced by his family, one of the main responsibilities of his office was the provisioning of food (it'am al-ta'am).[98] If one can judge by the estate of Hamid al-'Imadi, an earlier mufti, this injunction was taken quite seriously. A glance at his many possessions brings to life his extensive social commitments: numerous cups, plates, pans, cushions, pillows, and other domestic equipment, far beyond the requirements of even the largest households.[99] It was a natural outgrowth of his position. In the minds of all Damascenes, food, privilege, and piety were inextricably linked.

DOMESTIC INTERIORS

Eating habits and the values attached to them were unusual, insofar as local authors were occasionally willing to discuss them as illustrations of ethical and religious ideals. Few other household routines received the same attention, and except in rare and random comments they were passed over as too mundane or obvious to be edifying or worth discussing at length. As we look into other areas of eighteenth-century domesticity, most of our knowledge will therefore have to be drawn from official documents, which can only present a rather static and impersonal view of the home.

Let us start with the arrangement of the interior. Upon first inspection, there is little to distinguish one room from another. Legal records such as sales deeds, which offer the most direct descriptions, contain nothing like a detailed floor plan. Scribes always mentioned whether rooms were on the first or second story, but omitted physical dimensions or other salient characteristics. They usually contented themselves with generic terms (like *maskan, uda,* or *murabbaʿ*) that indicate nothing more than four walls enclosing a living space; likewise, the main compartment on the upper floor appears simply as a *tabaqa*.[100] Only reception areas were likely to receive more specific names. One fairly standard feature, even in modest houses, was the *iwan,* a recessed section of the courtyard. As a rule, it was covered overhead; less frequently, decorated with a stone arch (*qaws hajr*).[101] In many courtyards, it was also accompanied by one or two small annexes (*qubba*) set off to the side, which offered additional warmth and privacy as the seasons and circumstances demanded. The most impressive room was the *qaʿa,* which was designed mainly for entertaining guests. Especially in the houses of notables such as ʿAbd al-Muʿti al-Falaqansi, it was a major showpiece which might be embellished with ornate woodwork and painted murals.[102] If located on the second floor, the same room was classified as a *qasr,* and in many families was customarily reserved for the master of the house. Ideally, the stairway leading to it was placed within easy access of the door, so that guests could be quickly spirited to their appointments, away from the bosom of family life.[103] Actual usage must have varied as considerably as it did with other rooms. ʿAbd al-Ghani al-Nabulsi, whose house contained both a qaʿa and qasr, liked to alternate between them according to the season, preferring the ground-floor shelter of the qaʿa in summer and moving to the warmth of his upstairs qasr in winter.[104]

Yet the venerable shaykh hardly qualifies as a guide to popular habits. He belonged to a privileged minority whose homes held an abundance of space, ready to be divided and defined as the owner pleased. Reception chambers simply did not exist in most houses (table 5.4). Even in those

TABLE 5.4. Windows and Reception Rooms in Damascene
Residences, c. 1738–63

(based on 261 floor plans)

VALUE OF HOME (PIASTERS)	<100	100–499	500–999	>=1000	TOTAL
window (1) (shabbak)	2	0	1	0	3
windows (2)	0	2	0	0	2
windows (3)	0	3	2	4	9
qaʿa (1)	0	2	6	12	20
qaʿa (>=2)	0	1	0	3	4
qasr (1)	0	12	7	15	34
qasr (>=2)	0	1	3	4	8
iwan (1)	4	45	20	13	82
iwan (>=2)	0	1	5	9	15
qubba (1)	1	11	3	0	15
qubba (>=2)	1	4	3	4	12

SOURCE: Islamic Court Records

equipped with them, rooms had to serve the occasion at hand, regardless of custom or design. Only a few areas—kitchen, cellar, latrine—were
given over to specific tasks. Most interior space was flexible, and the same
room often fulfilled multiple functions. The lack of specialization was
quite striking to European visitors, whose upper-class culture was already
evolving towards a more elaborate domestic scheme.[105] Damascenes had
no equivalents for terms like dining room or sitting room. Most radical
(at least from a modern perspective) were the implications for sleeping
arrangements. Due to limitations of space that severely curtailed personal
privacy, family members never knew the luxury of individual bedrooms
and customarily slept together as a group. Moral commentators fretted
over these promiscuous sleeping arrangements and preached self-restraint
and modesty to elders. They found it necessary to caution couples against
passionate groping and touching: in the middle of the darkness, a husband

who "awakened his wife for sexual intercourse" might, they feared, easily squeeze the hand of his daughter.[106] Daylight brought no surer refuges for privacy. Except perhaps in a few exceptionally well-appointed homes, Damascenes seem not to have set aside anything like a study (even if we can assume a desire for solitude among the well educated). The practice had not yet arisen in a population where few people were habituated to literate pastimes. In our sample of estates, fewer than one-quarter of all men (hardly any women) owned writing implements such as a writing stand (*bashtakhta*) or inkwell (*dawayya*).[107] Books appeared even less frequently, in roughly 6 percent of male estates, and at a much lower rate than Western Europe, where the printing press had enabled mass publication.[108] In contrast to the rigid partitioning of space into studies and other specialized rooms that was slowly emerging in Europe, Damascene interiors were more fluid. It is impossible to say how the occupants of an eighteenth-century house might have used any one room. They saw no reason why they should assign it to a single activity, and disposed of it as they liked. Domestic life was ordered, above all, by a spirit of pragmatism.

Damascene furniture facilitated these rapid mutations of living space. It was lightweight and portable, due in part to the scarcity of local wood, which imposed an economy of materials.[109] To their European guests, accustomed to bulky trunks, dressers, and bedsteads, it seemed as though Damascenes barely owned possessions worthy of the name.[110] Cluttered interiors were rare, and decoration adhered to an extreme parsimony of taste. One factor was the general poverty of most households, whose resources had to be allocated overwhelmingly to food and other daily expenses. But it was more than a question of financial exigency, for local furniture also suited the manner in which Damascenes moved and held their bodies. At rest, their most common posture was to sit cross-legged on the ground, which required only the simplest accommodations. It was a crouching, squatting lifestyle typical of most of the Old World, but totally unlike European ways, which revolved around tables and elevated chairs. Only among the leading Greek families of Istanbul, who worked as translators and diplomats and had prolonged contact with Western embassies, did European furniture begin to gain any acceptance in the eighteenth century.[111] In Damascus, it made no headway until elite families began to adopt it in the late nineteenth century as part of a conscious effort to imitate Western models. Even then, the triumph of European

"The Letter-writer." Most of the urban population was illiterate. All documents and correspondence had to be drawn up by notaries, who made their services available in the marketplace. William Thomson, *The Land and the Book*. New York, 1886.

habits was never complete. As if to signal some private act of resistance, nearly all of these families continued to reserve at least one room of the house for traditional decorations.[112]

Prior to this intrusion of European fashions, Damascenes continued to relax on the objects most familiar to them: divans, cushions, and carpets. Divans (*takht*) were the heaviest pieces of furniture and represented the height of luxury. Built around a wooden frame, they stood just above the ground and were typically set against one of the walls. For comfort and decoration, people covered them with bolsters (*maqʿad* and *mindar*) and a profusion of pillows (*mikhadda* and *yastaqiyya*). But such opulence was quite exceptional. Divans were found mostly in the homes of the wealthy, where they served as seats of honor (or the favorite perch for the master of the house).[113] A more popular (and practical) alternative was to place the bolsters and various kinds of cushions (*tarraha* and *tawati*) on the floor. But for the poor even these objects often remained out of reach. When there was nothing better, people sat on pillows or, in the barest homes, directly on their carpets (*bisat*). It was a familiar act, full of rich cultural significance: when a Sufi shaykh assumed his position, he was said to "sit on the carpet of his office" (*sajjadat al-mashyakha*).[114] There were also numerous prayer rugs (*sajjada* or *kilim*) and woolen and felt mats (*tunfusa* and *libbad*) which occupied the whole range of designs, colors, and prices; the latter were so comfortable that the bedouin used them as beds.[115] The most precious rugs were worth many times the annual income of an ordinary artisan.[116] But most floor coverings were fairly inexpensive items, and their presence was virtually universal in Damascene homes. Less in evidence, at least among urban households, were the straw mats (*hasir*) manufactured throughout the Ghuta. Available in various fine and coarse weaves, they often adorned local coffeehouses, but found their biggest market among the peasantry.[117]

All these carpets and mats, together with their complement of cushions and pillows, constituted most of the interior décor. Eighteenth-century Damascenes felt no urge, or rather had no means, to stuff their homes with baubles, trinkets, and curiosities, which were the exclusive amusements of the rich. Among the wonders found in the home of ʿAbd al-Muʿti al-Falanqasi, the hedonistic scribe, was a crystal bowl of European origin, filled with wax fruit whose likeness drew the admiration of onlookers. Equally marvelous was his mechanical music box containing miniature musicians—"figures without souls"—also imported from Europe.[118] The tastes of Muhammad Bey al-Kurdi were more familiar: silver and crystal nargilas, presumably for the delectation of his eyes as well as his mouth.[119] As a wealthy military officer and merchant, he could easily

Court and iwan of a house in Damascus. The gathering takes place in a large
house equipped with a large fountain and decorated reception area. The women
of the household (and perhaps some female guests) are relaxing on carpets.
William Thomson, *The Land and the Book*. New York, 1886.

indulge his whims and fancies. But for most of his fellow townspeople,
function inevitably took precedence over form.

This emphasis on thrift and simplicity applied equally to accommodations for sleeping. There were no cumbersome bed frames or cano-
pies, only thin mattresses (*firash*) which were laid on the ground at night.
Depending on the season, people snuggled under layers of sheets (*shar
shaf* and *milhafa*), blankets (*lihaf*), and woolen coverlets (*ihram*) for warmth.
Cradling sleeping heads were the same pillows which doubled as furniture during the day; most were stuffed with straw (*qashsh*) shipped from
the Ghuta, and those of good quality contained an extra layer of cotton
padding.[120] These articles of bedding—mattresses, pillows, sheets, and
blankets—were among the most numerous objects in eighteenth-century
households. It should also be noted that they tended to turn up dispro-

portionately in the estates of women (Appendix B), for whom they were central possessions.[121] Cheap and easily transported, such textiles featured, then as now, as the main articles of a woman's trousseau, to be carried upon marriage to her new household.

Reinforcing this preference for textile furnishings were the requirements of domestic space. Multipurpose rooms had to be arranged according to the needs of the moment, and few things lent themselves to this flexible lifestyle better than lightweight fabrics, which were easily folded and put away for later use. Most households had at least some storage capacity. Families might rely partly on china racks (*matbaqiyya*) and recesses in the walls, but more often wrapped their possessions in cloth bundles (*buqja*) or placed them inside wooden trunks (*sunduq*). Though both of these items were sometimes embellished—bundles with embroidery, and trunks with paint or mother-of-pearl—their value lay far more in their practical use than any aesthetic effect. Particularly prominent were trunks, which were undoubtedly the largest objects in Damascene homes. To one foreign observer, their appearance overwhelmed everything else: "a family's whole stock of furniture consists of one or two trunks in which their goods and jewels are locked up."[122] From the standpoint of Damascenes, their popularity was really a matter of necessity. Closets and bureaus were nonexistent, and living space was nearly always at a premium.

Having surveyed the various components of Damascene interiors, is it possible to recreate them as a physical ensemble? Unfortunately, the information at our disposal does not permit us to place objects around houses, or even around a single room. Probate inventories, drawn up as goods were being auctioned, list things with little regard for classification or origin. The scribes in attendance were concerned strictly with ascertaining quantity and price and entering a brief (usually all too brief) description. An additional problem is that inventories mention only the personal effects of the deceased. All images of domestic interiors are necessarily incomplete because the belongings of spouses and other occupants remain out of the picture. Amid the inevitable frustrations, the only possible solution is to find spouses who died within a short time of each other, and therefore left estates which were recorded in close proximity in the records. These combined references offer an approximation of the full complement of furnishings to be found in local households. We still cannot see decoration in the true sense—the actual distribution of objects over the entire interior—but their combined possessions indicate a certain level of wealth and comfort. For present purposes, we can take the cases of four couples whose estates meet our criteria.

To start with an exceptional rather than a typical household, we can look at the registered possessions of Mustafa Agha al-Kilisli and his wife Fatima, whose inventories were recorded in 1761. Together, they held assets worth more than twenty-five thousand piasters. Nearly all of this immense sum belonged to the husband, who had extended numerous loans to villagers and others; if not a professional moneylender, he may very well have served as a tax farmer. His wife's fortune was much smaller, but, at 739 piasters, quite respectable in the eyes of local society, which honored her with the title *masuna* ("protected"), most likely because she was a secluded woman.[123] In other words, the husband and wife were an immensely fortunate couple. It may seem surprising, then, that their list of home decorations is not very substantial. Together with their four children, the couple slept on five "colored" mattresses and kept warm under six blankets and one sheet. Their floors were covered with a prayer rug and two carpets, and the family rested on a total of twenty-one bolsters and twenty-two pillows—probable indications of a more extensive household and frequent entertainments. Aside from the unusual number of seats, the objects which most reveal their status are the implements for lighting and heating. Three crystal lanterns and two candlestick holders (together with accompanying "trays") betrayed a touch of luxury while providing an unusual degree of illumination for an eighteenth-century household. Against the tribulations of winter, they owned a curtain and not one, but two, braziers for generating warmth; and in all seasons, there was a censer for freshening the rooms. Many of these possessions were undoubtedly put away in their three trunks, which, incidentally, belonged to Mustafa Agha even though the mattresses and most of the furnishings were actually the property of his wife. Thus we have the bare elements of the domestic scene. But did all these things, collected together in a household of considerable wealth, constitute anything like splendor in eighteenth-century eyes?

Before drawing any conclusions, let us examine the estates of the three other couples, all of whom lived in more modest circumstances. To take the case of a "middle-class" family: 'Abd al-Qadir al-Mutafji and his wife Sa'diyya died in 1756 with a combined fortune of over seven hundred piasters, which, though not impressive by the standards of local notables, must have offered them a fair degree of comfort and security.[124] Excluding a single candlestick mentioned among her husband's belongings, Saʿdiyya owned all of the household's furniture, which consisted of three felt carpets, two bolsters, three cushions, nine pillows, three mattresses, two sheets, two trunks, and a bundle, all of which she shared with her husband and two young children. The smaller number of items, at least in comparison to the much wealthier couple above, suggests that their furniture strictly served the needs of family life, as opposed to an extended household or network of peers and clients. But can anyone say that this was a uniquely "middle-class" interior? The estates of Mustafa al-Farraʾ (who worked as a barber) and his wife Fatima were valued in 1753 at slightly more than one hundred thirty-two piasters—less than a fifth of what ʿAbd al-Qadir and Saʿdiyya held—and yet their furniture was not much different.[125] Among the decorations noted by the scribes were two prayer rugs, a censer, and a trunk for the husband; and two mattresses, a prayer rug, a woolen rug, three felt rugs, three blankets, and seven pillows for his wife. A similar picture can be drawn from the household of ʿAbduh al-Harastani, a ropemaker, and his wife ʿAysha (d. 1762), whose joint wealth also stood at one hundred thirty-two piasters.[126] The husband's contribution to the living quarters amounted to only two blankets, whereas his wife provided two mattresses, two more blankets, two felt carpets, a woolen carpet, five pillows, and a trunk. The couple had only one daughter, with whom they shared their spartan household.

What do the estates of these four couples reveal about eighteenth-century interiors? To speak in the broadest terms: the repertoire of furnishings did not vary dramatically from one household to the next. In the homes of rich and poor, we find the same familiar collection of pillows, bolsters, cushions, carpets, blankets, mattresses, trunks. From one end of the social spectrum to the other, households differed mainly in the number of objects that they owned. Inventories conjure up an image of families who, for the most part, lived in rather spare lodgings. We do not need to take the preceding lists of items as exact counts. It is enough to note the similarities in types and quantities of furnishings, all of which were found in most other estates as well. Only the wealthy were able to surround themselves with a relative profusion of objects, justified, one may assume, by the requirements of extended households and social networks. In a world dominated by widespread and routine poverty, these deliberate redundancies would have acted as a quiet demonstration of social superiority.

A QUESTION OF PRIORITIES

To put it another way, Damascenes bestowed relatively little importance on domestic interiors. Over the course of the eighteenth century, there was no perceptible evolution in living space. Overall, it is difficult to detect any shifts in design, construction, or decoration. Builders continued to follow the well-worn tracks of their predecessors and were so dependent on received techniques that they had no need of formal plans and blueprints.[127] The same conservatism molded domestic furnishings. If we can judge from preliminary work on earlier probate inventories, household objects from the late-seventeenth century were virtually identical to those of the eighteenth, and rarely absorbed more than a small portion of personal wealth.[128] Furnishings had a predominantly utilitarian character and had not yet been converted into heirlooms and precious objets d'art, arrayed for a refined aesthetic effect or as part of a discreet social performance.

It would be a mistake, however, to assume an absolute uniformity in eighteenth-century decoration, as if notions of taste played no role whatsoever. In all objects, there were many gradations of price and style according to workmanship and materials. Social distinction continued to assert itself in small touches added to the humblest things: crystal candlesticks, cushions and pillows embroidered with gold thread, trunks inlaid with mother-of-pearl, woolen drapes imported from Salonika. All this petty finery must have generated some appeal, insofar as it attracted sporadic censure from moral commentators. Al-Nabulsi, who was no extremist, explicitly disapproved of decorative wall hangings (pl. *lubud*), which he dismissed as tokens of pride and ostentation. Their only legitimate purpose, he contended, was to act as barriers against the heat or cold, and to block flies and other pests from entering doorways.[129] Were townspeople responsive to these objections? Given the evidence at our disposal, it is impossible to know how residents actually arranged their belongings. Inventories show that hangings were very common, and if al-Nabulsi's criticisms can be taken as an indicator of domestic habits, it is hard not to conclude that at least some households used them in an ornamental fashion. In their dark and crowded rooms, Damascenes had not given up all hope of embellishing their homes. But could such small vanities really have created much of an effect in these impoverished conditions? By the standards of their distant descendants, even the grandest families lived in comparatively mean and plain quarters, where the main concern was to stave off the elements and maximize comfort through the crude means available to them.

VI

FASHION

&

DEPORTMENT

Ｉｎ an entry for 1730, ibn kannan noted some dis-
tressing news. In what would later be known as the Patrona Halil rebellion, mutinous soldiers in Istanbul had overthrown and imprisoned
the Ottoman sultan Ahmed III (r. 1703–30). These distant rumblings
prompted a naïve reverie, in which the chronicler complimented the
Ottomans for their relatively decent treatment of deposed sultans, "who
were locked up and given a stipend until they died or were poisoned." In
the more distant "time of the caliphs," he explained, palace coups were
often accompanied by lamentable acts, such as the blinding of the former
ruler, who would thereafter be disqualified from holding power. Equally
shocking and outrageous, the fallen monarch would be dressed in the
clothes of a commoner—sometimes little more than rags or unworked
cloth—and, as a final humiliation, paraded through the streets in front
of his former subjects.[1] It was a detail that Ibn Kannan would not have
overlooked. What offended him in these imaginary scenes was not merely

the demotion, disgrace, and display of a sultan, but the very notion of putting such an august figure in the clothing of the "flocks" (ra'aya)—that is, ordinary subjects.

In other words, clothing was not merely a matter of personal taste and style; it placed a person within an all-encompassing social hierarchy that fashion helped to make visible and explicit. As Ibn Kannan understood, and would not have needed to remind his contemporaries, clothing has always been much more than a physical necessity. It was inseparable from a whole system of values, manners, and attitudes, all of which can be summed up, in a word, as fashion. At the core of this enormous subject, which has never been concerned solely with shifting trends in taste and design, is the body itself, which provides clothing with its essential form and movement. Many elements of fashion can be traced directly to beliefs about the body—more specifically, to what could, or could not, be displayed or left open to the public gaze. These taboos, though hushed and implicit, surrounded people as much as the physical clothing that they wore. In reconstructing standards of dress, we will thus take the body as our guide, starting with the head and face, which always received especially intense scrutiny, and then going on to consider the human form as a whole. One final section will look at variations in material and color, which articulated fashion and enabled it to project distinctions of wealth and status that, in some cases, were mandated by Islamic law or the Ottoman state. Yet these legal and administrative regulations should not be taken as a full reflection of social practice. Far more than other possessions, clothing shows how material culture easily blurred imaginary social boundaries and, in matters of fashion and identity, tended towards a looser complexity grounded in a common local culture.

CLOTHING AND SELF-ADORNMENT: HEAD AND FACE

Among the most visible parts of the body were the head and face, whose appearance was a matter of the greatest sensitivity. The first rule, binding for both men and women, was that the head had to be covered in public. Exceptions were so rare that they demanded an explanation. Murad al-Muradi, a great Sufi master, went about bareheaded and escaped criticism only on account of his extraordinary piety.[2] In the case of Sulayman al-Majdhub, a local folk saint, it was taken as one more sign of his madness and listed with his other eccentric habits, such as talking incomprehensibly fast and loitering outside the bathhouse of Nur al-Din.[3] For ordinary townspeople, no such excuses were possible. Careless exposure of the head was always treated as an unseemly breach of custom and moral sensibility.

Headpieces were therefore an indispensable feature of local costume. In Damascus, which was no stricter than most other Middle Eastern towns, people did not wear hats in the Western sense, but rather a variety of turbans (*qawuq*). At the lower end of the economic ladder, turbans could be little more than a piece of cloth wrapped around the head. More elaborate models brought together several different components: a light skullcap (*taqiyya*) supporting a cylindrical cap (*tarbush* or *fas*), swathed in a long strip of cloth (*shadd, shash,* or *shal*[4]). Some attained a truly ponderous size and weight, involving several caps and many folds of fabric, and, according to al-Qasimi, "weighed heavily upon the head and created head colds and even blindness." A turban of this size, or one that was intricately wound, might require considerable skill to assemble. Even in the final decades of the Ottoman period, some Damascenes continued to turn to local experts, who handled the task for a fee.[5]

It is difficult to picture these turbans in any detail. Most of our knowledge comes from nineteenth-century sources, which speak for a time of accelerating change as old habits steadily yielded to new ones, primarily at the instigation of the Ottoman state, which viewed clothing—or at least the uniforms of its officials—as one more avenue for pursuing reform and creating a modern society. Reminiscing on the fashions of the early nineteenth century, al-Qasimi mentions six different kinds of turbans, mostly of elegant styles and materials.[6] Yet only one of them (the white *libada*) appears in eighteenth-century inventories. Were scribes, in hastily drawing up their lists, simply indifferent to the niceties of fashion? In everyday social life, Damascenes were certainly attentive to these distinctions in headgear. Turbans were an integral part of official dress and intimately tied to self-image and social rank. When the governor 'Uthman Pasha al-Muhassil expelled the kapıkulları from Damascus in 1740, he allowed small numbers of these imperial Janissaries to stay behind on the condition that they quit the military and enter the civilian population. In accepting his offer, the dismissed soldiers had to unwind their turbans, which helped to distinguish them from both rivals and civilians.[7] This link between turban and identity held true even in death. On the way to the cemetery, mourners customarily placed the turban of a scholar or Sufi on the bier next to his head, thereby announcing to passersby that an important man had died.[8] And touring the city's old cemeteries today, one still finds turbans carved atop the tombstones of prominent religious figures. In the language of fashion, the head was one of the main focal points of differentiation. Turbans ranked among the most conspicuous and effective means of defining and reaffirming status.

The size of a turban often introduced individuals before they ever opened their mouths, announced their titles, or spoke of their occupations and affiliations. In general, large turbans were one of the everyday emblems of political and religious authority, and it was mainly important members of the community who wore them. Al-Nabulsi took it for granted that high-ranking ulama would share this predilection. Though the fashion had no religious justification and, strictly speaking, might be regarded as an "innovation," he defended it as permissible on the grounds that "the common people should not scorn and despise [the ulama]."[9] Entranced by the distant glow of elite society, Mahmud al-Hanbali, a preacher in the village of Duma, found it natural to imitate this grand style. "He put on great airs, had a big turban, rode a horse, and dressed in fine clothes."[10] His preening was overlooked only because he was a scholar; outside the religious establishment, and other high social circles, fewer liberties were permitted. One local broker (dallal) tried to switch to an unusually tall turban, but soon made himself an object of public ridicule; he gave up the habit after a scholar began to circulate mocking verses.[11] People had little sympathy for such idiosyncrasies. For ordinary townsmen, standards of dress remained clear, if unspoken, and embodied the virtues of modesty and conformity. It was assumed that people would know their place and dress accordingly.

Feminine fashion had its own rules, which never insisted on an elaborate headpiece or required the equivalent of a turban. Many women simply preferred to drape themselves in large cloaks that they could draw around the head and face. The plainest covering might suffice—often little more than a white cloth capped with a kerchief. Depending on the effect that one wanted to create, kerchiefs might be wrapped around the head as a veil or tied more loosely as an ornament.[12] Women's estates reveal a fondness for these items, which came in a variety of colors, patterns, and brocades. The local craftsmen who handled this business were never at a loss for customers "in view of the fact that women are unable to do without kerchiefs."[13] At the end of the nineteenth century, many wealthy women were still fond of the *rabta*, which consisted of several scarves tied around a skullcap or tarbush. The ensemble sometimes bulked so large as to assume "the shape of a small bathhouse basin" and required informal specialists (always female) to assemble it.[14] Though it is not clear when this decoration had evolved, the presence of tarbushes and other caps in the estates of many eighteenth-century women seems to confirm that it was not a late-Ottoman innovation.[15]

The main purpose of all these cloaks and kerchiefs was to throw up an extra barrier against unwanted gazes, showing as little of the face and hair as possible and thereby projecting an air of modesty and respectability. Only on the fringes of the social order did women feel free to ignore these prohibitions. According to al-Budayri, one carefree prostitute, who had fallen madly in love with a "Turkish youth," organized a parade to celebrate his recovery from an illness. Holding censers, candles, and lanterns, she and her colleagues boldly gathered in the markets, singing and clapping and shaking tambourines as a large crowd looked on. Most disturbing to al-Budayri were the "open faces and unbound hair" that the "daughters of sin" made no attempt to hide.[16]

To remove the face from public view, women might resort to the veil as a supplemental headpiece. European travelers long marked it as one of the most curious and exotic features of women's clothing. In the modern world, it has acquired connotations of "Islamic" morality, but women around the Mediterranean basin have worn it in one form or another since antiquity.[17] As late as the eighteenth century, it was never a strictly Islamic prerogative; non-Muslim women might cover their faces just as readily as Muslims.[18] Beyond these generalizations, any discussion of premodern veiling has to overcome numerous challenges. One problem is that we have few descriptions of veils. Damascene authors rarely talk about them, and inventories provide little information about prices, materials, and other indications of quality. One study has argued that the Ottoman conquest brought a narrowing in the range of veils worn by Arab women: each region adopted its own version, which gradually supplanted the old medieval diversity.[19] Even if a certain uniformity had taken hold, some differences were still obvious. Burckhardt, the early nineteenth-century traveler, immediately noticed that the *barqu'*, the distinctive Egyptian face-veil that trailed down the front, "is not a Syrian fashion."[20] But within Syria itself, or a single town like Damascus, did veils follow a more or less standard design? As usual, the evidence from inventories cannot tell us anything about physical appearance, but the variety in terminology (*sha'riyya* and *khimar*, together with the much less frequently mentioned *hijab*) suggests a modest range in style. The fabrics were finely woven and covered the whole spectrum, from silk to horsehair.[21] The fanciest veils might be embellished with gold or silver pieces,[22] but most do not seem to have been very extravagant.

In eighteenth-century towns, veiling was quite common, but by no means universal or practiced according to a single definition of modesty. Speaking for many jurists, al-Nabulsi explained that women needed to cover themselves in the presence of unrelated men, but specifically allowed them to show the hands and face.[23] The evidence taken from inventories offers only partial clarification and, as always, reveals little about actual behavior. We cannot be sure how thoroughly and consistently women may have covered themselves in the course of their daily routine, or in whose presence they felt free to show themselves. The most lasting impression is that affluent women were much more likely to own face-veils and kerchiefs, which, in elite society, were treated as the surest guarantees of chastity and honor. Elite women were certainly the most reluctant to reveal themselves in public. In one of the most unusual decrees of the century, As'ad Pasha al-'Azm tried in 1749 to organize a mass expulsion of the city's prostitutes. To facilitate the search for suspects, he ruled that only the women of his own household and that of Musa Kikhiya, his lieutenant governor, would henceforth be allowed to place kerchiefs over their faces.[24] The measure was most notable for its futility: within days the prostitutes had returned to the streets.

Among various head coverings, the one item which failed to achieve much popularity was the long scarf known as a *ghitat shash*. Attached from the top of the head, it flowed down the neck and shoulders and, as al-Qasimi later maintained, was worn mainly as a means of screening the back of the neck from the sun and wind.[25] It must also have performed the function of concealing a woman's hair, which, under the mores of the day, was counted among her most enchanting attributes. For a woman, showing the hair was no less provocative than showing an open face.

Men's hair was never so intimately bound up with notions of decency and chastity, but remained subject to its own set of communal standards. Men were never free to grow their hair as they liked. The normal expectation was that they would keep it short and neatly trimmed. The ulama explained this preference not as a religious duty, but as a practical virtue which helped to maintain a neat appearance. Offering typical advice on grooming habits, al-Nabulsi recommended that men get a haircut once a week.[26] Barbers plied a busy trade. The chronicler al-Budayri, a barber, fondly memorialized Ahmad al-Hallaq, his mentor in the profession, who cut the hair of eminent ulama, including al-Nabulsi himself, and always offered his services free to indigent religious students.[27] Departures from the norm invited censure or at the very least carried the stigma of nonconformity. Long hair, in particular, was seen as an oddity. People might excuse this liberty in a few extraordinarily pious shaykhs and dervishes, but could also treat it as an indictment of character.[28] When al-Nabulsi suffered a mid-life bout of depression, lasting all of seven years, he confined himself almost entirely to his house and composed poetry mocking the "people"; equally disturbing to his peers, he refused to cut his hair and fingernails, further fueling rumors that he had lost his faith.[29]

The length of facial hair also came under the same close scrutiny. Learned opinion favored beards which were short enough to be grasped in one hand, and admonished men to keep them clean and free of odors.[30] The ability to grow a beard, as al-Nabulsi observed, was a "component of manhood [given] from God Almighty."[31] The sprouting of whiskers was a turning point in the life of a young boy and marked his age as much as any numerical measure. Returning with the pilgrimage caravan in 1699, one governor took the unusual step of sending ahead a youth as his official representative; Ibn Kannan remembered him only as being "near the age at which his beard would emerge."[32] Among adult men, a cleanshaven face seemed downright eccentric. Muhammad al-Maliki, for example, won notoriety not merely for his tall turbans and habit of bleeding himself two to three times per week, but also for his insistence on shaving his eyebrows, mustache, and beard.[33] So shocking was the absence of a beard that it was considered shameful and humiliating. When the Greek Orthodox patriarch of Aleppo ordered the arrest of priests who had defected to Roman Catholicism (1819)—which, to his consternation, had made significant inroads among local Christians—he vented his rage by shaving their beards and exiling them to Arwad Island off the Syrian coast.[34] Muslims shared the same views about the importance of a beard, and archconservatives might even dream of imposing it as a religious obligation. Genç Yusuf Pasha, whose zeal for moralizing knew few bounds, forbade all Muslims (1807) to shave their beards and threatened to cut off the hand of any barber who was found guilty of assisting. Mikha'il Mishaqa reports that many youths fled to the coastal regions to escape the decree. His explanation is revealing: once a man acquired a beard, custom demanded that he keep it.[35] Perhaps another reason that Damascene men were so reluctant to remove beards and mustaches was the poor quality of local razors and scissors. An admirer of modern barber shops, which first opened in Damascus near the end of his lifetime, al-Qasimi looked back on the older techniques with scorn. The barber would "shave with a blade like a saw. By the time the cutting was finished, the [customer's] head would be dyed with the henna of blood."[36]

While men grappled with their beards, women pursued ideals of beauty which emphasized facial decoration. One of the favorite choices was jewelry. Earrings appeared at nearly all economic levels.[37] The most expensive were made from gold or inlaid with pearls; lesser varieties, which ranged from silver to brass, could be fairly valuable as well.[38] Yet earrings were probably a little too common to rank among the gaudiest status symbols. Necklaces were almost certainly the true extravagance. Most were made from gold and therefore very costly—around twenty piasters, which could represent nearly an entire year's earnings for the most destitute Damascenes. It should come as no surprise that they turned up overwhelmingly in the estates of the most affluent women.[39]

The subtle pressure on women to attend to their appearance can be gathered from the distribution of mirrors, which showed up quite frequently in female estates. Most mirrors did not cost very much, just one to two piasters, and were probably small and hand-held, confirming their use as cosmetic tools.[40] Makeup was rudimentary. "To paint the face is an improvement unknown among the Oriental fair, save the Greeks alone"[41]—the assessment of one traveler, who was not, however, entirely accurate. Henna, a kind of reddish dye, might be daubed on the hands, feet, and face. It was also effective for coloring the hair, as was walnut oil, which was the choice of those who preferred black over red tones.[42] To accentuate their eyes, many women applied kohl, a substance derived from antimony, which served as the premodern equivalent of eyeliner. Folk medicine also recommended it as a remedy for eye diseases, which were treated by a whole network of popular specialists (*kuhhal*).[43]

In spite of the decidedly feminine connotations of makeup and other beautifying techniques, some men might openly resort to them. Genç Yusuf Pasha, who could not resist yet another opportunity for moral perfectionism, decreed for a time that all men should put kohl around their eyes and dye their beards with henna.[44] His order is surprising because it suggests that painting the face and coloring the hair were not confined solely to women—and, what is most interesting, that these practices might be acceptable even to conservative religious opinion. Perhaps it was a rural or tribal fashion, mostly alien to Damascus, for the governor himself was Kurdish and, as reported in local rumors, had fallen under the spell of a charismatic Kurdish shaykh. The mainstream of scholarly opinion clearly disapproved. Al-Nabulsi, who was normally flexible and accommodating in the tug-of-war between doctrine and custom, ruled out the use of facial palliatives by men, even to hide some embarrassing defect. "Man is not ordered [by God] to beautify [the face]. Indeed, he is probably forbidden from doing so in the manner of women."[45] Contemporaries seem to have agreed. The governor's embellishments never really caught on as a male aesthetic ideal. Though the boundaries between male and female fashion may not have always been exact or consistent, Damascenes clearly believed that some differences between men and women were too intrinsic to be ignored altogether.

CLOTHING AND SELF-ADORNMENT: THE BODY

Just as Damascenes were careful to garb the head in appropriate modesty, they showed the same concern for the body, which had to be kept discreetly covered at all times. Ibn Kannan could mention the death of Ahmad al-Misri (1720), a revered folk saint who "was always naked, summer and winter," but in the same breath hasten to explain the extraordinary "states and marvels" which placed him in a special category of humanity, beyond the normal rules of conduct.[46] Even among the antics of folk saints, this holy exhibitionism was an extreme eccentricity. Damascenes had very conservative ideas about dress. They regarded it improper to bare any more flesh than was absolutely necessary, and understood this precaution as a defense against the insidious passions, appetites, and instincts that the display of the human form might arouse. The greatest exponents of these attitudes were religious commentators, whose tone is unmistakably prudish. "In general," wrote Ibn Kannan, "it is the lust of the stomach and genitals which leads to dangers, scandals, dissolution, disgrace, and perdition of the soul."[47] The body was full of temptations which had to be fought, stifled, and conquered.

Nudity was especially upsetting. Ulama fretted over the moral, and even medical, consequences of exposing the body. At the center of this uneasiness were the sexual organs. A scholar like al-Nabulsi could gravely warn that little more than gazing upon them could cause forgetfulness; he added, moreover, that couples who took this liberty during marital intimacy could unwittingly blind their offspring, who might pay the price for the immodesty committed by their parents' eyes. It would be better, in fact, for husbands and wives not to undress fully, even for the purpose of sexual intercourse.[48] No safer was solitude, which bred its own dangers. During bathing, individuals ought to wrap themselves in a cloth and look directly at their genitalia only to wash them, submit to medical care, shave the pubic hair (as required by Islamic hygiene), or clean themselves after urination or defecation.[49] When these tasks were finished, they should dress again as quickly as possible. Though no one might seem to be looking, they could unwittingly find themselves in the company of angels or mischievous genies (*jinn*), who were always prowling about invisible and undetected.[50] Modesty demanded vigilance in a world where one could never be sure of being truly alone.

People might go to great lengths to preserve their sense of moral decency. During the ambush of the pilgrimage caravan in 1757, the bedouin raiders were so rapacious that they strip-searched pilgrims, leaving them to stagger into Damascus naked and exhausted. Some of the survivors coated their genitalia and buttocks with mud;[51] anything was better than abject self-exposure. In view of these sensitivities about the body, clothing had as much a moral as a practical function. Designs were intentionally loose and baggy. The aim was not merely to protect the body from heat and cold, but to de-emphasize its outline behind a decorous screen of cloth and embroidery. Alternatives were hard to imagine. European attire was seen as shocking, ridiculous, and somewhat lewd. Resistance to these foreign outfits, so tight-fitting by local standards, was prolonged and broke down only slowly and grudgingly. To avoid offending local opinion, all "Franks"—like the poet Nerval, who visited Damascus in 1841—continued to dress in Middle Eastern attire and dared not show themselves in their native outfits until at least the mid-nineteenth century.

Shaped by the same moral strictures and standards of taste, the clothing of men and women shared many features of cut and proportion, and in some cases were virtually identical. This rough convergence of design is evident in eighteenth-century probate inventories, in which many garments appeared with almost equal frequency in the estates of men and women. This is not to say that the clothing of this period failed to express distinctions of gender. Damascenes could tell men apart from women at a glance. In 1720, a spice merchant accused of murder tried to escape the city disguised as a woman; authorities nonetheless apprehended him after he was betrayed by several acquaintances.[52] That this subterfuge was at all possible is enough to show that men and women observed recognizably separate codes of fashion.

How exactly did one garment differ from the next? A detailed reconstruction of eighteenth-century dress is nearly impossible. We have few direct descriptions of clothes, especially for the most mundane articles, such as shirts and pants. A slightly later observer of Arab fashion, Reinhart Dozy, could offer (1845) only a few broad generalizations, which were most likely valid for the eighteenth century as well. Shirts, he noticed, were often made of thin fabric, and were worn in every season. Sleeves might extend to various lengths, but not customarily past the elbows. Unlike shirts found in Europe, moreover, the Middle Eastern version was rarely tucked into the pants; people allowed it to hang loose, primarily as a concession to the warm climate.[53] Inventories show that shirts (qamis) were common to both men and women, but make only the barest mention of cuts, styles, and colors. The same is largely true of pants, which came in several types: libas, jaqshir, and jirwal, which tended to show up in the estates of men, and rafiq and shintiyan for women. These were not full-length pants as modern consumers would know them, but loose-fitting drawers which might hang down to the knees.[54]

Regardless of season, people usually wore several layers of clothing. In winter, this precaution was an absolute necessity in view of ineffective heating techniques. Damascenes could hardly comprehend the sight of a folk saint like ʿAli al-Iskaf, who wandered through the streets and covered himself with nothing more than a simple cloak; in the most numbing chill, beads of perspiration reportedly dripped from his face, testifying to the divine grace (*baraka*) which suffused him.[55] Even as warm weather approached, few townspeople would have ventured out so lightly clad. They might shed their outermost clothes, but not their shirts and pants, which were never removed, in large part because wardrobes did not contain anything resembling modern underwear. This essential, if hidden, function probably explains why the ulama frowned on the use of green in pants, objecting that it was the color of the prophet Muhammad and therefore inappropriate for such a lowly purpose, which might bring it into contact with unclean parts of the body.[56]

Over these inner clothes, Damascenes wore multiple layers of robes and overcoats. Though measurements and designs were not always consistent, they conformed to the same general principle of loose fits and ample proportions. Several features were common to nearly all of these garments: no collars, few (if any) buttons, and no pockets (which later had to be borrowed from European clothing).[57] Many styles were popular among both men and women: the *jubba* and *qunbaz*, long smocks of ancient origin; the *ʿantari*, a short cloak; and the *milaya*, a wide wrap assembled from two or three pieces of cloth. A few of the loosest coverings were more strictly identified with women: the *izar*, *qaba*, and *milhafa*,[58] which were capable of shrouding the head and body. Most interesting is the large number of vests and cloaks belonging almost exclusively to men. The language of the inventories is quite terse, but at the same time leaves little doubt that they had more options than female consumers. Did this comparative freedom of choice reflect a greater freedom of movement outside the home? Is it evidence of a more public life, which required them to attend to appearances? The expense of many vests and cloaks—above all, the *binish*,[59] which was often decorated with precious fabrics and materials—suggests their great appeal to members of the elite, who liked to identify themselves through outer finery. Among other expensive overcoats, whose variety is a testimony to their distinctiveness, were the *farajiyya*, *qaftan*, *irtaya*, and *kartukiyya*, together with the *yaghmurluq* (which must have functioned as something like a raincoat).[60] In cold weather, many men also favored the *ʿabaya* (or *ʿaba*), a short, sleeveless overcoat made from wool. Regularly dyed black, it everywhere acquired a reputation as one of the favorite garments of the bedouin, and throughout Is-

"Syrian gentlemen of various sects." The scene shows the basic elements of local fashion. All the men have turbans or some other head-covering, and wear long, flowing cloaks. Only the presence of a European-style sofa reminds us of the nineteenth-century setting. William Thomson, *The Land and the Book*. New York, 1886.

lamic history served as a kind of rough uniform for itinerant Sufis.[61] The *yabanja*, which seems to have been a kind of cape, was much less popular, evidently because eighteenth-century men preferred longer cloaks that covered as much of the figure as possible.

Damascenes secured all these garments with belts and sashes, which came in several styles and might be heavily decorated. Most common was the *zunnar*,[62] which occupied the whole spectrum of luxury and taste. In its crudest form, it might be nothing more than a strip of leather or brass, or a thin kind of shawl wrapped around the waist. Fancier versions could be adorned with gold or silver, studded with pearls, or woven from *alaja*, a mixture of cotton and silk. Other types of belts seem much less luxurious: the *kamar* and *shala*, preferred overwhelmingly by men, and the *mihzam*, which could be worn by both sexes. Decoration for these lesser styles might consist of different dyes and weaves, but almost never featured metalwork or jewelry. Humblest of all was the *dakka*, a twisted cord or lace commonly used to hold up trousers.

The most virile ornaments were weapons, which were used not merely as a means of protection, but as a kind of status symbol. Some objects were beyond the reach of ordinary Damascenes and, in any case, had a highly specialized military function. Maces, for example, were quite expensive and turned up mostly in the estates of military officers and members of the social elite.[63] Far more common were a variety of swords, daggers, knives, pistols, and muskets. The owners were overwhelmingly Muslim and, for the most part, held ʿaskari status, suggesting that many were indeed members of military units or paramilitary groups. A few Christians might enter the trade in guns or knives, but apparently did not sell to their own communities.[64] What is surprising is the sheer number of people who owned guns—nearly a quarter of the male population. The Ottoman state had long tried to confine possession of firearms to its own officials and soldiers, but as early as the sixteenth century, this monopoly had become little more than a legal fiction. Subsequent attempts to disarm the population or curtail supplies, especially in the countryside, proved absolutely futile.[65] The trade soon became routine, if somewhat clandestine, and nourished itself on a wide array of smuggling networks, conniving officials, and opportunistic merchants. Some manufacture took place in Damascus itself, but most guns originated in Europe or were shipped from Istanbul.[66] By the eighteenth century, quarters such as the Midan, which had evolved into a hotbed of paramilitary activity, were notorious for being heavily armed.[67] Defiant Janissaries and mercenaries bristled with daggers and pistols and were always difficult to control. One Afghan shaykh, a long-time resident of Damascus memorialized by al-Budayri, appears almost as a caricature of these swaggering toughs. He rarely spoke—at most, uttering a few curses in Turkish—and was so attached to his weapons that he remained fully girded even while asleep or relaxing in the bathhouse.[68] Against the background of mounting factional violence, Ottoman regulations that forbade soldiers from appearing armed in the streets, except in time of war, had little meaning. Even shopkeepers and artisans began to carry guns openly. In 1760, they had no qualms about marching with their "weapons, equipment, and superb armor" under the nose of the governor himself, who, at the behest of Istanbul, had organized public festivities to celebrate the birth of the future Selim III (r. 1789–1807).[69]

Such a wide demand, meeting with an active trade, helped to depress prices. The fanciest guns fetched twenty to thirty piasters, but many (presumably of much poorer quality) could be bought for less than five. Concealed in these relatively affordable prices was a somewhat low regard for many firearms, which were of varying quality and not necessarily the weapon of first choice. Among local connoisseurs, swords earned the greatest esteem. Though firearms had been present in the Middle East since the fifteenth century, they sometimes proved cumbersome and unreliable in combat; especially in fighting at close quarters, pistols and muskets simply took too much time to reload.[70] Again, prices tell an interesting story. Swords ranked among the most prized possessions in the city—at the high end, more than twice the value of a good pistol. Silver daggers and knives could easily fetch more than an entire musket. Their appeal owed as much to their decorative as military properties. The finest blades were made from steel and often set in elaborate hilts of silver. Among soldiers and their paramilitary allies, these weapons were as integral to their sense of fashion as any article of clothing.

Few other objects were strapped or hung from outer clothing. Buttons were uncommon, and pins, brooches, and medallions made their first appearance only with the gradual adoption of European styles in modern times. Handkerchiefs were dismissed as an affectation. Religious authorities agreed that it was perfectly acceptable to wipe the nose or sweaty skin with the sleeve of a garment or a free hand. Etiquette was even looser with nose blowing and spitting, which were tolerable as long as one was not standing inside a mosque or facing in the direction of Mecca. The rules were strictest with yawning, which was treated as the height of rudeness, best covered with a hand and emitted silently.[71] No extra accessories were needed to accommodate these bodily urges. Good manners, as understood at the time, did not require them.

The one exception to this minimalism in decoration was the craze for watches, all of which were imported from Europe, the world's sole producer. This monopoly was slow to be broken. At the end of the nineteenth century, al-Qasimi was still lamenting the small number of craftsmen in Damascus who had the tools and qualifications to repair watches properly.[72] For most owners, it probably did not matter much; they were simply not in the habit of keeping such precise track of time. There was, to be sure, a practical method of reckoning in hours, which were divided into two separate sets of twelve, one for daytime, and the other for night, causing the length of each respective set of hours to vary with the season. But it was not the same as the evenly divided hours on the face of a European watch. Moreover, the desire for such precision remained restricted to specialists. As al-Nabulsi explained about a trip to Tripoli (1693), "We went to the aqueduct there; it is far away [from town] by a measure of half an hour according to the system of the astronomers."[73] More convenient was religious time, which, for Muslims, corresponded to the five daily calls to prayer issued at dawn, midday, mid-afternoon, sunset, and evening. Like the seasonal "hours," the intervals lengthened toward summer, contracted toward winter. When al-Nabulsi and his traveling companions entered the town of Latakia, he recalled not the hour, but merely that it was "at the time of the afternoon call for prayer."[74] On many other occasions, it was easiest and most natural to mark time by the passage of the sun across the sky. 'Uthman al-Sham'a, a renowned and indefatigable teacher, held most of his lessons "from the rising of the sun till afternoon, summer and winter."[75] As his students understood, he did not need to set his schedule to anything more accurate and rigorous than these simple diurnal rhythms. Nighttime, on the other hand, posed bigger logistical problems. The only attempt to maintain anything like a public sense of time after dark came from the citadel: the period from sunset to sunrise was conventionally divided into thirds, each of which was announced by the sounding of drums.[76] More exact measurements, kept in hours and minutes on watches and clocks, were superfluous. Damascenes had more relaxed notions of time, which did not require mechanized accuracy or constant monitoring. The modern era of "time discipline," as one historian has put it, still lay in the distant future.[77]

How, then, can we make sense of the demand for watches? What possible use would ordinary people have for devices which could not have told time for them in any meaningful way? The main answer is that watches performed an essentially aesthetic function. This may, in turn, explain why religious authorities never viewed them as a challenge to "Islamic" traditions and spared them the hostility that they reserved for the printing press, another mechanical import from Europe. Indeed, fancy timepieces appeared in the estate of the mufti Hamid al-'Imadi himself, along with other prominent ulama.[78] These scholars belonged to a wealthy clientele who provided most of the demand for these strange mechanisms, which provoked such admiration that poets might even celebrate them in verse.[79] Most models were expensive and made of gold or silver; a timepiece from the top of the line could easily command more than fifty piasters. Some estates contained cheaper versions of silver or brass available for less than ten piasters, but it was really a luxury market driven more by personal vanity than workaday efficiency. Watches were chic. Consumers valued them mainly as appurtenances of elite fashion, as exotic toys and baubles for the amusement of the wealthy and privileged.[80]

To move beyond these elite affectations and talk about popular techniques of self-adornment, we need to turn to other options, which, for most Damascenes, meant jewelry in all its manifold forms. Most numerous were rings, which ran the usual gamut of metals, from gold and silver at the high end to brass among the less fashionable. Gender decisively shaped preferences. As the contents of estates make absolutely clear, rings appeared more frequently on the fingers of women than men. Further skewing the distribution were religious norms, which ruled out gold rings for men.[81] Though custom seems largely to have gone along with these prohibitions, it never yielded entirely. One can talk only of broad trends: women owned the great majority of gold rings (about two-thirds), whereas those made from silver belonged mostly to men (in roughly the same proportion).[82] Many Damascenes who wore rings were quite affluent, but it was not a prerequisite. Silver rings, in particular, were rather modestly priced. Nothing, of course, carried the cachet of gold. Creating the biggest splash were gold bracelets and bands (*siwar*), a favorite decoration of wealthy women that represented potentially extravagant sums—in the upper range, roughly the price of a modest home. So feminine were bracelets that women might direct the trade themselves. Among the surviving estates from the period, the single biggest dealer was Mukrima Qadin, a wealthy woman from the notable Safarjalani family, who presumably sold to a female clientele.[83]

In general, the hands were decorated with relative simplicity. One ring, placed discreetly on the small finger of the left hand (never the right), was deemed sufficient in polite society.[84] Most Damascenes seem to have agreed; few estates contained more than one ring. And apart from jewelry and women's use of henna tattoos, there were few other refinements. Stylish men, especially attentive about appearance, might make an impression simply by manicuring their nails properly. In their eagerness to prescribe and regulate daily routines, the ulama have left behind lengthy debates about the correct techniques, which were taken as yet another mark of civility and distinction.[85]

Among all the parts of the body, Damascenes probably showed the least concern for adorning the feet, which were treated as a bigger problem for the rules of etiquette than those of fashion. When people sat, politeness required that they squat or keep their legs primly tucked under their bodies. More relaxed positions were potentially offensive. Al-Nabulsi cautioned pious Muslims against extending their legs in the direction of Mecca, or pointing them at the Quran or other religious books.[86] Guests received the same consideration. Despite having ridden nearly a full day on horseback, which left him sore and exhausted, the bedouin chieftain Zahir al-'Umar felt it necessary to apologize for extending his legs in the presence of an Ottoman emissary.[87] Footwear was part of this subtle choreography, and came off at the entrance of homes and shops. In mosques, where these mundane rituals held the greatest significance, the gesture was treated as a matter of respect for religion itself.[88] Violations were a cause of public outrage. In the confusing aftermath of the Egyptian occupation of Damascus, in 1771, Druze and Christian soldiers from Lebanon brazenly forced their way into the Umayyad Mosque and, in a deliberate touch of insolence, refused to take off their boots. The entry of Christians was doubly provocative because the precincts of the mosque were normally off-limits to non-Muslims. Local Muslims did not take long to react. Several days after the Lebanese troops left the city, bands of Muslim vigilantes began harassing Damascene Christians, who had seen the trouble coming. Some families fled to safety, but most tried to stay out of sight and weathered the crisis in their homes.[89]

At first glance, shoes seem rather unremarkable elements of the wardrobe. Inventories mention only four or five basic varieties, but this simple terminology conceals a much greater potential for inventiveness and self-expression. Take the *jazma*, the "curious gondola-shaped red overshoes" noticed by one mid-nineteenth-century traveler.[90] Made of leather and designed for men, they came in different sizes: low, medium, and high, the latter of which could cover "most of the leg."[91] Cheaper and suitable for both sexes was the *babuj*, a low-cut leather shoe which claimed the largest market among local footwear. Popularity spawned an almost countless variety: "every village has its own version different from the others."[92] Much harder to find were *sarmaya*, heelless shoes that resembled slippers more than boots.[93] For extra protection and comfort, people might resort to *mast* (or *mazd*), leather wrappings that rose above the ankles and took the place of socks, which were not introduced into Syria until the nineteenth century.

Some shoes seem to have been clearly identified as feminine. Thin slippers for the house (*tarlik*) appeared mostly in the estates of women and were presumably judged unfit for men. Exuding the same lack of masculinity were elevated clogs (*qabqab*) which, cheap and rather plain, were made from wood. "All the women and small children of Damascus wear clogs at home," and wooden shoes were an essential part of the equipment of bathhouse attendants, who worked in a perpetually damp environment. Many of the poor also preferred clogs during the rainy season, when they offered protection from the mud and filth of the streets.[94] Perhaps for this reason, the qabqab were viewed as rather plebian objects. Upon discovering his Damascene wife in a pair of clogs, the warlord al-Jazzar was reputed to have exclaimed (in the secondhand account of an English traveler), "Are you the wife of an Arabian [*sic*] peasant? Do you forget that you are the wife of a pasha?"[95] Utility seems to have triumphed over image. His wife, as it turns out, was the daughter of Muhammad Pasha al-ʿAzm, a long-time governor of Damascus, and would have needed no initiation into the niceties of fashion. And as probate inventories repeatedly demonstrate, wealthy women had no discernible prejudice against clogs regardless of their humble connotations.

Shoes were simply not that central to the prevailing code of fashion. In contrast to the wide range of outer garments, which were the most visible and expressive items in the wardrobe, they seem to have possessed a relatively functional quality, and as a general rule were cheap and plentiful. The shops of shoemakers (*qawwaf*) tell an interesting story. Unlike many artisans, who feared sudden economic downturns and warily minimized their stocks, they tended to keep relatively large quantities of shoes on hand.[96] Their trade offered a cheap, easily manufactured commodity that met a steady demand and was not likely to sit long on shelves. Shoes very much fit this description in suffering rapid wear and tear. Buyers were constantly coming for replacements, which were available at very affordable prices, typically well under one piaster. Long before the ravenous consumerism of modern times, some goods were clearly more disposable than others.

This is really saying something because, for most Damascenes, clothes were assets as much as necessities, investments as much as adornments, and could not be lightly discarded.[97] Even the cheapest garments could represent a sizable purchase, especially at the lowest rungs of the economic scale. Shirts, pants, undergarments, and belts were generally the most affordable items; standard varieties were priced at roughly one to one and a half piasters. Among the poorest of the poor, one of these basic pieces of clothing might nonetheless consume up to 5 percent of annual earnings. Mid-range clothing required a more serious decision about household resources. A simple cloak could easily cost between three and five piasters—sometimes putting it at more than 10 percent of disposable income. More luxurious apparel naturally fetched prohibitive prices, which in the eyes of an ordinary consumer could represent a once-in-a-lifetime purchase. As families grew larger, the potential budgetary strains can easily be imagined.

Given the obvious value of the most ordinary garments, prominent townspeople won much credit for making donations to the poor, for whom the expenses of a wardrobe posed a difficult burden. It was a meritorious act which fell under the category of religious alms and thereby fulfilled an obligation incumbent upon all good Muslims. Hamza al-Dumi, a noted scholar, earned praise not only for making the pilgrimage twice, but for distributing gifts, including hundreds of shirts and shoes, to the needy of Mecca and Medina.[98] As governor, Nasuh Pasha dispensed largesse on an incomparably grander scale. In addition to charity for the Holy Cities, he showered funds on Damascene mosques, religious schools, and scholars. His munificence even touched ordinary townspeople. During a dramatic tour of the markets in 1714, he handed out a gold coin to every artisan and shopkeeper and, accompanied by pack animals, gave away shoes and clothing to the poor, most notably to children whom he encountered in the streets.[99] Even in the obvious service of power, such extravagance was bound to win public approbation.

The authorities were quick to appreciate the symbolic uses of clothing. In official circles, new appointees might receive ceremonial robes. The act passed into ordinary language, allowing chroniclers to refer to governors who "dressed" (labbasa) their nominees for formal posts.[100] Among the most frequent targets of these gifts were leading ulama, who wielded considerable prestige and influence, both as local notables in their own right and no less significantly as the voice of Islam, which conferred legitimacy on power. After his first Friday prayer as governor (1714), Yusuf Pasha Topal bestowed a cloak of purple wool on the chief preacher at the Umayyad Mosque, while not forgetting to offer "customary" gifts to the muezzins.[101] These lavish gestures, transmitted in so much fabric and thread, were bound to impress their audience, which understood the value of fine clothes.

Such signals were hard to miss. Townspeople felt few inhibitions against displays of status and wealth, and were often inclined to flaunt what they had, particularly during holidays, feasts, and celebrations. As late as the opening of the twentieth century, people often chose these special occasions to bring out new clothes or show off the finest items in their wardrobe.[102] Urban culture was largely unmarked by the gnawing anxieties about material indulgence that bedeviled many consumers in early modern Europe. Few people considered living like Abu Yazid al-Halabi, who wore the same shirt for twelve straight years without removing it.[103] He needs to be classed among a small number of spiritual adepts, practicing an austere regimen of fasting and solitary meditation and turning their backs on the temptations of the material world. Within the larger social order, shows of strict piety were never sufficient to recast popular tastes. These ideals were admired, but not widely emulated.

The impulse to display was thwarted only by fear of official fines and depredations. Most vulnerable were the city's non-Muslims, whose position as a religious minority made them occasional prey to grasping officials and soldiers. So as not to advertise their wealth, some families resorted to the expedient of concealing it within their homes. The main beneficiaries of this self-imposed modesty were non-Muslim women. Deprived of the opportunity to flaunt their own wardrobes, affluent Christians and Jews showered their wives and daughters with precious clothes and jewels, which could be safely worn within the family circle or under the cover of voluminous wraps in the streets.[104] Through such stratagems, they were able to satisfy a taste that was, at least for a time, inadvisable to indulge in public. Yet Muslims were not necessarily immune to these extortions, either, especially during prolonged periods of political violence and flux. As Janissary factions openly battled on the streets in 1804, many affluent Damascenes began to wear plainer clothing simply to escape the notice of rapacious troops, who were roaming neighborhoods at will and terrorizing the civilian population.[105] Styles which in earlier times had proudly announced high status now invited unpleasant harassment. We should not, however, make too much of these passing disturbances, which, apart from reinforcing a certain wariness towards the state and its agents, did little to dampen popular exuberance in personal dress.

Even in the eighteenth century, before the rise of mass consumerism, Damascenes had very definite notions of taste and style. All these preferences ultimately constituted a sense of fashion whose significance was not merely aesthetic, but intensely social as well, for fashion was not, and never has been, egalitarian. Different combinations of fabric, color, pattern, texture, and workmanship acted as an intricate semaphore of power, rank, and self-image. All clothes (and by extension, their wearers) took their place in a hierarchy that everyone recognized and the market constantly reaffirmed. These gradations of taste and affectation were most visible, of course, among the affluent, who had the means to indulge their fancies. But traces can be found even at the bottom of the economic scale, where people had to make their choices count.

The most desirable qualities could be very subtle. Rich and poor wore roughly the same kinds of clothes, from shirts and pants to cloaks and belts, all of which adhered to the same basic cut and design. There were no brand names which might lure consumers and confer prestige on certain shops and artisans over others. Nor did artisans, in any noticeable way, try to distinguish themselves from their competition by regularly perfecting or promoting new designs and styles, which seem to have evolved with no great urgency. One finds nothing like the "fashion dolls" (sometimes of life-sized proportions) which annually made their way from Paris to English towns in the eighteenth century so that consumers across the Channel could follow all the latest fads and styles and adjust their wardrobes with timely purchases.[106] The very idea of sales promotions was alien to the commercial culture of Ottoman towns, where artisans generally had to answer to watchful guilds. Fashion had not yet become frenetic.

Even without such intensive commercialization, Damascene consumers were able to draw on fashion systems of very diverse origin. Place of manufacture could make a big difference in the value of a garment. But tracking this sense of discernment is another matter. Due to the usual difficulties in reading documents, which are quite taciturn about these points, it is often impossible to tell where particular pieces of clothing were actually made. And when geographical labels were attached, these might just as easily refer to a certain style or pattern, known throughout the region and copied in local workshops. The few distinctions which emerge from the probate lists are nonetheless instructive. Not surprisingly, long-distance imports won great admiration. Indian shawls and belts commanded high prices and seem to have occupied a relatively small and privileged niche.[107] Conspicuous in their absence were European textiles. By the late eighteenth century, French cloth had begun to make inroads among upscale consumers in Cairo,[108] the largest Arab emporium of the eastern Mediterranean, but had apparently not gained much of a footing in the Syrian interior. European domination of these markets, led by British merchants and the immense output of their mechanized factories, would have to wait until the middle decades of the nineteenth century. In the meantime, Ottoman centers of production such as Salonika, celebrated for its woolen manufactures, continued to attract an appreciative clientele. Closer to home, textiles arrived from regional workshops in towns such as Nablus and Hama, which were renowned for their fine belts.[109] But most production came out of Damascus itself, whose textile industry was largely self-sufficient and handled every level of operations. It was by far the city's largest employer, and stood out as one of the chief pillars of the urban economy.

A more reliable indicator of fashion was the quality of material in clothing. It is true that design and color probably played a large part as well, but it is nearly impossible to reconstruct them or to recapture the exact nuances of taste that markets found most gratifying. Records pay most attention to the question of fabric, which could easily double or treble the price of a piece of clothing. Few other details provide such a predictable gauge of value and appeal.

Nothing had as complicated or storied a career as silk. In antiquity, it had been the stuff of dreams, and centuries after its diffusion throughout the medieval Middle East, it continued to epitomize opulent dress. For precisely this reason, it evoked a deep ambivalence. Islamic jurists treated it as morally dubious and declared that pure silk was strictly forbidden; they relented only for mixed weaves such as alaja, which had become fairly commonplace by the Ottoman era.[110] The marketplace paid little heed to these legal debates and apprehensions. Silk was big business, and Syria was one of the major producers within the Ottoman domains. Leading the way were the towns around Mount Lebanon—the most notable of which were Tripoli, Beirut, and Baalabek—where silk had risen to prominence in the local economy by the seventeenth century, presaging its far more dramatic expansion in the nineteenth century under the stimulus of French capital. In Aleppo, caravans from Persia brought the most precious cargoes, judged highest in quality by European traders such as the factors of the British Levant Company. By the 1740s, however, this long-distance commerce had fallen into a deep crisis. Two decades of intermittent warfare along the Ottoman-Persian frontier had driven prices to exorbitant levels, and the gradual collapse of central authority inside Iran doomed any prospects for a recovery for the remainder of the century.[111] Unattached to these international networks, artisans in Damascus seem to have been relatively unaffected, and may have participated in the broader expansion of silk production which occurred throughout most of the Ottoman Empire over the eighteenth century. The city continued to meet its needs with regional production, which everywhere took up much of the slack.[112] On the local market, silk remained popular, often being woven into outer garments such as the 'antari, qunbaz, and karmasutiyya. Other materials might be produced with variants such as zarkash (silk stitched with silver thread). Demand came not merely from the wealthy, but from across the population, which meant that even relatively poor Damascenes might own one or two garments which contained a certain amount of silk. Only the purest grades, worked up as robes or scarves, would have remained entirely beyond reach. Though it retained a whiff of decadence, this ancient luxury product had, in large measure, been democratized by the eighteenth century.

Silk captured and titillated the imagination. In comparison, other materials were innocuous, respectable, even a bit pedestrian. Cotton had flourished in Syria throughout most of the Islamic period. It was a favorite of local artisans, who valued its lightness and versatility and wove it into everything from shirts and pants to cloaks and wraps. In combination with silk and wool, they used it extensively in mixed weaves, such as *alaja* and *qutniyya*, which were very popular in local markets. By Ottoman times, regional output had grown to such a magnitude that cotton became a major export, particularly in parts of northern Syria and Palestine, which sent their harvests to markets throughout the Ottoman Empire and as far abroad as Western Europe.[113] Less frequently mentioned was flax, one of the most affordable fibers. Regular imports came from Egypt, where it was grown and processed nearly everywhere, from Delta ports such as Rosetta to regions farther south, above all the Fayyum oasis.[114] Spanning the widest range in prices was wool. Damascus was fortunate in having supplies so close at hand, owing to the numerous bedouin who stopped at the city during their long migrations. Blended with either silk or (more typically) cotton, wool was the indispensable basis for broadcloth (*jukh*), one of the mainstays of the eighteenth-century textile industry. Artisans wove it into sturdy cloaks and overcoats and lighter items such as pants and skullcaps. They also converted large amounts of raw wool into household furnishings such as blankets, carpets, and stuffing for pillows.[115] Fine woolens, which alone could match the appeal of silken garments, were prized for their warmth and could be quite costly. So for consumers of nearly all ranks and means, wool generated significant demand, ensuring that Damascus (as well as most of the Ottoman market) would fall somewhere between broader "Asian" patterns of consumption, which heavily favored cotton and silk, and those prevalent in Western Europe, where linens and light woolens were the norm.[116]

Without a doubt, the most valuable material used in clothing was fur. Far more than other materials, it came in a sumptuous variety, which offers proof of its place at the pinnacle of fashion. Mainly coveted for overcoats, it might be sewn in patches, sometimes in combination with other furs, or inserted as a lining. The most luxurious garments, crafted from a single large skin, might fetch as much as one hundred piasters or more—a sum exceeding the entire value of many poor estates.[117] Fur was not, however, the monopoly of any one social group. Many of the indigent were able to own at least one fur-lined garment, showing that both supply and demand must have been fairly considerable. This was possible only because of a wide-ranging selection in quality and taste. Most esteemed were fox, ermine, mongoose, marten, and sable, which were chiefly imported from the northern provinces of the Ottoman Empire or from Europe and Russia. Cheaper substitutes, available from nearby sources, made use of rabbit, squirrel, sheep, and even ordinary cat. Furriers also offered the option of "false" furs (*farwa yalanja*), which, like the real thing, covered the whole breadth of the market, from the shoddiest to the most costly imitations.

It is not difficult to understand the attraction and demand. Given the primitive heating technology of the times, clothing was the primary defense against the cold. In the depths of winter, warmth was a constant obsession, pursued in the smallest ways. It explains why furs were the garments most frequently identified as "tattered" (*kuhna*) in inventories; the owners were usually the poor, who had to take—and keep—whatever they could get. Indeed, one of the biggest advantages of the wealthy, amply borne out by their estates, was their possession of numerous furs and other heavy pieces of clothing such as cloaks made from wool and broadcloth.

By no coincidence, expensive fur was synonymous with power and wealth. Among the elite, it was one of the supreme gifts, one of the highest compliments and rewards for service, which removed all doubts about a patron's goodwill. Acknowledging the unwavering loyalty of local notables to the Ottoman dynasty during the Egyptian occupation of the city in 1771, Mustafa III issued an imperial rescript (Tk. *hatt-ı şerif*) thanking the qadi, mufti, and chief of the *ashraf* (the legally recognized descendants of the prophet Muhammad) and presenting each of them with a fur of black ermine.[118] The significance of this gift would not have been lost on the recipients. An imperial decree of 1727 had reserved ermine exclusively to members of the elite, whose privileged bonds with the Ottoman dynasty were thereby ceremonially confirmed.[119] In this eighteenth-century world of privation, which knew none of the conveniences of modern times, comfort was one of the most tangible measures of power.

More vivid, and yet more abstract, was the role of color, which spoke its own complex language of status and rank. It is difficult, however, to interpret these subtle signals because of the extreme inconsistencies in record-keeping. Few textiles were identified as having a color, and even when a piece of clothing was as plain as white or black, scribes hardly bothered to note it. Scattered references reveal only that Damascenes had at their disposal a fairly broad palette of hues: red, green, yellow, blue, gold, pink, purple, brown, and black, together with various combinations and patterns. As far as prices were concerned, no single color was especially prized; but like other strong visual cues, such as fabrics, they came almost inevitably under the scrutiny of political and religious authorities, who regarded them as markers of social boundaries conceived as eternal and immutable.

Always alert to potential transgressions, moralists treated some colors as inherently more suspect than others. Al-Nabulsi fretted that unscrupulous dyers (who typically specialized in a single color) sometimes produced red fabrics by using mixtures of blood. He accused the craftsmen of Diyarbakir of being the worst violators of this religious taboo, which classified blood as an impure substance, but conceded that guilds in other towns (and probably in Damascus itself) may have copied the technique.[120] Other ulama held strict views not only about production techniques, but about colors themselves. Following an old debate, they questioned whether men should be allowed to wear any piece of clothing containing red or yellow, regardless of the methods used by dyers. As mufti, Hamid al-ʿImadi issued a fatwa in which he attempted a compromise, disapproving of these two colors, but declining to outlaw them altogether.[121] His fellow townsmen barely took notice. Both red and yellow were extremely popular and appeared in everything from overcoats and pants to headbands and shoes.[122] Even high-ranking ulama were known to ignore these restrictions. In spite of his fatwa, al-ʿImadi himself owned two red cloaks.[123]

One color which stood beyond reproach, and thus appealed widely to the ulama, was white. As al-Qasimi noted for nineteenth-century society, many scholars made a point of wearing white turbans as a badge of identity.[124] The ultrapious, never to be outdone, preferred to dress entirely in white. Ilyas al-Kurdi, a humble and devout figure, refused to wear anything except white clothes and a turban of white wool.[125] For his own devotion to white attire, ʿAbd al-Rahman Mughayzil was remembered as "the dove" (al-hamama).[126] As a symbol of unalloyed piety and renunciation of material pursuits, whiteness reassuringly mirrored the self-image of the ulama, who naturally identified themselves with the loftiest spiritual ideals.

Among all colors, the most Islamic was green. Ceremonies and processions proclaimed their religious character in green emblems and decorations.[127] But it was really the ashraf (sing. *sharif*) who were most closely identified with this color. By virtue of their special connection with the prophet Muhammad, they alone were entitled to wrap their turbans with a green shash, which became the symbol of their venerable lineage.[128] It was an honor that they jealously guarded. Any affront to the green turban was treated as an outrage that all ashraf had to avenge. In one particularly flagrant episode in 1748, imperial Janissaries arrested a group of ashraf and had them whipped three hundred times.[129] The soldiers then deposited their victims "like corpses" in the streets and, as a crowning insult, left them with green headbands stuffed into their pants. Furious ashraf filled the streets for several days before the governor could finally restore peace through mediation. Though it was the brutal beating which had actually touched off the uprising, the soldiers' gesture with the green turbans had not gone unnoticed. Indeed, the chronicler of the event, al-Budayri, was careful to mention it as one of the main provocations. Everyone understood exactly what the act meant and why it was so inflammatory.

The use of colors was not restricted to the green of the ashraf. Religious minorities observed their own dress code, which announced religious affiliation at a glance and signaled their "protected" status. The key item of clothing was the headband in the turban. In the eighteenth century, the standard color scheme was blue for Christians and red for Jews.[130] Muslims were free to wear these colors as long as they remained faithful to their religion.[131] Mikha'il Burayk reported the scandal caused by a visitor from Homs, who walked through the streets as a member of the ashraf, but in secret professed Christianity. He used to "change his clothes"—most likely switching from Muslim to Christian colors—and come to the Greek Orthodox church, where he would pray and reassure nervous priests about the sincerity of his faith.[132]

All these laws predated Ottoman rule, which had inherited them from early Islamic history. Throughout the long centuries, enforcement had varied from one period to another and depended mostly on political conditions. For most of the eighteenth century, it seems to have been quite lax. Mikha'il Burayk remembered the rule of As'ad Pasha al-'Azm (r. 1743–57) as a particularly tolerant time, when Christians could don any color except green. He also went on to mention that some Christian women openly ignored this restriction, wearing jackets of broadcloth and wool dyed in this most Islamic color.[133] The policies were not consistent. In fact, the authorities might periodically redefine the dress code according to their whims. Rumelian soldiers, pouring into Damascus in response to Napoleon's invasion of Syria in 1799, demanded that Jews swath their turbans in black like the Christians.[134] Soon afterwards, in 1807, Genç Yusuf Pasha launched his infamous campaign to promote public morality. Among other measures, he forbade non-Muslims from raising their voices in the streets and applied the old version of the color scheme: Jews were told to wear red again, but Christians kept their original black.[135] He made a great show of upholding the Islamic sartorial order and punishing violations. To demonstrate his firmness, he detained three Lebanese Christians who had been found wearing green belts. Despite their protests that it was the custom of their homeland, he gave them a choice between death or conversion to Islam. Two chose to save their necks; the other was beheaded.[136] Without a doubt, this severity was extremely unusual in the annals of Ottoman rule, but other provisions of the restored dress code seem to have persisted for decades. Visiting in the 1830s, de Lamartine noted that his ragged Armenian guide had to wear a black turban, "as all the Christians at Damascus are obliged to do."[137] Many of these restrictions had softened or disappeared altogether by the end of the nineteenth century, mostly as a result of Ottoman reforms which, in theory, had promised equality to non-Muslims. But even at this late date, local inhabitants were still aware of differences in dress between Muslims and religious minorities.[138] In fixing social identity, nothing could communicate as discreetly or instantaneously as the color of a turban or belt.

ANOTHER LESSON IN LOCALISM

The regulation of fashion was by no means peculiar to the Ottoman world. In medieval and early modern Europe, for example, vestimentary laws were practically universal until the nineteenth century and lost their relevance only in the great social and economic transformations of the modern period. Like their European counterparts, the Ottomans were sensitive to shifts in fashion, which seemed to erode imaginary boundaries between social groups and invite challenges to established authority.

One early round of regulation took place in the late sixteenth century, as the empire came under numerous military, financial, and administrative stresses. After a respite of nearly one hundred fifty years, Ottoman interest in clothing seemed to intensify again in the eighteenth and early nineteenth centuries. The first flurry of renewed legislation dated to the 1720s, and apparently came in reaction to wealthy Istanbul ladies who had begun to imitate non-Muslim fashions. The prohibitions had a primarily moral character: restraining lavish spending, fighting corruption, and containing new patterns of consumption which undermined traditional habits of dress. In the late eighteenth century, official attention turned to economic considerations. The state began to punish members of the elite for excessive consumption of foreign fabrics. Most disturbing was the suspected popularity of Persian and Indian garments, which were feared as a challenge to domestic industry. Donald Quataert has interpreted this eighteenth-century burst of sartorial decrees as a bid to shore up Ottoman legitimacy. It was a period which witnessed major setbacks for the empire's arms and prestige. In pressuring subjects to conform to an official dress code, the state saw itself as upholding a just and eternal social order.[139]

Did the provincial administration follow the same rhythms in regulating clothing? Local chronicles report few such proclamations. When officials bothered to issue restrictions, their concerns had to do mostly with perceived transgressions in women's fashion. One governor (1694–95) formally forbade women from wearing a certain kind of *taqiyya*, which was the "size of a tray" (and apparently imitated those worn by local paramilitary gangs). Shoring up well-known gender distinctions, he commanded them to revert instead to the usual *qalbaq*, a tall black hat made of goat skin.[140] They seem to have complied. In the middle of the eighteenth century, the qalbaq still had a loyal following, especially among wealthy women. After this fleeting edict, more than a century passes before anything like it comes to our attention again. The silence was broken by Genç Yusuf Pasha, who tried in 1807 to prevent women from wearing jewelry and gold-embroidered fabrics, which must have seemed far too ostentatious to his puritanical eye. Jewelry was always held in high esteem, and so was gold embroidery, which might raise the value of a shirt, cloak, or kerchief as much as ten times. Damascenes apparently did not share the governor's alarm over these adornments. The decree, like many others issued at this time, aroused quiet opposition, and was eventually repealed after a committee of ulama persuaded the governor that he had exceeded the proper bounds of Islamic law.[141]

Genç Yusuf's social legislation, which went beyond clothing, was far more radical than anything introduced by his predecessors. Most striking is its timing, which, like the sartorial regulations of the central state, coincided with a period of deep social and political crisis. By the first decade of the nineteenth century, the Wahhabis were raiding from the south into the Ghuta and had captured the Holy Cities, preventing the pilgrimage caravan from entering for nearly a decade. The economic consequences were extremely disruptive. Prices quickly jumped to new heights, and business slowed. Not to be deprived of his usual revenues, the governor continued to collect taxes for pilgrimage escorts that never left the city, began hoarding grain, and went on to establish, in 1810, an unprecedented monopoly on the production of soap.[142] As the city came under these unusual economic and political stresses, his campaign acted symbolically to reinforce the social order, reminding townspeople, especially subordinate groups, of their assigned place and rank, and soothing disgruntled opinion with appeals to Islamic morality and displays of public piety. So legal trends can be identified for Istanbul, and perhaps the core provinces of the empire as well; but if Damascus is typical of other Arab towns, more distant provincial centers must have responded to their own anxieties and social pressures, which could easily assert themselves in entirely different cycles. The localism which was so visible in economic and cultural life had its parallel in the legal and administrative affairs of the empire, which was too vast and unwieldy to be bound together by a single, internally consistent set of edicts and policies.

The point is not that "Ottoman"—or, for that matter, "Islamic"—sartorial ideals were irrelevant. Townspeople in Damascus and elsewhere in the Ottoman Middle East were very conscious of official styles and hierarchies in clothing. In accounting for all the persistent variations, two important qualifications need to be kept in mind. The first is that less privileged social groups constantly sought to align themselves with general standards of taste and deportment and, in moments of official inattention, to appropriate symbols of high status. The other is that, from one place to the next, the dress code was very much subject to local inflections and interpretations, which ensured uneven application throughout the wider Ottoman and Islamic dominions. The resulting distortions were perhaps inevitable, for eighteenth-century material culture was incapable of absolute uniformity, which never existed beyond the pages of administrative manuals and law books.

CONCLUSION

A T FIRST GLANCE, THE EIGHTEENTH CENTURY SEEMS to have offered nothing new or unfamiliar to the residents of Ottoman Damascus. One cannot point to any major innovation which would have marked a memorable turning point in their daily routines. Nearly everywhere one looks, an overwhelming continuity reigned: in dietary regime, sartorial tastes and fashions, infrastructure, and architectural design and interior decoration, all of which would have been fully recognizable to their parents and grandparents. The world of physical things and mental expectations was quite stable—not rigid and inflexible, as it might first seem, but very loyal to old habits and preferences.

For this reason, the eighteenth century can more accurately be characterized as a time of consolidation, not innovation. The most dramatic breakthroughs in Ottoman material culture had undoubtedly come earlier, in the form of coffee and tobacco, which had quickly entrenched themselves and seduced adherents from across the population. Perhaps more revolutionary than either of these commodities alone was the six-teenth-century advent of the coffeehouse, which, with the partial excep-tion of the tavern, had no precedent in the regional culture. One author has gone so far as to treat the coffeehouse as one of main harbingers of modernity in the Middle East, opening up an entirely new and public domain for sociability.[1] The eighteenth century merely built on these earlier advances and more fully routinized them. Opponents might still denounce coffee and tobacco, which were no longer so novel and shock-ing, but their hostility had clearly retreated to the margins of mainstream opinion, which was unwilling to forgo its newfound pleasures. The cof-feehouses stayed open, and coffee drinking and smoking had, by this time, evolved into utterly ordinary pastimes. After the furor of the initial controversies, this quiet acceptance was an unsung achievement which is all too easy to underestimate.

These successes did not occur in isolation, but as part of a rising trade in luxury goods which was making progress on a worldwide scale. In various parts of Western and Mediterranean Europe, where the new trends were most pronounced, the seventeenth and eighteenth centuries brought not only coffee and tobacco, but tea, sugar, and chocolate (origi-nally drunk as a beverage) to growing numbers of consumers. Even if all these imports first made their mark as luxuries, not yet qualifying before the nineteenth century as articles of mass consumption, their significance was far reaching for both economy and culture. Speaking of early mod-ern Britain, one historian has hailed the popularization of new foods and drugs as "the most striking development in consumer buying," far over-shadowing shifts in other spheres of demand.[2] In much of Western Eu-rope and colonial North America, affluent consumers were slowly eating and drinking their way towards a modern consumer culture.

In contrast to Western Europe, the Ottoman world had to content itself with only coffee and tobacco. Were these two newcomers, even if offering a narrower range of choices, able to remake Ottoman consumer culture in the same way? So novel were these products, and so complete and seem-ingly irresistible their victory, that some historians have indeed begun to discuss the possibility of an Ottoman "consumer revolution," launched from coffee pots and tobacco pipes. But before the banner can be raised, and the Ottoman Middle East proclaimed among the early frontiers of modern consumerism, basic questions have to be resolved. Setting aside cultural factors which would explain the huge popularity of coffee drinking and smoking, we still do not understand something as simple as the way in which people paid for these new diversions. Were households, as Donald Quataert has suggested,[3] simply working harder for extra income, in an "industrious revolution" concurrent with that proposed for early modern Europe? The hypothesis is intriguing but, like its European progenitor, faces numerous difficulties. Perhaps most frustrating is the task of counting work hours and measuring the intensity of labor in premodern populations, which, as nearly all historians concede, followed more irregular and cyclical work schedules. For early modern Europe itself, empirical research has so far produced mixed results, which have indicated marginal or rather late gains in productivity.[4] Beyond these attempts at rough calculations, the argument has rested mainly on indirect evidence about values, customs, and material possessions. One clue is the emergence of an increasingly diverse and affluent material culture, extending even to parts of the early modern countryside. Another is the spread of a new sense of time throughout the most advanced economies, such as eighteenth-century England. People were becoming more meticulous about counting time and acquiring sterner attitudes about leisure. Among the working classes, many were simply compelled to work harder and longer, according to fixed hours. In their grinding toil, the modern work day was beginning to take shape.

Were comparable trends taking place in the eighteenth-century Middle East? Having confined itself to a single town, this study cannot furnish much evidence about the material culture of peasants, which is surely one of the critical tests of any thesis about an industrious revolution. It can only talk reliably about the urban environment, where its findings, however, raise doubts about potential parallels with northwestern Europe. If Damascus was representative of other Ottoman towns, no new notions of time were beginning to take root. Urban culture showed no interest in more precise methods of timekeeping, and produced little rhetoric that might betray an obsession with greater diligence, punctuality, and self-discipline. One index for this new sensibility was ownership of personal watches, which, in Damascus, was restricted mainly to affluent townspeople, who kept them for ornamental uses. The general population had no practical need for them, and began no noticeable reorganization of their working habits. Nowhere do we hear of the loss of holidays or other forms of customary leisure. The cultural indicators of a more industrious economy, insofar as they can be glimpsed, would seem to have gained no new ground.

It seems improbable, moreover, that coffee and tobacco, or any other tandem of commodities, could launch such a dramatic cultural transformation by themselves. Even in Western Europe, increased consumption never revolved exclusively around luxury items. It penetrated and stimulated the lower ends of the marketplace as well. In places like eighteenth-century Paris, consumers acquired a passion for what one historian has branded "populuxe goods"—cheap imitations of upper-class ornaments and accessories sold to an eager public that wished to seem more refined and sophisticated. Shops began to offer an array of fans, snuffboxes, umbrellas, stockings—petty commodities which were easy to produce and yet carried a touch of aristocratic cachet.[5] At the same time, in England, consumers were beginning to buy household goods such as tableware, mass-produced pottery, and heavy furniture on an unprecedented scale. Demand surged mainly from the urban "middle ranks," at whom these products were explicitly aimed. More than a binge of eager spending, their behavior revealed a very new outlook. As one historian has put it, they showed a full-blown "acceptance of modernity," whose most distinctive characteristic was an open embrace of novelty and experimentation for their own sake.[6]

In Damascus, economic culture was less adventurous. A deeply rooted conservatism—not to be confused with immobility—sought its most cherished models and ideals in past generations and regarded tradition (or whatever passed for tradition) as the ultimate arbiter of value and taste. Damascenes liked to imagine that they lived just as their ancestors had—and indeed as people everywhere, at all times, had. In reality, this fidelity to the past was never absolute or unshakable; given the right incentives, townspeople could quietly assimilate new goods, tastes, and habits. ʿAbd al-Ghani al-Nabulsi once found it necessary to remind his readers that nearly all the clothing of their generation departed in some way from the example of the prophet Muhammad. He quickly explained that none of these deviations were wrong or immoral in themselves, and that innovation was objectionable only when it contravened the precepts of the Islamic faith.[7] And yet one cannot mistake the suspicion and faint sense of danger which continued to cling to the word. In principle, innovations were greeted with mistrust and misgiving, as potential departures from the one true path, and had to be evaluated with great care. Thus novelty might prove acceptable, but was not automatically charged with positive meaning or the allure of fresh thinking and experience. Only after acquiring the patina of religious tradition, recalling the wisdom of time immemorial, might new usages take their place, unchallenged, in local culture. No social group rose to question these comfortable values. "Middling" consumers, though not absent in Damascus, did not stand out in any discernible way and seem not to have generated their own distinctive class of goods.[8]

In view of all these difficulties, one might justifiably wonder whether simpler factors could explain how Damascenes successfully adopted coffee and tobacco. Might the supply side have something to say? One look at coffee and tobacco shows that both held steady in their respective price ranges from the late seventeenth to the late eighteenth century (before the onset of intense inflation throughout the entire Ottoman Empire). This stability is all the more impressive when set against bread, which doubled in price over the same period, or meat, which increased tenfold. Even if productivity in towns like Damascus was somehow climbing, the proportion of household expenses set aside for recreations like coffee and tobacco would have actually been falling. One can only surmise that supplies were expanding, or at least keeping pace with demand. The reasons are not hard to find. Both commodities were grown within the Middle East itself. Tobacco had been domesticated throughout several parts of the region by the late seventeenth century and was plentiful in local markets. The coffee trade had gotten its start along the Red Sea, and by the middle of the eighteenth century was receiving cheap imports from the New World, which further held down prices. One might, for good measure, challenge the foundations of the argument altogether and ask whether urban households had ever had much trouble affording these goods. To take coffee: was it a coincidence that it entered the diet on the heels of the fifteenth-century crisis in the Middle Eastern sugar industry? Did Middle Eastern consumers, deprived of one luxury product, opportunistically switch to another? The question is worthy of closer examination, together with the possibility that people simply tightened their belts and spent less on food and other necessities.

A much longer perspective on the arrival of coffee and tobacco would certainly be useful. We should remember that these breakthroughs in Ottoman material culture followed earlier waves of imports and innovations which were no less profound in reshaping Middle Eastern culture. Within the Islamic period, the original Arab conquests, starting in the seventh century, had created a political and economic zone of unprecedented dimensions, intensifying commercial contacts across much of Eurasia. These exchanges soon unleashed what one historian has called the "green revolution" of the early medieval period.[9] New plants and fibers were brought from the eastern reaches of the Islamic world and found a ready reception throughout the Middle East. By the eleventh century, silk and cotton had completely reordered the region's textile industry, leading to the wholesale replacement of the rough linen and hemp garments in which the region had formerly clothed itself. As part of the same migration, foods of entirely foreign provenance—most noticeably rice, eggplant, spinach, and sugar—established themselves, to one degree or another, in the Middle Eastern diet and agrarian order. Were the economic and cultural implications of these new commodities any less "revolutionary" than the later reactions to coffee and tobacco? In the end, it may be better to treat the Ottoman period as the final stage in a long and irregular series of premodern innovations that followed the formation and growth of new commercial networks. These advances, in turn, were made possible by the expansion and consolidation of huge empires straddling several continents. Gradually reshaping notions of luxury and taste, the new commodities may have stimulated not so much a consumer revolution as an uneven "evolution" in material culture, full of little shifts and accelerations, together with occasional setbacks, over many long centuries.

Perhaps the greatest imprint that Ottoman rule left on consumer culture was not so much an increase in the range of available goods as in aggregate levels of demand. Throughout the Middle East, the long Ottoman peace brought several generations of economic growth and security. With varying degrees of intensity and success, the empire integrated regional markets which, in earlier times, had been divided, contested, or stunted. In Syria and elsewhere, it oversaw a pronounced expansion in urban population and trade. The biggest beneficiaries were undoubtedly members of the urban elite. As recent scholarship has demonstrated, a great deal of wealth had begun to accumulate in the provinces by the beginning of the eighteenth century, if not sooner, both following and hastening the decentralization of power within the empire. One outcome of this process, which had parallels throughout much of early modern Asia, is that urban notables were able to convert their growing resources into impressive purchasing power.[10] In Damascus, they seemed to relish demonstrations of magnificence, regarding them both as a perquisite of power and a necessary bulwark to their social standing. They eagerly staged lavish banquets, picnics, and entertainments for one another. The wealthiest grandees deliberately drew attention to themselves for acts of charity and generosity, offering relief for the poor or undertaking projects for the benefit of the public. The admiration of contemporaries always increased with the scale of the gesture, whether it was hundreds of loaves of bread at a banquet, hundreds of shirts donated to the poor, or a new minaret adorning a local mosque.

By the eighteenth century, this extravagance seemed to be acquiring a new urgency. It certainly caught the attention of contemporaries such as Ahmad al-Budayri, who found it noteworthy precisely because it seemed so novel. In 1743, Sulayman Pasha al-ʿAzm sponsored public celebrations upon the occasion of his son's circumcision. He decorated the markets and arranged for seven days and nights of singing, dancing, and other amusements. On the final day, he staged a mass circumcision for poor youths and, as an act of almsgiving, showered two gold coins and a new garment on each boy. The proceedings then culminated with the distribution of food to the "high and low, poor and unfortunate." But what made the event truly extraordinary was the rapid response of his rival, Fathi al-Daftari, the city's treasurer, who was determined not to be outdone. That very same month, he put together a week of revelry in honor of his daughter's marriage.[11] Even more shocking was another episode, in 1747, in which the chief administrator of the Umayyad Mosque held an enormous feast upon the marriage of his daughter and went so far as to illuminate nearby markets and the minarets of the mosque. Public opinion was taken aback by the magnitude of the festivities, which were unprecedented for a person of his position.[12] Was this negative reaction nothing more than a perception of decadence, which common townspeople like al-Budayri may have been all too eager to attribute to the social elite? Perhaps, but such excessive displays of power and wealth also coincided with a marked rise in social and political competition, which had become quite noticeable by the mid-eighteenth century. The splendor of banquets and celebrations may be taken as a subtle measure of change in the provincial political order, which was invisibly realigning itself, elevating local notables to a new prominence that everyone, for the first time, was beginning to see and understand. The urban landscape itself left little doubt about this massive redistribution of resources. The city underwent a building boom in the eighteenth century that left behind an architectural legacy as distinguished as that from any part of the city's medieval past.[13]

The ascendancy of the notables did not, however, imply an ineluctable fraying of the Ottoman order, which, even at its most trying moments, continued to reach deep into provincial society. Consumer culture helps to clarify the essentially Ottoman framework in which economic life unfolded, for the larger distribution of wealth and opportunity was very much bound up with political status. In Damascus, these advantages appeared most notably in the spending and affluence of the "Ottoman class." In the early days of Ottoman rule, these Damascenes must have formed a fairly compact group within local society, not extending beyond the immediate servants of the state. Membership later broadened and ramified into the local population and, in the process, lost much of its military relevance. By the eighteenth century, the old Ottoman service class had evolved into what was, in effect, an Ottoman entitlement class.

The economic benefits accruing to this group were widely coveted. With their official honors and exemptions, 'askari Damascenes tended to hold greater wealth or enjoy more direct access to prized consumer goods. Some in this category truly qualified as members of the urban elite; but for many others of humbler rank and fortune, the most token affiliation with the state was no less capable of delivering material benefits, which, in the smallest ways, made for a better lifestyle. Most telling was the security and variety of their diet. One need only think of ordinary soldiers' superior access to grain, meat, and recreational luxuries such as coffee. Their choices were quite deliberate and had as much to do with the quest for greater comfort and nourishment as the broader motivation to control resources and accumulate wealth. In the hands of the Ottoman class, state privileges could serve essentially consumerist ends.

As townspeople understood, such privileges also offered valuable insurance against economic instability and predatory speculation. Political decentralization during the eighteenth century fomented local rivalries and opened the door wider to military and political interference in the marketplace. As factionalism intensified, so too did the insecurity of ordinary consumers. In the case of Damascus, it is enough to consider the fate of the grain and meat trades, where officials and other big dealers (most of whom had 'askari status) had a freer hand in bending rules and regulations to their own purposes. And Damascus was hardly an aberration. In eighteenth-century Cairo, for example, this interference was, if anything, more extreme and extortionate. As André Raymond has shown in great detail, the Janissaries derived most of their wealth from the double-edged exploitation and "protection" of the urban economy, where they obtained lucrative tax farms and customs offices, seized a percentage of registered inheritances, and brought important guilds under their control.[14]

If trade and production bowed to weighty military and political interests, at least in large Ottoman towns,[15] patterns of consumption were no more immune to the very same pressures. Urban material culture was thus inescapably tied to questions of political economy. To understand the flow of goods—particularly of the most select goods—one must first trace out all the different forms of political leverage that were available to households. Best prepared for this competition were members of the Ottoman class, who automatically qualified for state tax exemptions and, as yet another advantage, were far more likely than other townspeople to reap the rewards of service or clientage in political networks. As the bearers of these key contacts and entitlements, 'askari Damascenes inevitably took their place as favored consumers within the urban economic order.

It seems highly unlikely, however, that their preeminence as consumers led to a wider redefinition of consumer culture. Throughout the urban population, the deep structures of demand, which summed up all the constraints and exigencies faced by ordinary households, were very slow to change. Whatever new habits Damascenes might have acquired by the eighteenth century, their overriding concerns remained food and drink, which were mirrored in the very possessions that they kept. These priorities are easy to understand. Many households lived at or near the level of subsistence, husbanding their wealth for day-to-day expenses—mostly on food. In comparison, everything else seemed an afterthought, a secondary outlay whose wisdom and necessity had to be carefully weighed against family resources. In the contemporary Arab world, these habits of the hearth have not entirely faded away. One can still catch glimpses of this

older and poorer lifestyle in the spending patterns of working-class families, who, in cities like Cairo, set aside roughly three-fifths of their income
for food.[16] For eighteenth-century households, disposable income must
have been at least as small. With what remained, preferences were fairly
consistent. Clothing and other textiles, which comprised most household
furnishings, took second place. Ranking a distant third were metal and
wooden objects, most of which, as further proof of basic priorities, were
connected with cooking and eating. This hierarchy of material life was by
no means confined to the Ottoman Middle East. In the few household
budgets that historians have been able to reconstruct from eighteenth-
century Europe, for example, food always represented over half, sometimes as much as three-quarters, of all expenditures; and when people
had extra money, they were heavily inclined to lavish it on their diets.[17]

People were constantly thinking and talking about food. It was an
obsession that inserted itself into all manner of conversation and correspondence and silently hung over all other affairs. When Muhammad
Tabi'a al-Dimashqi, a religious scholar, set out for Istanbul, he instructed
a friend to keep him informed about recent openings at local mosques
and madrasas; while he stayed in the imperial capital, he could then apply to officials and patrons on the spot. His friend badly disappointed
him. Instead of writing about jobs and vacancies, he used every letter to
ramble on about the local price of bread and other foods. These aimless
jottings so infuriated Muhammad that, upon his return to Damascus, he
took his revenge by composing sarcastic verses about his friend's stupid-
ity.[18] The story, for all its amusing touches, reminds us that the people of
the eighteenth century were endlessly preoccupied with these basic indicators. What was the price of bread? How were other prices responding
to this telltale benchmark? What would the harvest bring in the spring?
These were not idle questions. One bad year was enough to push many
households to the brink of ruin. The economy was prey to a wide range of
disruptions for which there were no truly effective defenses. The ravages
of epidemics, violent weather, and other natural disturbances were grim
facts of life, to which one could easily add the social and political turmoil
that periodically beset the city. Perhaps we can now begin to understand
the wild rumors which were swirling through the streets of Damascus
throughout 1741, a time of high prices.[19] It was said that the end of the
world was approaching. Great earthquakes would devastate the land, men

would turn into women, and—in one of the most revealing visions—the rivers would bear food on their waters. This last image of belated bounty, of food being carried to long-awaiting mouths, said everything about the premodern economy, in which a simple loaf of bread was an uncertain blessing, never to be taken for granted.

Though it is undoubtedly true that most years passed without major incident, and that local markets possessed considerable resilience, everyone remained fully aware of the inherent fragility of economic life. Prices and supplies could be highly variable from one year to the next, producing shocks and swings which, for most of the urban population, represented a short-term adjustment in their standard of living. In Syria and other parts of the Ottoman Middle East, these structural deficiencies persisted throughout the Ottoman period and were a hallmark of the premodern agrarian economy. Well into the early twentieth century, the cost of bread remained probably the single most reliable indicator of social and economic conditions. As late as the French Mandate, a bad harvest and its attendant economic downturn helped to ignite the Great Revolt (1925–27), and later precipitated the crisis which resulted in the stillborn Franco-Syrian Treaty of 1933.[20] Each of these upheavals was, in part, a lingering remnant of an ancien regime whose limitations and inadequacies were not fully redressed until after the Second World War.

In a society susceptible to sudden fluctuations in its standard of living, every expenditure carried weight and called attention to itself. In most households, every decision had to count. Every little thing had its value. People used and reused possessions such as clothes, blankets, and utensils until the objects were hopelessly worn out. Repairmen were ready to mend delicate cups and dishes made from porcelain or crystal, which, if broken, were thrown away only when it proved impossible to piece them back together. These same pressures help to explain the bustle of secondhand markets, such as the one in Suq al-Arwam, which did a thriving business in the sale of used garments during the nineteenth century.[21] The existence of this trade in the eighteenth century is confirmed in the inventories themselves, recorded at auctions in the same commercial district of the city. Even for the wealthiest estates, scribes sometimes mention items that were "tattered" (*kuhna*) and yet still managed to find buyers at auction. The reluctance to discard possessions was so powerful that many estates contained articles of clothing normally worn by the opposite sex. In an act of hard-bitten pragmatism, townspeople kept them for their financial if not personal utility, and might no doubt pass them down to relatives as timely gifts.

This frugality was integral to the urban moral code. Needless waste of the smallest things aroused horror and indignation. So sacred were the plainest morsels of food that many Damascenes observed the custom of kissing their bread prior to meals. One of the city's chief religious officials, the mufti Hamid al-'Imadi, publicly approved the practice, hastening to add that it was highly objectionable to throw bread on the ground or, even worse, to step on it.[22] The sight of spilled and discarded food was treated as an affront to the entire social order. Very much aware of this reaction, rioting imperial Janissaries pillaged the main market in al-Salihiyya in 1730 and helped themselves to an impromptu feast; they sacked the bakeries and butcher shops, and at least one band of troops was seen eating from a big pot of food in the streets. Their most impious gesture, recalling the old Janissary tradition of overturning cauldrons as a signal of revolt, was to dump out containers of olive oil, grape syrup, and spices into the streets.[23] More than a violent protest, it was a calculated act of vandalism, violating the equivalent of a taboo in a society where people were taught not to speak badly even about foods that they disliked eating.[24]

All these universal beliefs and inhibitions sprang from the same source: the ineradicable poverty and insecurity of the premodern economy, which left their mark everywhere on eighteenth-century thought and behavior. Though some authors might insist on religion as the defining feature of Middle Eastern culture, this is a highly idealized (and ideological) understanding of the past, which lays the emphasis on all the wrong places. It strips everyday experience of its gritty urgency and immersion in the demands and pressures of the moment. Townspeople were very much distracted by workaday routines, and in the midst of prayers, funerals, and other religious rituals, casually haggled, struck bargains, and prattled about their business.[25] They had other things on their mind, which continually called their thoughts back to household and marketplace, and required endless care and attention. More than religion, it was this struggle for survival and sufficiency which stood at the center of popular culture. It bred a mentality which, in coping with all the persistent challenges of premodern life, was unavoidably worldly and pragmatic.

APPENDIX A

MAJOR ARTICLES

OF FURNITURE

THE FIRST FIGURE FOLLOWING EACH ITEM ON THE LIST BELOW indicates the number of estates in the sample of one thousand that contains at least one of the article in question. The second figure, in parentheses, gives the number of these estates owned by women. The last figure, following the slash, is the total number of objects of this type found in the entire sample.

BLANKET *(lihaf)*

assorted	279(159)/636.5
silk	188(171)/720
cotton	33(31)/158
Yemeni-style	318(230)/913
tattered	56(40)/134

BOLSTER

maqʿad	140(87)/616
mindar	22(4)/115

BRAZIER

manqal	112(19)/151

BUNDLE *(buqja)*

nondescript	334(242)/501
gold-embroidered	14(13)/30
Yemeni-style	25(20)/41

CANDLESTICK

shamʿadan	281(185)/669
mishmaʿ	7(0)/23

CARPET
bisat   227(73)/469

CENSER
mibkhara   140(113)/195

CHEST
sahhara   47(6)/103
sunduq   455(302)/1026.5

CUSHION
tarraha   131(57)/259
tawati   323(236)/1049

DIVAN
takht   10(0)/30

DRAPES
burdaya   41(10)/58

FELT PIECES (libbad)
assorted   258(193)/637
Safad-style   15(15)/45
Salonika-style 14(12)/48

LANTERN
manara   25(10)/33
misbaha   24(3)/37

MAT
hasir   27(12)/62

MATTRESS (firash)
tattered   20(12)/49
Yemeni-style   82(65)/259
other   477(307)/1289

MIRROR
miraya   256(214)/309

PILLOW (mikhadda)
assorted   281(170)/1499.5
Yemeni-style   219(143)/1359
velvet   163(128)/1169

PILLOW
yastaqiyya   199(159)/729

PILLOW CASE
qalib mikhadda 47(37)/289
wajh mikhadda 90(70)/542

PRAYER RUG
sajjada   232(97)/394
kilim   7(1)/10

SHEET

milhafa   102(79)/156

sharshaf   368(279)/760

STOOL

kursi   92(65)/320

iskamla   37(5)/64

WOOLEN CARPET

tunfusa   242(190)/263

WOOLEN CLOTH

ihram   70(22)/99

MAJOR UTENSILS

FOR COOKING

AND EATING

THE FIRST FIGURE FOLLOWING EACH ITEM ON THE LIST
below indicates the number of estates in the sample of one thousand
that contains at least one of the article in question. The second figure,
in parentheses, gives the number of these estates owned by women. The
last figure, following the slash, is the total number of objects of this type
found in the entire sample.

AMPHORA
khabiyya   55(3)/594

BASIN
lakan   418(196)/729.5

BASKET
sabat   103(60)/112

BEAN ROASTER
mihmasa   36(8)/41

BOWL *(tasa)*
glass   195(175)/1719
copper   33(17)/200
with cover   12(4)/25
silver   13(9)/25
other   321(119)/832

BOWL *(zabdiyya)*
"Chinese" (sini)   203(154)/4761
Kutahya-style   46(42)/463
other   159(126)/2721

BUCKET
satl 211(54)/403.5

COFFEE POT
ibriq qahwa 284(64)/713.5

CONTAINER
ʿulba 90(44)/209

COVER FOR POT
ghita' 164(63)/414

CUP (*finjan*)
"Chinese" 84(46)/2052
Kutahya-style 28(18)/10,531
other 203(139)/3573

CUP
kasa 39(24)/372

CUP
kubbaya 26(2)/49

CUP
sharba 52(36)/127

DEEP DISH
lankari 43(16)/149

DISH (*sahn*)
"Chinese" 192(141)/4375
Kutahya-style 47(40)/542
copper 303(161)/4444
other 441(206)/5041

DISH (*tabaq*)
copper 158(42)/228
other 181(64)/1362

LARGE DISH
qabaq 69(12)/596.5

DISTILLING APPARATUS
(*karakah*) 29(2)/38

DRINKING VESSEL
mashraba 27(19)/56

FORK
shawka 20(11)/20

FRYING PAN
luhuq 153(38)/197.5

FRYING PAN			MORTAR	
miqlaya	198(55)/234.5		hawun	52(13)/59

FRYING PAN
miqlaya   198(55)/234.5

FRYING PAN
tava (Tk.)   82(10)/128

FRYING PAN
tawwaya   170(54)/229

JAR
martaban   18(7)/47

JUG
batiyya   15(4)/33
ibriq   326(164)/616

KETTLE
kukum   33(7)/39

KNEADING TROUGH
miʿjan   72(6)/85

KNIFE
sikkin   99(6)/151

LADLE
kabja   140(21)/170

MORTAR
hawun   52(13)/59

NAPKIN
futa   4(50)/158

PERFUME BOTTLE
qumqum   114(84)/183

PIPE
qasaba   25(3)/39

POT
hilla (Tk. kazan)   44(1)/82

POT
maʿun   285(81)/411.5

POT *(tanjara)*
copper   40(6)/124
with cover   54(11)/212
other   298(114)/946.5

POUCH
kis   54(9)/241

SACK			TRAY	
ʿidl	39(0)/128		*sadr*	93(44)/111

SCALE			TRAY	
mizan	76(2)/109		*sufra*	81(45)/106

SKIMMER			TRAY *(tabsiyya)*	
kafkir	125(23)/143		copper	50(27)/92
			glass	14(11)/17
			other	298(137)/561

SPOON				
máʿlaqa	40(10)/19,247			

			WASHING BOWL	
			tasht	52(35)/87

STRAINER				
misfaya	254(58)/283.5			

			WATER PIPE	
			arkila	27(0)/55

TONGS				
milqat	15(1)/24			

TOWEL	
bashkir	52(27)/96

APPENDIX C

MAJOR ARTICLES

OF CLOTHING

THE FIRST FIGURE FOLLOWING EACH ITEM ON THE LIST
below indicates the number of estates in the sample of one thousand
that contains at least one of the article in question. The second figure,
in parentheses, gives the number of these estates owned by women. The
last figure, following the slash, is the total number of objects of this type
found in the entire sample.

GARMENTS			*binish*	
ʿaba / ʿabaya	97(1)/331		red	19(0)/19
ʿantari			broadcloth	
white	62(39)/89		(*jukh*)	202(0)/510
cotton-silk			tattered	17(0)/18
(*alaja*)	83(30)/226		wool	25(0)/50
filigreed			other	316(7)/510
(*bi-ʿirq*)	27(19)/34		*dakka*	83(104)/318
tattered	26(16)/59		*dalmaya*	
colored	21(12)/101		*jukh*	24(0)/33
gold-threaded	24(24)/41		other	132(13)/164
mixed-cotton			*dishmaya*	68(63)/109
(*qutni*)	135(74)/517		*farajiyya*	4(0)/90
other	481(187)/1005			

242

farwa

squirrel	117(77)/161
tattered	133(68)/181
sheep	20(2)/24
maragha (?)	83(45)/86
fox (*nafa*)	110(7)/148
cat	99(50)/116
imitation (*yalanja*)	
	38(34)/47
other	304(113)/440

himayla	20(4)/25
irtaya	69(52)/79
içlik (Tk.)	76(17)/117
izar	70(70)/79

jubba

farwa	20(9)/24
jukh	132(9)/352
unrefined (*kham*)	39(31)/43
fox	21(0)/28
cat	38(9)/41
squirrel	51(14)/54
imitation	32(21)/44
wool	20(4)/32
other	311(108)/517

jaqshir

jukh	47(0)/89
tattered	16(0)/28
wool	17(0)/27
other	278(8)/411

jirwal	98(2)/183
jukha	96(12)/508.25
khuliyya	122(94)/236.5
kemer (Tk.)	

kemerbend (Tk.)	17(4)/21
other	59(0)/59
karamsutiyya	122(10)/219
kartukiyya	21(2)/58
libas	225(41)/503
mahrama	283(109)/1026
mihzam	177(104)/368
milaya	84(50)/130
milhafa	102(79)/156

mandil

embroidered	12(12)/26
other	112(103)/459

minshafa	188(134)/399
mast	90(61)/104
mastura	57(54)/74
qaba	45(35)/96

qaftan

gold-embroidered	
	10(9)/11
other	50(18)/204

qamis

tawny (*Tk. melez*)	27(17)/61
tattered	20(10)/46
other	579(247)/1276

qunbaz

white	14(12)/17
alaja	10(3)/21
tattered	24(16)/45
other	281(124)/523

qismaya	39(4)/52
rafiq	302(222)/696

saya

white	37(2)/62

blue	10(0)/18
other	196(26)/281
shabkan / jabkan	
jukh	26(10)/28
other	46(6)/62
shadd	26(8)/59
shintiyan	226(173)/508
sirtiyya	43(10)/86
tawila	
alaja	38(1)/55
other	102(14)/160
yan	110(54)/347
yabancı (Tk.)	18(1)/32
yağmurluk (Tk.)	37(0)/45
zunnar	
alaja	53(0)/65
with pearls	22(20)/36
gold	35(32)/38
silver	162(140)/255
Hama-style	14(0)/20
other	235(35)/526

SHOES

babuj	127(66)/140

jazma	57(1)/70
qabqab	84(72)/161
tarlik	136(133)/152

HEADGEAR/FACIAL
ORNAMENTS

fas	67(10)/172
ghitat shash	53(46)/73
hijab	7(5)/8
khimar	41(40)/51
qalbaq	96(90)/117
qawuq	277(1)/426
shal / shala	
red	17(0)/18
tattered	15(2)/22
other	246(27)/398
sha'riyya	106(100)/113
shash	
green	19(0)/38
used	43(0)/83
other	313(11)/573
taqiyya	70(7)/224.5
tarbush	86(29)/122

NOTES

INTRODUCTION

1. Ahmad Hilmi al-ʿAllaf, *Dimashq fi matlaʿ al-qarn al-ʿishrin*, ed. ʿAli Jamil Nuʿaysa (Damascus, 1976), 1.

2. See the discussion in Neil McKendrick, "The Commercialization of the Economy," in Neil McKendrick, John Brewer, and J. H. Plumb, *The Birth of a Consumer Society: The Commercialization of Eighteenth-Century England* (London, 1982), 30; Maxine Berg, "New Commodities, Luxuries, and Their Consumers in 18th-Century England," in *Consumers and Luxury: Consumer Culture in Europe, 1650–1850*, ed. Maxine Berg and Helen Clifford (New York, 1999), 64.

3. Thorstein Veblen, *The Theory of the Leisure Class*, 3rd ed. (New York, 1934); Werner Sombart, *Luxury and Capitalism*, trans. W. R. Dittmar (Ann Arbor, 1967).

4. For the seminal discussion, Jan deVries, "The Industrial Revolution and the Industrious Revolution," *Journal of Economic History* 54(1994): 249–70.

5. Daniel Roche, *A History of Everyday Things: The Birth of Consumption in France, 1600–1800*, trans. Brian Pearce (Cambridge, 2000), 54. For a similar opinion, Fernand Braudel, *The Wheels of Commerce*, trans. Sian Reynolds (New York, 1982), 177.

6. For a seminal discussion of the role of entitlements in distributing resources, especially during hard times, see Amartya Sen, *Poverty and Famines* (London: Oxford, 1981).

7. See, for example, Simon Schama, *The Embarrassment of Riches: An Interpretation of Dutch Culture in the Golden Age* (New York, 1987), esp. 290–322.

8. Craig Clunas, *Superfluous Things: Material Culture and Social Status in Early Modern China* (Urbana, 1991).

9. For a classic profile of the notables, Albert Hourani, "Ottoman Reform and the Politics of Notables," in *The Beginnings of Modernization in the Middle East: The Nineteenth Century*, ed. W. R. Polk and R. L. Chambers (Chicago, 1968), 41–68.

10. The main courthouse was located at al-Mahkama al-Kubra, inside the Madrasa al-Jawziyya in the neighborhood of al-Buzuriyya, until 1752–53. It was then transferred close by to Mahkamat al-Bab, located opposite the now-vanished

Madrasa al-Nuriyya in the southwest portion of the walled city. Brigitte Marino, *Le Faubourg du Midan à Damas à l'époque ottomane (1742–1830)* (Damascus, 1997), 30.

11. On the eighteenth-century courthouses, ʿAbd al-Karim Rafeq, "The Law-Court Registers of Damascus, with Special Reference to Craft-Corporations during the First Half of the Eighteenth Century," in *Les arabes par leurs archives*, ed. Jacques Berque and Dominique Chevallier (Paris, 1976), 143–44; Marino, *Le Faubourg*, 32–33; Linda Schatkowski Schilcher, *Families in Politics: Urban Factions and Estates of Damascus in the 18th and 19th Centuries* (Stuttgart, 1985), 116. For one other courthouse that reportedly operated into the early eighteenth century (al-Mahkama al-Bayaniyya, on the eastern end of the city near Bab Sharqi), Muhammad Khalil al-Muradi, *Silk al-durar fi aʿyan al-qarn al-thani ʿashar* (Beirut, 1988), 3:275.

12. For the "military" estates, MS, vol. 162 (covering the years 1759–67); for the "civilians," Al-mahkama al-Sharʿiyya (henceforth MS), vols. 131, 138, 143 (spread over 1750–58).

13. ʿAbd al-Karim Rafeq, "Mazahir min al-haya al-ʿaskariyya al-ʿuthmaniyya fi bilad al-sham min al-qarn al-sadis ʿashar hatta matlaʿ al-qarn al-tasiʿ ʿashar," in *Buhuth fi al-tarikh al-iqtisadi wa al-ijtimaʿi li-bilad al-Sham fi al-ʿasr al-hadith* (Damascus, 1985), 156–59; Karl Barbir, *Ottoman Rule in Damascus, 1708–1758* (Princeton, 1980), 89–93.

14. Ibn Kannan, *Al-Mawakib al-islamiyya fi al-mamalik wa al-mahasin al-shamiyya*, ed. Hikmet Ismaʿil (Damascus, 1992), 1:216–18. See also ʿAbd al-Karim Rafeq, "The Local Forces in Syria in the 17th and 18th Centuries," in *War, Technology, and Society in the Middle East*, ed. V. J. Parry and M. E. Yapp (London, 1975), 290.

15. Among the total number of estates found in the four volumes of mid-century inventories, women accounted for 44.8% (406 out of 906) among "civilians," and for 22.7% (68 out of 299) among ʿaskari Damascenes.

16. See the pointed criticism in ʿAbd al-Ghani al-Nabulsi, *Al-Hadiqa al-nadiyya: sharh al-tariqa al-muhammadiyya* (Lailbur, 1977), 2:474.

17. Al-Muradi, *Silk*, 2:309, 4:373.

18. Jan deVries, *European Urbanization, 1500–1800* (Cambridge, MA, 1984), 178.

19. In truth, we have no means of generating precise estimates of population for the eighteenth century, and have to extrapolate from various counts (usually of male taxpayers) conducted in the sixteenth and nineteenth centuries. In one survey for 1842 (closest in time to our period), the total population of the city stood at approximately 112,500; by religion, the breakdown was 84.5% (95,150) for Muslims, 11.1% (12,500) for Christians, and another 4.3% (4,850) for Jews. For a lengthy discussion of the difficulties of building estimates, Zouhair Ghazzal, *L'économie politique de Damas durant le XIXe siècle: structures traditionnelles et capitalisme* (Damascus, 1993), chap. 2.

20. Najwa al-Qattan, "*Dhimmis* in the Muslim Court: Legal Autonomy and Religious Discrimination," *International Journal of Middle East Studies* 31 (1999): 429–44.

21. On literary trends in eighteenth-century Syria, 'Anuti, *Al-Haraka al-adabiyya fi bilad al-Sham khilal al-qarn al-thamin 'ashar* (Beirut, 1970).

22. Even the unlettered recognized fatwas as legal weapons and occasionally brandished them at court. The fatwas of Ahmad al-Muhamandari, for instance, were "in circulation among the people." Al-Muradi, *Silk*, 1:187.

23. On Syrian Christian chronicles, Thomas Philipp, "Class, Community, and Arab Historiography in the Early 19th Century," *International Journal of Middle East Studies* 16(1984): 37–52.

24. See, for example, the findings of the self-proclaimed Garbage Project at the University of Arizona. Excavating modern landfills and sorting through neighborhood garbage cans, these remarkable researchers have demonstrated the clear divergence between what people say about their consumption and the patterns which emerge from the physical evidence that they leave behind. On their methods and results, William L. Rathje and Cullen Murphy, eds., *Rubbish! The Archaeology of Trash* (New York, 1992).

I. CITY AND ENVIRONMENT

1. Jean Sauvaget, "Esquisse d'une histoire de la ville de Damas," *Revue des études islamiques* 4(1934): 427.

2. Muhammad Kurd 'Ali, *Ghutat Dimashq* (Damascus, 1949), 86.

3. Muhammad Khalil al-Muradi, an eighteenth-century scholar, proudly ranked it among the four most fertile areas in the entire world. Al-Muradi, *Silk al-durar fi a'yan al-qarn al-thani 'ashar* (Beirut, 1988), 2:159. On the geographical features of the Ghuta, Kurd 'Ali, *Ghutat,* 13; Safuh Khayr, *Ghutat dimashq* (Damascus, 1957), 115–18; Anne-Marie Bianquis, "Damas et la Ghouta," in *La Syrie d'aujourd'hui,* ed. André Raymond (Paris, 1980), 363.

4. Ibn Kannan, *al-Mawakib al-islamiyya fi al-mamalik wa al-mahasin al-shamiyya,* ed. Hikmet Isma'il (Damascus, 1992), 1:394.

5. For a more detailed account of this system, Richard Thoumin, "Notes sur l'amenagement et la distribution des eaux à Damas et dans sa Ghouta," in *Bulletin d'études orientales* 4(1934): 1–26; Bianquis, "Damas et la Ghouta," 359–84; André Raymond, *Grandes villes arabes à l'époque ottomane* (Paris, 1985), 161; Nayif al-Siyagha, *Al-Haya al-iqtisadiyya fi madinat Dimashq fi muntasaf al-qarn al-tasi'ashar* (Damascus, 1995), 67–81.

6. For an eighteenth-century impression of al-Marj, Ibn Kannan, *Al-Mawakib,* 1:398.

7. Henry Maundrell, "A Journey from Aleppo to Jerusalem," in *Early Travels in Palestine,* ed. Thomas Wright (London, 1848), 485.

8. See, for example, Ibn Kannan, *Al-Muruj al-sundusiyya al-fasiha bi-talkhis tarikh al-Salihiyya*, ed. Muhammad Ahmad Dahman (Damascus, 1947), 34–35, 65–68.

9. Linda Schatkowski Schilcher, *Families in Politics: Damascene Factions and Estates in the 18th and 19th Centuries* (Stuttgart, 1985), 7.

10. During the period 1500–1800, the population of Damascus nearly doubled, rising from an original level of 50,000 to approximately 90,000. On population estimates, Schatkowski Schilcher, *Families*, 3; Antoine Abdel-Nour, *Introduction à l'histoire urbaine de la Syrie ottomane (XVIe–XVIIIe siècles)* (Beirut, 1982), 74; Zouhair Ghazzal, *L'économie politique de Damas durant le XIXe siècle* (Damascus, 1993), 45. On urban growth throughout the Arab provinces, Raymond, *Grandes villes arabes*, 57.

11. Schatkowski Schilcher, *Families*, 7; Colette Establet and Jean-Paul Pascual, *Familles et fortunes à Damas: 450 foyers damascains en 1700* (Damascus, 1994), 12.

12. R. Pococke, *A Description of the East* (London, n.d.), 118, cit. Brigitte Marino, *Le Faubourg du Midan à Damas à l'époque ottomane: espace urbain, société et habitat (1742–1830)* (Damascus, 1997), 119. On the growth of Damascus (ca. 1500–1900), Sauvaget, "Esquisse," Plates VIII and X.

13. ʿAbd al-Razzaq Moaz, "Domestic Architecture, Notables, and Power: A Neighborhood in Late Ottoman Damascus," in *10th International Congress of Turkish Art* (Geneva, 1995).

14. Marino, *Le Faubourg*, 106.

15. Elizabeth Thompson, *Colonial Citizens: Republican Rights, Paternal Privilege, and Gender in French Syria and Lebanon* (New York, 2000), 177–80.

16. Nuʿman Qasatli, *Al-Rawda al-ghannaʾ fi Dimashq al-fayhaʾ* (Beirut, 1876), 95.

17. For modern measurements, Khayr, *Ghutat*, 79–84; Abdel-Nour, *Introduction*, 251.

18. ʿAbd al-Ghani al-Nabulsi, *ʿAlam al-malaha fi ʿilm al-falaha* (Damascus, n.d.), 238.

19. Al-Muradi, *Silk*, 1:68. For another example, Ismaʿil al-Mahasini, *Safahat min tarikh Dimashq fi al-qarn al-hadi ʿashar al-hijri mustakhraja min kunnash Ismaʿil al-Mahasini*, ed. Salah al-Din al-Munajjid, in *Maʿhid al-makhtutat al-ʿarabiyya*, 6(1960): 131–32.

20. Ibn Kannan, *Yawmiyat*, 184, 471; al-Budayri, *Hawadith*, 163; Hasan Agha al-ʿAbd, *Tarikh Hasan Agha al-ʿAbd*, ed. Yusuf Nuʿaysa (Damascus, 1979), 30; al-Muradi, *Silk*, 4:98.

21. Al-Muradi, *Silk*, 4:27. See also ibid., 1:191; Muhammad al-Muhibbi, *Khulasat al-athr fi aʿyan al-qarn al-hadi ʿashar*, (Beirut, n.d.), 4:365. For other positive images of rain, ʿAbd al-Ghani al-Nabulsi, *Taʿtir al-anam fi tafsir al-ahlam*, ed. Taha ʿAbd al-Raʾuf Saʿd (Damascus, n.d.), 2:224–25.

22. Mikhaʾil Burayk, *Tarikh al-Sham*, ed. Ahmad Ghassan Sabbanu (Damascus, 1982), 100–101.

23. Al-Budayri, *Hawadith*, 85–86.

24. Ibn Kannan, *Yawmiyat*, 473; Muhammad Sa'id al-Qasimi, *Qamus al-sana'at al-shamiyya*, ed. Zafir al-Qasimi (Damascus, 1988), 216–17.

25. Raslan al-Qari, "Al-Wuzara' aladhina hakamu dimashq," in Salah al-Din al-Munajjid, ed., *Wulat Dimashq fi al-'ahd al-'uthmani* (Damascus, 1949), 89.

26. Ahmad al-Barbir, *Zahr al-ghida fi dhikr al-fida*, in Muhammad Dahman, ed., *Fi rihab Dimashq* (Damascus, 1982), 217. See also al-Budayri, *Hawadith*, 40.

27. Other major floods occurred in 1609, 1654, 1687, 1710, 1715, and 1755. Al-Muhibbi, *Khulasat*, 2:76, 4:227; al-Mahasini, *Safahat*, 89; Ibn Kannan, *Yawmiyat*, 166, 233; al-Budayri, *Hawadith*, 186.

28. For twentieth-century estimates, Sauvaget, "Esquisse," 426; Khayr, *Ghutat*, 63.

29. Burayk, *Tarikh*, 48–49; al-Budayri, *Hawadith*, 193–94. For a sixteenth-century cold snap, al-Muhibbi, *Khulasat*, 2:41.

30. Al-Mahasini, *Safahat*, 102–3.

31. Snow was recorded for 1706, 1711, 1715, 1716, 1718, 1721, 1728, 1729, 1735, 1737, 1756, 1759, 1768, 1779, and 1813. Ibn Kannan, *Yawmiyat*, 103, 184, 231–32, 249, 279, 333, 393, 398, 472, 481; al-Budayri, *Hawadith*, 188–89, 225; Burayk, *Tarikh*, 101, 119; Hasan Agha, *Tarikh*, 156.

32. Emmanuel Le Roy Ladurie, *Times of Feast, Times of Famine: A History of Climate Since the Year 1000*, trans. Barbara Bray (New York, 1971).

33. Al-Budayri, *Hawadith*, 10–11, 34, 138, 197; Burayk, *Tarikh*, 48–49, 110; Hasan Agha, *Tarikh*, 156.

34. Khayr, *Ghutat*, 80–81.

35. Burayk, *Tarikh*, 40, 86. See also Ibn Kannan, *Yawmiyat*, 299.

36. Quoted from al-Budayri, *Hawadith*, 162; see also Burayk, *Tarikh*, 44.

37. Burayk, *Tarikh*, 86.

38. Ibn Jum'a, "Al-Bashat wa al-qudat," in *Wulat Dimashq fi al-'ahd al-'uthmani*, ed. Salah al-Din al-Munajjid (Damascus, 1949), 63.

39. Muhammad al-Muhibbi, *Khulasat al-athr fi a'yan al-qarn al-hadi 'ashar* (Beirut, n.d.), 2:124–25; Ibn Jum'a, "Al-Bashat," 44, 52; Ibn Kannan, *Yawmiyat*, 138; al-Muradi, *Silk*, 3:213–15; al-Budayri, *Hawadith*, 73–74, 88–93; Burayk, *Tarikh*, 34, 118.

40. On at least one occasion, in 1682, the water was brought from a spring near Ankara, in Anatolia. For details on these rituals, al-Muhibbi, *Khulasat*, 2:124–25; al-Muradi, *Silk*, 3:213–15.

41. Al-Budayri, *Hawadith*, 89; Burayk, *Tarikh*, 34.

42. Al-Budayri, *Hawadith*, 74, 93–98.

43. 'Abd al-Ghani al-Nabulsi, *Burj babil wa shadw al-balabil*, ed. Ahmad al-Jundi (Damascus, 1988), 318; Ibn Kannan, *Yawmiyat*, 101, 197, 354, 471; al-Budayri, *Hawadith*, 180.

44. For different accounts of this earthquake, al-Qari, "Al-Wuzara'," 82; al-Budayri, Hawadith, 222–27; Burayk, Tarikh, 78–80; al-Muradi, Silk, 1:113, 3:82; Kamal al-Din al-Ghazzi, Al-Tadhkira al-musamma bi 'l-durr al-maknun wa al-jamal al-masun min fara'id al-'ulum wa fawa'id al-funun, in Fi rihab Dimashq, ed. Muhammad Ahmad Dahman (Damascus, 1982), 196–202; Anonymous (possibly Ahmad al-Barbir), untitled letter, in Dahman, ed., Fi rihab Dimashq, 203–13; 'Abd al-Karim Rafeq, The Province of Damascus, 1723–83 (Beirut, 1966), 227.

45. Burayk, Tarikh, 80; al-Budayri, Hawadith, 228, 232–33; al-Qari, "Al-Wuzara'," 83; al-Muradi, Silk, 4:245; Rafeq, Province, 232.

46. Epidemics struck in 1608, 1652, 1670–71, 1679, 1691–92, 1703, 1708–09, 1718–20, 1731–32, 1739, 1743–44, and 1793. Al-Muradi, Silk, 3:205, 4:24, 64; Ibn Jum'a, "Al-Bashat," 48, 52, 58, 65; Ibn Kannan, Yawmiyat, 308, 426; Burayk, Tarikh, 24, 29; al-Budayri, Hawadith, 56; Rafeq, Province, 114; Establet and Pascual, Familles, 18; Hasan Agha, Tarikh, 21.

47. Ibn Kannan, Yawmiyat, 308; Burayk, Tarikh, 80. Plagues in Damascus usually coincided with those in Aleppo. On their timing, Abraham Marcus, The Middle East on the Eve of Modernity (New York, 1989), 256.

48. Al-Budayri, Hawadith, 228.

49. Al-Budayri, Hawadith, 122–23, 184; Hasan Agha, Tarikh, 34.

50. Contemporaries were totally mystified by this disease, which they described as "an unknown fever with assorted chills." Burayk, Tarikh, 118. For a more general treatment, Sauvaget, "Esquisse," 427.

51. Ibn Kannan, Yawmiyat, 181–82; for the other sons, ibid., 364, 426. For another case, ibid., 57.

52. MS 131:185.

53. P. Green, Journey from Aleppo to Damascus (London, 1736), 44.

54. Qasatli, Al-Rawda, 100.

55. Laurent d'Arvieux, Wasf madinat Dimashq fi al-qarn al-sabi'ashar, trans. Ahmad Ibish (Damascus, 1982), 29–30.

56. Al-Qasimi, Qamus, 156.

57. Ibn Kannan, Yawmiyat, 223.

58. Al-Budayri, Hawadith, 17.

59. Al-Budayri, Hawadith, 167.

60. Establet and Pascual, Familles, 12.

61. John Bowring, Report on the Commercial Statistics of Syria (London, 1840), 28.

62. Maundrell, "Journey," 414.

63. Bowring, Report, 46.

64. Al-Qari, "Al-Wuzara'," 77; al-Muradi, Silk, 3:161. See also W. G. Browne, Travels in Africa, Egypt, and Syria, 1792–98 (London, 1799), 394.

65. Bowring, Report, 46.

66. Al-Budayri, *Hawadith*, 36–37.

67. Bruce Masters, *The Origins of Western Economic Dominance in the Middle East: Mercantilism and the Islamic Economy in Aleppo, 1600–1750* (New York, 1988), 112.

68. Bowring, *Report*, 47.

69. For an estimate of rental costs, ʿAbd al-Karim Rafeq, "Qafilat al-hajj al-shami wa ahimmiyatuha fi al-ʿasr al-ʿuthmani," in *Buhuth fi al-tarikh al-iqtisadi wa al-ijtimaʿi li-bilad al-Sham* (Damascus, 1985), 203–04.

70. Maundrell, "Journey," 404, 409; Bowring, *Report*, 47. See also Suraiya Faroqhi, "Camels, Wagons, and the Ottoman State in the Sixteenth and Seventeenth Centuries," *International Journal of Middle East Studies* 14(1982): 527.

71. Pack animals were listed in 100 out of 1000 estates. All 100 were owned by men.

72. Al-Qasimi, *Qamus*, 106–7, 156–57. For the estates of donkey drivers, MS 131:193; 138:22; 143:44.

73. The expense of mules was probably a long term and widespread feature of premodern Middle Eastern transport. On prices in seventeenth-century Anatolia, Suraiya Faroqhi, *Towns and Townsmen of Ottoman Anatolia: Trade, Crafts, and Food Production in an Urban Setting, 1520–1650* (New York, 1984), 50.

74. Only seven inventories listed mules among possessions. For estates of muleteers (*baghghal*), MS 143:145, 379. See also al-Qasimi, *Qamus*, 47–48, 466–67.

75. MS 162:22. For others who owned mules, MS 138:32; 143:384; 162:7.

76. For owners of camels, MS 138:73, 127; 143:226; 162:39, 239, 345. As with the muleteers, this sample represented roughly 1% of the male population. See also al-Qasimi, *Qamus*, 83.

77. Masters, *Origins*, 113.

78. ʿAbd al-Karim Rafeq, "Mazahir min al-haya al-ʿaskariyya al-ʿuthmaniyya fi bilad al-sham," in *Buhuth fi al-tarikh al-iqtisadi wa al-ijtimaʿi li-bilad al-Sham* (Damascus, 1985), 151; al-Budayri, *Hawadith*, 218; Ibn Jumʿa, "Al-Bashat," 82.

79. Rafeq, "Qafilat," 202. For an example of two brothers sharing a camel to Mecca, al-Muradi, *Silk*, 4:247.

80. Browne, *Travels*, 394–95.

81. Al-Muradi, *Silk*, 2:310, 4:16.

82. Richard Bulliet, *The Camel and the Wheel* (New York, 1990).

83. Al-Budayri, *Hawadith*, 144.

84. Al-ʿAllaf, *Dimashq*, 39–40.

85. Roger Owen, *The Middle East in the World Economy, 1800–1914* (London, 1981), 245–46.

86. Owen, *The Middle East*, 54.

87. See, for example, d'Arvieux, *Wasf*, 49.

88. One British observer claimed that Damascene merchants were beginning

to show confidence in sea routes only at the end of the eighteenth century. Browne, *Travels*, 397–98.

89. On the routes through northern Palestine, Thomas Philipp, *Acre: The Rise and Fall of a Palestinian City, 1730–1831* (New York, 2001), 10–16.

90. P. Green, *Journey*; W. G. Browne, *Travels*, 394; Maundrell, "Journey."

91. Ibn Kannan, *Yawmiyat*, 114–15; Rafeq, "Qafilat," 206.

92. Mikha'il Mishaqa, *Muntakhabat min al-jawab ʿala iqtirah al-ahbab*, ed. Asad Rustam and Subhi Abu Shaqra (Beirut, 1985), 6; Mikha'il Mishaqa, *Murder, Mayhem, Pillage, and Plunder: The History of the Lebanon in the 18th and 19th Centuries*, trans. Wheeler M. Thackston, Jr. (Albany, 1988), 15.

93. Al-Mahasini, *Safahat*, 111–12.

94. ʿAbd al-Ghani al-Nabulsi, *Al-Hadra al-unsiyya fi al-rihla al-qudsiyya*, ed. Akram al-ʿUlabi (Beirut, 1990).

95. For an overview of developments in Ottoman Palestine, Beshara Doumani, *Rediscovering Palestine: Merchants and Peasants in Jabal Nablus, 1700–1900* (Berkeley, 1995), 33–44; in Ottoman Transjordan, Eugene L. Rogan, *Frontiers of the State in the Late Ottoman Empire: Transjordan, 1850–1921* (New York, 1999), chap. 1.

96. On the dawra, Rafeq, *Province*, 21–23.

97. For detailed studies of these rulers, Philipp, *Acre*; Amnon Cohen, *Palestine in the Eighteenth Century* (Jerusalem, 1973).

98. Al-Budayri, *Hawadith*, 152. See also ibid., 147.

99. ʿAbd al-Ghani al-Nabulsi, *Al-Haqiqa wa al-majaz fi al-rihla ila bilad al-Sham wa Misr wa al-Hijaz*, ed. Ahmad ʿAbd al-Majid Haridi (Cairo, 1986), 101, 172; Maundrell, "Journey," 503.

100. Burayk, *Tarikh*, 60. For the same warning, al-Muhibbi, *Khulasat*, 3:393. See also al-Muradi, *Silk*, 4:236.

101. Maundrell, "Journey," 384–85. The Frenchman Volney made practically the same observation; C. F. Volney, *Travels in Syria and Egypt in the Years 1783, 1784, and 1785* (London, 1794), 2:420.

102. Al-Nabulsi, *Al-Hadra*, 47–48.

103. Al-Qasimi, *Qamus*, 405–6; see also Qasatli, *Al-Rawda*, 111.

104. Burayk, *Tarikh*, 111.

105. Al-Nabulsi, *Al-Haqiqa*, 177.

106. The line between bandits and rebels was sometimes hard to discern. Ottoman terminology refers simply to "outlaws" (Tk. *şaki*). For reports from Lebanon, Başbakanlik Arşivi (henceforth BA), Şam-ı Şerif Ahkam Defterleri, 1:67, 87, 104, 136, 142, 144, 214; 2:117, 217, 254, 294, 307; 3:50; from the area of Jenin, ibid., 1:148.

107. Karl Barbir, *Ottoman Rule in Damascus, 1708–58* (Princeton, 1980), Appendix IX.

108. Al-Qari, "Al-Wuzara'," 79–81; al-Budayri, *Hawadith*, 207–8; Burayk, *Tarikh*, 57–59.

109. Rafeq, "Qafilat," 207.

110. Rafeq, "Qafilat," 194; Barbir, *Ottoman Rule*, 155.

111. BA, Cevdet Zaptiye, 26, 633. For the comparable expenditures on the caravans of 1780 and 1796, BA, Cevdet Askeriye, 1586, 4724.

112. Hasan Agha, *Tarikh*, 150.

113. Al-Budayri, *Hawadith*, 44.

114. Al-ʿAllaf, *Dimashq*, 273.

115. ʿAbd al-Ghani al-Nabulsi, *Al-Hadra*, 299.

II. BREAD AND SURVIVAL

1. Ahmad al-Budayri, *Hawadith Dimashq al-yawmiyya*, ed. Ahmad ʿIzzat ʿAbd al-Karim (Cairo, 1959), 130.

2. ʿAbd al-Ghani al-Nabulsi, *ʿAlam al-malaha fi ʿilm al-falaha* (Damascus, n.d.), 140.

3. Linda Schatkowski Schilcher, *Families in Politics: Urban Factions and Estates of Damascus in the 18th and 19th Centuries* (Stuttgart, 1985), 77; Antoine Abdel-Nour, *Introduction à l'histoire urbaine de la Syrie ottomane, XVIe–XVIIIe siècles* (Beirut, 1982), 240.

4. Safuh Khayr, *Ghutat Dimashq* (Damascus, 1957), 383–89; Schatkowski Schilcher, *Families*, 77.

5. BA, Cevdet Dahiliye, 9010.

6. Based on observations of the "laboring classes" during the 1830s, John Bowring concluded that the majority of Damascenes "sometimes" ate rice; see his *Report on the Commercial Statistics of Syria* (London, 1840), 49–50. See also Abdel-Nour, *Introduction*, 219. On rice as a food at celebrations, Muhammad Kurd ʿAli, *Khitat al-Sham*, 2nd ed. (Damascus, 1983), 6:275.

7. C. F. Volney, *Travels through Syria and Egypt in the Years 1783, 1784, and 1785* (London, 1794), 2:412.

8. ʿAbd al-Ghani al-Nabulsi, *Al-Hadra al-unsiyya fi al-rihla al-qudsiyya* (Beirut, 1990), 67. See also Hasan Agha al-ʿAbd, *Tarikh Hasan Agha al-ʿAbd*, ed. Yusuf Nuʿaysa (Damascus, 1979), 53–54.

9. Animals also ate various mixtures of grains and seeds, like the *maʿmuk* fed to camels. As for hay, it was not grown in Syria. See al-Budayri, *Hawadith*, 31, f. 3; Henry Maundrell, "A Journey from Aleppo to Jerusalem," in *Early Travels in Palestine*, ed. Thomas Wright (London, 1848), 503.

10. Faruk Tabak, "Agricultural Fluctuations and Modes of Labor Control in the Western Arc of the Fertile Crescent, ca. 1700–1850," in *Landholding and Com-*

mercial Agriculture in the Middle East, ed. Çağlar Keyder and Faruk Tabak (Albany, 1991), 144–45.

11. Muhammad Sa'id al-Qasimi, Qamus al-sana'at al-shamiyya, ed. Zafir al-Qasimi (Damascus, 1988), 290.

12. On the spread of maize in Syria, Tabak, "Agrarian Fluctuations," 144–45.

13. For the new foods adopted in China, see Jonathan Spence, "Ch'ing," in Food in Chinese Culture: Anthropological and Historical Perspectives, ed. K. C. Chang (New Haven, 1977), 263.

14. 'Abd al-Ghani al-Nabulsi, Ta'tir al-anam fi tafsir al-ahlam, ed. Taha 'Abd al-Ra'uf Sa'd (Damascus, n.d.), 1:150.

15. Ahmad al-'Allaf, Dimashq fi matla' al-qarn al-'ishrin (Damascus, 1976), 355; Bowring, Report, 49–50.

16. Ibn al-Saddiq, Ghara'ib al-bada'i' wa 'aja'ib al-waqa'i', ed. Yusuf Nu'aysa (Damascus, 1988), 21; Hasan Agha, Tarikh, 76.

17. Volney, Travels, 2:460.

18. Al-Nabulsi, Ta'tir, 1:184.

19. Alphonse de Lamartine, De Lamartine's Visit to the Holy Land, trans. Thomas Phipson (London, n.d.), 2:63. See also Chevalier d'Arvieux, Wasf Dimashq fi al-qarn al-sabi' 'ashar, trans. Ahmad Ibish (Damascus, 1992), 23.

20. Eliyahu Ashtor, A Social and Economic History of the Near East in the Middle Ages (Berkeley, 1976), 41.

21. Ibn Kannan, Al-Mawakib al-islamiyya fi al-mamalik wa al-mahasin al-shamiyya, ed. Hikmet Isma'il (Damascus, 1992), 2:262–63.

22. Al-Budayri, Hawadith, 130.

23. Al-Budayri, Hawadith, 5, 182.

24. P. Green, A Journey from Aleppo to Damascus (London, 1736), 66–67. For examples of biscuit being ordered for official expeditions, BA, Cevdet Askeriye, 10,939; 16,128; 26,633. See also 'Abd al-Karim Rafeq, "Qafilat al-hajj fi al-dawla al-'uthmaniyya," in Buhuth fi al-tarikh al-iqtisadi wa al-ijtima'i li-bilad al-Sham fi al-'asr al-hadith (Damascus, 1985), 200. On the positive image of ka'k, al-Nabulsi, Ta'tir, 1:186.

25. Al-Budayri, Hawadith, 126–27.

26. Also known as qursa; Ibn Kannan, Al-Mawakib, 2:261.

27. Al-Nabulsi, 'Alam, 142. See also al-Qasimi, Qamus, 71; Abdel-Nour, Introduction, 235. For "cooked bread" (baked with an iron pot), Ibn Kannan, Al-Mawakib, 2:261; al-Nabulsi, 'Alam, 142–43.

28. Al-Nabulsi, Ta'tir, 1:185. For the recipe, Ibn Kannan, Al-Mawakib, 2:260–61. The latter was quite mindful of the need to keep the bread separate from its pungent fuel.

29. Ibn Kannan, Al-Mawakib, 2:261–62. See also al-Nabulsi, 'Alam, 143–44.

30. Ibn Kannan, Al-Mawakib, 2:262; al-Nabulsi, 'Alam, 143.

31. Al-Nabulsi, *Al-Hadra*, 91. See also al-Nabulsi, *Ta'tir*, 1:185.

32. Al-Budayri, *Hawadith*, 130.

33. Mikha'il Burayk, *Tarikh al-Sham*, ed. Ahmad Ghassan Sabbanu (Damascus, 1982), 70.

34. Al-Budayri, *Hawadith*, 106. See also ibid., 88.

35. Burayk, *Tarikh*, 70.

36. Hasan Agha, *Tarikh*, 20–21.

37. Al-Budayri, *Hawadith*, 149.

38. For the former, MS 162:165; for the latter, MS 143:265.

39. See also Brigitte Marino, *Le Faubourg du Midan à Damas à l'époque ottomane (1742–1830)* (Damascus, 1997), 140–45.

40. See, for example, MS 131:272–73; 143:167.

41. Fernand Braudel, *The Structures of Everyday Life*, 132–33; Massimo Livi-Bacci, *Population and Nutrition* (Cambridge, 1991), 11.

42. One kilogram of bread is equal to about 2500 calories; at 1.85 kilograms, one *ratl* therefore contains 4625 calories.

43. Linda Schilcher, "The Grain Economy of Late Ottoman Syria and the Issue of Large-Scale Commercialization," in *Landholding and Commercial Agriculture in the Middle East*, ed. Çağlar Keyder and Faruk Tabak (Albany, 1991), 174.

44. Youssef Khoury, *Prix et monnaie en Syrie* (Nancy, 1943), 159–61. This proportion is very similar to eating habits in Manchu China, where it was estimated that urban workers spent about 80% of their income on cereals alone; Spence, "Chi'ng," 270.

45. Livi-Bacci, *Population*, 27.

46. Braudel, *Structures*, 130.

47. Susan Hanley, *Everyday Things in Premodern Japan* (Princeton, 1997), 91–92.

48. İhsan Ekin, *A'dan Z'ye Dengeli Beslenme* (Ankara, 1996), 29–31, citing data from the U.S. National Research Council. The same study observes that adult men require significantly more calories than women. Premodern diets may very well have had similar imbalances.

49. Hamid al-'Imadi, *Al-'Uqud al-durriyya fi al-fatawa al-hamidiyya*, ed. Ibn 'Abdin (Beirut, 1883), 1:243, 246. All Ottoman administrative centers enjoyed this priority; André Raymond, "Les rapports villes-campagnes dans les pays arabes à l'époque ottomane (XVIe–XVIIIe siècles)," in *Terroirs et sociétés au Maghreb et au Moyen-Orient: Séminaire IRMAC, 1983–84*, ed. Byron Cannon (Lyon, 1987), 41; Abdel-Nour, *Introduction*, 253.

51. Al-Budayri, *Hawadith*, 157.

52. Ibn Kannan, *Yawmiyat shamiyya*, ed. Akram al-'Ulabi (Damascus, 1994), 143; Ibn Jum'a, "Al-Bashat wa al-qudat," in *Wulat Dimashq fi al-'ahd al-'uthmani*, ed. Salah al-Din al-Munajjid (Damascus, 1949), 52.

53. Al-Budayri, *Hawadith*, 96–98.

54. Volney, *Travels*, 2:416.

55. Ibn Kannan, *Yawmiyat*, 106. For another note of skepticism, al-Budayri, *Hawadith*, 163.

56. Steven Kaplan, *Bread, Politics, and Political Economy in the Reign of Louis XV* (The Hague, 1976).

57. Al-Budayri, *Hawadith*, 128–29.

58. Al-Budayri, *Hawadith*, 25, 48–49. See also ibid., 81–82, 197.

59. Raslan al-Qari, "Al-Wuzara' aladhina hakamu Dimashq," in *Wulat Dimashq fi al-ʿahd al-ʿuthmani*, ed. Salah al-Din al-Munajjid (Damascus, 1949), 77, 83. See also Burayk, *Tarikh*, 23; al-Budayri, *Hawadith*, 164.

60. Al-Budayri, *Hawadith*, 222. See also Hasan Agha, *Tarikh*, 57.

61. Al-Nabulsi, *Taʿtir*, 1:186.

62. Al-Budayri, *Hawadith*, 191; Hasan Agha, *Tarikh*, 57.

63. Al-Qasimi, *Qamus*, 290–92.

64. Ibn Kannan, *Yawmiyat*, 473–74. See also ibid., 221; al-Budayri, *Hawadith*, 97–98; ʿAbd al-Karim Rafeq, "Economic Relations Between Damascus and the Dependent Countryside, 1743–1771, in *The Islamic Middle East, 700–1900*, ed. A. L. Udovitch (Princeton, 1981), 655.

65. For references to each of the following methods for baking bread, al-Nabulsi, *Taʿtir*, 2:120–21.

66. Ibn al-Saddiq, *Gharaʾib al-badaʾiʿ fi ʿajaʾib al-waqaʾiʿ*, ed. Yusuf Nuʿaysa (Damascus, 1988), 49.

67. For specific references to food stored in cellars and pantries, MS 131:261; 138:167; 162:46, 89. For an example of a private granary, MS 90:73–74.

68. Al-Budayri, *Hawadith*, 49–50.

69. Al-Qasimi, *Qamus*, 291.

70. Al-Qasimi, *Qamus*, 121–22.

71. One measure of these habits is the distribution of kneading troughs, which were found in one-third of estates appraised at more than five thousand piasters (15 out of 45). At the bottom of the economic ladder, in estates valued at less than one hundred piasters, one hardly finds any mention of them at all (2 out of 285, or 0.07%).

72. Al-Qasimi, *Qamus*, 290–91.

73. Hand mills were fairly common among the poor of Aleppo; see Alexander Russell, *The Natural History of Aleppo* (London, 1794), 1:77.

74. Al-Budayri, *Hawadith*, 143.

75. See, for example, MS 138:112; 162:89, 104.

76. Ibn Kannan, *Al-Mawakib*, 2:260; al-Nabulsi, *ʿAlam*, 142.

77. Al-Qasimi, *Qamus*, 290.

78. André Raymond, *Grandes villes arabes à l'époque ottomane* (Paris, 1985), 190; James Reilly, "Property, Status, and Class in Ottoman Damascus: Case Studies from the Nineteenth Century," *Journal of the American Oriental Society* 112(1992): 11.

79. 'Abd al-Karim Rafeq, "Al-Buniyya al-ijtima'iyya wa al-iqtisadiyya li-mahallat Bab al-Musalla bi-Dimashq," *Dirasat Tarikhiyya* 25–26(1987): 29; Marino, *Le Faubourg*, 96.

80. Al-Qasimi, *Qamus*, 319.

81. MS 94:38, 70, 109, 170, 206, 222, 234, 244, 246; 110:26–27; 115:152, 205, 229; 122:61; 168:200.

82. MS 94:109, 170, 234; 115:152, 165; 168:127.

83. MS 94:4, 246; 110:26–27.

84. In our sample of inventories, twenty-one estates contained at least one ghirara of grain, but only two were non-'askari in status. For the latter, MS 131:285; 138:38. For grain dealers among the Ottoman class, MS 162:17, 27, 29, 33, 39, 47, 56, 58, 79, 87, 102, 130, 131, 147, 170, 194, 203, 242, 268. Only rice seems to have been exempt from this overwhelming 'askari bias, probably because it was grown in Egypt, which meant that the purchase of large consignments required no control over the Damascene hinterland. For the one big rice merchant in the sample, MS 143:118.

85. Ibn Kannan, *Yawmiyat*, 203–04. On the depradations of al-Jazzar, al-Qari, "Al-Wuzara'," 85; Mikha'il al-Dimashqi, *Tarikh hawadith al-Sham wa Lubnan.* ed. Ahmad Ghassan Sabbanu (Damascus, 1982), 14–15. See also Hasan Agha, *Tarikh,* 148–49.

86. MS 162:294. See also the estates of two soldiers, MS 162:17, 39.

87. On the workings of the malikane, Mehmet Genç, "Osmanlı Maliyesinde Malikane Sistemi," in *Osmanlı İmparatorluğunda Devlet ve Ekonomi* (Istanbul, 2000), 99–152.

88. MS 162:29. See also the estate of a certain 'Ali Efendi, who accumulated large quantities of grain while serving as secretary (*amin al-fatawa*) to the mufti 'Ali al-Muradi; MS 162:358.

89. MS 162:89.

90. Al-Budayri, *Hawadith*, 127.

91. Marino, *Le Faubourg*, 95–99. See also Jean-Paul Pascual, "The Janissaries and the Damascus Countryside at the Beginning of the Seventeenth Century According to the Archives of the City's Military Tribunal," in *Land Tenure and Social Transformation in the Middle East*, ed. Tarif Khalidi (Beirut, 1984), 357–70. He finds evidence of Janissary involvement throughout the Damascene hinterland at the opening of the seventeenth century, and possibly earlier as well.

92. MS 162:170.

93. MS 162:79. For the estates of other Janissaries who doubled as grain merchants, MS 162:27, 87, 131, 203.

94. In Damascus, one ghirara was approximately 204.5 kilograms (449.9 pounds); a mudd was one seventy-fifth of that amount, i.e., 2.72 kilograms (6 pounds).

95. Al-Budayri, *Hawadith*, 64–65.

96. See, for example, Ibn Kannan, *Yawmiyat*, 255.

97. See, for example, ʿAbd al-Ghani al-Nabulsi, *Burj babil wa shadw al-balabil*, ed. Ahmad al-Jundi (Damascus, 1988), 109–10.

98. al-Nabulsi, *ʿAlam*, 229–32.

99. Estimates for the price of rice were adjusted from the *qintar*, its standard unit of measurement, to the slightly heavier ghirara, which was used for wheat. In Damascus, one qintar was equal to 185 kilograms (407 pounds). See Walther Hinz, *Al-Mikayil wa al-awzan al-islamiyya wa ma yuʿadiluha fi al-nizam al-mitri*, trans. Kamil al-ʿAsli (Amman, 1970), 42, 64.

100. Al-Budayri, *Hawadith*, 126.

101. Abdel-Nour, *Introduction*, 247.

102. Ibn Jumʿa, "Al-Bashat," 52; Ibn Kannan, *Yawmiyat*, 204.

103. André Raymond, *Artisans et commerçants au Caire au XVIIIe siècle* (Damascus, 1974), 58.

104. Cited in Ashtor, *A Social and Economic History*, 293.

105. The odd weather did not escape the notice of Antoine Abdel-Nour. But as we will see, he was perhaps a little too hasty in identifying drought as the factor which "largely explains" subsistence crises in eighteenth-century Syria. See his *Introduction*, 250.

106. Al-Budayri, *Hawadith*, 31, 34.

107. Al-Budayri, *Hawadith*, 64.

108. Burayk, *Tarikh*, 70. For the earlier rumors, Ibn Jumʿa, "Al-Bashat," 47.

109. Fernand Braudel, *The Mediterranean and the Mediterranean World in the Age of Philip II*, trans. Sian Reynolds (New York, 1972), 245.

110. Al-Mahasini, *Safahat*, 92–93; Ibn Kannan, *Yawmiyat*, 398.

111. Ibn Kannan, *Yawmiyat*, 184. See also al-Budayri, *Hawadith*, 31.

112. Al-Budayri, *Hawadith*, 166.

113. Hasan Agha, *Tarikh*, 30.

114. Abdel-Nour, *Introduction*, 252.

115. Al-Budayri, *Hawadith*, 157.

116. BA, Cevdet Askeriye, 26, 101.

117. McGowan, "The Age of the Ayans, 1699–1812," in *An Economic and Social History of the Ottoman Empire: Volume 2, 1600–1914*, ed. Halil Inalcık and Donald Quataert (Cambridge, 1994), 721, 727.

118. Rafeq, *Province*, 95; Ibn Kannan, *Yawmiyat*, 382; Ibn Jumʿa, "Al-Bashat,"

63–64. See also Muhammad al-Muhibbi, *Khulasat al-athr fi aʿyan al-qarn al-hadi ʿashar* (Beirut, n.d.), 1:263.

119. Burayk, *Tarikh*, 107–8, 111.

120. Hasan Agha, *Tarikh*, 53–54.

121. Ibn Kannan, *Yawmiyat*, 357.

122. Al-Qari, "Al-Wuzaraʾ," 78; Ibn Kannan, *Yawmiyat*, 443; Burayk, *Tarikh*, 24–25; Rafeq, *Province*, 119–20.

123. Al-Budayri, *Hawadith*, 41.

124. Al-Budayri, *Hawadith*, 63–65.

125. James Grehan, "Street Violence and Social Imagination in Late-Mamluk and Ottoman Damascus (ca. 1500–1800)," *International Journal of Middle East Studies* 35(2003): 215–36.

126. E. P. Thompson, "The Moral Economy of the English Crowd in the Eighteenth Century," *Past and Present* 50(1971): 76–136.

127. For a detailed discussion of political trends in these years, Rafeq, *Province*, 144–54, 161–66.

128. Rafeq, *Province*, 146; Rafeq, "Economic Relations," 658.

129. Al-Budayri, *Hawadith*, 197, 200–202; Rafeq, *Province*, 209–12.

130. Al-Budayri, *Hawadith*, 214–19; Rafeq, *Province*, 222–25.

131. Though Antoine Abdel-Nour and Farouk Mardam-Bey tend to grant a more prominent role to climate as a cause for social discontent in these years, they too were somewhat aware of the connection with political events. See Abdel-Nour, *Introduction*, 124, 240, 247–49; Farouk Mardam-Bey, "Tensions sociales et réalités urbaines à Damas au XVIIIe siècle," in *La ville arabe dans l'Islam*, ed. Abdel-Wahhab Bouhdiba and Dominique Chevallier (Tunis, 1982), 118.

132. Hasan Agha, *Tarikh*, 121–32.

133. André Raymond, "Urban Networks and Popular Movements in Cairo and Aleppo (End of Eighteenth to Beginning of Nineteenth Century)," in *Urbanism in Islam*, ed. Yuzo Itagaki, Masao Mori, and Takeshi Yukawa (Tokyo, 1989), 2:219–71; Raymond, *Artisans*, 817–21; Abraham Marcus, *The Middle East on the Eve of Modernity: Aleppo in the Eighteenth Century* (New York, 1989), chap. 3.

III. LUXURY AND VARIETY: EVERYDAY FOOD

1. ʿAbd al-Ghani al-Nabulsi, *Taʿtir al-anam fi tafsir al-ahlam*, ed. Taha ʿAbd al-Raʾuf Saʿd (Damascus, n.d.), 2:202–3.

2. The same was true for other parts of the Arab world. See, for example,

Alexander Russell, *The Natural History of Aleppo* (London, 1794), 1:116; Edward Lane, *Manners and Customs of the Modern Egyptians* (London, 1908), 198.

3. On the provisioning of the capital, Anthony Greenwood, "Istanbul's Meat Provisioning: A Study of the Celepkeşan System" (PhD dissertation, University of Chicago, 1988). On the priority given to official palates, Suraiya Faroqhi, *Towns and Townsmen in Ottoman Anatolia: Trade, Crafts, and Food Production in an Urban Setting, 1520–1650* (New York, 1984), 221–22.

4. See, for example, BA, Cevdet Askeriye 16,492.

5. ʿAbd al-Karim Rafeq, "Mazahir min al-haya al-ʿaskariyya al-ʿuthmaniyya fi bilad al-Sham min al-qarn al-sadis ʿashar hatta matlaʿ al-qarn al-tasiʿ ʿashar," in *Buhuth fi al-tarikh al-iqtisadi wa al-ijtimaʿi li-bilad al-Sham* (Damascus, 1985), 84.

6. Ahmad al-Budayri, *Hawadith Dimashq al-yawmiyya*, ed. Ahmad ʿIzzat ʿAbd al-Karim (Cairo, 1959), 214–16. See also Raslan ibn Yahya al-Qari, "Al-Wuzura' aladhina hakamu Dimashq," in *Wulat Dimashq fi al-ʿahd al-ʿuthmani*, ed. Salah al-Din al-Munajjid (Damascus, 1949), 86.

7. Mikhaʾil Burayk, *Tarikh al-Sham*, ed. Ahmad Ghassan Sabbanu (Damascus, 1982), 93–94.

8. ʿAbd al-Ghani al-Nabulsi, *Al-Risala fi masʾalat al-tasʿir*, ed. Muhammad ʿAbd al-Latif al-Farfur, in *ʿAlam al-turath*, ed. ʿAbd Allah Muhammad al-Darwish (Damascus, 1984), 1:37–44.

9. C. F. Volney, *Travels in Syria and Egypt in the Years 1783, 1784, and 1785* (London, 1794), 2:413.

10. Al-Budayri, *Hawadith*, 25.

11. Mikhaʾil al-Sabbagh, *Tarikh al-shaykh Zahir al-ʿUmar al-Zaydani, hakim ʿAkka wa bilad Safad*, ed. Qastantin al-Basha al-Mukhlisi (Harisa, Lebanon, n.d.), 156.

12. Al-Budayri, *Hawadith*, 193–94.

13. Muhammad Saʿid al-Qasimi, *Qamus al-sanaʿat al-shamiyya*, ed. Zafir al-Qasimi (Damascus, 1988), 276–79.

14. See, for example, al-Nabulsi, *Taʿtir*, 1:198–99.

15. Al-Qasimi, *Qamus*, 331–32; BA, Şam-1 Şerif Ahkam Defterleri 2:292; ʿAbd al-Karim Rafeq, "Economic Relations Between Damascus and the Dependent Countryside, 1743–1771, in *The Islamic Middle East, 700–1900: Studies in Economic and Social History*, ed. A. L. Udovitch (Princeton, 1981), 676; Rafeq, "Aspects of Traditional Society in Preindustrial Ottoman Syria," in *La ville arabe dans l'Islam*, ed. Abdel-Wahhab Boudhiba and Dominique Chevallier (Tunis, 1982), 113; Antoine Abdel-Nour, *Introduction à l'histoire urbain de la Syrie ottomane, XVIe–XVIIIe siècles* (Beirut, 1982), 219–21.

16. Al-Qasimi, *Qamus*, 401; ʿAbd al-Ghani al-Nabulsi, *ʿAlam al-malaha fi ʿilm al-falaha* (Damascus, n.d.), 239.

17. Al-Qasimi, *Qamus*, 331–32.

18. MS 131:122–23.

19. Mikhaʾil al-Dimashqi, *Tarikh hawadith al-Sham wa Lubnan, aw tarikh Mikhaʾil al-Dimashqi*, ed. Ahmad Ghassan Sabbanu (Damascus, 1982), 18.

20. Of the ten individuals who held significant numbers of sheep or cows, eight belonged to the Ottoman class. MS 131:122; 143:196; 162:7, 27, 39, 103, 131, 170, 194, 281.

21. ʿAbd al-Karim Rafeq, "The Law-Court Registers of Damascus with Special Reference to Craft-Corporations during the First Half of the 18th Century," in *Les Arabes par leurs archives (XVIe–XXe siècles)*, ed. Jacques Berque and Dominique Chevallier (Paris, 1976), 159; Abdel-Nour, *Introduction*, 231.

22. Abdel-Nour, *Introduction*, 231–32. See, for example, MS 162:14.

23. Al-Nabulsi, *Taʿtir*, 2:202.

24. Al-Qasimi, *Qamus*, 437.

25. Abdel-Nour, *Introduction*, 220.

26. Al-Budayri, *Hawadith*, 88.

27. ʿAbd al-Karim Rafeq, *The Province of Damascus, 1723–1783* (Beirut, 1966), 94–95; Farouk Mardam-Bey, "Tensions sociales et réalités urbaines à Damas au XVIIIe siècle," in *La ville arabe dans l'Islam*, ed. Abdel-Wahhab Boudhiba and Dominique Chevallier (Tunis, 1982), 118.

28. Al-Budayri, *Hawadith*, 94–95.

29. Al-Budayri, *Hawadith*, 126.

30. See respectively Ibn Kannan, *Yawmiyat shamiyya*, ed. Akram al-ʿUlabi (Damascus, 1994), 13; Burayk, *Tarikh*, 111. One cannot rule out the possibility of deliberate price-fixing, as happened in Aleppo during the 1760s; Abraham Marcus, *The Middle East on the Eve of Modernity: Aleppo in the Eighteenth Century* (New York, 1989), 172; Herbert Bodman, *Political Factions in Aleppo, 1760–1826* (Chapel Hill, 1963), 64–65; Kamil al-Ghazzi, *Nahr al-dhahab fi tarikh Halab* (Aleppo, 1926), 3:303–4.

31. Al-Budayri, *Hawadith*, 171–72.

32. Of those who owned at least five cows in our mid-century sample of inventories, three-quarters (12 out of 16) were ʿaskari Damascenes. All the major goat dealers (six out of six holding at least five) fell into the same category.

33. MS 143:26.

34. Al-Qasimi, *Qamus*, 454.

35. MS 162:49.

36. For an example of the former, MS 143:165, 172; 162:147, 267; for the latter, MS 138:32.

37. Al-Qasimi, *Qamus*, 49.

38. Al-Qasimi, *Qamus*, 105; Abdel-Nour, *Introduction*, 229.

39. Al-Nabulsi, *Taʿtir*, 1:164.

40. Al-Qasimi, *Qamus*, 105.

41. Al-Qasimi, *Qamus*, 105.

42. Al-Budayri, *Hawadith*, 182.

43. Al-Nabulsi, *'Alam*, 242.

44. Al-Qasimi, *Qamus*, 352–53.

45. Al-Budayri, *Hawadith*, 182.

46. Al-Qasimi, *Qamus*, 398–99.

47. Muhammad Khalil al-Muradi, *Silk al-durar fi a'yan al-qarn al-thani 'ashar* (Beirut, 1988), 2:67.

48. As observed for Aleppo; Russell, *The Natural History of Aleppo*, 1:118.

49. Al-Qasimi, *Qamus*, 126; Kurd 'Ali, *Khitat al-Sham, 2nd ed.* (Damascus, 1983), 4:191; Abdel-Nour, *Introduction*, 221.

50. Al-Muradi, *Silk*, 2:133–34.

51. Al-Qasimi, *Qamus*, 161.

52. See, for example, Ibn Kannan, *Al-Mawakib al-islamiyya fi al-mamalik wa al-mahasin al-shamiyya,* ed.Hikmet Isma'il (Damascus, 1992), 2:266.

53. Ibn Kannan, *Yawmiyat*, 102.

54. Abdel-Nour, *Introduction*, 222.

55. For local techniques of pressing olives and storing the oil, al-Qasimi, *Qamus*, 456–57.

56. See, for example, MS 162:184.

57. Al-Qasimi, *Qamus*, 268–69; Kurd 'Ali, *Khitat*, 4:190. For an account of the soap trade between Damascus and the hill country of Palestine, Beshara Doumani, *Rediscovering Palestine: Merchants and Peasants in Jabal Nablus, 1700–1900* (Berkeley, 1995), 23–24, 72–77.

58. Al-Qasimi, *Qamus*, 173.

59. Better known to Americans as black-eyed peas.

60. On the varieties of beans eaten by Damascenes, al-Nabulsi, *'Alam*, 144.

61. Al-Qasimi, *Qamus*, 91.

62. For other variations, al-Qasimi, *Qamus*, 114–15; Ahmad al-'Allaf, *Dimashq fi matla' al-qarn al-'ishrin* (Damascus, 1976), 355

63. Al-Qasimi, *Qamus*, 115.

64. Al-Nabulsi, *'Alam*, 144; Muhammad al-Muhibbi, *Khulasat al-athr fi a'yan al-qarn al-hadi 'ashar* (Beirut, n.d.), 4:162.

65. See, for example, MS 131:251; 143:117; al-Qasimi, *Qamus*, 356–57.

66. Al-Nabulsi, *Ta'tir*, 1:185.

67. Ibn Kannan, *Al-Mawakib*, 2:263.

68. Ibn Kannan, *Al-Mawakib*, 2:264; Muhammad Khalil al-Muradi, *'Arf al-basham fi man waliya fatwa Dimashq al-Sham*, ed. Muhammad Muti' al-Hafiz and Riyad 'Abd al-Hamid Murad, 2nd ed. (Damascus, 1988), 22; al-Nabulsi, *'Alam*, 144–45.

69. Al-Nabulsi, 'Alam, 144.

70. MS 162:318.

71. Yusuf Nu'aysa, *Mujtama' madinat Dimashq, 1772–1840* (Damascus, 1986), 2:522; Faruk Tabak, "Agrarian Fluctuations and Modes of Labor Control in the Western Arc of the Fertile Crescent, ca. 1700–1850," in *Landholding and Commercial Agriculture in the Middle East*, ed. Çağlar Keyder and Faruk Tabak (Albany, 1991), 144–45.

72. Nu'man Qasatli, *Al-Rawda al-ghanna' fi Dimashq al-fayha'* (Beirut, 1876), 116–17. Among other crops which are familiar today but absent in the eighteenth-century sources are ochre (*bamiya*) and peas (*bisilla*).

73. Al-Qasimi, *Qamus*, 73–74.

74. Abdel-Nour, *Introduction*, 225.

75. For a detailed list of local fruits, Ibn Kannan, *Al-Mawakib*, 2:266–338. For later accounts, Qasatli, *Al-Rawda*, 116–17; al-Qasimi, *Qamus*, 333–34; al-'Allaf, *Dimashq*, 360–66.

76. Al-Qasimi, *Qamus*, 333–34.

77. Abdel-Nour, *Introduction*, 225–26.

78. Al-'Allaf, *Dimashq*, 365. Only *kızılcık* (Tk.), a type of very small, sour cherry, seems to have been available in the eighteenth century; see, for example, MS 162:335.

79. See, for example, MS 131:115, 164, 283; 138:32; 143:41, 129, 165, 376; 162:93; al-Qasimi, *Qamus*, 219.

80. See, for example, MS 90:5–6, 50, 78–79, 90, 147, 154–55, 161–62, 165, 170, 191, 194–95, 243–44, 246, 250–51; 109:3, 39, 50, 60, 87–89, 102–3; 112:42–43, 154, 173–74; 122:193–94; 168:12, 75, 122, 166, 174–75, 236, 283.

81. See, for example, MS 90:73–74; 112:42–43; 168: 287. Such channels were indicated with various terms such as *qanat ma'*, *majri ma'*, and *saqiyya bustaniyya*.

82. Al-Qasimi, *Qamus*, 322.

83. Al-Budayri, *Hawadith*, 82.

84. Ibn Kannan, *Yawmiyat*, 464, 484.

85. 'Abd al-Ghani al-Nabulsi, *Al-Tuhfa al-nabulusiyya fi al-rihla al-tarabulusiyya*, ed. Heribert Busse (Beirut, 1971), 58.

86. See, for example, MS 138:144; 162:39.

87. Al-Nabulsi, 'Alam, 251–56.

88. Al-Nabulsi, 'Alam, 246–50.

89. See, for example, MS 138:150.

90. For examples of grocers, MS 138:29; 143:141, 373.

91. Al-Qasimi, *Qamus*, 423–24.

92. For the making of vinegar from other base ingredients, al-Nabulsi, 'Alam, 267–69.

93. Al-Nabulsi, 'Alam, 252, 255, 269.

94. Burayk, Tarikh, 59.

95. Henry Maundrell, "A Journey from Aleppo to Jerusalem," in Early Travels in Palestine, ed. Thomas Wright (London, 1848), 512.

96. Abdel-Nour, Introduction, 224.

97. BA, Bab-ı Defteri Başmuhasebe Kalemi, Şam Hazinesi, 16,997; 17,025.

98. See, for example, MS 162:58.

99. MS 131:245; 138:29; 143:257; 162:164.

100. 'Abd al-Karim Rafeq, "Qafilat al-hajj al-shami wa ahammiyatuha fi al-'ahd al-'uthmani," in Buhuth fi al-tarikh al-iqtisadi wa al-ijtima'i li-bilad al-Sham (Damascus, 1985), 206–8.

101. See, for example, MS 131:144.

102. MS 162:335. For the estates of other spice merchants, MS 131:32, 77, 220; 138:74, 85, 103, 144; 143:15; 162:179, 198, 330, 335.

103. Al-Qasimi, Qamus, 73–74.

104. Al-Nabulsi, 'Alam, 164–65.

105. Al-Nabulsi, 'Alam, 156, 196–97. See also al-Budayri, Hawadith, 217.

106. Al-Nabulsi, 'Alam, 208–9; Ibn Kannan, Al-Mawakib, 2:233.

107. Fernand Braudel, The Structures of Everyday Life: The Limits of the Possible, tr. Sian Reynolds (New York, 1979), 220–24.

108. 'Abd al-Ghani al-Nabulsi, Al-Sulh bayn al-ikhwan fi hukm ibahat al-dukhan, ed. Ahmad Muhammad Dahman (Damascus, 1924), 35.

109. Al-Nabulsi, 'Alam, 260–63.

110. Al-Nabulsi, 'Alam, 165.

111. Al-Nabulsi, 'Alam, 260.

112. Al-Nabulsi, 'Alam, 159–60.

113. Al-Qasimi, Qamus, 456.

114. See, for example, MS 138:190.

115. One center of production was the Palestinian town of Safad; MS 68:294.

116. Abdel-Nour, Introduction, 225; Robert Paris, Histoire du commerce de Marseille, 1660–1789 (Paris, 1957), 5:557.

117. Paris, Histoire, 559. Other variations were powdered sugar (sukkar na'im), rock sugar (sukkar al-nabat), and sugar paste (ma'jun al-sukkar), which was a kind of candy.

118. Ibn Tulun, Mufakahat al-khillan fi hawadith al-zaman, ed. Muhammad Mustafa (Cairo, 1962), 1:41. On the collapse of the medieval sugar industries in Egypt and Syria, Eliyahu Ashtor, A Social and Economic History of the Near East in the Middle Ages (Los Angeles, 1976), 306–7.

119. On the fate of the sugar industry in Ottoman Egypt, André Raymond, "Le fabrication et le commerce du sucre au Caire au XVIIIe siècle," in Sucre, sucreries et douceurs en Méditerranée (Paris, 1991), 213–25. On sugar as a luxury for

Egyptian consumers, Raymond, *Artisans et commerçants au Caire au XVIIIe siècle* (Damascus, 1974), 315.

120. On the applications of sugar in Middle Eastern medicine, Da'ud al-Antaki, *Tadhkirat uli al-albab wa al-jami' li'l-'ajab al-'ujab* (Beirut, n.d.), 1:195. On the medicinal uses of sugar in Europe, Sidney W. Mintz, *Sweetness and Power: The Place of Sugar in Modern History* (New York, 1985), 79–80.

121. Ibn Kannan, *Yawmiyat*, 92–93.

122. See, for example, MS 131:261, 270; 138:151.

123. It was estimated that by the 1930s "working families" in Syrian cities were consuming nearly as much sugar as rice (in terms of weight); Youssef Khoury, *Prix et monnaie en Syrie* (Nancy, 1943), 161.

124. Kurd 'Ali, *Khitat*, 4:190; Abdel-Nour, *Introduction*, 223.

125. MS 138:32.

126. Ibn Kannan, *Yawmiyat*, 154.

127. Ibn Kannan, *Al-Mawakib*, 2:159.

128. Al-Qasimi, *Qamus*, 186; Kurd 'Ali, *Khitat*, 4:189.

129. For examples of sweet sellers, MS 131:41, 200, 240; 143:234, 266; 162:246. One can also find a grocer, carpenter, sawyer, bustani, and two merchants who participated in the trade; MS 131:245; 143:271; 162:6; 138:32; 131:90; 162:267.

130. MS 131:71; 143:124, 126, 361; 162:180. On the nineteenth-century decline of the trade, al-Qasimi, *Qamus*, 106.

131. For qata'if, Al-Nabulsi, *Ta'tir*, 2:170; for kunafa, bughaja, and baqlawa, Hasan Agha al-'Abd, *Tarikh Hasan Agha al-'Abd*, ed. Yusuf Nu'aysa (Damascus, 1979), 143.

132. Al-Nabulsi, *Ta'tir*, 1:186.

133. Al-Qari, "Al-Wuzara'," 86.

134. Al-Dimashqi, *Tarikh*, 39.

135. Al-Dimashqi, *Tarikh*, 41–42. For the diet imposed on his retinue, ibid., 39.

136. Hasan Agha, *Tarikh*, 143.

137. Braudel, *The Structures of Everyday Life*, 194–202.

138. John Bowring, *Report on the Commercial Statistics of Syria* (London, 1840), 49–50. As he summed it up, "the condition of the laboring classes is, comparatively with those in England, easy and good."

IV. LUXURY AND VARIETY: EVERYDAY DRINK

1. According to Islamic jurists, people "drank" whatever required no chewing; 'Abd al-Ghani al-Nabulsi, *Al-Sulh bayn al-ikhwan fi hukm ibahat al-dukhan*, ed. Ahmad Muhammad Dahman (Damascus, 1924), 20.

2. André Raymond, *Grandes villes arabes à l'époque ottomane* (Paris, 1985), 162–63.

3. Nuʿman Qasatli, *Al-Rawda al-ghanna' fi Dimashq al-fayha'* (Beirut, 1876), 113.

4. ʿAbd al-Ghani al-Nabulsi, *ʿAlam al-malaha fi ʿilm al-falaha* (Damascus, n.d.), 210; Ibn Kannan, *Al-Mawakib al-islamiyya fi al-mamalik wa al-mahasin al-shamiyya*, ed. Hikmet Ismaʿil (Damascus, 1992), 2:252, 258, 267.

5. ʿAbd al-Ghani al-Nabulsi, *Burj babil wa shadw al-balabil*, ed. Ahmad al-Jundi (Damascus, 1988), 331.

6. Al-Nabulsi, *ʿAlam*, 156, 165, 195, 214; Ibn Kannan, *Al-Mawakib*, 2:301.

7. Rida Murtada, "Miyah al-shurb fi madinat Dimashq min khilal hadarat al-tarikh," in *ʿIlm al-miyah al-jariyya fi madinat Dimashq*, ed. Ahmad Ghassan Sabbanu (Damascus, 1984), 146–47. Another source says that the project was completed in 1909; Muhammad Saʿid al-Qasimi, *Qamus al-sanaʿat al-shamiyya*, ed. Zafir al-Qasimi (Damascus, 1988), 185–86.

8. Al-Qasimi, *Qamus*, 351. For more about the system of pipes, see also Murtada, "Miyah," 141.

9. Al-Qasimi, *Qamus*, 364–65. The same techniques were prevalent in Aleppo; Abraham Marcus, *The Middle East on the Eve of Modernity: Aleppo in the Eighteenth Century* (New York, 1989), 263.

10. For a detailed description of a taliʿ, Murtada, "Miyah," 143–44.

11. Hamid al-ʿImadi, *Al-ʿUqud al-durriyya fi al-fatawa al-hamidiyya*, ed. Ibn ʿAbdin (Beirut, 1883), 2:215–16, 220–22.

12. Ibn Kannan, *Yawmiyat shamiyya*, ed. Akram al-ʿUlabi (Damascus, 1994), 340; Ahmad al-Budayri, *Hawadith Dimashq al-yawmiyya*, ed. Ahmad ʿIzzat ʿAbd al-Karim (Cairo, 1959), 168.

13. Al-Budayri, *Hawadith*, 181. See also ibid., 224.

14. Al-Budayri, *Hawadith*, 144–45.

15. See, for example, MS 109:58, 85; al-ʿImadi, *Al-ʿUqud*, 2:216, 221–22.

16. For examples of houses with multiple fountains, MS 109:34–35, 150; 112:103–4; 168:8, 12, 112–14, 137–38, 159–60, 236–37.

17. MS 90:138–39, 157; 109:85; 122:186–87; 168:12, 199–200.

18. Al-Nabulsi, *Burj*, 336–37. See also ibid., 127–28.

19. Al-Qasimi, *Qamus*, 61–62.

20. See, for example, MS 90:195; 109:3.

21. Ibn Kannan, *Al-Mawakib*, 2:200. For more about well water, Murtada, "Miyah," 146; Antoine Abdel-Nour, *Introduction à l'histoire urbaine de la Syrie ottomane (XVIe–XVIIIe siècles)* (Beirut, 1982), 194.

22. See, for example, MS 90:184.

23. ʿAbd al-Ghani al-Nabulsi, *Al-Haqiqa wa al-majaz fi al-rihla ila bilad al-Sham wa Misr wa al-Hijaz*, ed. Ahmad ʿAbd al-Majid Haridi (Cairo, 1986), 60.

24. MS 90:39, 99–100; 109:28, 112, 115, 132–33; 112:26, 163–64; 122:34–35.

25. See, for example, MS 168:202.

26. Al-ʿImadi, al-ʿUqud, 1:70–71.

27. Al-Qasimi, Qamus, 185–86, 273–74.

28. Murtada, "Miyah," 145; Safuh Khayr, Madinat Dimashq (Damascus, 1969), 498; Nayif al-Siyagha, Al-Haya al-iqtisadiyya fi madinat Dimashq fi muntasaf al-qarn al-tasiʿashar (Damascus, 1995), 80.

29. Al-Qasimi, Qamus, 72.

30. Ibn Kannan, Al-Mawakib, 1:395; al-Qasimi, Qamus, 72–73. For a qadi who used snow as part of a medical treatment, Muhammad al-Muhibbi, Khulasat al-athr fi aʿyan al-qarn al-hadiʿashar (Beirut, n.d.), 3:44.

31. Al-Siyagha, Al-Haya, 72.

32. Al-Nabulsi, Al-Haqiqa, 153.

33. Marcus, The Middle East, 298–303.

34. Mikhaʾil Niqula al-Sabbagh, Tarikh al-shaykh Zahir al-ʿUmar al-Zaydani, hakim ʿAkka wa bilad Safad, ed. Qastantin al-Basha al-Mukhlisi (Harisa, Lebanon, n.d.), 156.

35. ʿAbd al-Ghani al-Nabulsi, Taʿtir al-anam fi tafsir al-ahlam, ed. Taha ʿAbd al-Raʾuf Saʿd (Damascus, n.d.), 2:20. On rose water, Ibn Kannan, Al-Mawakib, 2:159.

36. Al-Qasimi, Qamus, 252–53. For examples of spice merchants selling sherbets, MS 138:144; 162:335.

37. Al-Sabbagh, Tarikh, 62.

38. Ibn Kannan, Yawmiyat, 25.

39. Al-Nabulsi, Taʿtir, 2:20.

40. Richard Thoumin, "Deux quartiers de Damas: le quartier chrétien de Bab Musalla et le quartier Kurde," Bulletin d'études orientales 1 (1931): 111.

41. ʿAbd al-Karim Rafeq, "Craft Organizations and Religious Communities in Ottoman Syria (16th–19th Centuries)," in Convegno sul Tema: La shiʿa nell'impero ottomano (Rome, 1991), 148.

42. Al-Qasimi, Qamus, 127.

43. Abdel-Nour, Introduction, 222–23.

44. Muhammad Khalil al-Muradi, Silk al-durar fi aʿyan al-qarn al-thaniʿashar (Beirut, 1988), 3:280.

45. Hasan Agha al-ʿAbd, Tarikh Hasan Agha al-ʿAbd, ed. Yusuf Nuʿaysa (Damascus, 1979), 122. See also ibid., 62–63.

46. Henry Maundrell, "A Journey from Aleppo to Jerusalem," in Early Travels in Palestine, ed. Thomas Wright (London, 1848), 494.

47. Mikhaʾil Burayk, Tarikh al-Sham, ed. Ahmad Ghassan Sabbanu (Damascus, 1982), 116. On the drunkenness and violence of Janissaries and their allies, al-Budayri, Hawadith, 125; Ibn Kannan, Yawmiyat, 411.

48. Al-Budayri, Hawadith, 57.

49. Al-Budayri, *Hawadith*, 137–38.

50. ʿAbd al-Ghani al-Nabulsi, *Al-Hadiqa al-nadiyya: sharh al-tariqa al-muhammadi-yya* (Lalipur, 1977), 2:518.

51. Burayk, *Tarikh*, 74.

52. Mikhaʾil al-Dimashqi, *Tarikh hawadith al-Sham wa Lubnan, aw tarikh Mikhaʾil al-Dimashqi (1782–1841)*, ed. Ahmad Ghassan Sabbanu (Damascus, 1982), 29.

53. Hasan Agha, *Tarikh*, 139.

54. Ralph S. Hattox, *Coffee and Coffeehouses: The Origins of a Social Beverage in the Medieval Near East* (Seattle, 1985), chaps. 1–4.

55. Rafeq, "Craft Organizations," 33.

56. On the cultural reactions to coffee in Europe, Wolfgang Schivelbusch, *Tastes of Paradise*, trans. David Jacobson (New York, 1992), 39–40.

57. Al-Nabulsi, *Al-Sulh*, 76–77.

58. Al-Nabulsi, *Al-Haqiqa*, 60, 172.

59. Al-Muradi, *Silk*, 1:186. For another sign of indifference, Ibn Jumʿa, "Al-Bashat wa al-qudat," in *Wulat Dimashq fi al-ʿahd al-ʿuthmani*, ed. Salah al-Din al-Munajjid (Damascus, 1949), 62.

60. MS 131:144; 138:124, 128, 151; 143:16, 377; 162:21, 39, 170, 271, 276, 313, 316, 321. Political involvement in the coffee trade was even more pronounced in Cairo; Jane Hathaway, *The Politics of Households in Ottoman Egypt: The Rise of the Qazdağlıs* (Cambridge, 1997), 134–38.

61. On the rise of the Egyptian coffee trade, André Raymond, *Artisans et commerçants au Caire au XVIIIe siècle* (Damascus, 1974), 1:289–91.

62. Raymond, *Artisans*, 1:157.

63. Bruce McGowan, "The Age of the Ayans, 1699–1812," in *A Social and Economic History of the Ottoman Empire: Volume Two, 1600–1914*, (ed.) Halil Inalcik and Donald Quataert (New York, 1994), 726–27.

64. For the first mention of "Frankish coffee" in Damascene inventories, MS 138:151.

65. MS 138:151; 143:196. On a similar differential in Egyptian prices, Raymond, *Artisans*, 1:157.

66. On the preferences of Egyptian merchants, Raymond, *Artisans*, 1:156; Robert Paris, *Histoire du commerce de Marseille, 1660–1789* (Paris, 1957), 5:559–60. On European tastes, Fernand Braudel, *The Structures of Everyday Life*, trans. Sian Reynolds (New York, 1979), 259.

67. See, for example, MS 131:155.

68. Coffee merchants occasionally carried ambergris in their stock; MS 143:377; 162:39.

69. For a description of the procedure, Lane, *Manners*, 141.

70. Michel Tuchscherer, "Les cafés dans l'Égypte ottomane (XVIe–XVIIIe

siècles)," in *Cafés d'Orient revisités*, ed. Hélène Desmet-Grégoire and François Georgeon (Paris, 1997), 105.

71. Lane, *Manners*, 141.

72. Schivelbusch, *Taste*, 179.

73. Tuchscherer, "Les cafés," 105.

74. In mid-century estates, most coffee cups were not identified according to style. Among those listed with more specific labels, "china cups" (*finjan sini*) appeared in three times as many inventories (84 vs. 28) as "Kutahya cups" (*finjan kutahi*). See also McGowan, "The Age of the Ayans," 704, 731.

75. Qasatli, *Al-Rawda*, 121.

76. Chinese cups and saucers were held in such high regard that, as far back as the early Abbasid period (eighth and ninth centuries), nearly all fine porcelain was called "Chinese," regardless of origin. M. M. Ahsan, *Social Life Under the Abbasids (786–902 AD)* (New York, 1979), 122–23.

77. Alexander Russell, *The Natural History of Aleppo* (London, 1794), 1:119–20.

78. See, for example, al-Muhibbi, *Khulasat*, 3:393. Cairenes had the same morning attachments; Tuchscherer, "Les cafés," 96.

79. Of the 281 coffee pots found in our sample of mid-century estates, more than half (153, or 54.4%) turned up in fortunes worth less than 500 piasters.

80. For example MS 162:331. See also al-Qasimi, *Qamus*, 107.

81. C. F. Volney, *Travels in Syria and Egypt in the Years 1783, 1784, and 1785* (London, 1794), 2:420–21.

82. John Bowring, *Report on the Commercial Statistics of Syria* (London, 1840), 29.

83. Ibn al-Siddiq, *Ghara'ib al-bada'i' fi wa 'aja'ib al-waqa'i'*, ed. Yusuf Nu'aysa (Damascus, 1988), 50.

84. 'Abd al-Ghani al-Nabulsi, *Al-Hadra al-unsiyya fi al-rihla al-qudsiyya*, ed. Akram al-'Ulabi (Beirut, 1990), 66–67.

85. Qasatli, *Al-Rawda*, 109.

86. Al-Budayri, *Hawadith*, 189–90.

87. Ibn Jum'a, "Al-Bashat," 56.

88. Al-Budayri, *Hawadith*, 145.

89. MS 162:204.

90. See, for example, MS 143:274.

91. See, for example, MS 143:329.

92. Maundrell, "Journey," 491. See also Ibn Kannan, *Yawmiyat*, 431.

93. Qasatli, *Al-Rawda*, 109.

94. Al-Qasimi, *Qamus*, 367.

95. For examples of individuals who owned coffeehouses merely as an investment, MS 162:30, 70, 347. For a coffeehouse funded by a waqf, MS 162:204.

See also al-Qasimi, *Qamus*, 367. He maintains that, in his day, the majority of operators had to rent.

96. MS 143:274; 162:321. In the nineteenth century, coffeehouses ranked among the most profitable investments for pious foundations; Randi Deguilhem, "Les cafés à Damas (XIXe—XXe siècles)," in Desmet-Grégoire and Georgeon, 131.

97. Al-Qasimi, *Qamus*, 51.

98. Among the thirteen individuals who could be identified (through ownership of a gedik or relevant supplies and equipment) in probate inventories as coffeehouse attendants (1750–67), five possessed estates worth more than one thousand piasters at the time of their death, and only two were so poor that they fell below one hundred piasters; MS 143:19, 86, 274, 329; 162:74, 130, 147, 245, 293, 299, 303, 321, 340.

99. Among the thirteen individuals identified as a qahwaji, nine held ʿaskari status. The ratio was even higher for those who owned coffeehouses (seven out of eight).

100. MS 162:147. See also MS 162:299, 340.

101. See, for example, Ibn al-Siddiq, *Gharaʾib*, 23. On the popularity of coffee drinking among the soldiers of Cairo, Tuchscherer, "Les Cafés," 97, 110.

102. Hasan Agha, *Tarikh*, 55.

103. Qasatli, *Al-Rawda*, 110.

104. Dice turned up in about one of every twenty estates (5.5%), which belonged mostly to men (44 out of 55, or 80%). Some dice were made from brass, but fancy ones were cast in silver. Most owners were affluent; 41 out of 55, or 74.5%, left estates worth at least one thousand piasters.

105. Al-Budayri, *Hawadith*, 95.

106. Al-Qasimi, *Qamus*, 112–14. For the biography of a poet who began his career as a *hakawati*, al-Muradi, *Silk*, 1:155.

107. See, for example, al-Muhibbi, *Khulasat*, 1:167; 3:225.

108. Ibn Kannan, *Yawmiyat*, 412.

109. Ibn Kannan, *Yawmiyat*, 19.

110. On the motives for the closure of the coffeehouses in Istanbul, Lewis V. Thomas, *A Study of Naima*, ed. Norman Itzkowitz (New York, 1972), 94; also Ayşe Saraçgil, "L'introduction du café à Istanbul (XVIe—XVIIe siècles)," in Desmet-Grégoire and Georgeon, 36–37.

111. Al-Dimashqi, *Tarikh*, 39.

112. See, for example, MS 168:12, 159–60.

113. Al-Qasimi, *Qamus*, 127.

114. Al-Muradi, *Silk*, 2:293. See also al-Qasimi, *Qamus*, 368.

115. Al-Muradi, *Silk*, 2:103.

116. Other names were *tabgh*, *dukhan* (smoke), *tanbak*, and *tubbaq*; al-Nabulsi, *Al-Sulh*, 18.

117. MS 68:379.

118. Al-Qasimi, *Qamus*, 337.

119. For an example of "Kurdish" tobacco (*tutun kurdi*), see MS 131:98; for the Persian kind (*tutun ʿajami*), MS 143:150. Praise for the latter can be found in al-Qasimi, *Qamus*, 70.

120. Al-Nabulsi, *Al-Sulh*, 19.

121. Among those who sold only tobacco, MS 131:98; 143:15, 362. For more diversified merchants, MS 131:201; 138:10; 143:269.

122. Al-Nabulsi, *Al-Sulh*, 19. For a description of Egyptian pipes, Lane, *Manners*, 138.

123. Al-Nabulsi, *Al-Sulh*, 19; al-Qasimi, *Qamus*, 36–37, 330.

124. For the scholar's estate, MS 162:123. Only twenty-six individuals from our sample owned water-pipes. Most of these men (there were no women) were affluent; nearly two-thirds of them (17 out of 27) held estates worth more than one thousand piasters; MS 131:261; 138:58; 143:124, 159, 199, 206, 239, 329; 162:7, 54, 68, 76, 95, 123, 127, 130, 138, 161, 184, 252, 276, 310, 325, 330, 334, 340. For an example of a coffeehouse stocked with glass water-pipes, MS 143:329.

125. On the use of snuff, Schivelbusch, *Taste*, 131.

126. Volney, *Travels*, 2:409.

127. Al-Nabulsi, *Al-Sulh*, 36. Cairenes showed the same attachment to tobacco (and coffee) as Damascenes; Lane, *Manners*, 137.

128. Al-Budayri, *Hawadith*, 130, 140.

129. Burayk, *Tarikh*, 74.

130. Al-Nabulsi, *Al-Hadra*, 235.

131. Al-Muradi, *Silk*, 1:254.

132. Al-Nabulsi, *Al-Sulh*, 5–14.

133. Al-Nabulsi, *Al-Sulh*, 34.

134. Al-Nabulsi, *Al-Sulh*, 53. Earlier, he had conceded that tobacco might have harmful side effects for some people, depending on their bodily constitution, but that this was sometimes the case with other permitted substances and therefore provided no basis for banning tobacco; ibid., 11.

135. Al-Nabulsi, *Al-Sulh*, 70.

136. Al-Muradi, *Silk*, 4:130.

137. Al-Muradi, *Silk*, 2:31.

138. Ibn Kannan, *Yawmiyat*, 21.

139. See respectively Ibn Kannan, *Yawmiyat*, 180, 203.

140. Al-Budayri, *Hawadith*, 130. The text is ambiguous and mentions only "drinking," which could refer to coffee, tobacco, or both. But since the coffeehouses were

not closed, and in fact were among the sites where copies of the decree were circulated, one can assume that it was tobacco alone that the governor intended to suppress.

141. ʿAbd al-Ghani al-Nabulsi, ʿAlam al-malaha fi ʿilm al-falaha (Damascus, n.d.), 152; al-Nabulsi, Al-Sulh, 71.

142. Al-Nabulsi, ʿAlam, 189–90; see also Ibn Kannan, Al-Mawakib, 2:254–55.

143. Al-Nabulsi, Al-Sulh, 70.

144. On Aleppo, Marcus, The Middle East, 233. For a firsthand account of the situation in Cairo, Lane, Manners, 341–42. On Anatolian towns, Suraiya Faroqhi, Osmanlı Kültürü ve Gündelik Yaşam: Ortaçağdan Yirmi Yüzyıla, trans. Elif Kılıç (Istanbul, 1997), 237–38.

145. MS 143:366.

146. ʿAbd al-Karim Rafeq, "The Local Forces in Syria in the 17th and 18th Centuries," in War, Technology, and Society in the Middle East, ed. V. J. Parry and M. E. Yapp (London, 1975), 305.

147. Al-Muradi, Silk, 4:210. Al-Nabulsi mentions that many ulama excused their addiction through the loophole cited above: if they were to quit suddenly, they might risk death; ʿAbd al-Ghani al-Nabulsi, Ajwiba ʿan khamsat as'ila, Süleymaniye Library, Esad Efendi 3607/25, 206–206b.

148. Al-Muradi, Silk, 1:41–42. For other aficionados of opium, al-Muhibbi, Khulasat, 3:17; 4:273, 290; al-Muradi, Silk, 4:185.

149. Charles Issawi, An Economic History of the Middle East and North Africa, 1800–1980 (New York, 1982), 125. By the late nineteenth century, teahouses (Tk. çayhane) had begun to appear in entertainment districts such as Direklerarası; François Georgeon, "Les Cafés à Istanbul à la fin de l'empire ottoman," in Desmet-Grégoire and Georgeon, 53–54.

V. DOMESTIC SPACE

1. Muhammad Khalil al-Muradi, Silk al-durar fi aʿyan al-qarn al-thani ʿashar (Beirut, 1988), 2:67. For a wali who lived in a cave, Muḥammad al-Muhibbi, Khulasat al-athr fi aʿyan al-qarn al-hadi ʿashar (Beirut, n.d.), 2:76.

2. Ownership of homes was widespread in other Arab towns as well. For the case of Aleppo, Abraham Marcus, The Middle East on the Eve of Modernity: Aleppo in the Eighteenth Century (New York, 1989), 189; for Cairo, Nelly Hanna, Habiter au Caire: la maison moyenne et ses habitants aux XVIIe et XVIIIe siècles (Cairo, 1991), 44.

3. Of 370 owners of residential property, only 99 (26.7%) were women.

4. Eugen Wirth, "Villes islamiques, villes arabes, villes orientales? Une problématique face au changement," in La ville arabe dans l'Islam, ed. A. Boudhiba and D. Chevallier (Tunis, 1982), 193–225.

5. Nu'man Qasatli, *Al-Rawda al-ghanna' fi Dimashq al-fayha'* (Beirut, 1876), 95.

6. Muhammad Sa'id al-Qasimi, *Qamus al-sana'at al-shamiyya*, ed. Zafir al-Qasimi (Damascus, 1988), 118.

7. Mikha'il Burayk, *Tarikh al-Sham*, ed. Ahmad Ghassan Sabbanu (Damascus, 1982), 47, 122.

8. Burayk, *Tarikh*, 77.

9. Al-Qasimi, *Qamus*, 148–49. On the decline of this artwork in the nineteenth century, Qasatli, *Al-Rawda*, 121.

10. 'Abd al-Ghani al-Nabulsi, *Al-Hadra al-unsiyya fi al-rihla al-qudsiyya*, ed. Akram al-'Ulabi (Beirut, 1990), 85.

11. Ahmad al-Budayri, *Hawadith Dimashq al-yawmiyya*, ed. Ahmad 'Izzat 'Abd al-Karim (Cairo, 1959), 141–43.

12. Among the markets which burned down were Suq al-'Attarin (1699), followed by Suq Tali' al-Qubba (1709) and Suq al-'Amara (1713). Ibn Kannan, *Yawmiyat shamiyya*, ed. Akram al-'Ulabi (Damascus, 1994), 16, 185, 193; Ibn Jum'a, "Al-Bashat wa al-qudat," in *Wulat Dimashq fi al-'ahd al-'uthmani*, ed. Salah al-Din al-Munajjid (Damascus, 1949), 53, 55.

13. Hamid al-'Imadi, *Al-'Uqud al-durriyya fi al-fatawa al-hamidiyya*, ed. Ibn 'Abdin (Beirut, 1882–83), 2:242.

14. André Raymond, *Grandes villes arabes à l'époque ottomane* (Paris, 1985), 153. Wooden houses were also standard throughout the towns of the Ottoman Balkans; Nikolai Todorov, *The Balkan City, 1400–1900* (Seattle, 1983), 33.

15. See, for example, MS 90:33–34; 109:14–15; 168:122–24, 216, 278–79. The materials were essentially the same for military architecture; BA, Bab-ı Defteri Başmuhasebe Kalemi, Şam Hazinesi, 16,993.

16. Al-Qasimi, *Qamus*, 52–53, 144–45, 294–95; Safuh Khayr, *Madinat Dimashq* (Damascus, 1969), 382–84.

17. A mixture of ash, lime, sand, and earth. Al-Budayri defined it simply as what "is extracted from the fuel of the bathhouse"; al-Budayri, *Hawadith*, 182.

18. Al-Qasimi, *Qamus*, 297.

19. Al-Qasimi, *Qamus*, 415; see also ibid., 66, 295–98.

20. Studying sales deeds from one neighborhood—the Midan—during the period 1742–52, Brigitte Marino has found that nearly half the houses had two or more owners; Marino, *Le Faubourg du Midan à Damas a l'époque ottomane (1742–1830)* (Damascus, 1997), 274–75. On Cairo, Hanna, *Habiter*, 150–52.

21. Marcus, *The Middle East*, 190. See also Abraham Marcus, "Privacy in Eighteenth Century Aleppo: The Limits of Cultural Ideals," *International Journal of Middle East Studies* 18(1986): 170–71.

22. See, for example, MS 94:8, 19, 21, 66, 67, 105, 148, 159, 170, 172, 174, 176, 179–80, 183, 185, 195, 202, 217, 221, 232, 236, 239, 240, 243, 245; 110:14, 16,

24–25, 51, 74, 133, 143; 115:106, 152, 230; 122:174; 137:1; 138:3–4; 143:109, 159–60; 168:32, 42, 67, 98, 110, 139, 287. One seventeenth-century waqf supervisor used to feel it necessary to patrol mosques and madrasas and discourage people from sleeping inside them; al-Muhibbi, *Khulasat*, 1:172.

23. Al-Muradi, *Silk*, 4:191. For further details on materials and techniques, ibid., 2:293; 3:216.

24. Al-Muradi, *Silk*, 3:21; 4:64–65, 142; Ibn Kannan, *Yawmiyat*, 190. For an example of a pilgrim, MS 143:314.

25. See, for example, MS 143:34, 98, 212–13, 229–30. André Raymond has concluded that these were the most common residents in the khans of Cairo; Raymond, *Grandes villes*, 321–23.

26. Al-Muradi, *Silk*, 4:131.

27. MS 138:157.

28. ʿAbd al-Karim Rafeq, "Qafilat al-hajj al-shami wa ahimmiyatuha fi al-ʿahd al-ʿuthmani," in *Buhuth fi al-tarikh al-iqtisadi wa al-ijtimaʿi li-bilad al-Sham fi al-ʿasr al-hadith* (Damascus, 1985), 194.

29. See, for example, MS 138:108. As for definitions, *hawsh* is an ambiguous term which can mean not only a large tenement, but a house located in a village—or, indeed, any house resembling a rural dwelling; Marino, *Le Faubourg*, 254–58; Antoine Abdel-Nour, "Types architecturaux et vocabulaire de l'habitat en Syrie aux XVIe et XVIIe siècles, in *L'espace social de la ville arabe*, ed. Dominique Chevalier (Paris, 1979), 70–71. For a general discussion of these tenements in Arab cities, Raymond, *Grandes villes*, 323–26; Antoine Abdel-Nour, *Introduction à l'histoire urbaine de la Syrie ottomane (XVIe–XVIIIe siècles)* (Beirut, 1982), 130–35; specifically for Ottoman Cairo, Hanna, *Habiter*, 70–71; for Aleppo, Marcus, *The Middle East*, 190, 318.

30. Khayr, *Madinat*, 387.

31. Ibn Kannan, *Yawmiyat*, 253–54. On the same sleeping habits in Aleppo, Alexander Russell, *The Natural History of Aleppo* (London, 1794), 1:146–47.

32. Drapes were found in just 30 out of 1,000 probate inventories. On their use, see Jean-Paul Pascual, "Meubles et objets domestiques quotidiens des intérieurs damascains du XVIIe siècle," in *Villes au Levant: hommage à André Raymond*, ed. Daniel Panzac (Aix-en-Provence, 1990), 203.

33. For one of these cases, MS 109:19–20. On neighbors' wariness towards chimneys, al-ʿImadi, *Al-ʿUqud*, 1:311–12.

34. Braziers were found throughout the population, but mostly in estates worth more than five hundred piasters (70 out of 112, or 62.5%).

35. Earthen stoves hardly ever appear in probate inventories. If al-Qasimi can be counted as a reliable guide, they were the first choice of the poor, presumably on account of their cheapness. He reports that by the end of the nineteenth

century, they had almost entirely disappeared in favor of iron braziers; al-Qasimi, *Qamus*, 396.

36. Al-Qasimi, *Qamus*, 100, 386–87.

37. Al-Qasimi, *Qamus*, 386–87.

38. Al-Qasimi, *Qamus*, 336; Abdel-Nour, *Introduction*, 221–22.

39. Al-Budayri, *Hawadith*, 10–11, 125, 172.

40. Al-Qasimi, *Qamus*, 364, 457.

41. Ibn Kannan, *Al-Mawakib*, 2:260.

42. On local techniques for glass-making and the fitting of these small windows (*nafidha* or *qumri*), al-Qasimi, *Qamus*, 163–65, 256, 363; Khayr, *Madinat*, 387. On the popularity of European glass, Raymond, *Grandes villes*, 265.

43. In a sample of 261 floor plans, windows appeared in only fifteen (5.3%). On the effect that they created in interiors, Alphonse de Lamartine, *De Lamartine's Visit to the Holy Land*, trans. Thomas Phipson (London, n.d.), 2:55.

44. Among all Arab cities, only Cairo had any tradition of street lighting; Raymond, *Grandes villes*, 151–52. For a brief description of Ramadan celebrations, al-Budayri, *Hawadith*, 23.

45. Al-ʿImadi, *Al-ʿUqud*, 2:326.

46. Al-Qasimi, *Qamus*, 256–57, 343.

47. Al-Muradi, *Silk*, 1:146.

48. Al-Qasimi, *Qamus*, 297.

49. ʿAbd al-Ghani al-Nabulsi, *ʿAlam al-malaha fi ʿilm al-falaha* (Damascus, n.d.), 167, 240.

50. Al-Nabulsi, *ʿAlam*, 156.

51. Al-Nabulsi, *ʿAlam*, 227–28; Ibn Kannan, *Al-Mawakib*, 2:215, 308–9.

52. For other suggestions, al-Nabulsi, *ʿAlam*, 226.

53. Al-ʿImadi, *Al-ʿUqud*, 2:258.

54. On the burning of trash to heat the water of bathhouses, al-Qasimi, *Qamus*, 163, 496. For references to depots in al-ʿAmara, MS 131:248–50.

55. Al-Qasimi, *Qamus*, 242; Abdel-Nour, *Introduction*, 208.

56. Al-Qasimi, *Qamus*, 142.

57. Al-Qasimi, *Qamus*, 365–66; Abdel-Nour, *Introduction*, 210.

58. Al-Budayri, *Hawadith*, 189.

59. For a discussion of the proper methods for cleaning oneself after defecation, ʿAbd al-Ghani al-Nabulsi, *Al-Hadiqa al-nadiyya: sharh al-tariqa al-muhammadiyya* (Lailbur, 1977), 2:494, 529.

60. Al-Nabulsi, *Al-Hadiqa*, 2:509. On the favoritism shown to the right side of the body, al-Nabulsi, *Al-Hadiqa*, 2:450–51, 482.

61. Al-Nabulsi, *Al-Hadiqa*, 2:493, 495.

62. Bathhouses were also to be found in many villages around the Ghuta.

Only the bedouin seem not to have bathed with any regularity. See, for example, Mikha'il al-Sabbagh, *Tarikh al-shaykh Zahir al-ʿUmar al-Zaydani, hakim ʾAkka wa bilad Safad,* ed. Qastantin al-Basha al-Mukhlisi (Harisa, Lebanon, n.d.), 62.

63. Ibn Kannan, *Al-Mawakib,* 1:238; Qasatli, *Al-Rawda,* 108–9.

64. MS 168:12, 159–60.

65. MS 90:5–6, 16, 227–28; 109:67, 135–36; 168:182.

66. Al-ʿImadi, *Al-ʿUqud,* 1:79.

67. See the description in al-Qasimi, *Qamus,* 119–20. His comments are almost certainly valid for the eighteenth century as well.

68. Only seven out of twenty-three slaveholders were registered as owning more than one slave. The highest number found in any single estate was six.

69. Only four out of thirty-five slaves (11.1%) contained in our sample of inventories were male. For a more detailed discussion of late-Ottoman slavery, Y. Hakan Erdem, *Slavery in the Ottoman Empire and its Demise, 1808–1909* (London, 1996); Ehud Toledano, *Slavery and Abolition in the Ottoman Middle East* (Seattle, 1998).

70. See, for example, al-Muradi, *Silk,* 1:109.

71. One finds confirmation of these trends in probate inventories at the end of the seventeenth century; Colette Establet and Jean-Paul Pascual, "Women in Damascene Families around 1700," *Journal of the Economic and Social History of the Orient* 45(2002): 301–19.

72. The total gross value of all one thousand estates in the sample was 1,174,920 piasters; of this amount, women held only 151,579.

73. For Cairo and Aleppo, Edward Lane, *Manners and Customs of the Modern Egyptians* (London, 1908), 137, 145; Russell, *The Natural History of Aleppo* 1:166, 172–76.

74. *Kursi* is a rather imprecise term, which also used to mean a sort of divan. Shorn of context, it remains hopelessly ambiguous; Pascual, "Meubles,", 200–201.

75. Badr al-Din al-Ghazzi, *Risalat adab al-muʾakala,* ed. ʿUmar Musa Basha (Rabat, 1984), 27.

76. On the manufacture of copper goods, al-Qasimi, *Qamus,* 413–14, 479–80.

77. For straw plates, al-Qasimi, *Qamus,* 484–85.

78. Lorna Weatherill, *Consumer Behavior and Material Culture in Britain, 1660–1760* (Cambridge, 1988), 8, 33–36; Carole Shammas, *The Pre–Industrial Consumer in England and America* (New York, 1990), 182–83. For a discussion of the evolution in manners which accompanied these new implements, Norbert Elias, *The Civilizing Process: The History of Manners and State Formation and Civilization,* trans. Edmund Jephcott 5th ed. (Cambridge, MA, 1994), 54–55, 99–105.

79. Al-Ghazzi, *Risalat,* 26.

80. Al-Ghazzi, *Risalat,* 39, 41. For modern observations of the same habit, P. L. Pellet and J. Jamalian, "Observations on the Protein-Calorie Value of Middle

Eastern Foods and Diets," in *Man, Food, and Agriculture in the Middle East*, ed. Thomas S. Stickley et al. (Beirut, 1969), 622.

81. Al-Ghazzi, *Risalat*, 15–50.

82. According to al-Nabulsi, violations of these rules were a cause of forgetfulness; ʿAbd al-Ghani al-Nabulsi, *Al-Kashf wa al-bayan ʿamma yataʿaliqu biʾl-nisyan*, ed. ʿAbd al-Jalil al-ʿIta (Damascus, n.d.), 29–30. On the virtues of moderation, al-Nabulsi, *Al-Hadiqa*, 2:465–73.

83. Al-Qasimi, *Qamus*, 114–15, 286–87, 310–11, 344–45.

84. Ibn Kannan, *Yawmiyat*, 222, 268, 300, 320, 323, 326, 327, 340, 367, 371, 374–75, 383, 394, 397, 399–400, 421, 431, 433, 437, 438, 439, 442, 443, 444, 445, 452, 462, 466, 498, 499.

85. Ibn Kannan, *Al-Mawakib*, 1:274. See also Qasatli, *Al-Rawda*, 116; al-Qasimi, *Qamus*, 305–7.

86. Al-Muradi, *Silk*, 3:135.

87. Al-Budayri, *Hawadith*, 145; Ismaʿil al-Mahasini, *Safahat min tarikh Dimashq fi al-qarn al-hadi ʿashar al-hijri mustakhraja min kunnash Ismaʿil al-Mahasini*, ed. Salah al-Din al-Munajjid, in *Maʿhid al-makhtutat al-ʿarabiyya* 6(1960), 85–86.

88. See, for example, Ibn Kannan, *Yawmiyat*, 255.

89. Ibn Jumʿa, "Al-Bashat," 57; al-Budayri, *Hawadith*, 38–39.

90. Ibn Kannan, *Yawmiyat*, 142, 162–63, 234, 289, 453.

91. Henry Maundrell, "A Journey from Aleppo to Jerusalem," in *Early Travels in Palestine*, ed. Thomas Wright (London, 1848), 405.

92. For one reaction to deliberately bad manners, al-Muradi, *Silk*, 3:59.

93. Burayk, *Tarikh*, 30–31. For other references to accusations of stinginess, together with the heated reactions that they might produce, al-Budayri, *Hawadith*, 131–32; al-Muradi, *Silk*, 3:275–76.

94. ʿAbd al-Ghani al-Nabulsi, *Al-Haqiqa wa al-majaz fi al-rihla ila bilad al-Sham wa Misr wa al-Hijaz*, ed. Ahmad ʿAbd al-Majid Haridi (Cairo, 1986), 28.

95. See, for example, Ibn Kannan, *Yawmiyat*, 190; al-Muradi, *Silk*, 3:223. For villagers showing hospitality to ulama, al-Nabulsi, *Al-Hadra*, 61–62, 67.

96. See, for example, al-Nabulsi, *Tahqiq*, 100.

97. Al-Muradi, *Silk*, 3:225–26. See also al-Budayri, *Hawadith*, 132.

98. Muhammad Khalil al-Muradi, *ʿArf al-basham fi man waliya fatwa Dimashq al-Sham*, ed. Muhammad Mutiʿ al-Hafiz and Riyad ʿAbd al-Hamid Murad, 2nd ed. (Damascus, 1988), 21.

99. See his estate, MS 162:89

100. For a discussion of these terms, Jean-Paul Pascual, "Du notaire au propriétaire en passent par l'expert: descriptions de la 'maison' damascène au XVIIIe siècle," in *L'habitat traditionnel dans les pays musulmans autour de la Méditerranée* (Cairo, 1990), 2:399–400.

101. It was possible, though extremely rare, for an iwan to be placed on the upper floor. See, for example, MS 168:236–37.

102. Ibn Kannan, *Yawmiyat*, 172–73. See also Qasatli, *Al-Rawda*, 95. On the adornment of walls, al-Qasimi, *Qamus*, 148–49.

103. Abdel-Nour, *Introduction*, 126.

104. Pascual, "Du notaire," 400. See also Marino, *Le Faubourg*, 227–28, 235.

105. Jean-Charles Depaule, "Deux regards, deux traditions: l'espace domestique perçu par les auteurs anglais et français au Levant," in *Les villes dans l'empire ottomane*, ed. Daniel Panzac (Paris, 1994), 2:197–98.

106. Al-Nabulsi, *Al-Hadiqa*, 2:437.

107. Writing implements were listed in 101 out of 1,000 estates; only two belonged to women, leaving the rate of ownership among men at approximately 16 percent (99 out of 606 male estates).

108. Books were found in only 40 out of 1000 estates. Most bibliophiles were affluent (leaving behind estates appraised at 500 piasters or more), and the overwhelming majority (all but two) were male. It is interesting to compare these figures with estates studied by Colette Establet and Jean-Paul Pascual for the late seventeenth century. They put the percentage of book owners at around 18 percent of men—only slightly inferior to the estimates of 25 percent from contemporary European inventories. Only further research on towns across the Ottoman Middle East will allow us to resolve these discrepancies and draw firmer conclusions. See Colette Establet and Jean-Paul Pascual, "Les livres des gens à Damas vers 1700," in *Livres et lecture dans le monde ottoman*, ed Frédéric Hitzel (Paris, 1999), 148.

109. Jean-Paul Pascual, "Aspects de la vie materielle à Damas à la fin du XVIIe siècle d'après les inventaires après décès," in *The Syrian Land in the Eighteenth and Nineteenth Centuries*, ed. Thomas Philipp (Stuttgart, 1992), 174.

110. Depaule, "Deux regards," 2:196–97.

111. Fatma Müge Göçek, *East Encounters West: France and the Ottoman Empire in the Eighteenth Century* (New York, 1987), 124–26. One exception to Old World decoration—or rather a partial one—was China, where well-to-do homes often kept a combination of low-slung and raised furniture; Fernand Braudel, *The Structures of Everyday Life*, trans. Sian Reynolds (New York, 1979), 288–92.

112. Qasatli, *Al-Rawda*, 95.

113. Depaule, "Deux regards,", 2:205–7. For references to divans, Maundrell, "Journey," 488; de Lamartine, *Visit*, 2:55.

114. Al-Muradi, *Silk*, 1:5, 39; 3:60; 4:50.

115. On the manufacture of *libbad*, al-Qasimi, *Qamus*, 399–400.

116. See, for example, MS 162:61–62. This wealthy estate recorded a single rug worth 200 piasters.

117. Al-Qasimi, *Qamus*, 98–99.

118. Ibn Kannan, *Yawmiyat*, 173.

119. MS 162:39–41.

120. Al-Qasimi, *Qamus*, 117, 473.

121. For identical patterns in inventories from the end of the seventeenth century, Establet and Pascual, "Women in Damascene Families," 301–19.

122. De Lamartine, *Visit*, 2:64.

123. MS 162:42–44.

124. MS 143:192–93.

125. MS 131:254–55.

126. MS 162:132.

127. Abdel-Nour, *Introduction*, 137–38. In the words of Ahmad al-ʿAllaf, who grew up at the turn of the twentieth century, his fellow Damascenes "were architects by instinct." Al-ʿAllaf, *Dimashq fi matlaʿ al-qarn al-ʿishrin* ed. ʿAli Jamil Nuʿaysa (Damascus, 1976), 142.

128. For a discussion of late-seventeenth century furniture, Pascual, "Meubles," 199–206; Pascual, "Aspects," 173–76. On the small percentage of personal wealth devoted to furniture (14.4% for "domestic goods"), Colette Establet and Jean-Paul Pascual, *Familles et fortunes à Damas: 450 foyers damascains en 1700* (Damascus, 1994), 89.

129. Al-Nabulsi, *Al-Hadiqa*, 2:534–35.

VI FASHION AND DEPORTMENT

1. Ibn Kannan, *Yawmiyat shamiyya*, ed. Akram al-ʿUlabi (Damascus, 1994), 414.

2. Muhammad Khalil al-Muradi, *Silk al-durar fi aʿyan al-qarn al-thani ʿashar* (Beirut, 1988), 4:129.

3. Al-Muradi, *Silk*, 2:183; also ibid., 1:249. For the comment attracted by the casual removal of a turban, Muhammad Amin al-Muhibbi, *Khulasat al-athr fi aʿyan al-qarn al-hadi ʿashar* (Beirut, n.d.), 3:101.

4. For descriptions, see R. P. A. Dozy, *Dictionnaire de noms des vêtements chez les Arabes* (Amsterdam, 1845), 213–15, 235–40, 244. The term *shal* also applied to a kind of belt.

5. Muhammad Saʿid al-Qasimi, *Qamus al-sanaʿat al-shamiyya*, ed. Zafir al-Qasimi (Damascus, 1988), 375.

6. Al-Qasimi, *Qamus*, 374–75.

7. Ahmad al-Budayri, *Hawadith Dimashq al-yawmiyya*, ed. Ahmad ʿIzzat ʿAbd al-Karim (Cairo, 1959), 5.

8. Al-Qasimi, *Qamus*, 374.

9. ʿAbd al-Ghani al-Nabulsi, *Kashf al-nur ʿan ashab al-qubur*, ed. Muhammad ʿAbd al-Hakim Sharaf Qadiri (Lahore, 1977), 13. For slightly earlier references to these attitudes, al-Muhibbi, *Khulasat*, 4:324, 393. See also R. Tresse, "L'évolution du costume syrien depuis un siècle," in *Entretiens sur l'évolution des pays de civilisation arabe: Communications présentées à la réunion tenue à Paris du 7 au 10 Juillet 1937 sous les auspices de l'Institut des Etudes Islamiques de l'Université de Paris et du Centre d'Etudes de Politique Etrangère* (Paris, 1938), 92.

10. Ibn Kannan, *Yawmiyat*, 287.

11. Al-Muradi, *Silk*, 2:253.

12. R. Tresse, "L'évolution du costume des citadines en Syrie depuis le XIXe siècle," *La Géographie* 71(1939):260.

13. Al-Qasimi, *Qamus*, 471.

14. Al-Qasimi, *Qamus*, 378–79.

15. For examples of women who owned a tarbush, MS 131:119, 180, 199, 246, 259; 138:55, 191; 143:52, 55, 56, 78, 115, 119, 136, 158, 228, 245, 257, 273, 280, 319, 338, 348, 358, 368, 374. For the *fas*, MS 131:213; 138:141; 143:35, 103; 162:103, 132, 149, 164, 254, 298, 355.

16. Al-Budayri, *Hawadith*, 112.

17. Yedida Stillman, *Arab Dress: A Short History*, ed. Norman Stillman (Boston, 2000), 140.

18. See, for example, MS 131:167.

19. Stillman, *Arab Dress*, 148.

20. John Lewis Burckhardt, *Travels in Syria and the Holy Land* (London, 1822), 407, 659.

21. Dozy, *Dictionnaire*, 169–70, 226–29; Colette Establet, "Les intérieurs damascains au début du XVIIIe siècle . . . sous bénéfice d'inventaire," in *Les villes dans l'empire ottomane: activités et sociétés*, ed. Daniel Panzac, (Paris, 1994), 2:41.

22. See, for example, MS 143:144.

23. The most conservative scholars debated whether women should show the entire hand or only the palm. ʿAbd al-Ghani al-Nabulsi, *Al-Hadiqa al-nadiyya: sharh al-tariqa al-muhammadiyya* (Lailbur, 1977), 2:420.

24. Al-Budayri, *Hawadith*, 134. The sample of mid-century inventories shows that 179 out of 394 women, or 45.4%, owned at least one face-veil or kerchief. Among those whose estates were assessed at five hundred piasters or more, the percentage rises to 66.1% (45 out of 68); for the rest, it stands at 41.1% (134 out of 326).

25. See al-Qasimi, who identified it as a *turra*; *Qamus*, 378. Among the 44 women recorded as owning a ghitat shash, half (22) left behind estates worth at least five hundred piasters.

26. 'Abd al-Ghani al-Nabulsi, *Ibanat al-nass fi mas'alat al-qass*, unpublished manuscript, Süleymaniye Library, Istanbul, Esad Efendi 3607/4, 89. For a discussion of the proper way to cut hair, al-Nabulsi, *Al-Hadiqa*, 2:447–48.

27. Al-Budayri, *Hawadith*, 24–25.

28. For other cases of unorthodox hairstyles, al-Muhibbi, *Khulasat*, 3:13; al-Muradi, *Silk*, 3:118.

29. Al-Muradi, *Silk*, 3:32.

30. For a summary of the ulama's basic position on beards, al-Nabulsi, *Ibanat al-nass*, 90b. For one scholar who defied these standards, al-Muhibbi, *Khulasat*, 3:223.

31. Al-Nabulsi, *Ibanat al-nass*, 89.

32. Ibn Kannan, *Yawmiyat*, 10.

33. Al-Muradi, *Silk*, 4:61. For others who dared to shave their beards, ibid., 2:183; al-Muhibbi, *Khulasat*, 1:111; 4:511.

34. Mikha'il Mishaqa, *Muntakhabat min jawab 'ala iqtirah al-ahbab*, ed. Asad Rustum and Habibi Abu Shaqra (Beirut, 1985), 77. See also the English translation by Wheeler M. Thackston, *Murder, Mayhem, Pillage, and Plunder: the History of the Lebanon in the 18th and 19th Centuries* (Albany, 1988), 118.

35. Mikha'il al-Dimashqi, *Tarikh hawadith al-Sham wa Lubnan, aw tarikh Mikha'il al-Dimashqi (1782–1841)*, ed. Ahmad Ghassan Sabbanu (Damascus, 1982), 39; Hasan Agha al-'Abd, *Tarikh Hasan Agha al-'Abd*, ed. Yusuf Nu'aysa (Damascus, 1979), 143; Mishaqa, *Muntakhabat*, 40–41; Mishaqa, *Murder*, 62.

36. Al-Qasimi, *Qamus*, 103–4.

37. Of the 393 estates which belonged to women, 118 registered earrings (30%). Hardly any men had earrings, confirming their essentially feminine appeal.

38. The contrast with early modern England, where diamonds were all the craze, is interesting; Marcia Pointon, "Jewellery in Eighteenth-Century England," in *Consumers and Luxury: Consumer Culture in Europe, 1650–1850*, ed. Maxine Berg and Helen Clifford (Manchester, 1999), 121.

39. Necklaces were found in the possessions of only 17 women (and one man); 13 estates were valued at more than 500 piasters.

40. The feminine connotation of mirrors is unmistakable: 206 out of 249 estates containing mirrors belonged to women. Few people felt the need to own more than one. Rare references to "big mirrors" hint that most were quite small.

41. W. G. Browne, *Travels in Africa, Egypt, and Syria, 1792–98* (London, 1799), 401.

42. Ibn Kannan, *al-Mawakib al-islamiyya fi al-mamalik wa al-mahasin al-shamiyya*, ed. Hikmet Isma'il (Damascus, 1992), 2:272.

43. Al-Qasimi, *Qamus*, 385–86.

44. Al-Dimashqi, *Tarikh*, 39; Mishaqa, *Muntakhabat*, 41; Mishaqa, *Murder*, 63.

45. Al-Nabulsi, *Ibanat al-nass*, 89.

46. Ibn Kannan, *Yawmiyat*, 314. The authorities might not always be so lenient; Mikha'il al-Sabbagh, *Tarikh al-shaykh Zahir al-ʿUmar al-Zaydani, hakim ʿAkka wa bilad Safad*, ed. Qastantin al-Basha al-Mukhlisi (Harisa, Lebanon, n.d.) 57–58.

47. Ibn Kannan, Yawmiyat, 325.

48. Al-Nabulsi, *Al-Hadiqa*, 2:418–20.

49. Al-Nabulsi, *Al-Hadiqa*, 2:528. For other exceptions to the rule, al-Nabulsi, *Al-Hadiqa*, 2:421–22, 529.

50. Al-Nabulsi, *Al-Hadiqa*, 2:528.

51. Al-Budayri, *Hawadith*, 208. For the uses of nudity as a means of humiliation, al-Muradi, *Silk*, 3:287; Ibn al-Siddiq, *Ghara'ib al-bada'iʿ fi ʿaja'ib al-waqa'iʿ*, ed. Yusuf Nuʿaysa (Damascus, 1988), 64.

52. Ibn Kannan, *Yawmiyat*, 324.

53. Dozy, *Dictionnaire*, 371, 374.

54. Dozy, *Dictionnaire*, 121–22, 233–34, 395–96; Stillman, *Arab Dress*, 75–77.

55. Al-Muradi, *Silk*, 3:230.

56. Dozy, *Dictionnaire*, 122.

57. Stillman, *Arab Dress*, 170.

58. Dozy, *Dictionnaire*, 24–38, 352–62, 401–3.

59. Dozy, *Dictionnaire*, 89–90.

60. Other terms from the inventories give a good impression of the broad range in price and taste: *karamsutiyya, jukha, sirtiyya* (presumably identical to the *sadriyya*), *dalmaya* (or *dalman*), *saya, tawila*.

61. Al-Muhibbi, *Khulasat*, 4:31. For a description, Dozy, *Dictionnaire*, 292–97.

62. Dozy, *Dictionnaire*, 196–98.

63. MS 131:11; 143:27, 260; 162:54, 60, 75, 79, 104, 130, 138, 147, 170, 212, 301, 313.

64. For the estates of two Christian arms dealers, MS 138:122, 157.

65. ʿAbd al-Karim Rafeq, "Mazahir min al-haya al-ʿaskariyya al-ʿuthmaniyya fi bilad al-sham min al-qarn al-sadis ʿashar hatta matlaʿ al-qarn al-tasiʿ ʿashar," in *Buhuth fi al-tarikh al-iqtisadi wa al-ijtimaʿi li-bilad al-Sham fi al-ʿasr al-hadith* (Damascus, 1985), 92.

66. Rafeq, "Mazahir min al-haya al-ʿaskariyya," 88–89. Another branch of the local gun trade was the manufacture of gunpowder; BA, Cevdet Askeriye, 42, 273.

67. Ibn Kannan, *Yawmiyat*, 113.

68. Al-Budayri, *Hawadith*, 174.

69. Al-Budayri, *Hawadith*, 234. See also Rafeq, "Mazahir min al-haya al-ʿaskariyya," 152; Rafeq, "The Local Forces in Syria in the 17th and 18th Centuries," in *War, Technology, and Society in the Middle East*, ed. V. J. Parry and M. E. Yapp (Lon-

don, 1975), 297. In the early eighteenth century, one governor was still reminding his men not to show their weapons about town; Ibn Kannan, *Yawmiyat*, 180.

70. Rafeq, "Mazahir min al-haya al-'askariyya," 86.

71. Al-Nabulsi, *Al-Hadiqa*, 2:394–95, 450, 480, 534.

72. Al-Qasimi, *Qamus*, 174.

73. 'Abd al-Ghani al-Nabulsi, *Al-Haqiqa wa al-majaz fi al-rihla ila bilad al-Sham wa Misr wa al-Hijaz*, ed. Ahmad 'Abd al-Majid Haridi (Cairo, 1986), 75. The day started officially at sunset, as did the counting of the hours. So when Ahmad al-Manini praised a colleague who "shone like the sun at four o'clock," he was actually comparing him to the bright sun of late morning as it steadily approached the zenith; al-Muradi, *Silk*, 1:135; also ibid., 1:174. Only astronomers had a system of twenty-four evenly divided hours. For other references to hours (and even "degrees," or minutes), Ibn Kannan, *Yawmiyat*, 354; al-Muradi, *Silk*, 2:18, 59, 157, 183, 294; 3:287.

74. Al-Nabulsi, *Al-Haqiqa*, 60. For other uses of religious time, ibid., 41, 61, 62; al-Muradi, *Silk*, 3:201, 215; 4:50, 67, 199, 223.

75. Al-Muradi, *Silk*, 3:167; 4:102. For other uses of diurnal time, ibid., 1:221; 2:189, 220; 3:60, 65, 81, 86, 180, 192, 219, 247, 304; 4:58, 102, 222, 247.

76. Ibn Kannan, *Al-Mawakib*, 1:221.

77. David Landes, *Revolution in Time* (Cambridge, MA, 1983), 7.

78. MS 162:89; for other ulama who owned watches, MS 162:68, 104.

79. Al-Muradi, *Silk*, 1:71. A clear majority of watch owners (34 out of 48, or 70.8%) left estates worth at least one thousand piasters. Even more interesting is the still higher number who came from an 'askari background (39 out of 48, or 81.2%). Only three women appeared in this sample; MS, 143:127; 162:148, 149.

80. It is interesting to note that in eighteenth-century England, one of the main manufacturing centers of the clock and watch industry at the time, the ownership of watches was also confined mostly to the patrician orders. Only toward the final decades of the century did it begin to extend on an appreciable scale to a more modest clientele. E. P. Thompson, "Time, Work-Discipline, and Industrial Capitalism," reprinted in *Customs in Common: Studies in Traditional Popular Culture* (New York, 1993), 366.

81. Al-Nabulsi, *Al-Hadiqa*, 2:451.

82. The figure for gold rings is 28 estates for men versus 80 for women; for silver rings, 41 for men and 14 for women.

83. MS 162:36. She owned 83 bracelets, priced around four to five piasters apiece and of no particular specification. The quantity is obviously far too large for strictly personal use. Deepening this impression is the price, which was fairly cheap for bracelets and almost certainly beneath the dignity of an elite woman.

84. Al-Nabulsi, *Al-Hadiqa*, 2:452–53.

85. Al-Nabulsi, *Al-Hadiqa*, 2:457; *Al-Tuhfa al-nabulusiyya fi al-rihla al-tarabulusiyya*, ed. Heribert Busse (Beirut, 1971), 88–90; *Ibanat al-nass*.

86. Al-Nabulsi, *Al-Hadiqa*, 2:506.

87. Al-Sabbagh, *Tarikh*, 155.

88. On the association of bare feet with humility, al-Muhibbi, *Khulasat*, 3:473.

89. Mikha'il Burayk, *Tarikh al-Sham*, ed. Ahmad Ghassan Sabbanu (Damascus, 1982), 105–6.

90. J. L. Porter, *Five Years in Damascus* (London, 1855), 58.

91. Al-Qasimi, *Qamus*, 81–82. Instead of the standard red, some jazma might be colored black, brown, or yellow.

92. Al-Qasimi, *Qamus*, 57–58; Dozy, *Dictionnaire*, 50–53.

93. Al-Qasimi, *Qamus*, 270–71.

94. Al-Qasimi, *Qamus*, 348–49.

95. Browne, *Travels*, 402.

96. See, for example, MS 131:24, 74, 103; 143:87, 162; 162:200, 304. Nearly all these shops contained at least 50 pairs of shoes, an unusually high number of goods.

97. The act of giving away clothes could be taken as a dramatic announcement of worldly renunciation or, more alarmingly, as a symptom of depression or madness; al-Muhibbi, *Khulasat*, 1:135

98. Al-Muradi, *Silk*, 2:76.

99. Ibn Kannan, *Yawmiyat*, 215–16.

100. Hasan Agha, *Tarikh*, 138.

101. Ibn Kannan, *Yawmiyat*, 222. See also al-Muhibbi, *Khulasat*, 4:138.

102. Ahmad al-'Allaf, *Dimashq fi matla' al-qarn al-'ishrin*, ed. 'Ali Jamil Nu'aysa (Damascus, 1976), 28. For the same behavior in eighteenth-century Aleppo, Abraham Marcus, *The Middle East on the Eve of Modernity: Aleppo in the Eighteenth Century* (New York, 1989), 229. On similar expectations in early modern Europe, Carlo Cipolla, *Before the Industrial Revolution: European Society and Economy, 1000–1700*, 3d ed. (New York, 1993), 25.

103. Al-Muradi, *Silk*, 1:73. For others who insisted on coarse and simple clothing, ibid., 1:272; 3:230; 4:115.

104. John Bowring, *Report on the Commercial Statistics of Syria* (London, 1840), 7, 25.

105. Hasan Agha, *Tarikh*, 100.

106. Neil McKendrick, "The Commercialization of the Economy," in Neil McKendrick, John Brewer, and J.H. Plumb, *The Birth of a Consumer Society: The*

Commercialization of Eighteenth-Century England (London, 1982), 23. On the rise of a French sense of fashion, Daniel Roche, *La culture des apparences: une histoire de vêtement, XVII-XVIIIe siècles* (Paris, 1989). We should definitely not assume that only Western Europeans were capable of such elaborate methods of advertising. On the "precocity" of Japanese fashion, S. A. M. Adshead, *Material Culture in Europe and China, 1400–1800* (New York, 1997), 27–29.

107. On the place of Indian textiles in Ottoman markets, Gilles Veinstein, "Commercial Relations between India and the Ottoman Empire (Late-Fifteenth to Late-Eighteenth Centuries): A Few Notes And Hypotheses," in *Merchants, Companies, and Trade: Europe and Asia in the Early Modern Era*, ed. Sushil Chaudhury and Michel Morineau (Cambridge, 1999), 107. See also Halil İnalcık, "The Ottoman Cotton Market and India: The Role of Labor Costs in Market Competition," in *The Middle East and the Balkans under the Ottoman Empire: Essays on Economy and Society* (Bloomington, 1993), 264–308.

108. André Raymond, *Artisans et commerçants au Caire au XVIIIe siècle* (Damascus, 1974), 182–83.

109. On the belts shipped by Hama, James A. Reilly, *A Small Town in Syria: Ottoman Hama in the Eighteenth and Nineteenth Centuries* (Oxford, 2002), 86.

110. Al-Nabulsi, *al-Kawakib al-mushriqa fi hukm istiʻmal al-muntaqa*, Süleymaniye Library, Esad Efendi 3607/16, 103b; al-Nabulsi, *Al-Hadiqa*, 2:530.

111. Robert Paris, *Histoire du commerce de Marseille, 1660–1789* (Paris, 1957), 5:507.

112. Daniel Panzac, "International and Domestic Maritime Trade in the Ottoman Empire during the Eighteenth Century," *International Journal of Middle East Studies* 24(1992): 192.

113. Roger Owen, *The Middle East in the World Economy, 1800–1914* (London, 1981), 29–30; Bruce Masters, *The Origins of Western Economic Dominance in the Middle East: Mercantilism and the Islamic Economy in Aleppo, 1600–1750* (New York, 1988), 195–96. Cotton was not grown in the Ghuta until the late nineteenth century, and only after cultivators overcame numerous difficulties; al-Qasimi, *Qamus*, 360.

114. Raymond, *Artisans et commerçants*, 189–90, 303–4.

115. Al-Qasimi, *Qamus*, 275–76.

116. On "Asian" patterns, Kenneth Pomeranz, *The Great Divergence: China and Europe and the Making of the Modern World Economy* (Princeton, 2000), 138–42.

117. See, for example, the wardrobes of two prominent ulama, MS 162:89, 104.

118. Ibn al-Siddiq, *Gharaʼib*, 58–59. For other official gifts of fur, al-Muhibbi, *Khulasat*, 4:303; al-Muradi, *Silk*, 2:85; al-Budayri, *Hawadith*, 194.

119. Donald Quataert, "Clothing Laws, State, and Society in the Ottoman Empire, 1720–1829," *International Journal of Middle East Studies* 29(1997): 409.

120. ʿAbd al-Ghani al-Nabulsi, *Al-Ghayth al-munbajis fi hukm al-masbugh bi-najis*, unpublished manuscript, Süleymaniye Library, Esad Efendi 3607, 41–44b.

121. Hamid al-ʿImadi, *Al-ʿUqud al-durriyya fi al-fatawa al-hamidiyya*, ed. Ibn ʿAbdin (Beirut, 1882–83), 2:323–24.

122. See, for example, MS 131:122, 155, 159, 210, 216; 138:11, 38, 61, 62, 127, 160, 175; 143:27, 39, 46, 99, 123, 126, 141, 144, 162, 188, 210, 229, 345, 372, 380; 162:24, 58, 68, 93, 101, 102, 103, 104, 123, 130, 133, 138, 178, 203, 242, 246, 250, 266, 268, 306, 308, 318, 319, 325.

123. MS 162:89. For prominent scholars who owned yellow garments, MS 162:68, 104.

124. Al-Qasimi, *Qamus*, 376–77.

125. Al-Budayri, *Hawadith*, 135–36.

126. Al-Muradi, *Silk*, 2:232.

127. Browne, *Travels*, 395–96.

128. See, for example, MS 131:207, 219, 226; 138:20, 34, 151; 143:7, 36, 46, 107, 118, 196, 206, 223, 243, 250; 162:29, 168, 194.

129. Al-Budayri, *Hawadith*, 108–10.

130. See, for example, MS 131:277; 138:58; 143:225. For more about these regulations, Yusuf Nuʿaysa, *Mujtamaʿ madinat Dimashq (1772–1840)* (Damascus, 1986), 2:624.

131. See, for example, MS 131:155, 216; 138:61, 127; 143:99; 162:24, 68, 104, 319. All of these individuals, though Muslim, owned yellow turbans.

132. Burayk, *Tarikh*, 38. Sartorial distinctions were so well known that people might incorporate them into insults; al-Muhibbi, *Khulasat*, 2:108.

133. Burayk, *Tarikh*, 73–74.

134. Al-Dimashqi, *Tarikh*, 23. The headgear of the Rumelians struck al-Dimashqi as quite odd. They wore a hat known as a *kulenk*, to which they fastened a small bell.

135. On the colors to be worn by non-Muslims, ibid., 38; also Mishaqa, *Murder*, 63 (left out altogether in the published Arabic version).

136. Al-Dimashqi, *Tarikh*, 41. For a less complete version of the story, Hasan Agha, *Tarikh*, 142.

137. Alphonse de Lamartine, *De Lamartine's Visit to the Holy Land*, trans. Thomas Phipson (London, n.d.), 2:50.

138. Al-ʿAllaf, *Dimashq*, 32–33. He reports that at the turn of the twentieth century, Christians and Jews of the older generation were partial to yellow.

139. Quataert, "Clothing Laws," 407–11.

140. Ibn Jumʿa, "Al-Bashat wa al-qudat," in *Wulat Dimashq fi al-ʿahd al-ʿuthmani*, ed. Salah al-Din al-Munajjid (Damascus, 1949), 49. This was probably the same incident mentioned in al-Muradi, *Silk*, 3:135. This association with female attire

is interesting because Damascene men had become very fond of the qalbaq by the nineteenth century; al-Qasimi, *Qamus*, 379–80.

141. Al-Dimashqi, *Tarikh*, 37–41.

142. Hasan Agha, *Tarikh*, 148–50.

CONCLUSION

1. Hélène Desmet-Grégoire, conclusion to *Cafés d'Orient revisités*, ed. Hélène Desmet-Grégoire and François Georgeon (Paris, 1997), 209.

2. Carole Shammas, "Changes in English and Anglo-American Consumption from 1550 to 1800," in *Consumption and the World of Goods*, ed. John Brewer and Roy Porter (London, 1993), 178–79.

3. Donald Quataert, introduction to *Consumption Studies and the History of the Ottoman Empire, 1500–1922* (Albany, 2000), 4, 10–11.

4. Hans-Joachim Voth, "Time and Work in Eighteenth-Century London," *Journal of Economic History* 58(1998): 29–58; Gregory Clark and Ysbrand van der Werf, "Work in Progress? The Industrious Revolution," *Journal of Economic History* 58(1998): 830–43. See also E. P. Thompson, "Time, Work-Discipline, and Industrial Capitalism," reprinted in *Customs in Common: Studies in Traditional Popular Culture* (New York, 1993), 352–403; Douglas Reid, "The Decline of St. Monday, 1776–1876," *Past and Present* 71(1976): 76–100.

5. Cissie Fairchilds, "The Production and Marketing of Populuxe Goods in Eighteenth-Century Paris," in *Consumption and the World of Goods*, ed. John Brewer and Roy Porter (London, 1993).

6. On the "middle ranks" as the most dynamic consumers in eighteenth-century England, Lorna Weatherill, *Consumer Behavior and Material Culture in Britain, 1660–1760*, 2nd ed. (London, 1996), 191–94. On the rise of a modern economic culture, J. H. Plumb, "Part Three: Commercialization and Society," in Neil McKendrick et al., *The Birth of a Consumer Society: The Commercialization of Eighteenth-Century England* (London, 1982), 284–85, 332–34.

7. 'Abd al-Ghani al-Nabulsi, *Kashf al-nur 'an ashab al-qubur*, ed. Muhammad 'Abd al-Hakim Sharaf Qadiri (Lahore, 1977), 22–23.

8. For a very different view of the prospects for finding a "middle-class" culture, Nelly Hanna, *In Praise of Books: A Cultural History of Cairo's Middle Class, Sixteenth to the Eighteenth Century* (Syracuse, 2003).

9. Andrew M. Watson, "A Medieval Green Revolution," in *The Islamic Middle East, 700–1900*, ed. Abraham Udovitch (Princeton, 1981), 29–58; "The Arab Agricultural Revolution and Its Diffusion, 700–1100," *Journal of Economic History* 34(1974): 8–35; *Agricultural Innovation in the Early Islamic World* (Cambridge, 1983).

10. Among the recent contributions to this debate: Dina Rizk Khoury, *State and Provincial Society in the Ottoman Empire: Mosul, 1540–1834* (Cambridge, 1997); Margaret Meriwether, "Urban Notables and Rural Resources in Aleppo, 1770–1830," *International Journal of Turkish Studies* 4(1987): 55–73; Ariel Salzmann, "An Ancien Regime Revisited: Privatization and Political Economy in the 18th-Century Ottoman Empire," *Politics and Society* 21(1993): 393–423; Jean-Pierre Thieck, "Décentralisation ottomane et affirmation urbaine à Alep à la fin du XVIIIe siècle," in *Passion d'Orient* (Paris, 1992), 113–76.

11. Ahmad al-Budayri, *Hawadith Dimashq al-yawmiyya*, ed. Ahmad 'Izzat 'Abd al-Karim (Cairo, 1959), 38–39. For a comparison of Ottoman decentralization with transformations occurring in Iran and India, C. A. Bayly, *Imperial Meridian: The British Empire and the World, 1780–1830* (London, 1989), chap. 2.

12. Al-Budayri, *Hawadith*, 103.

13. Steve Tamari, "Ottoman Madrasas: the Multiple Lives of Educational Institutions in Eighteenth-Century Syria," *Journal of Early Modern History* 5(2001): 120–25.

14. André Raymond, *Artisans et commerçants au Caire au XVIIIe siècle* (Damascus, 1974), chaps. 13–15; Raymond, "Soldiers in Trade: The Case of Ottoman Cairo," *British Journal of Middle Eastern Studies* 18(1991):16–37. On Janissary abuses in Aleppo, Abraham Marcus, *The Middle East on the Eve of Modernity: Aleppo in the Eighteenth Century* (New York, 1989), 88–92, 133–34.

15. In smaller towns such as Jerusalem, paramilitary intervention in the marketplace may have been more restrained, or altogether absent. See, for example, Amnon Cohen, *The Guilds of Ottoman Jerusalem* (Leiden, 2001), 6.

16. As estimated for "lower-income budgets" in Cairo during the 1990s; Diane Singerman, *Avenues of Participation: Family, Politics, and Networks in Urban Quarters of Cairo* (Princeton, 1995), 167.

17. Weatherill, *Consumer Behavior*, 135.

18. Muhammad Khalil al-Muradi, *Silk al-durar fi a'yan al-qarn al-thani 'ashar* (Beirut, 1988), 4:118. For evidence of the same obsessions among twentieth-century townspeople, Unni Wikan, *Life among the Poor in Cairo*, trans. Ann Henning (New York, 1980), 34.

19. Al-Budayri, *Hawadith*, 4. On food and popular imagination in Europe, Piero Camporesi, *Bread of Dreams: Food and Fantasy in Early Modern Europe*, trans. David Gentilcore (Chicago, 1989).

20. Philip S. Khoury, *Syria and the French Mandate: The Politics of Arab Nationalism, 1920–1945* (Princeton, 1987), 168–69. For the harvest of 1932, ibid., 375, 399.

21. Muhammad Sa'id al-Qasimi, *Qamus al-sana'at al-shamiyya*, ed. Zafir al-Qasimi (Damascus, 1988), 422–23; Ahmad al-'Allaf, *Dimashq fi matla' al-qarn al-'ishrin*, ed. 'Ali Jamil Nu'aysa (Damascus, 1976), 12.

22. Hamid al-ʿImadi, *Al-ʿUqud al-durriyya fi al-fatawa al-hamidiyya*, ed. Ibn ʿAbdin (Beirut, 1883), 2:334. See also ʿAbd al-Ghani al-Nabulsi, *Al-Hadiqa al-nadiyya: sharh al-tariqa al-muhammadiyya* (Lailbur, 1977), 2:482.

23. Ibn Kannan, *Yawmiyat shamiyya*, ed. Akram al-ʿUlabi (Damascus, 1994), 411–12.

24. Al-Nabulsi, *Al-Hadiqa*, 2:375.

25. See the laments in al-Nabulsi, *Al-Hadiqa*, 1:130–31; 2:317.

BIBLIOGRAPHY

ARCHIVAL COLLECTIONS

Başbakanlık Arşivi (Prime Ministry Archives), Istanbul, Turkey.
Markaz al-Watha'iq al-Tarikhiyya (Center for Historical Documents), Damascus, Syria.
National Library, Damascus, Syria.
Süleymaniye Library, Istanbul, Turkey.

UNPUBLISHED MANUSCRIPTS

al-Nabulsi, 'Abd al-Ghani, Ajwiba 'an khamsat as'ila, Süleymaniye Library, Esad
    Efendi 3607/25.
———. Al-Ghayth al-munbajis fi hukm al-masbugh bi'l-najis, Süleymaniye Library, Esad
    Efendi 3607/9.
———. Ibanat al-nass fi mas'alat al-qass, Süleymaniye Library, Esad Efendi 3607/13.
———. Ishraq al-ma'alim fi ahkam al-mazalim, Süleymaniye Library, Esad Efendi 3607/8.
———. Al-Kawakib al-mushriqa fi hukm isti'mal al-muntaqa, Süleymaniye Library, Esad
    Efendi 3607/16.
———. Al-Majalis al-shamiyya fi muwa'iz al-bilad al-rumiyya, Süleymaniye Library, Esad
    Efendi 1677/1.

PUBLISHED SOURCES

Abdel-Nour, Antoine. Habitat et functions urbaines en Syrie, XVIe–XVIIIe
    siècles. Paris, 1979.
———. "Habitat et structures sociales à Alep aux XVIIe et XVIIIe siècles." In
    La ville dans l'Islam, ed. A. Bouhdiba and D. Chevallier, 69–102. Tunis, 1982.
———. Introduction à l'histoire urbaine de la Syrie ottomane (XVIe–XVIIIe siècles). Beirut,
    1982.

————. "Types architecturaux et vocabulaire de l'habitat en Syrie aux XVIe et XVIIe siècles." In *L'espace social de la ville arabe*, ed. Dominique Chevalier, 59–92. Paris, 1979.

Abou el-Haj, Rifaʿat ʿAli. *Formation of the Modern State: The Ottoman Empire, Sixteenth to Eighteenth Centuries*. Albany, 1991.

Abu Husayn, Abdul-Rahim. "Problems in the Ottoman Administration of Syria in the 16th and 17th Centuries." *International Journal of Middle East Studies* 24(1992): 665–75.

Abu Shanab, ʿAdil. *Dimashq ayyam zaman*. Damascus, 1991.

Abu Zahra, Muhammad. *Al-Ahwal al-shakhsiyya*. Damascus, 1957.

Adshead, S. A. M. *Material Culture in Europe and China, 1400–1800*. New York, 1997.

Ahsan, M. M. *Social Life under the Abbasids (786–902 AD)*. New York, 1979.

Aladdin, Bakri. "ʿAbd al-Ghani al-Nabulsi: Ouevre, vie, et doctrine." 2 vols. Thèse: Université de Paris, 1985.

al-ʿAllaf, Ahmad. *Dimashq fi matlaʿ al-qarn al-ʿishrin*. Edited by ʿAli Jamil Nuʿaysa. Damascus, 1976.

al-Antaki, Daʾud. *Tadhkirat uli al-albab wa al-jamiʿ liʾl-ʿajab al-ʿujab*. 3 vols. Beirut, n.d.

ʿAnuti, Usama. *Al-Haraka al-adabiyya fi bilad al-Sham khilal al-qarn al-thamin ʿashar*. Beirut, 1970.

Appadurai, A., ed. *The Social Life of Things: Commodities in Cultural Perspective*. Cambridge, 1986.

Artan, Tülay, ed. *Eyüp'te Sosyal Yaşam*. Istanbul, 1998.

Ashtor, Eliyahu. *A Social and Economic History of the Near East in the Middle Ages*. Berkeley, 1976.

al-Aswad, Nizar. *Al-Amthal al-shaʿbiyya al-shamiyya*. Damascus, 1992.

al-ʿAttar, Muhammad Husayn. *ʿIlm al-miyah al-jariyya fi madinat Dimashq*. Edited by Ahmad Ghassan Sabbanu. Damascus, 1984.

al-ʿAzm, ʿAbd al-Qadir. *Al-Usra al-ʿAzmiyya*. Damascus, 1960.

Baer, Gabriel. *Population and Society in the Arab East*. New York, 1966.

al-Barbir, Ahmad. "Zahr al-ghida fi dhikr al-fida." In *Fi rihab Dimashq*, ed. Muhammad Dahman. Damascus, 1982.

Barbir, Karl. "From Pasha to Efendi: The Assimilation of Ottomans in Damascene Society, 1516–1783," *International Journal of Turkish Studies* 1(1979–80): 68–83.

————. *Ottoman Rule in Damascus, 1708–1758*. Princeton, 1980.

————. "Wealth, Privilege, and Family Structure: The ʿAskeris of 18th-Century Damascus According to the Qassam ʿAskeri Inheritance Records." In *The Syrian Land in the 18th and 19th Century*, ed. Thomas Philipp, 179–96. Stuttgart, 1992.

Bartlett, W. H., William Purser, et al. *Syria, the Holy Land, Asia Minor &c., Illustrated*. London, 1836.

Bayly, C. A. *Imperial Meridian: The British Empire and the World, 1780–1830.* London, 1989.

———. *Rulers, Townsmen, and Bazaars: North Indian Society in the Age of British Expansion, 1770–1870.* New York, 1983.

Beck, Lois, and Nikki Keddie, eds. *Women in the Muslim World.* Cambridge, 1978.

Berg, Maxine, and Helen Clifford, eds. *Consumers and Luxury: Consumer Culture in Europe, 1650–1850.* New York, 1999.

Bianquis, Anne-Marie. "Damas et la Ghouta." In *La Syrie d'aujourd'hui,* ed. André Raymond, 359–84. Paris, 1980.

Bowring, John. *Report on the Commercial Statistics of Syria.* London, 1840.

Boyer, Pierre. *La Vie quotidienne à Alger à la veille de l'intervention française.* Monaco, 1962.

Braudel, Fernand. *The Mediterranean and the Mediterranean World in the Age of Philip II.* Trans. Sian Reynolds. 2 vols. New York, 1972.

———. *The Structures of Everyday Life: The Limits of the Possible.* Trans. Sian Reynolds. New York, 1981.

Bray, Francesca. *Technology and Gender: Fabrics of Power in Late Imperial China.* Berkeley, 1997.

Brewer, John, and Roy Porter, eds. *Consumption and the World of Goods.* London, 1993.

Brown, K., et al., eds. *Middle Eastern Cities in Comparative Perspective.* London, 1986.

Browne, E. G. *Arabian Medicine.* Cambridge, 1962.

Browne, W. G. *Travels in Africa, Egypt, and Syria, 1792–98.* London, 1799.

al-Budayri, Ahmad. *Hawadith Dimashq al-yawmiyya.* Edited by Ahmad 'Izzat 'Abd al-Karim. Cairo, 1959.

Bulliet, Richard. *The Camel and the Wheel.* New York, 1990.

Burayk, Mikha'il. *Tarikh al-Sham.* Edited by Ahmad Ghassan Sabbanu. Damascus, 1982.

Burke, Peter. *The Historical Anthropology of Early Modern Italy: Essays on Perception and Communication.* Cambridge, 1987.

———. *Popular Culture in Early Modern Europe.* New York, 1978.

Camporesi, Piero. *Bread of Dreams: Food and Fantasy in Early Modern Europe.* Trans. David Gentilcore. Chicago, 1989.

Chartier, Roger, ed. *A History of Private Life.* Vol. 3, *The Passions of the Renaissance.* Trans. Arthur Goldhammer. London, 1989.

Chatila, Khalid. *Le mariage chez les musulmans en Syrie.* Paris, 1934.

Chaudhuri, K. N. *Asia Before Europe: Economy and Civilization of the Indian Ocean from the Rise of Islam to 1750.* New York, 1990.

Chevalier, Dominique. *Villes et travail en Syrie.* Paris, 1982.

———, ed. *L'espace social de la ville arabe.* Paris, 1979.

Cipolla, Carlo. *Before the Industrial Revolution: European Society and Economy, 1000–1700.* 3d ed. New York, 1976.

Çizakça, Murat. *A Comparative Evolution of Business Partnerships: The Islamic World and Europe, with Specific Reference to the Ottoman Archives.* New York, 1996.

Cuno, Ken. *The Pasha's Peasants: Land, Society, and Economy in Lower Egypt, 1740–1858.* Cambridge, 1992.

Daghestani, K. *Étude sociologique sur la famille musulmane contemporaine en Syrie.* Paris, 1932.

Dahman, Muhammad Ahmad, ed. *Fi rihab Dimashq.* Damascus, 1982.

Dalton, George, ed. *Primitive, Archaic, and Modern Economies: Essays of Karl Polanyi.* Garden City, NY, 1968.

——. *Tribal and Peasant Economies: Readings in Economic Anthropology.* Garden City, NY, 1967.

D'Arvieux, Laurent. *Wasf madinat Dimashq.* Trans. Ahmad Ibish. Damascus, 1982.

De Grazia, Victoria, ed. *The Sex of Things: Gender and Consumption in Historical Perspective.* Berkeley, 1996.

Deguilhem, Randi. "Waqf Documents: A Multi-Purpose Historical Source— The Case of 19th-Century Damascus." In *Les villes dans l'empire ottomane: activités et sociétés,* ed. Daniel Panzac. 1(67–95). Paris, 1991.

De Lamartine, Alphonse. *De Lamartine's Visit to the Holy Land.* Trans. Thomas Phipson. 2 vols. London, n.d.

Depaule, Jean-Charles. "Deux regards, deux traditions: l'espace domestique perçu par les auteurs anglais et français au Levant." In *Les villes dans l'empire ottomane,* ed. Daniel Panzac. 2(189–228). Paris, 1994.

Desmet-Grégoire, Hélène, and François Georgeon, eds. *Cafés d'Orient revisités.* Paris, 1997.

DeVries, Jan. *European Urbanization, 1500–1800.* Cambridge, MA, 1984.

al-Dimashqi, 'Abd al-Rahman ibn 'Abd al-Razzaq. *Hada'iq al-in'am fi fada'il al-Sham.* Edited by Yusuf Bidiwi. Damascus, 1995.

al-Dimashqi, Mikha'il. *Tarikh hawadith al-Sham wa Lubnan, aw tarikh Mikha'il al-Dimashqi (1782–1841).* Edited by Ahmad Ghassan Sabbanu. Damascus, 1982.

Doumani, Beshara. *Rediscovering Palestine: Merchants and Peasants in Jabal Nablus, 1700–1900.* Berkeley, 1995.

Dozy, R. P. A. *Dictionnaire de noms des vêtements chez les Arabes.* Amsterdam, 1845.

Ensminger, Jean, ed. *Theory in Economic Anthropology.* Lanham, MD, 2002.

Establet, Colette. "Les intérieurs damascains au début du XVIIIe siècle . . . sous bénéfice d'inventaire." In *Les villes dans l'empire ottomane: activités et sociétés,* ed. Daniel Panzac. 2(14–46). Paris, 1994.

Establet, Colette, and Jean-Paul Pascual. "Damascene Probate Inventories of the 17th and 18th Centuries: Some Preliminary Approaches and Results." *International Journal of Middle East Studies* 24(1992): 373–93.

———. *Familles et fortunes à Damas: 450 foyers damascains en 1700*. Damascus, 1994.

———. "Les livres des gens á Damas vers 1700." In *Livres et lecture dans le monde otto-man*, ed. Frédéric Hitzel, 143–71. Paris, 1999.

———. "La mesure de l'inegalité dans la societé ottomane: utilisation de l'indice de Gini pour le Caire et Damas vers 1700." *Journal of the Economic and Social History of the Orient* 37(1994–95): 171–82.

Faroqhi, Suraiya. "Camels, Wagons, and the Ottoman State in the Sixteenth and Seventeenth Centuries." *International Journal of Middle East Studies*, 14(1982): 523–39.

———. "Crisis and Change, 1590–1699." In *An Economic and Social History of the Ottoman Empire: Volume 2, 1600–1914*, ed. Halil Inalcık and Donald Quataert. Cambridge, 1994.

———. *Making a Living in the Ottoman Lands, 1480–1820*. Istanbul, 1995.

———. *Men of Modest Substance: House Owners and House Property in 17th-Century Ankara and Kayseri*. Cambridge, 1987.

———. *Osmanlı Kültürü ve Gündelik Yaşam: Ortaçağdan Yirmi Yüzyıla*. Trans. Elif Kılıç. Istanbul, 1997.

———. *Towns and Townsmen of Ottoman Anatolia: Trade, Crafts, and Food Production in an Urban Setting, 1520–1650*. New York, 1984.

Fine, Ben, and Ellen Leopold. *The World of Consumption*. New York, 1993.

Friedland, Roger, and A. F. Robertson, eds. *Beyond the Marketplace: Rethinking Economy and Society*. New York, 1990.

Gerber, Haim. *Economy and Society in an Ottoman City: Bursa, 1600–1700*. Jerusalem, 1988.

———. "The Monetary System of the Ottoman Empire." *Journal of the Economic and Social History of the Orient* 25(1982):308–24.

———. "The Social and Economic Position of Women in an Ottoman City: Bursa, 1600–1700." *International Journal of Middle Eastern Studies* 12(1980): 231–44.

———. *The Social Origins of the Modern Middle East*. Boulder, CO, 1987.

———. *State, Society, and Law in Islam: Ottoman Law in Comparative Perspective*. Albany, 1994.

Gerber, Haim, and N. Gross. "Inflation or Deflation in 19th-Century Syria and Palestine." *Journal of Economic History* 40(1980): 351–57.

Ghazzal, Zouhair. *L'économie politique de Damas durant le XIXe siècle*. Damascus, 1993.

al-Ghazzi, Badr al-Din. *Risalat adab al-mu'akala*. Edited by 'Umar Musa Basha. Rabat, 1984.

al-Ghazzi, Kamal al-Din. "Al-Tadhkira al-musamma bi'l-durr al-maknun wa al-jamal al-masun min fara'id al-ʿulum wa fawa'id al-funun." In *Fi rihab Dimashq*, ed. Muhammad Dahman. Damascus, 1982.

Göçek, Fatma Müge. *East Encounters West: France and the Ottoman Empire in the Eighteenth Century*. New York, 1987.

Goffman, Erving. *The Presentation of Self in Everyday Life*. New York, 1959.

Goitein, S. D. *A Mediterranean Society: The Jewish Communities of the Arab World as Portrayed in the Documents of the Cairo Geniza*. 5 vols. Los Angeles, 1967–88.

Green, P. *A Journey from Aleppo to Damascus*. London, 1736.

Greenwood, Anthony. "Istanbul's Meat Provisioning: A Study of the *Celepkeşan* System." PhD dissertation, University of Chicago, 1988.

Grehan, James. "Street Violence and Social Imagination in Late-Mamluk and Ottoman Damascus (ca. 1500–1800)." *International Journal of Middle East Studies* 35(2003): 215–36.

———. "The Mysterious Power of Words: Language, Law, and Culture in Ottoman Damascus (17th–18th Centuries)." *Journal of Social History* 37(2004): 991–1015.

Halstead, Paul, and John O'Shea, eds. *Bad Year Economics: Cultural Responses to Risk and Uncertainty*. Cambridge, 1989.

Hammami, Hasan. *Al-Azya' al-sha'biyya wa taqaliduha fi Suriya*. Damascus, 1971.

Hanley, Susan. *Everyday Things in Premodern Japan*. Princeton, 1997.

Hanna, Nelly. *Habiter au Caire: la maison moyenne et ses habitants aux XVIIe et XVIIIe siècles*. Cairo, 1991.

Hasan Agha al-'Abd, *Tarikh Hasan Agha al-'Abd*. Edited by Yusuf Nu'aysa. Damascus, 1979.

Hathaway, Jane. *The Politics of Households in Ottoman Egypt: The Rise of the Qazdağlıs*. Cambridge, 1997.

Hattox, Ralph S. *Coffee and Coffeehouses: The Origins of a Social Beverage in the Medieval Near East*. Seattle, 1985.

Hodgson, Marshall. *The Venture of Islam*. Vol. 3, *The Gunpowder Empires and Modern Times*. Chicago, 1974.

Hinz, Walther. *Al-Mikayil wa al-awzan al-islamiyya wa ma yu'adiluha fi al-nizam al-mitri*. Trans. Kamil al-'Asli. Amman, 1970.

Holt, P. M. *Egypt and the Fertile Crescent, 1516–1922: A Political History*. London, 1966.

Hourani, Albert. *Arabic Thought in the Liberal Age, 1798–1939*. London, 1962.

———. "Culture and Change: the Middle East in the Eighteenth Century." In *Islam in European Thought*. Cambridge, 1991.

———. *A History of the Arab Peoples*. London, 1991.

———. "Ottoman Reform and the Politics of Notables." In *The Beginnings of Modernization in the Middle East: The Nineteenth Century*, ed. W. R. Polk and Richard Chambers. Chicago, 1968.

Ibesch, Ahmad N., and Koutaiba Shihabi. *Ma'alim Dimashq al-tarikhiyya*. Damascus, 1996.

Ibn 'Abdin. *Radd al-muhtar 'ala darr al-mukhtar.* 6 vols. Beirut, 1987.

———. *Rasa'il Ibn 'Abdin.* 2 vols. Beirut, n.d.

———. *Al-'Uqud al-durriyya fi tanqih al-fatawa al-hamidiyya.* 2 vols. Beirut, 1882.

Ibn Jum'a. "Al-Bashat wa al-qudat." In *Wulat Dimashq fi al-'ahd al-'uthmani,* ed. Salah al-Din al-Munajjid. Damascus, 1949.

Ibn Kannan. *Al-Mawakib al-islamiyya fi al-mamalik wa al-mahasin al-shamiyya.* Edited by Hikmet Isma'il. 2 vols. Damascus, 1992.

———. *Al-Muruj al-sundusiyya al-fasiha bi talkhis tarikh al-salihiyya.* Edited by Muhammad Ahmad Dahman. Damascus, 1947.

———. *Yawmiyat Shamiyya.* Edited by Akram al-'Ulabi. Damascus, 1994.

Ibn al-Siddiq. *Ghara'ib al-bada'i' fi 'aja'ib al-waqa'i'.* Edited by Yusuf Nu'aysa. Damascus, 1988.

al-'Imadi, Hamid. *Al-'Uqud al-durriyya fi al-fatawa al-hamidiyya.* Edited by Ibn 'Abdin. 2 vols. Beirut, 1882–83.

İnalcık, Halil. "Capital Formation in the Ottoman Empire." *Journal of Economic History* 19(1969): 97–140.

———. "The Ottoman Cotton Market and India: The Role of Labor Costs in Market Competition." In *The Middle East and the Balkans under the Ottoman Empire: Essays on Economy and Society,* 264–308. Bloomington, 1993.

Institut français d'archeologie orientale. *L'habitat traditionnel dans les pays musulmans autour de la Méditerranée.* 2 vols. Cairo, 1988.

Issawi, Charles. *An Economic History of the Middle East and North Africa, 1800–1980.* New York, 1982.

Jennings, Ronald. "Loans and Credit in Early 17th-Century Ottoman Judicial Records—The Shari'a Court of Anatolian Kayseri." *Journal of the Economic and Social History of the Orient* 16(1973): 168–216.

———. "Women in Early 17th-Century Ottoman Records—The Shari'a Court of Anatolian Kayseri." *Journal of the Economic and Social History of the Orient* 18(1975): 53–114.

Johansen, Baber. *The Islamic Law on Land Tax and Rent.* London, 1988.

———. "Urban Structures in the View of the Muslim Jurists: The Case of Damascus in the Early 19th Century." *Villes au Levant: Revue du monde musulmane et de la Méditerranée* 55–56(1990):94–100.

Kandiyoti, Deniz. "Bargaining with Patriarchy." *Gender and Society* 2(1988): 274–90.

———. "Islam and Patriarchy." In *Women in Middle Eastern History,* ed. Nikki Keddie and Beth Baron. London, 1991.

Kayyal, Munir. *Ramadan wa taqaliduhu al-dimashqiyya.* Damascus, n.d.

Keddie, Nikki. Introduction to *Women in Middle Eastern History,* ed. Nikki Keddie and Beth Baron. London, 1991.

———. "Problems in the Study of Middle Eastern Women." *International Journal of Middle East Studies* 11(1979): 225–40.

Kelly, Walter Keating. *Syria and the Holy Land, Their Scenery and Their People*. London, 1844.

Khayr, Safuh. *Ghutat Dimashq*. Damascus, 1957.

———. *Madinat Dimashq*. Damascus, 1969.

Khoury, Philip S. *Syria and the French Mandate: The Politics of Arab Nationalism, 1920–1945*. Princeton, 1987.

Khoury, Youssef. *Prix et monnaie en Syrie*. Nancy, 1943.

Kurd 'Ali, Muhammad. *Ghutat Dimashq*. Damascus, 1949.

———. *Khitat al-Sham*. 2nd ed. 6 vols. Damascus, 1983.

Lane, Edward. *Manners and Customs of the Modern Egyptians*. London, 1908.

Lapidus, Ira. *Muslim Cities in the Later Middle Ages*. Cambridge, MA, 1967.

Lecerf, Jean. "La famille dans la monde arabe et islamique." *Arabica* 3(1956): 31–60.

———. "Transformation en Orient sous l'influence de l'Occident du costume et des modes." In *Entretiens sur l'évolution des pays de civilisation arabe: communications présentées à la réunion tenue à Paris du 7 au 10 Juillet 1937 sous les auspices de l'Institut des Etudes Islamiques de l'Université de Paris et du Centre d'Etudes de Politique Etrangère*. Paris, 1938.

Leibenstein, Harvey. *Beyond Economic Man: A New Foundation for Microeconomics*. Cambridge, 1976.

Le Roy Ladurie, Emmanuel. *Times of Feast, Times of Famine: A History of Climate Since the Year 1000*. Trans. Barbara Bray. New York, 1971.

Lewis, Bernard. *The Emergence of Modern Turkey*. New York, 1961.

Livi-Bacci, Massimo. *Population and Nutrition*. Cambridge, 1991.

Lortet, L. *La Syrie d'aujourd'hui: voyages dans la Phénicie, le Liban, et la Judée, 1875–1880*. Paris, 1884.

Mabro, Judy. *Veiled Half-Truths: Western Travellers' Perceptions of Middle Eastern Women*. London, 1991.

al-Mahasini, Isma'il. "Safahat min tarikh Dimashq fi al-qarn al-hadi 'ashar al-hijri mustakhraja min kunnash Isma'il al-Mahasini." Edited by Salah al-Din al-Munajjid. *Ma'hid al-makhtutat al-'arabiyya* 6(1960): 77–160.

Marcus, Abraham. *The Middle East on the Eve of Modernity: Aleppo in the Eighteenth Century*. New York, 1989.

———. "Privacy in Eighteenth-Century Aleppo: The Limits of Cultural Ideals." *International Journal of Middle East Studies* 18(1986): 165–83.

Mardam-Bey, Farouk. "Tensions sociales et réalités urbaines à Damas au XVIIIe siècle." In *La ville arabe dans l'Islam*, ed. Abdel-Wahhab Bouhdiba and Dominique Chevallier, 117–96. Tunis, 1982.

Marino, Brigitte. *Le Faubourg du Midan à Damas à l'époque ottomane: espace urbain, société et habitat (1742–1830)*. Damascus, 1997.

Massignon, Louis. "La Structure du travail à Damas en 1927." *Cahiers internationaux de sociologie* 15(1953): 34–52.

Masters, Bruce. *The Origins of Western Economic Dominance in the Middle East: Mercantilism and the Islamic Economy in Aleppo, 1600–1750*. New York, 1988.

Maundrell, Henry. "A Journey from Aleppo to Jerusalem." In *Early Travels in Palestine*, ed. Thomas Wright. London, 1848.

Maury, B. "La maison damascène au XVIIIe et au début de XIXe siècle." In *L'habitat traditionnel dans les pays musulmans autour de la Méditerrannée*, 1:1–42. Cairo, 1988.

Mayer, Ann Elizabeth, ed. *Property, Social Structure, and Law in the Modern Middle East*. Albany, 1985.

McGowan, Bruce. "The Age of the Ayans, 1699–1812." In *An Economic and Social History of the Ottoman Empire: Volume 2, 1600–1914*, ed. Halil Inalcık and Donald Quataert. Cambridge, 1994.

McKendrick, Neil, John Brewer, and J. H. Plumb. *The Birth of a Consumer Society: The Commercialization of Eighteenth-Century England*. London, 1982.

Meriwether, Margaret L. *The Kin Who Count: Family and Society in Ottoman Aleppo, 1770–1840*. Austin, 1999.

Minchinton, Walter. "Patterns and Structure of Demand, 1500–1750." In *The Fontana Economic History of Europe: Volume 2, The Sixteenth and Seventeenth Centuries*, ed. Carlo Cipolla. Glasgow, 1974.

Mintz, Sidney W. *Sweetness and Power: The Place of Sugar in Modern History*. New York, 1985.

Mishaqa, Mikha'il. *Muntakhabat min al-jawab 'ala iqtirah al-ahbab*. Edited by Asad Rustum and Subhi Abu Shaqra. Beirut, 1985.

Moaz, 'Abd al-Razzaq. "Domestic Architecture, Notables, and Power: A Neighborhood in Late Ottoman Damascus." In *10th International Congress of Turkish Art*. Geneva, 1995.

———. "The Urban Fabric of an Extramural Quarter in Damascus and Its Change during the 19th Century." In *Second International Conference: The Syrian Land*. Erlangen, 1995.

al-Muhibbi, Muhammad. *Khulasat al-athr fi a'yan al-qarn al-hadi 'ashar*. Beirut, n.d.

al-Munajjid, Salah al-Din. *Al-Mu'arrikhun al-dimashqiyun fi al-'ahd al-'uthmani*. Beirut, 1964.

al-Muradi, Muhammad Khalil. *'Arf al-basham fi man waliya fatwa Dimashq al-Sham*. Edited by Muhammad Muti' al-Hafiz and Riyad 'Abd al-Hamid Murad. 2nd ed. Damascus, 1988.

———. *Silk al-durar fi aʿyan al-qarn al-thani ʿashar.* 4 vols. Beirut, 1988.

Murtada, Rida. "Miyah al-shurb fi madinat Dimashq min khilal hadarat al-tarikh." In *ʿIlm al-miyah al-jariyya fi madinat Dimashq,* ed. Ahmad Ghassan Sabbanu. Damascus, 1984.

al-Nabulsi, ʿAbd al-Ghani. *ʿAlam al-malaha fi ʿilm al-falaha.* Damascus, n.d.

———. *Burj babil wa shadw al-balabil.* Edited by Ahmad al-Jundi. Damascus, 1988.

———. *Al-Hadiqa al-nadiyya: sharh al-tariqa al-muhammadiyya.* Lailbur, 1977.

———. *Al-Hadra al-unsiyya fi al-rihla al-qudsiyya.* Edited by Akram al-ʿUlabi. Beirut, 1990.

———. *Al-Haqiqa wa al-majaz fi al-rihla ila bilad al-Sham wa Misr wa al-Hijaz.* Edited by Ahmad ʿAbd al-Majid al-Haridi. Cairo, 1986.

———. *Kashf al-nur ʿan ashab al-qubur.* Edited by Muhammad ʿAbd al-Hakim Sharaf Qadiri. Lahore, 1977.

———. *Al-Kashf wa al-bayan ʿamma yataʿaliqu bi'l-nisyan.* Edited by ʿAbd al-Jalil al-ʿIta. Damascus, n.d.

———. "Al-Risala fi mas'alat al-tasʿir." In *ʿAlam al-turath,* ed. ʿAbd Allah Muhammad al-Darwish. Damascus, 1984.

———. *Al-Sulh bayn al-ikhwan fi hukm ibahat al-dukhan.* Edited by Ahmad Muhammad Dahman. Damascus, 1924.

———. *Tahqiq al-qadiyya fi al-farq bayn al-rashwa wa al-hadiyya.* Edited by ʿAbd al-Jalil al-ʿIta. Damascus, 1990.

———. *Taʿtir al-anam fi tafsir al-ahlam.* Edited by Taha ʿAbd al-Ra'uf Saʿd. Damascus, n.d.

———. *Al-Tuhfa al-nabulusiyya fi al-rihla al-tarabulusiyya.* Edited by Heribert Busse. Beirut, 1971.

Nashat, Guity. "Women in the Ancient Near East." In *Restoring Women to History,* ed. Nikki Keddie. Bloomington, 1988.

Nuʿaysa, Yusuf. *Mujtamaʿ madinat Dimashq, 1772–1840.* 2 vols. Damascus, 1986.

Okawara, Tomoki. "Size and Structure of Damascene Households in the Late-Ottoman Period as Compared with Istanbul Households." In *Family History in the Middle East: Household, Property, and Gender,* ed. Beshara Doumani. Albany, 2002.

Owen, Roger. *The Middle East in the World Economy, 1800–1914.* London, 1981.

Panzac, Daniel. *La peste dans l'empire ottomane, 1700–1850.* Leuven, 1985.

———, ed. *Les villes dans l'empire ottomane.* 2 vols. Paris, 1994.

Pardailhé-Galabrun, Annik. *The Birth of Intimacy: Privacy and Domestic Life in Early Modern Paris.* Trans. Jocelyn Phelps. Philadelphia, 1991.

Paris, Robert. *Histoire du commerce de Marseille, 1660–1789.* Vol. 5. Paris, 1957.

Pascual, Jean-Paul. "Aspects de la vie materielle à Damas à la fin du XVIIe siècle d'après les inventaires après décès." In *The Syrian Land in the 18th and 19th Century*, ed. Thomas Philipp, 165–78. Stuttgart, 1992.

———. "Du notaire au propriétaire en passent par l'expert: descriptions de la 'maison' damascène au XVIIIe siècle." In *L'habitat traditionnel dans les pays musulmans autour de la Méditerrannée*, 2:387–403. Cairo, 1990.

———. "The Janissaries and the Damascus Countryside at the Beginning of the Seventeenth Century According to the Archives of the City's Military Tribunal." In *Land Tenure and Social Transformation in the Middle East*, ed. Tarif Khalidi. Beirut, 1984.

———. "Meubles et objets domestiques quotidiens des intérieurs damascains du XVIIe siècle." In *Villes au Levant: hommage à André Raymond*, ed. Daniel Panzac, 197–207. Aix-en-Provence, 1990.

Pellet, P. L., and J. Jamalian, "Observations on the Protein-Calorie Value of Middle Eastern Foods and Diets." In *Man, Food, and Agriculture in the Middle East*, ed. Thomas S. Stickley et al., 621–48. Beirut, 1969.

Philipp, Thomas. *Acre: The Rise and Fall of a Palestinian City, 1730–1831*. New York, 2001.

———, ed. *The Syrian Land in the 18th and 19th Centuries*. Berlin, 1992.

Pococke, R. *A Description of the East*. London, n.d.

Polanyi, Karl, Conrad M. Arensberg, and Harry W. Pearson, eds. *Trade and Market in the Early Empires: Economies in History and Theory*. New York, 1957.

al-Qari, Raslan ibn Yahya. "Al-Wuzara' aladhina hakamu Dimashq." In *Wulat Dimashq fi al-'ahd al-'uthmani*, ed. Salah al-Din al-Munajjid. Damascus, 1949.

Qasatli, Nu'man. *Al-Rawda al-ghanna' fi Dimashq al-fayha'*. Beirut, 1876.

al-Qasimi, Muhammad Sa'id. *Qamus al-sana'at al-shamiyya*. Edited by Zafir al-Qasimi. Damascus, 1988.

al-Qattan, Najwa. "The Damascene Jewish Community in the Later Decades of the 18th Century: Aspects of Socio-Economic Life Based on the Registers of the Shari'a Courts." In *The Syrian Land in the 18th and 19th Century*, ed. Thomas Philipp, 197–216. Stuttgart, 1992.

———. "*Dhimmis* in the Muslim Court: Legal Autonomy and Religious Discrimination." *International Journal of Middle East Studies*, 31(1999): 429–44.

Quataert, Donald. "Ottoman Women and Manufacturing, 1800–1914." In *Women in Middle Eastern History*, ed. Nikki Keddie and Beth Baron. London, 1991.

Rafeq, 'Abd al-Karim. *Al-'Arab wa al-'uthmaniyun, 1516–1916*. Damascus, 1974.

———. "Aspects of Traditional Society in Preindustrial Ottoman Syria." In *La ville arabe dans l'Islam*, ed. A. Bouhdiba and D. Chevallier, 103–16. Tunis, 1982.

———. *Buhuth fi al-tarikh al-iqtisadi wa al-ijtima'i li-bilad al-Sham*. Damascus, 1985.

———. "Changes in the Relationship Between the Ottoman Central Administration and the Syrian Provinces from the 16th to the 18th Centuries." In *Studies in 18th-Century Islamic History*, ed. Thomas Naff and Roger Owen, 53–73. London, 1977.

———. "City and Countryside in Ottoman Syria." In *Urbanism in Islam*, ed. Yuzo Itagaki, Masao Mori, and Takeshi Yukawa. Vol. 3. Tokyo, 1989.

———. "Craft Organization, Work Ethics, and the Strains of Change in Ottoman Syria." *Journal of the American Oriental Society*, III (1991): 495–511.

———. "Craft Organizations and Religious Communities in Ottoman Syria (16th–19th Centuries)." In *Convegno sul Tema: La shi'a nell'impero ottomano*. Rome, 1991.

———. "Economic Relations Between Damascus and the Dependent Countryside, 1743–1771." In *The Islamic Middle East (700–1900): Studies in Economic and Social History*, ed. A. L. Udovitch, 653–85. Princeton, 1981.

———. "Land Tenure Problems and Their Social Impact in Syria around the Middle of the 19th Century." In *Land Tenure and Social Transformation in the Middle East*, ed. T. Khalidi, 371–96. Beirut, 1984.

———. "The Law-Court Registers of Damascus, with Special Reference to Craft-Corporations during the First Half of the 18th Century." In *Les Arabes par leurs archives (XVIe–XXe siècles)*, ed. Jacques Berque and Dominique Chevallier, 141–59. Paris, 1976.

———. "The Local Forces in Syria in the 17th and 18th Centuries." In *War, Technology, and Society in the Middle East*, ed. V. J. Parry and M. E. Yapp, 277–307. London, 1975.

———. "Mazahir min al-haya al-'askariyya al-'uthmaniyya fi bilad al-Sham min al-qarn al-sadis 'ashar hatta matla' al-qarn al-tasi' 'ashar." In *Buhuth fi al-tarikh al-iqtisadi wa al-ijtima'i li-bilad al-Sham fi al-'asr al-hadith*. Damascus, 1985.

———. "Mazahir min al-tanzim al-hirafi fi bilad al-Sham fi al-'ahd al-'uthmani." In *Buhuth fi al-tarikh al-iqtisadi wa al-ijtima'i li-bilad al-Sham*. Damascus, 1985.

———. *The Province of Damascus, 1723–83*. Beirut, 1966.

———. "Public Morality in 18th-Century Damascus." In *Villes au Levant: Revue du monde musulmane et de la Méditerranée*, 180–96. Aix-au-Provence, 1990.

———. "Qafilat al-hajj wa ahammiyatuha fi al-dawla al-'uthmaniyya." In *Buhuth fi al-tarikh al-iqtisadi wa al-ijtima'i li-bilad al-Sham fi al-'asr al-hadith*. Damascus, 1985.

———. "Social Groups, Identity, and Loyalty, and Historical Writing in Ottoman and Post-Ottoman Syria." In *Les arabes et l'histoire creatice*. Paris, 1995.

Raymond, André. *Artisans et commerçants au Caire au XVIIIe siècle*. 2 vols. Damascus, 1974.

———. "La conquête ottomane et le développement des grandes villes arabes." *Revue de l'occident musulman et de la Méditerranée* 27 (1978): 115–34.

———. "Espaces publics et espaces privés dans les villes arabes traditionnelles."
Maghreb-Machreq 123(1989):194–201.

———. *Grandes villes arabes à l'époque ottomane.* Paris, 1985.

———. *The Great Arab Cities in the 16th to 18th Centuries: An Introduction.* New York,
1984.

———. "Groupes sociaux et geographie urbaine à Alep au XVIIIe siècle." In *The
Syrian Land in the 18th and 19th Centuries,* ed. Thomas Philipp, 147–63. Stuttgart,
1992.

———. "The Population of Aleppo in the 16th and 17th Centuries According
to Ottoman Census Documents." *International Journal of Middle Eastern Studies*
16(1984): 447–60.

———. "Les provinces arabes (XVIe–XVIIIe siècles)." In *Histoire de l'empire ottoman,* ed. Robert Mantran, 341–420. Paris, 1989.

———. "Les rapports villes-campagnes dans les pays arabes à l'époque ottomane
(XVIe–XVIIIe siècles)." In *Terroirs et sociétés au Maghreb et au Moyen-Orient,* ed.
Byron Cannon, 21–58. Lyon, 1987.

———. "Soldiers in Trade: The Case of Ottoman Cairo." *British Journal of Middle
Eastern Studies* 18(1991): 16–37.

———. "Urban Networks and Popular Movements in Cairo and Aleppo (End
of Eighteenth to Beginning of Nineteenth Century)." In *Urbanism in Islam,*
ed. Yuzo Itagaki, Masao Mori, and Takeshi Yukawa. Vol. 2. Tokyo, 1989.

Reilly, James. "Properties around Damascus in the 19th Century." *Arabica*
37(1990): 91–114.

———. "Property, Status, and Class in Ottoman Damascus: Case Studies from
the Nineteenth Century." *Journal of the American Oriental Society* 112(1992):9–21.

———. "Status Groups and Propertyholding in the Damascus Hinterland,
1828–80." *International Journal of Middle Eastern Studies* 21(1989): 517–39.

———. "Women in the Economic Life of Late Ottoman Damascus." *Arabica*
42(1995):79–106.

Rodinson, Maxime. "Recherches sur les documents arabes relatifs à la cuisine."
Revue des études islamiques 17(1949): 95–165.

Russell, Alexander. *The Natural History of Aleppo.* 2 vols. London, 1794.

al-Sabbagh, Mikha'il. *Tarikh al-shaykh Zahir al-ʿUmar al-Zaydani, hakim ʿAkka wa bilad
Safad.* Edited by Qastantin al-Basha al-Mukhlisi. Harisa, Lebanon, n.d.

Sahillioğlu, H. "The Role of International Monetary and Metal Movements
in Ottoman Monetary History, 1300–1750." In *Precious Metals in the Later
Medieval and Early Modern Worlds,* ed. J. F. Richards, 269–304. Durham, 1983.

Sauvaget, Jean. *Dimashq al-Sham.* Trans. Fu'ad Afram al-Bustani. Damascus, 1989.

———. "Esquisse d'une histoire de la ville de Damas." *Revue des études islamiques*
4(1934): 421–80.

Sauvaget, Jean and J. Weulersse. *Damas et la Syrie sud.* Paris, 1936.

Scarce, Jennifer. *Women's Costume of the Near and Middle East.* London, 1987.

Schama, Simon. *The Embarrassment of Riches: An Interpretation of Dutch Culture in the Golden Age.* New York, 1987.

Schatkowski Schilcher, Linda. *Families in Politics: Urban Factions and Estates of Damascus in the 18th and 19th Centuries.* Stuttgart, 1985.

Schilcher, Linda. "The Grain Economy of Late Ottoman Syria and the Issue of Large-Scale Commercialization." In *Landholding and Commercial Agriculture in the Middle East,* ed. Çağlar Keyder and Faruk Tabak. Albany, 1991.

Schivelbusch, Wolfgang. *Tastes of Paradise: A Social History of Spices, Stimulants, and Intoxicants.* Trans. David Jacobson. New York, 1992.

Seng, Yvonne. "The Üsküdar Estates (Tereke) as Records of Everyday Life in an Ottoman Town, 1521–1524." PhD dissertation, University of Chicago, 1991.

Şevket, Mahmud. *Al-Tashkilat wa al-azya' al-'askariyya al-'uthmaniyya mundhu bidayat tashkil al-jaysh al-'uthmani hatta sanat 1825.* Trans. Yusuf Nu'aysa and Mahmud 'Amer. Damascus, 1988.

Shamir, Shimon. "As'ad Pasha al-'Azm and Ottoman Rule in Damascus (1743–58)." *Bulletin of the Society of Oriental and African Studies* 26(1963):1–28.

Shaw, Thomas. *Travel or Observations Relating to Several Parts of Barbary and the Levant.* Oxford, 1738.

Singerman, Diane. *Avenues of Participation: Family, Politics, and Networks in Urban Quarters of Cairo.* Princeton, 1995.

al-Siyagha, Nayif. *Al-Haya al-iqtisadiyya fi madinat Dimashq fi muntasaf al-qarn al-tasi' 'ashar.* Damascus, 1995.

Sombart, Werner. *Luxury and Capitalism.* Trans. W. R. Dittmar. Ann Arbor, 1967.

Spence, Jonathan. "Chi'ng." In *Food in Chinese Culture: Anthropological and Historical Perspectives,* ed. K. C. Chang. New Haven, 1977.

Stillman, Yedida. *Arab Dress: A Short History.* Edited by Norman Stillman. Boston, 2000.

Tabak, Faruk. "Agricultural Fluctuations and Modes of Labor Control in the Western Arc of the Fertile Crescent, ca. 1700–1850." In *Landholding and Commercial Agriculture in the Middle East,* ed. Çağlar Keyder and Faruk Tabak. Albany, 1991.

Thieck, Jean-Pierre. "Décentralisation ottomane et affirmation urbaine à Alep à la fin du XVIIIe siècle." In *Passion d'Orient,* 113–76. Paris, 1992.

Thompson, E. P. "The Moral Economy of the English Crowd in the Eighteenth Century." *Past and Present* 50(1971): 76–136.

———. "Time, Work-Discipline, and Industrial Capitalism." Reprinted in *Customs in Common: Studies in Traditional Popular Culture,* 352–403. New York, 1993.

Thomson, William. *The Land and the Book, or Biblical Illustrations Drawn from the Manners and Customs, the Scenes and Scenery, of the Holy Land: Lebanon, Damascus, and beyond Jordan.* New York, 1886.

Thoumin, Richard. "Deux quartiers de Damas: le quartier chrétien de Bab Musalla et le quartier Kurde." *Bulletin d'études orientales* 1(1931): 99–135.

———. "Notes dur la repartition de la population par origine et par religion." *Revue de geographie alpine* 25(1937): 663–97.

———. "Notes sur l'amenagement et la distribution des eaux à Damas et dans sa Ghouta." *Bulletin des études orientales* 4(1934): 1–26.

Tlas, Mustafa, ed. *Al-Muʿjam al-jughrafi liʾl-qutr al-ʿarabi al-suri.* 5 vols. Damascus, 1990.

Todorov, Nikolai. *The Balkan City, 1400–1900.* Seattle, 1983.

Tresse, R. "L'évolution du costume syrien depuis un siècle." in *Entretiens sur l'évolution des pays de civilisation arabe: Communications presentées à la reunion tenue à Paris du 7 au 10 Juillet 1937 sous les auspices de l'Institut des Études Islamiques de l'Université de Paris et du Centre d'Études de Politique Étrangère*, 87–96. Paris, 1938.

Tucker, Judith. "Marriage and Family in Nablus, 1720–1856: Towards a History of Arab Muslim Marriage." *Journal of Family History* 13(1988): 165–79.

———. "Problems in the Historiography of Women in the Middle East." *International Journal of Middle Eastern Studies* 15(1983): 321–36.

———. "Ties That Bound: Women and Family in 18th and 19th-Century Nablus." In *Women in Middle Eastern History*, ed. Nikki Keddie and Beth Baron. London, 1991.

al-ʿUlabi, Akram Hasan. *Khitat Dimashq.* Damascus, 1989.

Van der Woude, A. D., and Anton Schurman, eds. *Probate Inventories: A New Source for the Historical Study of Wealth, Material Culture, and Agricultural Development.* Wageningen, 1980.

Vatter, Sherry. "Journeymen Textile Weavers in 19th-Century Damascus: A Collective Biography." In *Struggle and Survival in the Modern Middle East*, ed. Edmund Burke III, 75–90. New York, 1993.

Veblen, Thorstein. *The Theory of the Leisure Class.* New York, 1899.

Veinstein, Gilles. "Commercial Relations between India and the Ottoman Empire (Late-Fifteenth to Late-Eighteenth Centuries): A Few Notes and Hypotheses." In *Merchants, Companies, and Trade: Europe and Asia in the Early Modern Era*, ed. Sushil Chaudhury and Michel Morineau, 95–115. Cambridge, 1999.

Veinstein, G., and Y. Triantafyllidou-Baradié. "Les Inventaires après décès ottomans de Crète." In *Probate Inventories: A New Source for the Historical Study of Wealth, Material Culture, and Agricultural Development*, ed. A. D. van der Woude and Anton Schurman, 191–204. Wageningen, 1980.

Voll, John. "Old Ulama Families and Ottoman Influence in 18th-Century Damascus." *American Journal of Arabic Studies* 3(1975): 48–59.

Volney, C. F. *Travels in Syria and Egypt in the Years 1783, 1784, and 1785.* London, 1794.

th, Eugen. "Villes islamiques, villes arabes, villes orientales? Une problématique face au changement." In *La ville arabe dans l'Islam*, ed. A. Bouhdiba and D. Chevallier, 193–225. Tunis, 1982.

Wirth, Eugen. "Villes islamiques, villes arabes, villes orientales? Une problématique face au changement." In *La ville arabe dans l'Islam*, ed. A. Bouhdiba and D. Chevallier, 193–225. Tunis, 1982.

al-Budayri, Ahmad, 19, 35, 54, 73, 83, 134, 204, 218; and apocalyptic rumors, 229; and coffeehouses, 141, 144; and his diet, 104, 109, 119, 121, 123; market inspections, 71, 87, 111; and his mentor, 197; and morality of women, 149, 195; and prices, 62, 67, 77–78, 103, 165

bulgur, 59

bundles, 172, 186, 188

buqsumat. *See* biscuit

Burayk, Mikha'il, 50, 62, 96, 112, 135, 150, 159, 178, 218

Burckhardt, John Lewis, 195–96

bustani, 110, 117

butchers, 96, 97, 100, 102; and yerliyya, 99

butter, 117, 118, 119, 121; clarified. 60, 104–5; pricing of, 103, 105

buttons, 202, 205

Cabbage, 109

Cairo, 10, 11, 12, 136, 148, 174, 213, 231, 232

camels, 42–43, 97

candles, 114, 167, 195

candlesticks, 167, 187, 188, 189

cannibalism, rumors of, 83

cannon, 42

caravan: commercial caravans, 45, 46, 51–52. See also *hajj*

caravansaray. *See* khan

cardamom, 114, 137

Caribbean Sea, 116

carpets, 177, 183–84, 187–88, 215

carriages, 43

carrots, 109

cats, 168, 216

cattle. *See* cows

cauliflower, 109

cellars. See *kilar*

cemeteries, of Damascus, 28–29, 194

censers (*mibkhara*), 168, 187, 188, 195

Central Asia, 12

cereals. *See* grain

charcoal, 165

charity: with clothing, 210; with food, 178–79

cheese, 104, 121

cherries, 110

chess, 144

chickens, 97

chick peas, 107–8, 140

chimneys, 164

China, 58, 137

china racks, 186. *See also* housing: storage

chocolate, 224

cholera, 125

Christians, 163, 178, 208; and alcohol, 133–35; and clothing, 211–12, 218–19; and consumption of meat, 96; historians, 19; and urban population, 16; and weapons, 204

chronicles: as source for history writing, 18–19

cigarettes, 148

cinnamon, 114

Circassians, 43

circumcisions, 178

cisterns, 125

citadel, of Damascus, 14–15, 28, 141, 206

cloaks. *See* garments

clogs, 209. *See also* shoes

clothing. *See* garments; headgear; pants; shirts; shoes

cloves, 114

coconuts, 115

coffee, 52, 77, 124, 138, 146, 154–55,

Ibn Jumʿa, 141

Ibn Kannan, 23, 45, 128, 197; on bathhouses, 170; on bread, 61; death of sons, 35; on fruit, 111; on lust, 199–200; on Patrona Halil rebellion, 191–92; and prices, 70, 72; his social life, 177–78

Ibrahim ibn Saʿd al-Din, 153–54; Saʿd al-Din family (Banu Saʿd al-Din), 15

Ibrahim Pasha al-Muhassil, 135

Iltizam. See tax farming

al-ʿImadi, Hamid, 77, 179, 206, 217, 234

imperial Janissaries. See *kapıkulları*

incense, 113

India, 12, 116, 146, 148, 153

Indian Ocean, 113

"industrious revolution," 5–6, 225–28

inheritance law, 15, 66–67, 157

ink, 114

innovation, and Islam. See *bidʿa*

Iraq, 53, 54, 110

Iran, 34, 85, 146, 214

Ismaʿil Pasha al-ʿAzm, 12, 100

Istanbul, 46, 75, 84–85, 90, 92, 96, 159, 182, 204, 221, 232

Al-Jabawi, Mustafa ibn Saʿd al-Din, 15

al-Jaʿfari, Saʿid, 105

Jaffa, 45

jammal, 42

jams, 111, 114, 117

Janissaries, 13, 87, 118, 231; factionalism of, 85, 89–92; fondness for alcohol, 134; and local population, 14–15. See also *kapıkulları*; *yerliyya*

Japan, 68

al-Jazzar, Ahmad Pasha, 48–49, 91, 209

Jedda, 113

Jerusalem, 46, 51, 54, 140, 150

jewelry, 198, 207, 220

Jews: and alcohol, 133, 135; and clothing, 211–12, 218–19; musicians, 144; and urban population, 16

jinn, 200

Jordan River, 43

Judaism, 97. *See also* Jews

Judge. See *qadi*

jugs. See pitchers

jukh. See broadcloth

Kaʿk, 60

Kadızadeli movement, 118, 145

Kafr Susa, 110

Kaplan, Steven, 70

kapıkulları, 13, 73, 165, 218, 234; exile from Damascus, 89, 193; rations, 96

Karbala, 53

kerchiefs, 194–95, 196

kethüda, 76

kettles, 172

Khadr, 103

khans, 50–51, 163, 176; of Asʿad Pasha, 49, 90; Khan al-Haramayn, 163; Khan Hasan Pasha, 163; Khan al-Jubn, 104; Khan al-Thulj, 169; Khan al-Tutun, 147

khazzan, 75

khubz al-abariz, 60

khubz al-milla, 61

al-Kibrisli, Butrus, 108

kilar, 73, 172, 181

kishk, 59

kitchens, 172–73, 181

knives, 175, 204–5

kohl, 198–99

kunafa, 118

al-Misri, Khalil, 146
misriyyas, 67
modernization theory, 9
mongoose, 216
"moral economy," 88
mortars, 172
Mosul, 112
mother-of-pearl, 186, 189
Mount Lebanon. *See* Lebanon
Mount Qasyun, 25, 27, 34
mufti, 18, 77, 216, 234
Mughayzil, ʻAbd al-Rahman, 217
Muhammad ʻAli, 49, 53
Muhammad Bey Abuʼl-Dhahab, 140
Muhammad Pasha al-ʻAzm, 12, 98, 209
muhasabat, 66–67
mujaddara, 59
Mukha, 137
mulberries, 110, 111
mules, 41–42, 117
al-Muradi, ʻAli, 167–68
al-Muradi, Muhammad Khalil, 15,
    136, 145, 146, 154, 179
al-Muradi, Murad, 151, 192
Musa Kikhiya, 196
musicians, 144, 177
Mustafa Agha, 76
Mustafa Agha al-Hawasili, 77
Mustafa Agha ibn al-Qabani, 77
Mustafa III, 216
mustard, 114, 115
myrtle, 125, 133

Al-Nabak, 109
Nablus, 107, 159, 213
al-Nabulsi, ʻAbd al-Ghani, 112, 114–
    15, 127, 168; on *barsh*, 153; on
    beards, 197; on bread, 60, 61; on
    chickpeas, 108; on coffee, 135–36;
    domestic habits of, 180; on dyeing,

217; on interior decoration, 189;
    on innovation, 226; on *kunafa*, 118;
    on makeup, 199; on meat, 96–97;
    on milk supply, 103; on nudity,
    200; on posture, 208; on tobacco,
    148–51; travels of, 46, 51, 54, 58,
    111, 128, 140, 150, 159, 179, 206; on
    turbans, 194; on veiling, 196
Nadir Shah, 54
nafaqa, 66
Napoleon Bonaparte, 49, 57, 85, 144,
    219
narcotics, 153
nargilas. *See* hookahs
narnaj. *See* oranges
Nasuh Pasha, 76, 117, 152, 210
necklaces, 198
Nerval, Gérard de, 201
Nile River, 85
North Africa, 11
North Africans, 85
notables, 8, 12, 13; and hospitality,
    133, 176–77, 179; and their houses,
    160–61, 180; and urban economy,
    75, 77, 92–93, 229–30; and urban
    protest, 86
nudity. *See* body
Nur al-Din, 65, 75
nutmeg, 114
nuts, 115–16, 120–21, 123

Olive, 112, 114; groves 103; pits, 165;
    presses, 105; trees, 54, 105
olive oil, 105–08, 167, 234
onions, 109, 114, 115, 168
opium, 153
oranges, 110, 111, 178; bitter (*narnaj*),
    110
orchards, of Damascus, 23–24, 103,
    123, 125, 135, 160, 169, 177

Oriental despotism, 9
Orontes River, 32, 43
orphans' estates. See *muhasabat*
Ottoman class. See 'askari Damascenes
oxen, 43

Pails, 172
palace of As'ad Pasha al-'Azm, 43, 90, 127, 159
Palestine, 12, 27, 47, 48, 105, 107, 215
Palmyra, 113
pans, 172, 174, 177, 179
pants, 201–2, 210, 215, 217, 218. *See also* garments; shirts
paper, 114, 167
Paris, 68, 212, 226
parsley, 109
pastries, 104, 117, 118
Patrona Halil rebellion, 191
peaches, 110, 111, 125
pears, 110, 111
peasants, 31, 49, 59, 61, 62, 69, 103, 104
peddlers, 54, 104, 107, 112, 114, 165, 177
pepper, 114
perfume, 113, 175
Persia. See Iran
Persian Gulf, 116
Persians, 11
pestles, 172
pickling, 111–12, 114, 115
pigs. See pork
pillows, 179, 184–85, 187, 188, 215
pine nuts, 107, 115
pipes, 148
pistachios, 107, 115, 116, 118, 120
pistols. See weapons
pitchers, 174, 175

plague, 34–35
plates, 142, 174, 177, 179
plums, 110, 111
pockets, 202
poetry, 19, 127
pomegranates, 110, 111, 112; juice of, 107
pork, 97
postal service, 45–46
potatoes, 58, 68, 121, 154
pots, 172, 174
prayer beads, 54
privacy. See housing
probate inventories: as source for history writing, 14–17
prostitutes, 134, 195, 196
Protestant work ethic. See Weber, Max
puppeteers, 144

Al-Qabun, 32
qadama, 108
qadi (also *qadi al-qudat*), 12, 14, 134, 179, 216; and markets, 71–72, 88; and orphans, 66; and urban protest, 86–87
al-Qalamun, 130
Qal'at Jibril, 105
Qalit River (*nahr qalit*), 169
qamr al-din, 118, 121
al-Qanawat, 28, 99
Qanawat River, 127, 129
Qasatli, Nu'man, 30, 125, 140, 141, 158, 170
al-Qasimi, Muhammad Sa'id, 139, 165; on chickpeas, 107; on female attire, 196; on milk supply, 103; on sheep supply, 99; on turbans, 193, 217; on watches, 205
al-Qatrana, 39

Tripoli, 39, 45, 107, 113, 146, 206, 214
trunks, 186, 187, 188
tujjar, 13, 77
Tunis, 125
Tunisia, 85
Tura River, 32, 129
turbans, 193–94, 217, 218
Turkomans, 11, 43, 98
Turks, 11
turmeric, 114
turnips, 109, 112, 114
Tyre, 146

Ulama, 13, 221; and grain, 75–77; and
hospitality, 179; job-holding, 65–
66; and turbans, 194, 217; and urban protest, 86; worldliness of, 211
ʿulba. See containers
al-ʿUmari, 81
Umayyad Mosque, 28, 113, 152, 208,
211, 229
al-Ustuwani, Muhammad, 118
utensils. *See* eating habits
ʿUthman Pasha al-Kurji, 39, 71, 76
ʿUthman Pasha al-Muhassil, 193
Uzbekistan, 45

Veblen, Thorstein, 5
vegetables, 109, 111–12
veils, 195–96
vetch, 58, 59, 62, 76
vinegar, 112, 115
Volney, C. F., 69, 97, 140, 148

Wahhabi movement, 53, 91–92, 134,
135, 221
wall hangings, 189
walnuts, 115, 120; oil, 198
waqf, of Nur al-Din, 75

washbowls, 175
watches, 205–7
water, 124; under French Mandate,
125; interior taps, 172; piping of,
126
water buffalo, 97, 102
water-carriers, 130
watercress, 125
water-lily, 114
watermelons, 110, 111; seeds, 115
waterwheels, 43
wealth: in general population, 63–
64; disparities between men and
women, 174, 185–86
weapons, 204–5
weather, 32–33, 79, 97, 165; drought,
33, 62, 127–28; floods, 31–32;
rainfall, 30–31, 62, 81–84; psychological effects of, 31, 83–84;
snowfall, 32–33, 83
Weber, Max, 9
weddings, 177–78
wells, 125, 127–30, 132, 179
wheat, 57, 59, 76–78, 80, 82, 84,
96, 140
wheeled transport, 43
windows, 165–66
wine, 133–35, 145
women: and bathhouses, 170; and
clothing, 202–3; and facial decoration, 198–99; and headgear,
194–95; and jewelry, 198, 207,
220; non-Muslim, 16; and public
recreation, 23, 149–50, 177; and
shoes, 209; and smoking, 149–
50, 152; and urban population, 15;
and veiling, 196; and wealth, 174,
185–86
wood, 159, 165

wool, 98, 215, 216, 217

worms, 112, 114

writing. *See* literacy